ALSO BY FELIPE FERNÁNDEZ-ARMESTO

THE CANARY ISLANDS AFTER THE CONQUEST

BEFORE COLUMBUS

THE SPANISH ARMADA

BARCELONA: A THOUSAND YEARS OF THE CITY'S PAST

COLUMBUS

THE TIMES ATLAS OF WORLD EXPLORATION (GENERAL EDITOR)

COLUMBUS ON HIMSELF

EDWARD GIBBON'S ATLAS OF THE WORLD

THE TIMES GUIDE TO THE PEOPLES OF EUROPE (EDITOR)

THE EUROPEAN OPPORTUNITY (EDITOR)

THE GLOBAL OPPORTUNITY (EDITOR)

MILLENNIUM: A HISTORY OF THE LAST THOUSAND YEARS

THE TIMES ILLUSTRATED HISTORY OF EUROPE

ALSO BY DEREK WILSON

A TUDOR TAPESTRY—MEN, WOMEN AND SOCIETY IN REFORMATION ENGLAND

ENGLAND IN THE AGE OF THOMAS MORE

SWEET ROBIN: ROBERT DUDLEY, EARL OF LEICESTER 1533–1588

THE WORLD ENCOMPASSED: DRAKE'S GREAT VOYAGE

THE TOWER 1078–1978

HANS HOLBEIN—PORTRAIT OF AN UNKNOWN MAN

THE CIRCUMNAVIGATION

ROTHSCHILD: A STORY OF WEALTH AND POWER

THE ASTORS: LANDSCAPE WITH MILLIONAIRES

EAST AFRICA THROUGH A THOUSAND YEARS

A HISTORY OF SOUTH AND CENTRAL AFRICA

AFRICA—A MODERN HISTORY

THE ILLUSTRATED BOOK OF WORLD HISTORY

Reformations

A Radical Interpretation

of Christianity and the World,

1500–2000

Felipe Fernández-Armesto

and

Derek Wilson

SCRIBNER

SCRIBNER
1230 Avenue of the Americas
New York, NY 10020

Originally published in Great Britain by Bantam Press
Published by arrangement with Transworld Publishers Ltd.

SCRIBNER and design are trademarks of Simon & Schuster Inc.

Manufactured in the United States of America

1   3   5   7   9   10   8   6   4   2

Library of Congress Cataloging-in-Publication Data
Fernández-Armesto, Felipe.
[Reformation]
Reformations : a radical interpretation of Christianity and the world,
1500–2000 / by Felipe Fernández-Armesto and Derek Wilson.
p.   cm.
Originally published: Reformation. London : Transworld Publishers, 1996.
Includes bibliographical references and index.
1. Reformation. 2. Christianity and culture. 3. Religious
pluralism—Christianity. I. Title.
BR305.2.F47   1997
270—DC21   96-40940
CIP

ISBN 0-684-83104-X

Unity is the agreement not of minds, but of wills.
                                            – Thomas Aquinas

CONTENTS

PREFACE

The death of God has often been prematurely reported and the withering of religion confidently predicted. Instead, today, secularism is on the defensive, while religions are back – active powers in the reshaping of a spiritually charged world. Christianity, in particular – until recently divided and beleaguered – has made an unpredictable comeback. In Eastern Europe, the churches have emerged in strength from the ruins of communism. In the West, they are challenging the new paganism of consumer societies. In Latin America they have made and contained political revolutions. They have launched the most dynamic movement ever to have convulsed Africa. They have helped to wrench public policy into new directions in the USA. Their evangelizing power has broken out in patches in East Asia.

A generation ago, the history of Christianity could be indulged as an antiquarian pursuit; now it is an urgent part of the agenda of anyone who wants to be ready for the future. This book is an attempt to approach that history from a fresh perspective.

The Reformation used to be seen as a divisive event, which inaugurated a conflictive era. Here, it becomes a continuing story, embracing the common religious experiences of Christians of different traditions worldwide, moulding their relations with the world and with each other. During the last half-millennium the work of the sixteenth-century reformers has been presented as a triumph over superstition and an assault on faith; as the seedbed of democracy and the scapegoat of capitalism; as the breaker of dogma and a maker of anarchy; as a solvent of society and a liberator of the individual. The witness of people's senses, meanwhile, for most of the time, has been to a Europe and a world sundered by rival nationalisms and ideologies, many or most of which were thought to have originated, in varying degrees, in the cataclysm of the sixteenth century. Now, we can discern common features rippling the rival communions, spawned sects and proliferating traditions that have competed for the evangelization of the world. The Reformation looks like a stage in a long transformation of Christianity, a common project of Catholic, Protestant and Orthodox reformers. The last five hundred years of Christianity are seen in these pages as they will surely come to be seen in the perspective of lengthening time: not as a period dominated by disunity and decline, but as an era of creative diversity, overarching unity and dynamic promise. Paradoxically, it is only when we stop trying to identify the points at issue between the Churches that we can see them clearly, like a fine powder in suspension: if the container is shaken, we observe only a swirling, discoloured fluid. When the sediment is allowed to settle, we can see what it is.

The climate of these last-gasp years of our millennium suits – perhaps determines – the re-evaluation attempted here. We have frightened ourselves into reconciliation. We have seen what modern wars of religion can do to people. We have watched while theological squabbles undermine belief in the churches' teaching and erode their moral influence. In starting a reconquest against secularism most denominations are trying to let the particles of ancient struggles settle. In the closing years of this century it has become possible for Protestants and Catholics to behold each other with unprecedented fellow-feeling. Vatican II closed an era of mutual limit-drawing opened at Trent. Ecumenical discussions over the last thirty years have focused not on the divisive formulas of the past but on new, shared definitions for the future.

According to the Second Vatican Council, 'Christ summons the Church, as she goes her pilgrim way, to that continual reformation of which she always has need, insofar as she is an institution of men here on earth.' These words are our starting point. In challenging and serving a changing world, the Church (and the same holds true for the standard-bearers of other major religions) has to attempt something very difficult: to remain true 'to the faith once given to the saints', while, in life and teaching, presenting that faith in ways that are meaningful to each passing generation. This 'continual reformation', in effect, becomes sporadic reformation, since churches, like any man-made organization, slide into corruption or ineffectiveness or ossify into institutionalism. Brave radicals purge or re-enliven them.

What has been traditionally called 'the Reformation' was only the most violent of these jolts. Luther, Zwingli and Calvin or their Catholic counterparts, like Erasmus, Cisneros and Contarini, were arguing for some of the same ingredients of spiritual renewal which Bernard, Francis and Wycliffe had advocated. Later reformers such as Wesley, Newman and William Booth would take some of them up in the centuries ahead. If we accept that vital continuities overarch the history of the Church, then the Reformation ceases to be central in the sense that we see some events 'leading up' to it and others 'flowing from' it, or certain figures as 'forerunners' of the Reformation and later ones as its 'heirs'. This does not mean that the Reformation, as traditionally understood, never happened or that its importance has been exaggerated: only that it did not happen as commonly supposed and that its importance has been wrongly assigned.

Religion can do harm as well as good and the best intentions can get warped. But reformation is – and the Reformation was – a spiritual movement: spiritual in the sense of being a convulsion of the human spirit; spiritual also in strengthening the ties that bind individuals and society to the divine spirit. Reformation, through renewal of the Church, is an attempt to admonish the world and ultimately our attention is focused not on the differences between the denominations but on the successes and failures of the Church *as a whole* to fulfil its proper function in and against the world.

This book is about the issues which for nearly half a millennium have divided Christian from Christian and the Church from the world. This is not meant to be a simply academic quest. We want to approach spiritual, moral and intellectual problems which matter both for the Church and for the nations that have been shaped by its love-hate relationship with reformation. People are putting some tough questions to today's Churches: what have they to offer morally deprived societies – a healing cup or a poisoned chalice? What divides them? What unites them? Are they preaching different gospels? Are they, in effect, different religions? Are schemes of reunification clownish faces painted over the scowls of suspicion? To us these questions look a little less daunting – and the answers, perhaps, more hopeful – against the background we describe.

As far as we know, this is the only book on the subject produced by a collaboration between two authors starting squarely either side of the Catholic–Protestant divide. One of us is an evangelical Protestant of charismatic sympathies sparingly indulged; the other a Roman Catholic of Tridentine temptations wistfully resisted. For us, it has been a journey of exploration, discovery, re-evaluation and mutual exasperation resolved in tolerance. After a chapter which sets modern divisions in a long context of Christian diversity, Christianity is considered as a system of authority in Chapters Two and Three, of belief in Chapter Four, of worship in Chapters Five and Six, and, in Chapters Seven to Eleven, of human relationships, both individual and collective. These are not meant to be watertight categories. The contents seep into each other or flow into the stream of the book, which is meant to lead the reader towards an unconventional way of looking at Christian history.

The last two chapters focus on the common enterprise of Christians today: the struggle with sects and secularism. The message for our time – for readers who want one – is ecumenical. As publication approaches, this looks increasingly urgent. Catholics properly proud of the privilege of being Catholics are anxious that ecumenism has gone too far – diluting truth and easing the pressure on Protestants to reconsider their own attitudes. Traditions – traced, by Christians of different persuasions, to saints and apostles and defended for so long at the cost of so much blood and anguish –

are threatened with immersion in a post-modern mish-mash which needs no further stirring. Protestant traditionalists of all shades suspect that hallowed customs and hard-won beliefs are being trampled in a panic induced by falling numbers. Identities should be passionately felt; but first they must be properly understood. The writers of this book have learned from each other and want other Christians to go on doing the same.

Chapter One

SPLINTERS OF THE CROSS:
The Tradition of Christian Diversity

PLUS ÇA CHANGE

In the afternoon, the water will get choppy. It always does. In the morning, to singers on the lakeside, the surface seems stretched like a drumskin, as if the people queuing at the ramshackle jetty for baptism by total immersion were sure to bounce off. Rolling up sleeves and jeans, the minister sways into the water; his assistant does not bother to remove his battered straw hat for the occasion. To the dancing rhythm of the hymns, women spread a festival picnic. In the distance, the jagged volcanoes which rim this little world of Lake Atitlán in Guatemala slumber or brood.

In the prow of the approaching motorlaunch, Anastasio curls his lip. He is a high-class tourist-guide. His blood is all Indian and he recognizes the christening party as his kin. His skin is as brown, his hair as black as theirs, his stature almost as short. But he is a city-dweller, a *Ladino* descended from generations of Spanish-speaking city-dwellers. His ancestors were Maya artisans who took service with the conquistadores, just as he, a thoroughly modern professional, now serves a new wave of foreign intruders. He makes a display of disapproval, not in order to align himself with his customers, but to distance himself from the rites in the water. 'Those are evangelicals,' he says, as his face slips back into its usual smile. 'I don't understand their ceremonies.'

Further up the shore, in a big stone church dark with candleblack, pilgrims are gathering around the makeshift shrine of a murdered Catholic priest. To get to it, you thread through streets bright with life and sunlight, dotted with the huts and halls of radical sects. The Jehovah's Witnesses are here, the Assemblies of God, 'the Evangelical Church of Central America', the 'Bible Way Church', Baptists and Pentecostalists. The church at the top of the town, presiding indulgently over the colourful profanities of the market in the main square, still gives an impression of dominance, and Anastasio's smile broadens. He feels at home here, in the cool and dark of the sacred space, where the painted statues gleam like flares and, on the floor, the splashes of wax and smears of petals, fallen from the offerings of the faithful, shine like puddles. For him, this is the tradition of his own people – imported by the Spaniards but adapted over the centuries by an indigenous spirit. The conquistadores who are threatening it today are not the foreigners he serves in the tourist trade, but the gringo missionaries with their insidious dollars and alien politics. For the pastors, the powers that be are ordained of God; the priests are barely tolerated voices of social criticism. The victim commemorated in the shrine in this church was – almost everyone believes – murdered by army agents.

Deeper in the back streets of Santiago Atitlán, older, darker forms of devotion are in conflict. Sodalities of the worshippers of cult-images of the Virgin welcome you into their carefully swept hovels with anxious eyes. Their statues are displayed on trestles covered with baize, lit by candles, humoured by incense. Offerings in coin are solicited in shallow dishes. The cause of the fear lurks in a nearby house, where a grotesque doll, man-sized, stuffed with straw, with a cigar-butt stuck under his rigid moustache, is attended by minders with bulging belts. 'Má Ximón' is the effigy of an unchristian deity – a corrupt version of Simon Magus, generated by a warped understanding, an attempt to perpetuate the presence of the magician who defied the apostles and who believed that spiritual power can be bought. The shrine of Má Ximón is housed and arranged like those of the Virgin, but his devotees are sleeker and more comfortable. The offerings are more copious, the coins more deeply piled and complemented by fat cigars and pungent rum. This is a cult combined with a protection racket.

Though thronged with tourists and thick with evangelical missions, lakeside Atitlán is still, by the standards of today's world, remote and self-contained, stitched tight inside its hem of volcanoes. Each lakeside community is a culture-capsule with its own language and its own distinctive pattern of weaving, worn as a badge of identity by the local womenfolk. Yet the religious mixture – Catholic, Protestant, syncretic – and the tension within it, are typical of Christendom as a whole.

The diversity of beliefs and practices of those who call themselves Christian makes a pretty effective mask for the unity of the Church. Glossolalia slide from Pentecostalist tongues in an excited blather; awaiting the spirit in silence, old-fashioned Quakers tighten their lips and may go through a Sunday morning without saying anything at all. On a vast dirt plaza in Zaire, barefoot women in uniform bonnets and skirts dance in formation in honor of a latter-day prophet of Christ; in a hotel banqueting hall in Seoul, hundreds of couples line up in look-alike, western-style bridal dress to be blessed by a supposed Messianic incarnation. At Mass in a Dominican priory in Peru, the kiss of peace seems to have replaced communion as a focal point of the service, while the suspense of behatted Scottish lady Presbyterians at St Columba's kirk, where monthly communion is taking place today, is directed at the collection. At a neat Unitarian church in Concord, the service begins with a poem written by a Bengali Hindu; in 'Bibliopolis', 'south of Tuscaloosa', the congregation is using rattlesnakes as maracas to the tune of 'Faith in the Lord and the Snakes Won't Bite'.

On a Swiss mountainside, meanwhile, Catholic schismatics of Archbishop Lefebvre's allegiance prepare for induction as bishops in robes of cloth of gold and prostrate themselves before the altar, revealing red slippers like Dorothy's that seem to glitter with magic; at a Capuchin mission in New Guinea, the priest vests for solemn high mass in a grass skirt, attended by churchwardens with bones through their noses. In a weatherboard chapel on a private island in Massachusetts bay, children lead a clannish congregation of white Anglo-Saxon Protestants in loud hymns; in a crematorium in a London suburb, a family who never go to church are at the mercy of a vicar with a drink problem, gabbling impersonally from *The Alternative Service Book* before muzak from trite tapes restores their sense of belonging. Amid incense and candle flames, after an hour and a half of liturgical overkill, old women in St Petersburg, glimpsing the mysteries of the eucharist through a screen hung with icons, prod worshippers whose posture droops or who cross themselves at the wrong moment; at a charismatic service in Toronto, ecstatic confessants testify to their faith by collapsing in apparently anarchic giggles. For some, this colourful diversity is stains from the bloody fragments of a dismembered church. For others, it is the hues of a rainbow, distinguishable by a trick of the light.

Many or most of the differences between Christian congregations today can be and have been traced back to the Reformation – a series of movements traditionally said to have been launched by a dissident theologian in Saxony in 1517, which divided the Western Church into two mutually hostile, mutually exclusive camps, commonly labelled 'Roman Catholic' and 'Protestant'. By those who took part in it, the Reformation was recognized within a few years as a reform of unprecedented power to change the Church, the world and the soul of the worshipper. 'For more than a century,' said Luther,

> men have been talking about reform, but I have accomplished it. By the grace of God, I have brought about such a change that . . . I have

established the right order for all estates in society so that each will know how to live and serve God in his appointed role. And to those who have accepted it, my reformation has brought not a little benefit, peace and virtue.

Ever since, the Reformation has been almost universally regarded as one of the great decisive changes of world history, from which flowed consequences of immeasurable importance. It is said to have helped transform medieval Christendom – inertly unified – into the scandalously, emulously, productively competitive Western world of modern times: it helped prepare the world for the reception of other revolutionary ideas, including – according to the analyst's tastes – individualism, capitalism and imperialism, or constitutionalism, socialism and democracy. At the very least, it turned a monolithic church into a fiery, cloudy pillar, from which sparks shot off and wisps floated away, to form the bewilderingly numerous Christian churches and sects of today. At about the time the Reformation started, Erasmus of Rotterdam, criticizing the pious excesses traditionally condoned by the Church, joked that there were enough fragments of the True Cross abounding in collections of relics to build a battleship. In another sense, the splintering of the Cross was about to begin.

At one level, this book is written to subvert traditional views of the Reformation's importance: we find the origins of Christian diversity not in any particular events in the Church's past, but in the very nature of Christianity. At another level, we make the Reformation out to be even more significant than traditionally supposed: we understand it not just as a series of movements confined to the past, but as a theme overarching the whole history of the Church and still active and influential – indeed, powerfully reverberant – in the present. At a third level, we propose a thorough reformation of what the term means, in line with historical scholarship and the perspective of our times. The decisive, transforming features of Christian history in and since the sixteenth century have not been those which have divided the Catholic, Protestant and Orthodox traditions, but, we believe, those which they had in common.

The first deficiency of traditional Reformation historiography is its indifference to the history of the Eastern churches except where they were influenced by or against Protestantism. The schisms started by Luther did not shatter a single, all-encompassing Church. Populous parts of Christendom were already outside the Roman communion. Roman efforts to make converts and establish intercommunion with the Orthodox had never been very persistent or more than patchily successful. Further east and south, the Georgian and Ethiopian churches were medieval models of what 'national' churches might be; that of Armenia was only faintly mottled with Roman influence. The Coptic and other Monophysite communions, the Nestorians and the Jacobites were large or, at least, largely dispersed groups, stretching, in the Nestorian case, into the far corners of India and China; since the early fourteenth century Nestorianism had been almost untouched by Roman missions, and the Ethiopians, though they were in constant touch with Rome through the community established for them at the church of San Stefano dei Mori by Sixtus IV, showed little interest in Catholic blandishments. Even before the Reformation, most of Christendom lay beyond the reach of Rome.

There was almost as much diversity in the West, within the supposedly homogenous Catholic communion. Reformation historiography has been a confessional battlefield and it has suited both sides to exaggerate pre-Reformation unity. For Protestants, it enhances the impression of the uniquely powerful impact ascribed to their movement; for Catholics, it increases the scandal of the Reformation. It is true that there were no lasting national Churches in the Latin west in the middle ages: in the throes of the first secessions by reforming Churches in the sixteenth century, Thomas More went to the block rather than 'conform my conscience to the Council of one realm against the general Council of Christendom.' But the general trend was towards increasingly discrete national or State Churches, as ec-clesiastical offices came to be monopolized by natives of the countries to which they belonged, and as ecclesiastical appointments were devolved into the hands of rulers. The latest experiment in national church-building was still largely intact when the Reformation began. The Hussite Church in Bohemia anticipated the national Churches of the Reformation era in start-ling ways: the Catholic doctrine of the eucharist was abjured; communion was given in both kinds; the liturgy was celebrated in the vernacular; Church property was secularized; the unity of the reformed Church dissolved in its turn amongst dissident tendencies.

There were earlier precedents, too. It is not clear what, if anything, was doctrinally distinctive about the Bosnian Church in the fourteenth century – but this was a clear case of the secession of a well defined province of the Church from Roman allegiance. In the early fifteenth century, the English State was almost captured by adherents of the heresies of John Wycliffe, the Oxford don whom Protestants came to see as their forerunner. In the twelfth century the Cathar heresy – generally but insecurely presumed to have been a form of dualism – got close to being a State church in lands of the counts of Toulouse. In the tenth century, Bulgaria had its own Church, devoted to the heresy of the priest Bogomil – an allegedly dualist faith with which early Cathars may have been in touch.

Medieval Latin Christendom was also dappled with heterodox beliefs. At a popular level, where Christian doctrine is easily garbled or warped, heresy may have had a long prehistory before its continuous record began in the West in the eleventh century. Some of the dissenting Churches of early modern Europe originated before the Reformation and blended or co-existed with Protestantism. The Waldensians assimilated Calvinism; the Lollards merged into English non-conformity; the Moravian brethren began as a tendency within Hussitism. Three of the most powerful forms of radical Christianity in early modern Europe all had medieval origins: Anabaptism, peasant millenarianism and the antinomianism of free spirits liberated from discipline by their sense of spiritual superiority.

Every generation of academics had its theological revisionists who invented new heresies or revived old ones. It is hard – perhaps impossible – to find a doctrine associated with the sixteenth-century reformers that had not been anticipated from within the world of medieval Catholicism. As debate unfolded and doctrine evolved there was never a moment at which the faith could be said to have been definitely expounded – though later, after the Reformation, Catholics looked back to the golden age of theological compendia in the thirteenth century and elevated St Thomas Aquinas to the role of near-perfect arbiter of truth. In his own day, he was a politically canny man of the world with his feet firmly on the ground, but painters of the baroque age boosted the 'angelic doctor' up to the clouds. In the meantime, the dividing line between heresy and orthodoxy remained vague and in the absence of objective tests it was easy to get trapped on the wrong side of it.

Some medieval careers illustrate this: Francis of Assisi might have been – almost was – classified as a heretic for his uncompromising version of the doctrine of apostolic poverty, yet instead he became a saint; Bogomil had also addressed his message to 'the poor of Christ'. Meister Eckhart, commended in his lifetime for his mystical writings, was condemned after his death. Savonarola, who founded his 'godly republic' in Florence in defiance of the pagan style of the Renaissance, trumpeted the independence of his conscience: he was impugned for it but never condemned. Botticelli's 'Calumnia' is a touching defence of the revolutionary friar from the hand that had formerly been employed to paint erotica for the *jeunesse dorée* of the Medici villa. Cardinal Cisneros had the same taste in devotional reading as Luther, but he became Grand Inquisitor of Spain while his Saxon counterpart became the model heresiarch: Cisneros paid for the printing of a dozen late medieval works which – by their emphasis on Scripture, mysticism and the appeal from a profoundly penitent conscience to the direct exercise of God's grace – explore radical means of cultivating and extending personal devotion. Among them was a commentary of Savonarola on the penitential psalm which was edited by Luther and became the mainstay of early English Protestant primers. The sixteenth-century reformers were not just echoing their medieval predecessors: they were consciously fulfilling their prophecies. 'God will purify Holy Church,' prophesised St Catherine of Siena, 'by awakening the spirit of the elect. This will lead to such an improvement in the Church of God and such a renewal in the lives of her holy pastors that at the mere thought of it my spirit exalteth in the Lord.'

Diversity in doctrine and emotion was not only a *cumulative* feature of

Christianity: it was an *original* feature, too, which can be documented from Scripture in the earliest recorded phase of the Church's history. Heresy had always been around. In a sense, it was older than orthodoxy, which had not been part of the armour of a Church born fully equipped, but rather the imperfect product of a long process of debate and refinement. An array of opinions had to be available first, from which orthodoxy was subsequently selected. Heterodoxy can claim paradoxical priority; orthodoxy was defined in relation to it, rather than the other way round.

Debate in a Church convulsed by differences of opinion can be glimpsed in some of the earliest Christian writings. The gospel of John tries to appropriate dualist language – language of 'light in darkness' and of a cosmic conflict with 'the prince of this world'. The first council of the Church at Jerusalem was convened to settle a doctrinal point: whether gentiles 'should be instructed to keep the law of Moses'. Under the sanitized account in Acts, the odour of fierce and unresolved controversy is obvious. Paul's report to the Galatians makes it explicit: those who try to enforce the law 'are seeking to pervert the gospel . . . I opposed Peter to his face, since he was clearly in the wrong.' The very debate about Paul's apostolic credentials and the numerous denunciations of false apostles are evidence of the range of opinion in a Church 'carried hither and thither by every new gust of teaching'. Titus was advised to excommunicate those who chose wrong doctrines. When Peter wanted to change the teaching of his fellow apostles on dietary matters, he appealed to the authority of a vision – a sure sign of the tenacity of opposition, as well as the fluidity of doctrine. 'It is no bad thing', Paul advised the Corinthians, 'that there should be sects and differences [heresies] among you' so that the truth could be identified: this conjures up a convincing picture of how orthodoxy began to be refined out of the crude ore of primitive differences.

The Reformation did not therefore introduce the kinds of novelty commonly ascribed to it: it did not break up a monolithic Church; it did not initiate unprecedented heresies; it did not create the first national Churches. Rather than a new departure in Church history, it was a growth out of long traditions, a form of age-old diversity. The post-Reformation Church was more variegated than before, but it was a difference of degree rather than kind. Nor were the new divisions between Catholic and Protestant of the nature commonly supposed. The Catholic and Protestant movements of the period have traditionally been called 'Reformation' and 'Counter-Reformation' as if to emphasize their conflictive relationship and to represent one as a reaction against the other. A recent generation of historians recognized the movements as parallel and substituted the term 'Catholic Reformation' for 'Counter-Reformation'; but the enmity of the two camps – whose members executed each other and followed their leaders into war in alliances formed, at least in part, along confessional lines – has continued to dominate our picture of the times and to make it hard for us to see how much

ᴼmine ne in furoꝛe tuo arguas me:
neꝗ in ira tua corripias me. Ⅿiſere
re mei domie quoniam infirmus ſum

they had in common. In some ways, 'Reformation' – defined as a search for a purer Christianity, more conformable to primitive models, or as a movement to communicate Christian verities more deeply and widely to Christian people – was less a source of division than a common theme spanning hostile groups. Even the term 'Reformation' is now being discarded as misleading by some historians. The current trend in Reformation historiography is towards a re-evaluation of the sixteenth- and seventeenth-century experience as an age of 'transition' – encompassing both Catholics and Protestants and, to a lesser extent, the Orthodox – towards a more active and committed Christianity than prevailed before. Luther spoke for the élite of Christendom at the time, irrespective of denomination, when he claimed that 'a conscious and informed assent' to the call of faith was necessary for salvation. To sharpen that consciousness, expand that information and enhance that assent was the common project of the Churches on both sides of the Reformation divide. Alike in the Catholic, Protestant and Orthodox worlds, the Reformation era was defined by the reorientation of devotional life towards the personal and individual quest for God: a liberation of the soul, in which the Christian was encouraged to find a personal relationship with God, without bypassing his fellow Christians. The disagreements which have made the Catholic and Protestant traditions distinguishable from one another arose in the course of a common venture.

The story of the Reformation is an old one and most of its historians think it was over long ago. During the near half-millennium since it began, new problems have elicited new responses from the Churches and new circumstances have produced new initiatives, new movements, new projects. The opening of worldwide mission fields, in which Protestants, Catholics and Orthodox have variously competed and collaborated, has made the European Reformation look like a little local difficulty. The Churches have had to adapt their styles and messages to answer challenges from more-or-less new 'isms' which were non-existent or very immature when the Reformation began. Empiricism and rationalism have encouraged people to see transcendence in ways incompatible with Christianity or to deny its existence altogether. Liberalism and socialism have made promises of satisfaction in this world that have eclipsed hopes of salvation in the next. Humanism, which, when the Reformation began, meant study of the humane arts, has come to mean the doctrine that people can solve their problems without reference to God. Science and psychiatry have usurped some of the

1.1 One indication of the spread of lay devotion in the late fifteenth century is the large number of primers from the period which still exist. The books of psalms and prayers were for private devotion. They were used by members of religious orders, by beginners and people in lay confraternities and by ordinary people. This fine example from a Sarum primer shows David and Bathsheba, a suitable illustration for the beginning of the penitential psalms. Bathsheba turns her back on attendants who bear eucharistic images. She clutches a symbol of sin and stares into a mirror which represents vanity. Discarded footwear is part of the standard iconography of unchastity.

1.2 Pre-Reformation English devotional life. The advent of printing made possible the publication of educational aids for popular consumption. The London printer Wynkyn de Worde (ob. 1534) specialized in small, cheap books to meet the demands for religious instruction. They were heavily illustrated in order to appeal to the illiterate and semi-literate. *The Craft to Live Well and to Die Well* (1505) contained sections on many aspects of Catholic teaching, including confession (left), marriage (right) and the Lord's Prayer (below). Each scene is validated by an allusion to scripture. Soon after the publication of this book Wynkyn had to open additional premises to cope with the demand.

Churches' traditional functions in explaining the world and easing the mind. Christianity's struggle against worldliness has been deflected into courses unforseeable in Luther's day by secularism, consumerism and crass materialism. The rise of relativism – the doctrine, at its crudest, that one opinion is as good as another – has buried the Churches' claims to an exclusive truth or a comprehensive morality. Most recently, Christianity, which was received in the Western world nearly two thousand years ago as one of a number of fashionable mystery religions, has been challenged in turn by a new Western vogue for oriental thought.

The Reformation has reverberated through all these changes and challenges. Despite its reputation for having divided the Church, we think it has been the great unifying theme of Christian history in modern times. The Reformation projects have continued. The Churches have gone on reforming their own practices under the inspiration of the Bible, the model of the early Church and the influence of each on others. They have continued to work to make pagans into Christians and Christians into better Christians – more deeply aware, more actively committed. They have gone on encouraging individuals to make straight their own ways to God within and alongside the collective disciplines of Christian life. Alongside condemnation and reproof, the Catholic and Orthodox Churches have flattered Protestantism with a great deal of imitation. The theme of this book unites our times with Luther's and our Churches with each other.

Colours of the Canvas

Augustine of Canterbury and his little band of companions were justifiably nervous at the prospect of proclaiming the Gospel to the English and setting up a Church in 'a barbarous, fierce and pagan nation, of whose very language they were ignorant.' In addition to the obvious dangers of venturing beyond the fringe of Christendom there were problems of ecclesiology: how could Augustine be sure of 'getting it right' when he was largely out of touch with the time-hallowed certainties of Roman practice? And, anyway, what was right? As he agonized in a letter to Pope Gregory I, 'Since we hold the same faith, why do customs vary in different churches? Why, for instance, does the method of saying mass differ in the holy Roman church and in the church of Gaul?' The monk's journey towards his appointed area of mission proved to be something of an eye-opener. As he travelled through mountain passes, meadows and forests he found the cultural landscape no less varied than the physical and its contrasts and nuances reflected in the liturgies of the abbeys along his route.

Liturgy – and therefore the degrees of emphasis placed on various elements of the salvation story – not only varied from place to place; it was also in a state of constant development. The Roman rite which Augustine regarded as the norm was itself an amalgam and the pope was in the process of simplifying it even as Augustine began his work in distant Britain. The differences which the travellers noticed in the 'Gallican rite' (a misnomer since regional variations were considerable throughout Gaul) would have been the extensive use made of processions, more prayers, a more flexible Canon, the communion of the laity in both kinds and a greater sense of drama. There was, perhaps, something about this flamboyant style of worship that appealed even south of the Alps for elements of the Gallican rite had already become incorporated in the Ambrosian mass used in northern Italy. In the semi-isolated centres where Christ was worshipped, the clergy identified with liturgical traditions which, to their satisfaction, expressed the way they and their people wanted to express themselves.

Nor was there any official mistrust of these rich variations on a theme. Gregory, in reply to his young protégé, took a very relaxed attitude:

> If you have found customs, whether in the church of Rome or of Gaul or any other that may be more acceptable to God, I wish you to make a careful selection of them, and teach the church of the English . . . whatever you have been able to learn with profit . . . For things should not be loved for the sake of places, but places for the sake of good things.

Gregory's nice distinction proved too subtle for most people. A sense of place is a vital ingredient in a community's experience of identity and therefore of an individual's feeling of belonging. In reality, 'places' and 'good things' become cemented together in the edifices men call 'home', 'neighbourhood', 'country'; the psychological realities which inspire their loyalty and patriotism; the emotion-loaded entities for which they are prepared to fight and die. Gregory realized the power of special localities and their associated activities. In subsequent instructions to the English missionaries he advised sanctifying temples with holy water, appropriating them with altars and colonizing them with relics. Christian believers were also a part of the culture which their message challenged. Powerful local loyalties worked in them, too. Sub-cults rapidly developed within the Church. Augustine found it necessary to confront the Celtic monks over a range of customs in which they differed from Roman usage. Only after seventy years of rivalry did the two traditions achieve a measure of unanimity at the Synod of Whitby. At the end of the eighth century Charlemagne suppressed the Gallican rite in favour of the Roman mass. In 1085 Gregory VII abolished the Mozarabic rite used in a large area of Spain. But such attempts to impose uniformity were sporadic and far from successful. Nor did they have the unqualified support of leading churchmen. In particular the religious orders were allowed their own liturgies. Innocent III had to mount a fresh Romanizing crusade at the beginning of the thirteenth century, employing the friars as his agents. Yet even by the Reformation epoch, when centralized control became a matter of urgency, there were still senior clergy making pleas for creative variety. Cisneros of Toledo tried to resurrect the Mozarabic rite, while Charles Borromeo of Milan staunchly defended the Ambrosian use.

If medieval worship and devotion was a patchwork, doctrine was an intricate pattern of contrasting shapes and colours. Three influences were brought to bear on what Christians believed – the pronouncements of Rome, the deliberations of the schools and the thrust of popular religion. The interaction of these three produced a broad consensus within which local variants were more or less tolerated. The clearest example of this is the development of the cult of the Virgin.

On the eve of the Reformation the country around Berne was abuzz with scandal. In the Dominican convent a recently admitted friar received a vision in which Mary appeared in order to make it clear to him and the world that the circumstances of her own birth were perfectly normal. She had not been immaculately conceived. She even handed the quaking friar a letter for the pope making the same point. This appeared to settle an issue which had been debated fiercely in the schools for over two hundred years. That was precisely what the 'vision' was intended to do. For, of course, it was a fraud. Four senior members of the convent had drugged their poor brother and one of them had donned woman's attire to masquerade as the Virgin. Various other signs and wonders had been manufactured to add to the effect and the whole charade had worked beyond its instigators' wildest imaginings until the dupe discovered the deception and confessed all. The ringleaders were subsequently examined by the Inquisition, found guilty and burned. The incident was only the most bizarre in a long series of confrontations between the Dominicans and the Franciscans on the subject of the immaculate conception.

If we juxtapose two powerful images, we can see clearly how popular understanding of the roles of Christ and the Virgin changed during the pre-Reformation millennium. In the Catacomb of Calixtus in Rome there is a third century wall-painting of the Good Shepherd, leading his flock and carrying a sheep across his shoulders. This was a comforting and treasured gospel image for the unestablished Church, when Christians were in peril of denunciation to the authorities by angry fellow citizens or scheming neighbours who coveted their goods. The other equally haunting picture is a mid-fifteenth century polyptych by Piero della Francesca, now in the museum of Borgo San Sepolcro in Umbria. The central panel portrays the Virgin as a majestic *magna mater* receiving the adoration of kneeling devotees, around whom she casts her protective cloak. The Mother of Mercy was as popular a figure in the late medieval world (especially after the Black Death) as the Good Shepherd had been a thousand years before. She was now the one who knew the sheep by name and led them into the eternal fold. The Virgin had become, in popular devotion if not in official theology, a goddess in her own right and the supreme intermediary for sinful mortals before the judgement seat.

Accretions of exuberant mythology gradually built up around the meagre core of knowable fact. Mary was *perpetually* virgin, both before and after the birth of Jesus. At the end of her earthly life she was spared the normal process of death and decay by being assumed into heaven. There she was installed as the chief of intercessors. There she was recognized as Queen of Heaven, a doctrine first realized artistically in a superb mosaic on the west front of Santa Maria in Trastevere in Rome towards the middle of the twelfth century. The Virgin became an allegory of the community of faith. If Mary was mother, mediatrix, queen, virgin and miracle-worker, so, by mystical allusion, was the Church. The increasingly chaotic aggregate of popular Marian doctrines and legends was supported, sometimes reluctantly, by pastors, bishops and popes. The immaculate conception was widely believed long before it became an approved doctrine in 1662 or an official dogma nearly two hundred years later. Theology from below was being appropriated by the hierarchy to define and enhance the Church's self-image.

Theologically the medieval Church was far from being a monochrome canvas of approved beliefs. Splodges of colour were applied by different scholastic traditions, Dominicans, Franciscans, cloistered ascetics, hierarchs, humble believers and defenders of local interests. When Luther issued his Ninety-five Theses against indulgences he was not shouting defiance at a united Catholic establishment. His protest was a theological one but it made a deliberate appeal to local sentiment. Luther spoke for many of his countrymen when he objected to the raising of funds for rebuilding St Peter's:

> Before long all the churches, palaces, walls and bridges of Rome will be built out of our money. First of all we should rear living temples, next local churches, and only last of all St Peter's, which is not necessary for us. We Germans cannot attend St Peter's. Better that it should never be built than that our parochial churches should be despoiled.

This was not meant as a plea to dissolve the universal Church into national and local communities and congregations which would no longer form one communion, whole and entire; Luther's was a programme to rebuild the Church from the foundations upwards, by an evangelical assault on parishes and localities – to gather up the splinters of the Cross where they lay, and to try to put them together again.

SACRED TOPOGRAPHY

The clergy try to make the rough places plain but you can still visit the un-levelled hollows and hummocks of local religion. Sometimes the shrines are ruins or names on a map, like those of the extraordinary plethora of saints, unknown elsewhere and barely remembered in their own patches, who once blessed the sacred topography of the coves of Cornwall and the hilltops and valley bottoms of Wales. Yet, even today, scraps and wrecks of medieval religion survive where they are protected by mountains or particularist traditions. A devotional map of Bavarian customs and devotions – could such a thing be constructed – would be a patchwork of three levels of variety: assertions of local, regional and national allegiance to particular saints and patrons, in distinction from – sometimes in defiance of – the universal programme of the Church. On the Klopfersnacht, the night, unhonoured elsewhere, of the Thursday before the second Sunday before Christmas, wassailing children celebrate. At Berchtesgaden, where Hitler's is not the only shrine to attract modern pilgrims, the practice is spread over four weeks and accompanied by a fair. The end of the Christmas season is celebrated by the mummery of *Sternsinger* and chalked invocations to the magi on doorways. Local patrons, like St Nicholas in Schrobenhausen and St Leonard in Bad Tölz, have annual feasts which rival or excel those of universal cults. The region's principal shrine, which houses a cult of strongly patriotic Bavarian flavour, is that of the candle-blackened Virgin of Altötting, who is a focus of genuinely regional pilgrimage – though even on her feast-day not much comes from further afield than Upper Austria. The cathedrals of Passau and Friesing, the Cistercians of Ebrach and the Benedictines of Benediktbeuren all guard numinous regional shrines, but the last, which was the resting-place of the manuscript of the Carmina Burana, has also channelled pan-German sentiment, which, in a land that values Catholic devotion more than Catholic dogma, sometimes challenges loyalty to the Church: Martin Luther appears in the old kings' gallery of German heroes at Hohenschwangau. Except around Feldkirchen, which had a particularly active pastorate in the nineteenth century, Protestants are few, but in neighbouring Swabia, Protestantism co-exists with a regional religion at least as ancient and almost as riven by local allegiances as in Bavaria: a bride-theft ritual precedes weddings; umbilical cords are treasured as trophies of birth; death is celebrated with a wake. St Walburga, the eighth-century Abbess whose rocky tomb was said to secrete a healing fluid, is honoured on Walpurgis night, when her memory blurs with that of the pagan goddess Waldborg and witches are said to emerge for an annual mountain rendezvous.

Some of the most tenacious survivals can be seen in Spain. In worship – more than in any other activity except war – Spaniards have forged their collective identities. A Spaniard's sense of being Spanish, for instance, could formerly be measured – in some cases, can still be measured – by the intensity of his devotion to national cults, like those of the Virgin of the Pillar or St James the Slayer of Moors. Certain ethnicities can be identified to some extent with particular cults, like that of St Fermín for the Navarrese or the Virgin of Candelaria for the Canarians. Civic loyalties are linked to the veneration of celestial patrons: St Froilán is hardly known outside León; in Bilbao, civic pride is focused on the shrine of Our Lady of the Begonia, where the football club celebrates its victories. When Barcelona football club wins a major championship, the team go to the shrine of the Virgin of La Mercé to sing a Salve in her praise, and on her feast day Socialist councillors swallow their secularism and file and stoop before her feet.

Half a millennium of unification, evangelization, secularization and, latterly, industrialization has failed to prise Spaniards from their adherence to local religion. In a Cantabrian valley studied by William Christian, Jr., the post-Tridentine clerical élite brought the universal cults of the Virgin Mary and the suffering Christ as part of their effort to make the Church 'truly one'. The villagers responded, as had their ancestors, to the first missionaries' message, by adapting the proffered symbols to their local need for tutelary deities. Christ and His mother were stripped of their universal significance and relocalized, as it were, under advocations drawn from comforting local toponyms. They became the Christ of this place, the Virgin of that. In short, they displaced the patron saints only in the same limited way as once the saints had replaced pagan gods. In mid-nineteenth-century Spain, regionalist intellectuals sometimes advocated solutions to the country's problems more in terms of concessions to local religious feeling than of political devolution. 'Leave the provinces their local cults, their beliefs and their laws,' was a typical cry, 'their truths and their household gods!'

This was the kind of Christianity late medieval and early modern reformers were up against. In the Lyonnais, from the thirteenth century, the region's favourite saint was a dog: St Guinefort, unjustly slaughtered for the death of a baby he had really been trying to save, could never be canonized by the official Church but was a perfect martyr for the assertion of lay sensibilities in a world dependent on the friendship of dog and man. In Flanders, from the fourteenth century, people adored St Wilgefortis, a bearded lady who never existed but who was supposed to have protected her virginity by prayers to be ugly. She was especially popular with wives who wanted to be rid of their husbands. In Lucca, the Church finally surrendered in the sixteenth century, after centuries of struggle to control or disavow the cult of St Zita, a serving-maid whom angelic understudies liberated from her chores to give her time for ecstatic raptures. At North Rona in Scotland, the shrine of St Ronan was a symbol of local resistance, for he was said to have enlisted animals in defending it against the attacks of monsters during his life in the seventh century; at another level of resistance, St Magnus, the martyred Earl of Orkney, served as a patron of Scottish resistance against England, appearing to Robert Bruce on the eve of Bannockburn.

Out of the friable earth of medieval Christianity, reformers – from Innocent III to Luther and later – tried to make the solid bricks of a single edifice. But at least until the great clerical offensives of the sixteenth century, the fragments seemed to get smaller, the foci of devotion more minute. By the fifteenth century, group culture had ensconced itself securely within the parish church. Eamon Duffy has given us a vivid picture of the typical English building crammed with side altars and subsidiary chapels, each the responsibility of a local guild or family which kept the images fresh-painted and richly decked and paid priests to say regular masses. The installation of a new altar might be a thank-you offering, such as one erected to St James at Burgh, Lincolnshire, by a group of men preserved by the saint from ship-wreck on the way back from a pilgrimage to Compostela. It might be the expression of a family's new-found prosperity (gratitude mingled with osten-tation). It might be in response to changing fashion: in late medieval England, St Erasmus, a Syrian martyr, enjoyed a sudden surge of popularity – perhaps because he was credited with the healing of bowel complaints. This privatized religion involving small groups of devotees rather than the parish as a whole provided the principal worship focus for many. The Victorian image of the bareheaded medieval peasant standing in the furrow behind his restive workhorse listening in silent adoration to the Angelus bell will not do as a good picture of medieval Christianity.

THE GRAIL QUEST

This reformation and restoration in ecclesiastical affairs must needs begin with you, our fathers, and then afterwards descend upon us your priests and the whole clergy. For you are our chiefs – you are our examples of life. To you we look as waymarks for our direction. In you and in your lives we desire to read, as in living books, how we ourselves should live. Wherefore, if you wish to see our motes, first take the beams out of your own eyes; for it is an old proverb, 'Physician, heal thyself.' Do you, spiritual doctors, first assay that medicine for the purgation of morals, and then you may offer it to us to taste of it also.

When John Colet preached before the convocation of Canterbury in 1512 he used the words 'restoration' and 'reformation'. His was only one voice in what had become a Babel of urgent entreaty. Preachers across Europe were pleading, begging, praying for the wholeness and wholesomeness of the Church. But fewer and fewer of them thought only in terms of Christendom *restored*. Restoration suggested the renewal of old institutions. What was needed was something much more radical – *reform*. The old order had to be reconstituted; partly because it was corrupt and corrupting; partly because the world was changing. Gianfrancesco Pico della Mirandola, erstwhile champion of Savonarola, warned Leo X, 'If you fail to heal these wounds, I fear that God himself, whose place on earth you take, will not apply a gentle cure, but with fire and sword will cut off those diseased members and destroy them; and I believe that He has already clearly given signs of his future remedy.'

We who are in a position to take the longer view need to ask, 'Was there anything to restore or reform?' Was 'Christendom' ever anything more than a pious idea? If Catholic West was permanently sundered from Orthodox East; if liturgy and, to a certain extent, theology were syncretistic, amalgams of Jewish, Christian and pagan concepts about the divine; if doctrine was created 'on the hoof' by gullible peasants and ecclesiastical politicians as well as scholars; if the Holy Trinity or the Apostles and the Fathers were only figures, and not always prominent figures, in a passing cavalcade of wonder-working saints; if rival preachers under papal licence thundered contradictory sermons; if worship varied from place to place according to local tradition; if the ecclesiastical institution was a mess of competing authorities and jurisdictions; if attempts from the top to reimpose unity and uniformity consistently failed; if men's loyalty had to be constrained by threat of the stake or public humiliation (and even then many preferred death to subscribing to articles against which their intelligence rebelled); was Christendom any more than an elaborate shell from which the living organism had long since departed?

The answer is in the spiritual forces which throbbed within medieval society, inspiring, impelling, driving individuals, groups and sometimes whole communities to acts of heroism, works of charity and visions of glory: the spiritual continuum of the late Middle Ages into which the Reformation fits.

Over the last two centuries quantities of academic ink have been expended in attempts to prove that genuine Christianity was either flourishing or floundering in the pre-Reformation centuries. Gothic nostalgia created the myth of the Age of Faith. Sceptics like Robert Browning ridiculed such romantic propaganda.

> How should you feel, I ask, in such an age,
> How act? As other people felt and did;
> With soul more blank than this decanter's knob,
> Believe – and yet lie, rob, kill, fornicate
> Full in belief's face, like the beast you'd be!

More recently Keith Thomas in *Religion and the Decline of Magic* has presented a picture of an age in which, 'Many medieval clergy and laity had been beset by overwhelming temptations to blasphemy and atheism and a wide range of popular scepticism was uncovered by the fifteenth-century church courts.' With such theories very much in mind rival historians have considered it necessary to counterattack vigorously: 'My object . . . is to map the range and vigour of late medieval and early modern English Catholicism, and in the process to exorcise certain types of writing about the English Reformation', Eamon Duffy asserted in *The Stripping of the Atlas*.

The truth, as William Temple observed in a different context, lies in neither extreme; nor does it lie in the middle; but in both extremes. The late fifteenth century was a time of widespread religious fervour – of localized manifestation without doubt, intermittent to be sure, of varied intensity and duration certainly, but widespread nevertheless.

The Reformation did not come as a torrent in a parched land. People responded to the challenging ideas of emancipated preachers and propagandists because they appeared to meet already perceived needs.

Of course, there was much that *was* new in the sixteenth century. *Post tenebrae lux* was the watchword of Calvin's Geneva. The new opportunities for evangelization in growing towns, under-explored hinterlands and expanding frontiers could be exploited with new tools: printed catechisms, woodcuts and tracts, and, above all, vernacular scriptures. Those caught up in the exciting new movements were certainly not wrong in believing that they lived in revolutionary times. But that does not mean that they were right in their assessment *de l'âge passé*. In a vulgar altercation over the efficacy of requiem masses which was reported from Rotherham in 1537, one of the combatants shouted defiantly, 'Thy father was a liar and is in Hell, and so is my father in Hell also; my father never knew Scripture and now it is come forth.' From a post-1517 perspective the religious life of recent generations seemed torpid and drugged with error. What few, if any, contemporaries could see was that the momentum of spiritual exploration had begun long before. The vehicle might have been thrust suddenly from second into fifth gear in the 1520s, but it was already moving.

A traditional place for men and women who wanted to get closer to God was the cloister. Thousands of religious preceded Luther, Erasmus and other later reformers along the paths of daily worship, self-denial, contemplation and study. Worldliness, however, could overtake the most holy institution. John Wesley warned the early Methodists that their industry and thrift would inevitably bring them wealth, social standing, the envy of their neighbours and a host of new temptations. The same fate overtook some of the religious orders: frugality, careful husbandry and the gifts of pious patrons swelled their coffers and, unless they were vigilant, their pretensions and their pride. The religious life of the Middle Ages revolved in a cycle of corruption and reform. Founders tried to keep orders small or poor; some imitated the lives of hermits or beggars. St Francis aspired to copy the apostles and hoped vainly that his order would be able to do without a rule.

One aim of religious innovators was to bring spirituality closer to the common people. What became the Brethren of the Common Life began as a small group of lay preachers whom Gerard Groot gathered round him to teach a spiritual discipline capable of being followed in the workaday world. His close contemporary, Catherine of Siena, a Dominican tertiary, firmly refused blandishments to live in a convent. As well as attracting around her fervent disciples who were overawed by her ecstatic experiences, she kept up an enormous correspondence with popes, clerics, politicians and people of low degree. The great mystical writers of the fourteenth and fifteenth centuries were avidly read by the cloistered religious but their popularity rested on their offering spiritual paths to God which were not dependent on keeping the canonical hours and certainly not dependent on any initiation into speculative theology. Many of the contemplative masters either bypassed the intellect or regarded it as but a ladder to the upper realms of spiritual experience which transcended human thought: as Meister Eckhart said, 'To nothing but the Divine Being, directly and without mediation'.

It was this apparent encouragement of indifference to the standard means of grace which so often attracted the hostility of the religious establishment. If inquisitors were hard put to it to distinguish between heresy and orthodoxy; if Eckhart could be condemned; if jealous fellow-Dominicans could haul Catherine of Siena out of church and fling her down in the dust of the market place; if politically motivated clerics could order Joan of Arc to be burned as a witch, then it is clear that ordinary people could not be expected to draw simple demarcation lines between the exponents of truth and error. Medieval Europe was just as rich as modern America in prophets, visionaries and gurus offering sure-fire guides to heaven. Could a crowd of moderately intelligent townsmen hanging on the words of Eckhart tell the difference between his teachings and those of an equally compelling orator such as Gerald Segarelli who was captivating audiences on the other side of the Alps? Segarelli's Apostolic Brethren lived a life of mendicant poverty, like the friars. Segarelli also spoke about the indwelling Spirit of God. The fact that he was burned at the stake scarcely marked him out from the German who recanted under pressure, or from the holy men and exhorters of semi-official brotherhoods and beguinages that operated within, on the fringes of and outside what popes and bishops called 'the Church'. Some established identities of their own by schism; others remained as black sheep within the folds of Rome or Orthodoxy. Diversity was not the privilege of radicals, but the pattern of Christianity. The fringe was parti-coloured, but the quilt was also a patchwork of many hues.

Chapter 2

STAYING FOR AN ANSWER:
Scripture and Tradition

THE ECCLESIASTICAL MONOPOLY

In Dostoevsky's *The Brothers Karamazov,* Ivan, the idealistic revolutionary, tells a story which he calls *The Grand Inquisitor.* The setting is late-sixteenth-century Seville. In the title role stands a venerable cardinal, iron sentinel of an iron church; inflexible guardian of received tradition. The old man unexpectedly finds himself confronted with a new prisoner in his dungeon: a troublesome, itinerant pedlar of heresies. It is Christ himself.

The two men – one the representative of the Church, the other its founder – confront each other in the torture chamber, littered with the terrifying machines used for generations to extract confessions from wayward believers. Jesus, as at his former trial, remains accusingly mute. It is the Inquisitor who does the talking. Carefully, with nice logic, and quite without remorse, he explains to his unwelcome intruder why it is necessary to have him executed:

> You rejected the only way by which men might be made happy, but, fortunately, in departing, you handed on the work to us. You have promised and you have confirmed it by your own word. You have given us the right to bind and unbind, and of course you can't possibly think

IDEM IMPETRAVIT A DEO VT MAGVS A DEMONIBVS DISCERPERETVR ·

2.1 Religious and nationalistic feelings are unleashed in this engraving by Pieter van der Heyden after Pieter Brueghel the Elder (c1525-69). It depicts St James, patron saint of Spain, in league with the demons of hell, a scarcely veiled reference to the persecutions and violence perpetrated by the occupying power in the southern Netherlands.

of depriving us of that right now. Why, then, have you come to interfere with us? . . .

We have corrected your great work and have based it on *miracle, mystery, and authority*. And men rejoiced that they were once more led like sheep and that the terrible gift which had brought them so much suffering had at last been lifted from their hearts. Were we right in doing and teaching this? Tell me. Did we not love mankind when we admitted so humbly its impotence and lovingly lightened its burden and allowed men's weak nature even to sin, so long as it was with our permission? Why, then, have you come to meddle with us now? And why are you looking at me silently and so penetratingly with your gentle eyes? Get angry. I do not want your love because I do not love you myself. And what have I to hide from you? . . . Perhaps it is just what you want to hear from my lips. Well, then, listen. We are not with you but with *him*. Exactly eight centuries ago we took from him what you rejected with scorn, the last gift he offered you, after having shown you all the kingdoms

2.2 In a popular book of 1509, Ulrich Tengler's *Mirror for Laypeople*, a traditional image of Mary a *schultzmantelbild* was used. She was shown representing the Church, protecting people of all kinds of ranks from devils, while the evangelists work in the foreground and the Doctors of the Church attend Christ.

of the earth: we took from him Rome and the word of Caesar and proclaimed ourselves the rulers of the earth, the sole rulers.

We do not have to accept Dostoevsky's cynical assessment of Rome's deliberate distortion of the Gospel to agree that throughout Latin Christendom the medieval Church claimed a monopoly of truth. Not just religious truth. In a world in which the material was shot through with the spiritual, issues of politics, personal morality, legal obligation, business dealings, marital relationships, war and peace were all susceptible to ecclesiastical direction. Of course, what the Church asserted and what its lay members accepted by no means made a close, consistent match. It is difficult, if not impossible to make an accurate correlation between the belief system people acquiesce in, what they really believe in and how they behave as a result. In this chapter our objective is considerably more modest: we seek only to map the terrain of religious truth; to indicate what, by their own profession, people who thought about Christianity claimed to base their beliefs on.

Truth as a Given

'Whoever undertakes to set himself up as a judge in the field of truth and knowledge is shipwrecked by the laughter of the gods.' Einstein's dictum serves us well if we take it as a warning against intellectual arrogance. But we could read it as an affirmation of a world-weary scepticism; nothing is knowable; nothing is certain; nothing is proved which may not, in the fulness of time, be disproved. This is certainly a common perception. We live in a world of failed theories. Time and again we have been let down by scientists, politicians, economists, social theorists, educationalists. Inured to the regular dethroning of past certainties, we may readily come to rest our weight on the crooked staff of doubt and to link arms with disillusion. Certainly we consider it only prudent to be very wary of all experts.

This fixes a gulf between us and our sixteenth-century forbears. We are the heirs, not only of rationalism, which invites us to question the very idea of God, but also of empiricism which conditions us to believe only what we can discern with our senses; and of existentialism which demands that we fix our own, subjective concepts of truth. This makes it very difficult for us to grapple with the mind set of a thinker such as Francis Bacon, who could affirm, 'the inquiry of truth, which is the love-making, or wooing of it, the knowledge of truth, which is the presence of it, and the belief of truth, which is the enjoying of it, is the sovereign good of human nature.' Reformation man, whether he stood in the Catholic or Protestant camp, accepted the existence of God and that he was the fount of all truth – which was, therefore, objective. With the exception of some mystics, Christians

2.3 The tower of knowledge as depicted by Gregor Reisch in *Margarita philosophica* (1503). Under the scholastic system a university student proceeded from grammar, by way of logic, rhetoric, arithmetic, music, geometry, astronomy and physics to theology, the queen of the sciences.

believed that God revealed himself and his purposes to those who sought him. Theology was the queen of the sciences because it alone defined the parameters of knowledge and indicated which lines of enquiry led to the enhancement of the human condition and the greater glory of God (which two could not be disentangled).

Church authorities gave practical support to this containment of the world of ideas, through a system of censorship. By the terms of a papal bull of 1487 every new-printed book had to bear the name of its author and the place of its publication and had to be approved by the local bishop. Anonymous publications were outlawed in several decrees promulgated by ecclesiastical and secular authorities. From time to time bishops banned the works of certain authors and visited universities and schools to ensure that subversive material was not being circulated. Public burnings provided dramatic demonstrations of the Church's determination to protect people from dangerous false teaching. Lists of forbidden writings were issued, culminating in the first *index librorum prohibitorum* in 1559. Catholic authorities were not alone is seeking to shape public attitudes with the fires of persuasion and the hammers of coercion. Luther responded to the condemnation of his works by publicly burning the papal bull and throwing in the canon law for good measure. Henry VIII secularized book licensing but left it in the hands of churchmen. Calvin's Geneva and those regions which took their inspiration from it exercised a rigid censorship. There was no nation in sixteenth-century Europe in which either Church or State was not involved in the shaping of public opinion.

There was, however, room for speculation. Copernicus could dedicate his *De revolutionibus orbium coelestium* (which, in 1616, would be found on the Index) to Pope Paul III. It was common form for scholars to insist that their novel ideas existed to serve ancient truth. So, for example, Etienne de la Roche's textbook on arithmetic, offered to the world in 1516, was set forth 'For the gratification and glory of God the creator, and the most glorious Virgin Mary His most holy mother, and my lord Saint Stephen, my most revered patron, and the whole heavenly host in Paradise'. Sixteenth-century scholars were able to remain faithful Catholics or Protestants while advancing theories which, in the fulness of time, would oblige the theologians to reformulate their beliefs. They knew they were dealing in mysteries emanating from the Godhead. They accepted that all their strivings for truth were subsumed within that greater quest in which holy doctors and students of sacred Scripture led the way. Truth was something much more profound than a mere set of propositions which happened to be verified by observation and experimentation. In 1549 Melanchthon tried to make this clear to a new generation: 'Men of science with subtle minds like to discuss a lot of questions on which they exercise their ingenuity, but the young should be aware that these scientists have no intention of affirming such things.'

TONVS QVARTVS. LXXIII

decantat ipfum arbitrum undis:Sic etiam planctaҩ ordo exquirit:ut poſt
Lunam terream fit Mercurius aqueus:Venus aerea:Sol igneus.Et iterũ/
Mars igneus:Iupiter aereus:Saturnus aqueus:Signifeҩ cœlũ terreũ:Pri/
mum mobile igneum.Quo ordine etiã Angelicæ mentes ſuccedunt:Ha
bent.n.Angeli naturam terream cum Luna:Archãgeli aqueam cũ Mer/
curio:Principatus aereã cũ Venere:Poteſtates igneam eũ Sole : Virtutes
irerum igneam cum Marte:Dominatióes aereã cum Ioue:Throni aqueã
cum Saturno:Cherubini terream cum firmamento:Seraphini igneã cum
primo mobili:& cum Archetypo in ignea ui Spiritui ſancto conueniunt:
Throni uero cũ filio,qui eſt aqua ſupramundana,de qua omniũ philoſo/
Moſes phoҩ,& theologoҩ facile Princeps Moſes pertractat/quando aquas ſub
globo,aut cortina cœloҩ ſegregat ab iis,quæ deſup erant:Quæ ſunt aquę
Angelicæ Deũ/teſte Dauide/laudantes:Sunt & ſumma affluétia bonita/
tis diuinę,quæ ne plus ǫ inferioҩ gradus,& opera merentur effundaέ/in/
terpoſita eſt cõtinens illa cœleſtis:in qua tanǫ in tribunali quodã diiudica
tur/ǫcum ex ipſa aqua cuiǫ tribui debeat.Sed huiuſmodi arcana Moſes
ſub teſta recluſit pribus/populiſǫ illis /quibus in figura omnia continge/
bant:Ex ǫbus multigenis,& occultiſſimis ſacramétis antiqui philoſophi,
& uates aliquos cortices extrahentes ſibi multa uendicarunt:adeo/ut cre/
datur Pythagoræ,Socratis,Platonis,Ariſtotelis/& alioҩ ſapientia/quæ a
ſũmo fonte Deo per Moſem ad mortales emanauit,ut ipſe Moſes,& non
Cicero Socrates (ſicut ſcribit Cicero) ſapientiã uocauerit de cœlo/& primus lite
ris publicis cõmendauerit.Sed clarius hæc explicata habent a Chriſto/&
eius aſſeclis/ quibus eadé credidit. Et forſitã hæc aqua ſapientiæ ſalutaris
diffuſius adhuc propinabiέ mortalibus/quãdo ſuperiores Dei miniſtri in
aqueũ cœli atriũ conuenient omnes/quibus a ſupremo fonte dabiέ facul/
tas aperiendi excelſos illos canales/nũc ob infœlicia tempora conclſos:
immo ob mala merita illoҩ/qui his deterioribus offuſcati,ipſœliceſǫ te/
nebræ effecti illã ſupremam luce,& aquam apprehendere nequeunt:nec
merenέ:Quos canales iubeat Deus ſua clemétia aperiri : quia terrena fa/
cieſã in ſumma ariditate reperiέ,& propineέ,ſicut propinauit Moſi:qui
mérito ſumptus ex aquis diciέ:Profundatǫ ipſam Dei filius aqua ſupre/
ma per miniſtros in cubiculum aqueũ colligendos/ſicut olim tanta copia
propinauit diſcipulis,ut flumina de uentre eoҩ ſcaturirét aquæ uiuentis:
unde fieret fons ſaliens in uitã æternam.Sed ad noſtrũ Mercuriũ redeun/
do,naturã ſapit aqueã:Nam ſicut hæc laudãdo auterέ obtegenté maculã:
ut appareat nuda rei forma:ſic ille Hermes uerus interpres ãmouet teſtã
extranei idiomatis/obſcuritatem ęnigmatũ/& parabolaҩ,aut cuiuſcunǫ
detruſi ſermonis difficultaté:Et apiés ea,quæ in penetralibus arcanis Dei:
& naturæ recondita ſunt,nudam offert ueritatem contuendam.Et ut cum

K

2.4 A page of Francesco Giorgio's *De Harmonia Mundi* (Venice 1525) after an ecclesiastical
censor had been at it.

Melanchthon's friend, Martin Luther, began his protest in a conventional way: the ninety-five theses were an invitation – albeit a very truculent invitation – to other scholars to debate specific issues. He was taking advantage of the latitude enjoyed by academics. Melanchthon's other friend, Desiderius Erasmus, was doing the same with his satirical and controversial writings. Of the two men Erasmus was, initially, far more sweeping in his criticisms, but their attitudes to the religious life point to a deeper divergence. Both men had taken vows. Both came to loathe monasticism. The German Augustinian abandoned the cowl because he could find no scriptural justification for the monastic vocation: because he could find no scriptural justification for the monastic vocation, he advocated the dissolution of religious houses. The Dutch Augustinian just as effectively escaped from the rule. He declined to live in the cloister or to wear the habit. But he did so by virtue of papal dispensation.

There was a doctor in Constance who bought a portrait engraving of Erasmus so that he could pin it to his wall and spit at it whenever he passed by. For such orthodox Christians the great scholar was a corrupter of the Church. For the growing body of Protestants, Erasmus was a betrayer of the Gospel. His reputation has never escaped from the bearpit of controversy. As religious views polarized, Erasmus was castigated as a sitter on the fence; an arrogant intellectual content to recline on Olympus and snigger at the follies of mankind; a savage critic who, when taken to task, whined that he had been misunderstood; a man who lacked the courage of his convictions. He was jealous of his scholarly privacy and tranquillity. He resisted being dragged from the spectator's bench into the arena. When he heard of Thomas More's imprisonment his response was that his old friend should not have set himself up as a papal champion. But alongside his emotional disinclination for conflict went a commitment to the world as it was and the truth system which held it together. He would point out the flaws in that system. He would urge reform. But he would not overthrow the system – not even for the sake of the Gospel. In a letter to Luther he condemned the German reformer for doing just that: 'you are shattering the whole globe in ruinous discord . . . so carrying on the cause of the Gospel as to throw all things sacred and profane into chaos.'

Luther was condemned by the pope as the wild boar in the vineyard. He preferred to see himself as a labourer carrying out essential pruning and weeding. He was a prophet and it is the fate of prophets to stir up trouble. Day after day, week after week, letters and snippets of news arrived in Wittenberg telling of the spread of his revolution. He could not fail to be moved by accounts of tragedies and triumphs, heroism and barbarism, distortions of the message and pledges of support. Increasingly, he found the history of the old Israel a comfort in turbulent times. God's ancient people had been divided ever since Jacob and Esau. Apostasy and the call to repentance were repeated themes in the song sung by men and angels.

> . . . at all times we are either Esauites or Jacobites . . . and even if we
> were to conquer the Pope and his men, and if our doctrine which is
> proper to the true Church were to triumph; yet from our own midst
> would arise Papists and Turks who would sell the title of 'Church'. Thus
> the Anabaptists and Sacramentaries have arisen . . . thus always, Cain or
> Abel, Esau or Jacob.

The prophet had been laid hold of by a higher truth, a truth the whole
Church was pledged to uphold; a truth which now, as often in the past was
guarded only by a faithful remnant. He had no choice whether or not to
proclaim it and to recall wayward Christians from their disobedience. Nor
did he have any doubt about the outcome.

> This world's prince may rave.
> However he behave,
> He can do no ill.
> God's truth abideth still.
> One little word shall fell him.

THE WORD

Luther's higher truth was the word of God. The well-known account of his
enlightenment which he wrote in later years tells of his bitter struggle with
the concepts of law, sin, judgement and grace and his liberating realization
that acceptance by God is not earned but given in response to faith as a
result of the work of Christ the sin-bearer. This truth overturned the religion
of works which conventional devotion had become for Luther. From that
moment, everything had to be put under the microscope of Scripture – the
penitential system, the sacraments, the writings of the Fathers, the claims of
the papacy, everything.

Luther was very far from being either the first or the last to find his whole
being resonating to the dynamic of the word of God written. Throughout
the Christian centuries men and women have shared the experience of J.B.
Phillips who likened rendering the New Testament into modern English to
rewiring a house without disconnecting it from the mains.

> Ignorance of the Scriptures is ignorance of Christ . . . I beg you, dear
> brother, live with them, meditate on them, make them the sole object of
> your knowledge and inquiries.

So insisted Jerome who devoted the greater part of his long life (c.347–c.420)
to the study and translation of the Bible. For him the canonical Christian
writings were not only the staple diet of the individual believer, they were

the nutrients of divinely inspired truth which built up the Church and gave it the strength to overthrow heresy.

The Bible inspired the great monastic reform movements of the eleventh and twelfth centuries and every renewal, whether local or widespread, was connected with revived interest in Scripture. Archbishop Fitzralph of Armagh, one of the leading international churchmen of the early fourteenth century, testified to the way the Scriptures broke through his conventional studies and dazzled him with the radiance of truth.

> I used to think that I had penetrated to the depths of Your Truth with the citizens of Your Heaven; until You, the Solid Truth, shone upon me in Your Scriptures, scattering the cloud of my error, and showing me how I was croaking in the marshes with the toads and frogs.

These very writings – divinely inspired and Church-honoured – gave the impetus to heresy. Seekers of a deepened faith grabbed the bare wires of Scripture and were thrown right out through the doorway of the Catholic household. Dissidents, overwhelmed by holy writ, claimed that the Church had distorted or abandoned its essential truth. Spokesmen for orthodoxy accused the heretics of corrupting the divine message and departing from its traditional interpretation. The reality is more complex.

As far as we can tell from extant records, heresy seems not to have been perceived in the West as a serious problem for seven hundred years after the patristic era – not, at least, a problem worth kindling a pyre or launching a crusade for. The great enemy of the faith was paganism and compared with the worship of false gods variations of Christian doctrine were of less concern to the authorities. Meanwhile, independent reflection on the Bible was a spiritual luxury which was not widely available: one of the great sources of heretical inspiration was cut off.

Throughout what used to be called the Dark Ages, when the Latin church was in missionary mode, the Bible was brandished aloft and yet its contents were obscured from public view. Scripture was central to the Church's life both in its monastic fortresses and its mission outposts. The Bible was revered. Liturgy was steeped in it. Monks spent long hours copying portions of it and adorning the text with sumptuous illustrations. Scholars sufficiently versed in Latin pored over it in abbeys and cathedral schools. Its more dramatic episodes were depicted in murals and expatiated upon in sermons. All who could were encouraged to read it.

In reality, there were not many who could. Passages the clergy and travelling preachers chose to expound were freely mixed with quotations from uncanonical books and stories from the lives of the saints. Sometimes psalters carried glosses to aid understanding. Verse paraphrases were popular. It is clear from surviving fragments that some erudite preachers incorporated translated passages in their homilies and sermons. Even in the late Middle Ages, experience of regular worship did not provide this. As one modern scholar has observed, 'Medieval liturgies are bewildering mosaics cut and shaped for a purpose out of the Scriptures; and if this process gives a prodigious enrichment to meaning, it obscures almost completely the flow and scope of the original.' The biblical material presented to the people was like the gauze screen used in pantomime transformation scenes, sometimes concealing, sometimes displaying parts of the set behind. Veneration for the holy text turned the book itself, as a physical object, into an icon. A vestige of this attitude survives in many churches – Catholic and Protestant – today, where the Bible is set in a beautifully carved lectern or ceremonially carried in procession during worship. Even in Pentecostal circles it is not unknown for the Bible to be wielded almost as a material weapon during exorcism or spiritual healing. Such thinking was more common – even the norm – in an age when *any* book was a thing of wonder, commanding the price of a noble's ransom. People expected their priests to read out Bible passages over the sick and women in labour, or if that was beyond their powers, at least to touch them with the sacred tome.

Where the Bible was studied men brought to it a reverence which could lead to spiritual enlightenment but which could also stifle understanding. Generations of contemplatives meditated on holy writ in a disciplined atmosphere, bound and studded by liturgy and prayer. The reader only undertook the ascent of the majestic pinnacles of divine revelation clinging firmly to the interpretative rope which linked him to those expert climbers and guides, the Church fathers. Each order had its own library of devotional literature and this, too, indicated the traditional crevices and toeholds the man of prayer should follow. The reader was involved in was a devotional exercise; seeking the spiritual significance beneath the text and seeking it in ways prescribed by the masters. There was nothing unique in this rigidity. On the contrary, ever since rival Christians claimed 'I am of Paul' and 'I am of Apollos' distinct schools have gathered around leaders of outstanding erudition or holiness. Origen, Augustine, Luther, Calvin, Wesley, Jonathan Edwards – all through printed commentaries, sermons and treatises influenced students in the 'proper' way to approach and study the Bible.

There were places in late medieval Europe where the Bible could be studied with remarkable intellectual freedom and even with some scope for individual reinterpretation: not only in heretical conventicles, where vernacular translations were cherished, but also in Constantinople, where in the fifteenth century Cardinal Bessarion learned techniques of textual criticism which threw up new readings shocking to his auditors in the West; or in Observant Franciscan friaries, where hostility to unnecessary learning as a kind of corrupting surplus wealth excluded deadening commentaries from the reading lists; and in the many schools where the commentaries of Nicholas of Lyra were relied on – for these works, despite their early date, were of considerable humanist flair, tackling problems of the real meaning of the text in the vital context of the Holy Land as it was or might have been in the time of Christ and the prophets. Routine Bible teaching, however, was no doubt dull or deadly. Scripture was placed on a pedestal. The student (unless he belonged to one of the mendicant orders, which offered a less rigorous prior training) had to master grammar, rhetoric, logic, Greek philosophy, music, astronomy, arithmetic and geometry before he could proceed to the exploration of theology. Then he approached the Vulgate in a spirit of fundamentalism more rigid than anything to be found today in the American Bible Belt. It sprang from a deep reverence for *every* word of Scripture. Since no part of holy writ was superfluous, all was given for man's instruction. Parts were straightforward but others were mutually contradictory, obscure or even apparently hostile to Christian teaching. To take an obvious example the Song of Songs, with its exaltation of sexual love, was a potential embarrassment to a Church which prized virginity as a higher calling than marriage. Scholars contributed glosses which not only gave the Bible internal cohesion, but also made it support orthodox doctrines. It was the intellectual equivalent of Gothic fan tracery, feeding into a structural pillar.

All this activity was directed to the training of the Church's specialists. What degree of biblical knowledge was considered appropriate for educated laymen (whose numbers were increasing), whose vocation lay in the world? Two attitudes existed which, if not exactly mutually exclusive, certainly did not sit easily together: the word of God existed to comfort, challenge and inspire every human soul. At the same time, the average human soul was not equipped to discern the Bible's truth. What took a priest years of hard study to achieve with the guidance of the Church's treasury of past scholarship could not be gained by prince, courtier or merchant in his spare time. Extant examples of vernacular psalters, gospels and books of scriptural meditations indicate a growing demand among pious ladies and gentlemen who could afford such luxuries. There are also surviving copies of medieval 'strip cartoons' which were probably first produced in the thirteenth century. These *Biblia Pauperum* depicted scenes from the life of Christ associated with vignettes drawn from the Old Testament to show how earlier personalities and events prefigured the coming of the Saviour. The illustrations were accompanied by a minimum of text. These small books were probably intended as one answer to the problem of substandard preaching. They provided the semi-educated priest with a simple guide to the standard system of biblical exegesis and some pictures he could show to his flock to fix the lessons in their minds.

Alongside this went reluctance to allow portions of Scripture to fall into the hands of the unlearned. The shadowy figure of the scholar-monk Aelfric of Eynsham, who flourished in England in the early years of the present millennium was obviously a man of lively and independent mind. In the controversies of the sixteenth and seventeenth centuries he was adopted by

Protestant writers because of his rejection of transubstantiation. He was concerned to banish the ignorance of ordinary people about the Gospel and, to this end, translated sermons and scriptural extracts into the common tongue. Yet he was very aware of the potential danger of making the Bible available to men who had no religious vocation. When his patron, a nobleman named Sigeweard, asked for a translation of the New Testament, Aelfric tactfully but firmly explained that mere possession of the word of God was of little value. The Jews had had the Old Testament – and look what had happened to them! God had ordained three pillars of society: warriors, labourers and men of prayer. It would be dangerous to tamper with this arrangement.

Not all scholars and church leaders saw the situation so clearly or, if they

2.5 Martin Schongauer (c.1445-90) revolutionized the art of engraving and made possible the dissemination of religious images much more powerful than any that had been available before. These brought religious books to life for semi-literate readers.

did, they did not share Aelfric's reticence. Just as there was no coherent policy throughout Christendom regarding the attitude towards heretics, so reactions towards Scripture translation ranged from the nonchalant to the proscriptive. Some clergy could see little danger in lords and ladies and the members of religious communities possessing portions of holy writ for their own edification. After all, the economic considerations would always restrict the numbers of potential readers. By the mid-fifteenth century, in parts of Europe, notably northern Italy and northern France, several versions circulated with either the approval or indifference of the authorities. What those authorities failed to foresee was the spread of literacy and the invention of the printing press.

Those developments proved Aelfric right. The word of God, as the Epistle to the Hebrews testified, is a keen and devastating weapon. Its power for good or ill is incalculable. The history of Christian missions proves that when the Bible, unqualified by 'approved' interpretation, 'hits' a society the effects can be devastating. The massive contemporary expansion of Christianity in Asia owes much to the impact of the Bible unaided by missionary endeavour. In China, where colporteurs cannot keep up with the demand, there are stories of Red Guards being converted simply by exposure to the sacred text. One student who read the King James version as part of his English studies is now a Christian pastor. In Korea the growth rate of conversions has exceeded that of the population on both sides of the border ever since the war of 1950-53 and Christianity is poised to take over from Buddhism as the majority religion. In the north of that country, where no Christian denomination is permitted to function officially, and where statistics are hard to gather, it is estimated that there are millions of Christians sustained largely by smuggled Scriptures. There is a similar story to be told in the ex-Communist lands of Europe. In the early 1990s American evangelicals shipped over fifty million Bibles to Russia and the Ukraine. As a result there was a rapid growth of Protestant congregations in marked contrast to the less dramatic expansion of the longer-established and numerically stronger Orthodox and Catholic churches.

These effects were foreshadowed in early sixteenth-century 'Bible mania'. The illiterate went to school in order to gain access to the divine message. Farmers read the Bible to their workers and landowners to their tenants. 'Gospellers' stood up in churches to recite passages of the sacred text. When Church and State authorities banned the vernacular versions, threatening imprisonment and death to those who bought and sold them, this only added a frisson of excitement for the devotees who gathered in secret around the sacred page and formed links in the chain of clandestine colportage. Later in the century John Foxe looked back nostalgically on the heady days of the 1520s and 1530s in England.

> The fervent zeal of those Christian days seemed much superior to these our days and times, as manifestly may appear by their sitting up all night in reading and hearing: also by their expenses and charges in buying of books in English, of whom some gave five marks (roughly equivalent to £500 in modern currency), some more, some less, for a book; some gave a load of hay for a few chapters of St James or of St Paul in English.

Unlimited access meant undisciplined reading. Innocent III who, two hundred years after Aelfric, found himself having to deal with severe

2.6 Low German Bible (Lübeck 1494). By the end of the fifteenth century the demand for vernacular Scriptures resulted in many fine, well-illustrated publications.

Dat boek

Jonas de alter schoneste dume.myt siner
vtwerpyng.glе vth deme schepe ys vor=
betekende dat lytent des heren.he wed=
der eschet de werlte to penitencien.vn
de vnder deme name nyniue vorkundi
ghet den heydenen heyl.

¶ Hyr heuet sik an de profete Jonas.

Dat erste capi secht wo ionas

ghesant ward to predeken den van nyniue. vn wo he
vlo in tharsis. vn wo he ume siner vnhorsamheit wil
len in dat meer gheworpen ward.

nde des here wort
schach to ionas de een sone was
amathy.segghete.Sta vp vn
gha yn te groten stad niniue.
vn predike dar inе ere vmme
werpinghе.wete ere boszheit is
vp ghesteghen vor mi.ſ de boz=
heit erer inwaner hefft ere vmmekeringhe vordenet.
Vn ionas stunt vp vmme to vleen in tharsis.ſyn te
stad dar sunte pawel af ghebare was.vn angesicht
te des herе.vn is nedder ghesteghе in iope.ſ in de haue
des merеs.vn hefft ghevute een schip varēte in tarsis
vn ghaf sin schiplon. vn stech nedder in dat schip vm
me mit en to vare in tharsis va de anghesichte des he
ren.Me de here hefft ghesand ene groten wint in dat
meer.vn een grot vnweder is worte in de mere.vnte
dat schip was in angste dat dat vorderue scholte. vn
de schippers vruchtetе. vn de meine hebbе gheropе to
ere gade.ſ een islik to te gade de he erede.vn se hebben
vtgheworpеn in dat mer te vate.ume dat schip to vor
lichtеdе.Vn ionas is nedder ghesteghе to de binnen
stе des schepes.vn slep mit swarе slapе. vn de sturmа
is ghegha to em. vn hefft ghesecht.wat slapestu. Sta
vp vn rop an dine god.efte god bi enctire wil denkе
vp vns dat wi nicht envorderuе.vn een iewelyk man
sede to synе ghesellе Ramet latet vns werpе dat loth
dat wi wetе worume dyt quad vp vns kamen is. vn
se worpе dat lot.vn dat lot vyl vp ionas.vn se hebben
ghesecht to emе.Segghе vns vmme wat sake is vns
dyt quad ghekamе.wat is dyn werk. welk is din lat
vor gheistu.efte va wat volk bistu. vn ionas hefft ghe
secht to en.ick byn een ebreisch minsche. vn ick vruchte
den here god des heimels.de ghemaket hefft dath meer
vn ertе.vn de meine vruchtetе mit grotе vruchtе.ſ to

vortornēte den god ione.vn hebben ghesecht to emе.
Worume hefstu dit ghedа.Wete de mаne bеkāte dat
he vlo va de anghesichte des herе.wete ionas hadde
dat en gheapеnbaret. vn se setе to emе.wat schоеle wy
dy do dat dat meer vpholde va vns.Wete dat meer
bulgerde vn vpvloyete vp se.vn he hefft ghesecht tho
en.nemet vn werpet my in dat meer.ſ he wolte leuer
allene steruе wen dat de anderе mit em vorghinghе
vn dat scal vpholtе va iuw.wete yk wet dat ume my
dit grote vnwеdеr ys vp iuw.vn se mēne remetе vmi
wedder to kamе to lādе.vn se enmochten nicht.wente
dat meer ghik vn vpvloyede vp se.vn se repе to deme
here vn setе.Wi bidde here dat wi nicht envorghа in
te leuetе desses mаnеs.vn enwil nicht ghatеn dat vn
schuldighe blot vp vns.wete du here hefft ghedа alse
du woldеst.vn se hebbе ghenamе ionа.vn hebben ene
ghеworpе in dat meer.vn dat mer led va siner vpvlо
yenghе. vn de meine vruchtetе mit grotе vruchtе den
herе.vn offertе offeringе te herеn. vn laudе loeftе.

Dat ii. capit.secht wo de visch

yonam vorslock. vnte wo yonas dorch sin bed wed
ter to lante quam.

Vn de here hadde bered
ene groten visch dat he ionа vorsluken
scholdе.vn ionas was in des visches bu
kе drе daghe vn drе nacht. vnde ionas
hefft ghebedet to dem here sinеme gade vt des visches
buke. vn hefft ghesecht Jk hebbe gheropеn in mine vor
driete to de herеn. vn he hefft my horet. Jf hebbe ghe
ropеn va de buke des waluisschеs.vnde du hefst mine
stemme horet. vn du hefst my gheworpеn in dat dе pе.
vn in dat herte des merеs.vn te vlod hefft my vmme
vaghen.Alle dine storme vn vlodе sint vp mi ghеgа
vn ik hebbe ghesecht.ik byn gheworpеn van deme an=

outbreaks of heresy, insisted that the Bible is not 'for all men in all places'. When the sacred text was available to men and women who did not submit their understanding of it to their spiritual superiors, a diversity of views emerged which the broadest church could not contain. Protestant reformers later ran into the same problem. Heinrich Bullinger in Zürich told his congregation that the Bible was 'difficult or obscure to the unlearned, unskilful, unexercised, and malicious or corrupted wills' and that professional guidance was necessary to prevent people choosing 'such sense as every one shall be persuaded in himself to be most convenient'.

Every Christian church has had to defend itself, from time to time, against the 'anarchy' of the open Bible. Catholic hierarchies consistently tried to prevent Scripture escaping from the control of the clergy on the not always reliable assumption that priests were easier to discipline. Protestant denominations drew up confessions of faith, setting out official interpretations of Scripture on a wide range of doctrines. All such restrictions were imposed in the interests of unity and truth and in the conviction that the body in question had inherited the promised gift of Jesus, the Holy Spirit who leads disciples into 'all truth'. Embarrassingly, dissenters always claim to be guided by that same Holy Spirit.

STRICTLY BY THE BOOK

In 1116 a ragged, barefoot preacher entered Le Mans, preceded by two disciples carrying a large cross. In appearance Henry the Monk was little different from other wandering preachers who travelled through Europe, like John the Baptist, calling people to repentance. The citizens hurried to hear him and, caught up by his eloquence, were soon making bonfires of their ornaments and other luxuries. But before long it became clear that Henry's message went dangerously beyond the denunciation of vanities. He opposed the pomp and wealth of the Church and called upon it to cast off all post-New Testament accretions – vestments, large buildings, elaborate rituals, external objects of devotion such as images, and anything which interposed itself between the believer and Christ. This included the clergy. Not only did Henry want to see them stripped of material possessions, he also denied them their sacerdotal functions. All believers, he insisted, were simple brothers and sisters in Christ and needed no special caste of mediators.

Henry the Monk was unusual only in his doctrinal excesses. Several wandering holy men and preachers of repentance appeared from time to time in different parts of Europe. They represented what are the most obvious truths to emerge from even a cursory reading of the gospel narratives: Jesus lived a life of utter simplicity; he called his disciples to give up everything and follow him; and he had some uncompromising things to say about the rich. These are truths which challenge every thinking Christian. Over the centuries they have inspired individuals and groups to live lives uncluttered by worldly cares and possessions. They have also provided motivation for reform movements. The background from which Henry emerged was still strongly coloured by the reform of Pope Gregory VII which had vigorously attacked every kind of profanation of church life. He could stir his hearers to self-abnegation but he could also arouse them to indignation at corrupt and luxury-loving clergy.

Pulpit denunciations are not necessary to point up this particular Gospel truth. Holy simplicity is always a reproof to religious establishments which, by their very nature, are incapable of imitating the lilies of the field. No-one could have held together more successfully than Francis of Assisi orthodoxy and papal obedience with the unworldliness of the first disciples. Yet his literal adherence to the precepts of Jesus and his popularity with ordinary people made him a threat to Church authorities in North Italy. There were conflicts enough during the saint's lifetime but after his death inherent tensions produced rebellion, persecution and divisions within the Franciscan order. The purists – dubbed *fraticelli* – in their determination to 'sit loose' to this world, rejected not only personal possessions, but the very idea of possession. They were determined to have nothing to do with the gifts of money and land bestowed on the order by wealthy patrons and grateful benefactors. They counted it obscene that Christ's ambassadors should be comfortably provided for while so many for whom he died lived in abject poverty.

The poor loved them for this. The rich and powerful could see only anarchy in their teaching and the crowds who flocked to hear them. Politically they were right. Society and order break down when pragmatism gives way to the idealism of Rousseau: 'You are undone if you once forget that the fruits of the earth belong to us all, and that the earth itself belongs to nobody.' But visionaries like the *fraticelli* – like 'revolutionary' priests in Latin America who will have no truck with papal concordats made with dictators; like evangelical preachers in communist lands who are indifferent to the delicate balance between Church and State – could not regard Christianity as the art of the possible. It was, rather, a call to attempt the impossible. Their politics was that of the kingdom of heaven. Their constitution was written in the gospels. When Pope John XXII formally decided against them, the simple logic of their position forced them to defiance. If Rome was setting itself up against the clear word of Scripture, then Rome must be the sect of Antichrist. Four *fraticelli* were burned at Marseille in 1318 and persecution continued for several years. But there was no question of the distinctive teaching of the *fraticelli* dying out when its last adherents were hunted down in the Midi and Alpine foothills. The poverty ideal was shared by Cathars, Waldensians, Beguins and lay and clerical sympathisers over a wide area of northern Italy and southern France.

By the end of the thirteenth century a bewildering array of dissidents and separatists had been identified. The range of their beliefs and practice is as wide as that of the kaleidoscopic religious groupings operating in Europe and America in the seventeenth and eighteenth centuries. Yet, it is clear that the striving for personal holiness, often associated with poverty, was an almost universal factor. One opponent of a heretical congregation alleged that they claimed that

> theirs alone is the Church, inasmuch as only they are following in the footsteps of Christ. They continue to be the true imitators of the apostolic life, seeking not those things which are of the world, possessing no house, or lands, even as Christ had no property . . . 'You, however,' they say to us, 'add house to house, field to field, and seek the things that are of this world. You do this to the point that they who are considered the most perfect among you, such as monks and canons regular, although owning nothing of their own and holding everything in common, nevertheless possess all these things.' Of themselves they say, 'We, the poor of Christ, who have no fixed abode and flee from city to city like sheep amidst wolves, are persecuted as were the apostles and the martyrs.'

Any survey of alternative lifestyles in late-twentieth century Europe would have to cover a wide variety of groups and individuals from eccentric recluses, drop-outs and members of closed religious orders to gypsies, New Age travellers and the Jesus People. The only common factor linking them all would be renunciation of society. The same holds true of the pre-Reformation centuries. Among the thousands of men and women who turned their backs on the familiar world, there were mystics, angry protesters, fanatics, visionaries, the emotionally inadequate and the mentally unhinged. Their only shared thread was rejection of attitudes and practices prevailing in the day-to-day world. That made them potentially or actually dangerous.

Most religious drop-outs were driven by devotional intensity to the hermitage, the cloister, the heretical conventicle or to holy vagabondage. Many – most, perhaps – were safely catered for within the ecclesiastical system. Others were driven by Scripture into heresy. The originator of England's contribution to pre-Reformation dissent was an Oxford scholar, the

> . . . pestilent and wretched John Wyclif, of cursed memory, that son of the old serpent [who] endeavoured by every means to attack the very faith and sacred doctrine of Holy Church, devising – to fill up the measure of his malice – the expedient of a new translation of the Scriptures into the mother tongue.

Wycliffe appeared to be a giant at Oxford in the 1360s and 1370s. His breathtaking innovations and uncompromising lecturing style caught up his students and turned them into disciples. Resurrecting an unfashionable philosophy, he saw Scripture as a *universal,* and immutable idea in the mind of God before all time. This could be distinguished from the written word into which human error could creep. The Church, too, was a universal existing in the mind of God and distinguishable from the visible organization.

Several members of the royal and noble establishment had their own reasons for patronizing Wycliffe. He found support in Scripture for their protests over ecclesiastical taxes and clerical appointments. His language appealed to the fashionable piety of self-abasement in which the rich contemplated visions of their own worm-eaten bodies while distributing fortunes in their wills. For his part Wycliffe looked to the temporal powers to lead the work of Church reform. He called upon them to assert their God-given authority to eradicate abuses. He urged them to appropriate ecclesiastical endowments and divert them into charitable and educational channels. And so that his followers would be better equipped to put his ideas into practice, he instigated the translation of the Vulgate into English.

From the inner core of Wycliffite scholars there came, before and after the reformer's death, a succession of vernacular versions. Within a few decades there were thousands of Bibles and biblical extracts in circulation. Some were elegant copies made for noble sympathizers but the vast majority were small, modest, practical volumes designed to be carried around the country by preachers who, from the last years of the fourteenth century, went on evangelistic tours, instructing secret conventicles from the written word. Some copies of the gospels were made very small so that they could be easily hidden if an unsympathetic parish priest or neighbour came to call.

One remarkable fact about these translations is that they were free of partisan glosses. Such aids as did appear in the text simply explained obscure words and provided spiritualized interpretations of some passages in line with orthodox patterns of exegesis. This restraint was a result of the movement's scholarly origins and its respect for the unadorned word of God.

Such self-control did not apply to other writings circulated within the sect. The 'Lollard' leadership – the name, of uncertain meaning, was coined in derision – seems to have been very adept in the techniques of nurturing the faithful at all levels. For preachers and the more educated there were Bible commentaries and compendia of Wycliffite theories. To instruct the simple there were vigorous tracts and a whole sermon cycle built around the designated lessons for the Mass on Sundays and saints days. This fact indicates that there was no hard and fast line drawn between these English heretics and their more conventional neighbours. From the pages of Foxe and episcopal registers we read of belligerent Lollards often made more recalcitrant by persecution. But Lollardy was more than the sum of its more extremist parts. It was one aspect of that body of lay and clerical religious enthusiasts which embraced reformers, anti-clericals, free-thinkers and mystics.

We only know, from the proceedings of heresy trials, the names and opinions of extremist, belligerent or unlucky Lollards who fell foul of the authorities. If we exclude the eccentrics and simpletons who got caught up in persecution by accident, it seems clear that what united them and the brethren who managed to avoid prosecution was that they were book-based Christians: 'a reading sect', strong where literacy was incipient.

The problem they presented was as much intellectual as doctrinal. Between simplistic, amateur Bible students and long-trained school theologians there existed a gulf of understanding and sympathy. A frustrated William Tyndale expressed it thus:

> I had perceived by experience, how that it was impossible to establish the lay-people in any truth, except the scripture were plainly laid before their eyes in their mother-tongue, that they might see the process, order and meaning of the text: for else, whatsoever truth is taught them, these enemies of all truth quench it again. . .partly in juggling with the text expounding it in such a sense as is impossible to gather. . .the process, order and meaning thereof.

When he published his English New Testament, his rendering of certain Greek words challenged, not just the Vulgate understanding of those same words, but also the doctrines and ceremonies built up over the centuries on the foundation of that understanding. Thus Tyndale rendered *ecclesia* as 'congregation' rather than 'church' and *presbyteros* as 'senior' or 'elder' instead of 'priest'. Such renderings changed the emphasis of Scripture from the institutional and sacramental to the local and the internal. The reformer spoiled his case when, in later editions of the New Testament, he added Lutheran glosses to the text. His critics were, thus, to some extent justified in claiming that the new version had opened a postern gate through which heresy was infiltrating the citadel.

Orthodox apologists could produce a growing body of evidence to show that when the unlearned meddled with the Bible they fell into all manner of error. The same concern was voiced, as we have seen, by later champions of Protestant orthodoxy, pledged though they were to the principle of the open book.

'UNDERSTANDED OF THE PEOPLE'

> We do not publish upon erroneous opinion of necessity, that the holy
> Scriptures should always be in our mother tongue, or that they ought or
> were ordained by God to be read indifferently of all. . . but upon special
> consideration of the the present time, state and condition of our country,
> unto which divers things are either necessary, or profitable and medicin-
> able now, that otherwise in the peace of the church were neither much
> requisite, nor perchance wholly tolerable.

The Catholic framers of the Rheims-Douai English version in their somewhat ingenuous preface acknowledged that, now that the open Bible was
free, it could neither be coaxed nor driven back into its cage. This version
(New Testament 1582, complete Bible 1609–10) was a product of that school
of Catholic thought which asserted that heretics should be fought on their
own ground. It was set forth as a direct counterblast to the Geneva Bible
(1560) and employed the same technique of partisan readings and notes.
The rival versions trundled around the theological battle-field like tanks
bombarding the enemy positions with highly contentious glosses and
marginalia. It was largely this unedifying spectacle which prompted James
I, on his accession, to authorize a new translation which would strive for
maximum accuracy and be wholly devoid of controversial notes.

By the time the Authorized Version hit the bookshops a powerful and
irreversible process of cultural infiltration was well under way. As is often
the case, businessmen had been among the first to see the potential of the
printed Bible. When Tyndale fled to northern Germany to continue his translation work, he sought the patronage of a shadowy group of wealthy
merchants and shipowners who called themselves the Christian Brethren.
These capitalists, motivated by a mix of religious radicalism and entrepreneurship, were prepared to lay out risk capital to finance the printing
and smuggling into England of Tyndale's books. It was a shrewd investment.
The scholar's backers ordered six thousand copies of the first edition of
Tyndale's New Testament (1526), knowing that, despite the dangers their
distributors and customers were running, they had a ready market. The
books, infiltrating east coast ports concealed in bales of cloth, sacks of grain
and barrels of wine, were soon being eagerly bought. The Christian Brethren
had more to fear from the publishers of pirate editions than from the ecclesiastical authorities. For example, the Endhoven brothers of Antwerp brought
out fourteen printings of the 1526 edition in the next ten years. The profit
motive, allied with religious zeal, pragmatic government policy and widespread demand, placed vernacular Bibles in churches, vicarages, manor
houses and a growing number of humbler homes. In Protestant lands the

Bible became the major pillar of common culture. It infused language and, therefore, coloured the way people – including non-religious people – thought. It was made even more popular through the medium of music. Luther realized the importance of hymns for implanting the words of Scripture in people's minds. Congregational singing of both psalms and free settings of biblical passages became a vital part of Protestant worship. On a higher musical plane, the sacred oratorio achieved great popularity in the eighteenth century. Although the form had its origins in Italy, it was transformed in the North into something much more subservient to the vernacular text. Italian oratorios were, almost without exception, settings of Latin words. In the hands of such composers as Schütz, Bach and Handel the full emotional impact of German and English Bible passages was driven home. Catholic church music was also reformed to clear the text of obscuring polyphony. Where medieval people relied on pictures and stories to aid their biblical understanding, their post-Reformation descendants possessed the very cadences of Scripture.

Despite the occasional, reluctant sanctioning of translation work, the official attitude in Rome continued to centre on the all-sufficiency of the Vulgate. The Council of Trent called for an improved edition of the Latin text and a committee of scholars laboured over the task for many years, finally presenting the result to Sixtus V in 1588. The pope did not like it. The academics had done their job too well, found too many errors to correct, identified too many dubious readings for which they had suggested variants. Sixtus would have none of it. He was a true Reformation man, who could not allow the perfection of the Bible to be impugned by the exposure of human errors in the transmission of the text. The revised text was not clear, incisive, unequivocal, authoritative. He dismissed the experts and set about a scissors and paste job on their draft. Sixtus V was one of the great administrative reformers of the Roman church but he was no biblical scholar. The text which he completed months before his death was a disaster. Fortunately his demise absolved the Church from having to issue it. As soon as Gregory XIV was elected, he ordered a revision of the revision of the revision. Thus the Vulgate which was eventually issued at the end of 1592 was a work which had twice been put through the papal mincer and had not benefited from the experience. Yet it was the official Catholic Bible for over three centuries.

Even when vernacular translations were given curial approval any implication that this sanctioned their dissemination to ordinary believers was firmly rejected. Between 1667 and 1702 the Jansenists of Port Royal worked painstakingly and lovingly to produce a new French Bible. Yet, in 1713, Clement XI reacted hotly to a whole range of Jansenist suggestions, including those relating to the use of the Bible, such as that it should be available to all; that lay people should be encouraged to devote Sundays to the reading of Scripture and religious books; and that it was wrong to forbid God's word to God's people. Such statements were denounced in the bull, *Unigenitus*, as

> false, captious, ill-sounding, offensive to pious ears, scandalous, perni-
> cious, rash, injurious to the Church and its practices, not only outrageous
> against the Church but even against the secular powers, seditious,
> impious, blasphemous, suspected of heresy and savouring of heresy . . .
> and lastly also heretical.

One of the long-term trends of modern Church history, however, has been Catholic absorption and domestication of Protestant influence. The Catholic world made its peace with the Bible specifically as a result of contributions to biblical studies by Protestant scholarship in the nineteenth century. Ironically, the man who did most to reconcile Protestant and Catholic perceptions was the anti-Catholic propagandist, Ferdinand Christian Baur, who, as professor of theology at Tübingen from 1826, revolutionized Biblical criticism. He took the traditions of Renaissance humanism to their logical conclusion, subjecting the text of scripture to the same scrutiny as any other purportedly historical document. What Renaissance humanism had done for the Vulgate – exposing its textual imperfections and the distortions of its time – the Tübingen school did for the earliest available versions of the Scriptures. Previous erosion of the authenticity of scripture by rationalist critiques had been objectively convincing, but had been rejected by believers as written *a parti pris*. No-one could impugn the faith of Baur or the Christian commitment underlying his approach; though he was profoundly wrong in some of his theories about the chronology and circumstances of the writing of the books of the New Testament, the general effect of his work was to demonstrate beyond reasonable doubt the errors of human hands and the distortions of human purposes in the text we have inherited. Baur would have hated to admit it, but the 'higher criticism' he represented justified the reserve with which Catholics treated the Bible. Protestant criticism had proved that the Bible was not an apodictic gift, but a collection which it had taken time and human editorship to refine: the 'word of God', but selected and interpreted by the Church of the first Christian centuries.

Two important results ensued: first, Catholics could relax their guard. The Bible was no longer a rival but an ally. Secondly, the views of Catholics and moderate Protestants converged, leaving biblical fundamentalists isolated in intellectually disreputable wastes. It was no longer reasonable to suppose that scripture could put every man in direct touch with the mind of God, without critical reading, expert guidance and undogmatic interpretation.

Scripture in Tradition

But for the Church, said Cardinal Hosius, the holy scriptures would have no more authority than the fables of Æsop. Even for Christians convinced of the divine origins of the Bible, the problems of defining its contents, establishing the texts and interpreting their meaning demand human solutions. The fundamentalist innocent who thinks the Holy Spirit whispered every word of scripture into a scribe's ear has still to reckon with the textual corruptions introduced by copyists and translators, editors and arrangers. The most insidious intrusions are those of human readers, missing or misconstruing the divine message. No Protestant could be more unbending than Jean Calvin in his defence of the unique and sufficient authority of the Bible: he declared, 'Scripture bears upon the face of it as clear evidence of its truth as white and black do of their colour, sweet and bitter of their taste'; he dismissed the Church's claim to be able to authenticate scripture as 'ravings' intended to bolster tyranny and subject the Holy Spirit to the judgement of men. Yet, even from so trenchant a starting-point, it is hard to dissent from Calvin's conclusion that 'although the Holy Scriptures contain a perfect doctrine to which nothing can be added . . . still every person, not intimately acquainted with them, stands in need of some guidance and direction, as to what he ought to look for in them, that he may not wander up and down, but pursue a certain path, and so attain the end to which scripture invites him.' This caution has scriptural authority behind it in its turn: 'the interpretation of scriptural prophecy is never a matter for the individual.'

Before he converted to Roman Catholicism, the future Cardinal Newman laid bare every critical reader's anxieties about Scripture. Among doctrines widely accepted by Protestants, the divinity of the Holy Spirit, the necessity of infant baptism and the observance of the Lord's Day are all without clear or specific scriptural endorsement. Indeed, the inspiration of Scripture is in the same category of doctrines which can be found in the Bible, if at all, only by a prejudiced judgement. The internal contradictions of the Bible are alarming: there are two uneasily combined accounts of the creation in Genesis. Chronicles contradicts Kings and Exodus is at odds with Deuteronomy. St Matthew disagrees with the writer of Acts about the death of Judas Iscariot. A reader of a frankly uninspired text would have no doubt that Jesus's feeding of the multitude was a single episode described in discrepant versions and that St Luke was using a different tradition from St Matthew's of the content of the sermon on the mount.

Though the Bible is the common ground of Christians, it seems too shifting to support the foundations of unity. The practical problems were demonstrated in 1566 in Hosius's native Poland, when the Catholic bishops proposed a compromise to the Protestant communities. Reformed ministers would be allowed to preach in private houses and in buildings of their own, erected at their patrons' expense, but were not to usurp Church property or deflect or discourage the payment of tithes. Catholics and Protestants would join in a common profession of faith, based on the gospels alone, unalloyed by the pronouncements of synods or councils and uninterrupted except by the authority of Saints Jerome, Augustine, Ambrose and Chrisostom. To this apparently handsome offer, one reformer replied by asking who was to settle the questions of interpretation raised in turn by the writings of the fathers. The bishops' reply, which scuppered the discussions, was that their words should be understood only in the sense the Catholic Church attached to them.

'Tradition', said Chesterton, 'is the democracy of the dead' and to judge from the texts collected by the early Church, Christ himself was unimpressed by it. In a text much loved by the Protestant reformers, the Pharisees came to Jesus and said, 'Why do your disciples break away from the tradition of the elders?' Jesus replied with a characteristically pungent indictment, which Protestants have gleefully applied to the Church in its turn: 'And why do you break away from the commandment of God for the sake of your tradition? . . . You have made God's word ineffective by means of your tradition. Hypocrites! How rightly Isaiah prophesied about you when he said, "This people honours me only with lip-service. . . . The lessons they teach are nothing but human commandments."'

Tradition needs vigilant correction but Christians cannot do without it. Scripture and tradition are not rival sources of authority: the one is part of the other. Everything we know about Jesus is traditional – recorded in texts by followers, written after his time, partly from memory, partly from hearsay, partly from compendia of sayings attributed to Jesus, partly from adaptation of pre-Christian messianic prophecy. The claim that these writings were divinely inspired, even if true, would not make the methods by which they were compiled and transmitted any less traditional. A further layer of tradition was interposed when, as time went on, they were selected for special reverence, and others discarded or relegated to a less numinous category. Only one of the gospel-writers includes in his account of Jesus a claim to the authenticity of an eye witness, and even his account is declared to have passed through editorial hands. Even St Paul – the most vivid Christian witness, perhaps, of all time, who insists on his status as an apostle and cries, 'Have I not seen the Lord?' – never met Jesus in his lifetime; he therefore carefully distinguishes, from time to time, between what he 'knows' by revelation, what he has 'heard' from tradition, what he has originated himself for the benefit of his correspondents, and what is 'modelled' on the earliest congregations in Judaea by Christian communities elsewhere. 'Stand firm then, brothers,' is the adjuration of the Second Letter from Paul's circle to the Thessalonians, 'and keep the traditions we have taught you.' Any line drawn through time in purported distinction of 'primitive' Christianity, pristine and pure, from 'traditional' Christianity, diluted or corrupted, is arbitrary. Renunciation of Catholic traditions has not immunized Protestant churches against developing in externals traditions of their own: thus Methodist preachers wear tabs modelled on Wesley's, Amish wear seventeenth-century clothes; Protestants in the Church of England treat as unalterable truths a check-list of Elizabethan orthodoxy known as the Thirty-Nine Articles; Lutherans and Calvinists are guided in their interpretation of Scripture by commentaries a few hundred years old and Pentecostalists keep alive the music of Negro spirituals and original New Orleans Jazz. The dispute about tradition had a certain convincing freshness in the sixteenth century, when the Protestant reformers really did feel it was possible to scrape off 'accretions' and get back to a smooth tablet of wax: paradoxically, this emerges from Luther's confession to a young audience that his generation was so steeped in 'papist' teaching that he could no longer tell what was traditional from what was true; but he hoped that unspoiled young listeners would genuinely be able to reconstruct primitive Christianity, whole and pure. Experience since then makes this seem an unrealistic dream – albeit no less noble and worthwhile for that.

Chapter Three

ACCESS TO GOD:
External *versus* Internal Authority

EXPERIENTIALISM

Jung's dictum that religion is a substitute for religious experience strikes a warning that informed Christians have always been aware of, or, at least, that they have no excuse for not being aware of. The Bible contains numerous exhortations against empty formalism and there cannot be a saint or preacher or doctor of the Church who has not repeated the teaching of Jesus, 'It is not everyone who says to me "Lord, Lord" who will enter the Kingdom of Heaven, but he who does the will of my Father'. Erasmus' satires of the state of Christendom were the reverse side of his personal quest for a deeper spiritual life:

> Who is truly Christian? Not he who is baptized or anointed, or who attends church. It is rather the man who has embraced Christ in the inner-most feelings of his heart, and who emulates him by pious deeds.

Erasmus remained a loyal, if not very respectful, son of the Church. Yet his life and writings reveal that tension between interiority and commitment to the Christian body which many others over the centuries have found intolerable. The third source of truth to be set alongside Church and Bible is the direct revelation claimed usually by the more intensely devout. Most

Christians have managed somehow to live within the triangle framed by these three but some have been driven by their inner vision to challenge both written word and orthodox tradition. Andreas Carlstadt made the point with unflinching directness; 'I do not need the outward witness; I want to have the testimony of the Spirit within me . . . The Spirit of God, to which all things ought to be subjected, cannot be subject even to Scripture.'

The range of what, for want of a better word, we will call experientialism is rainbow-like. At one extreme are the eremetics who shut themselves away from the world to do their own religious thing. At the other stand the bizarre, sometimes tragic, figures who lead others along their own eccentric paths to destruction.

MYSTICS

It could be a scene of martyrdom or the expiration of some perverted voluptuary. St Teresa subsides in an excess of ecstasy. A divine wind ruffles her habit into sinuous curls, while a smiling angel, delicately poising a dart between thumb and forefinger, aims to thrust it into her breast. Bernini's sculpture has been acclaimed or derided as the epitome of baroque extravagance; yet it faithfully depicts the saint's own description of a mystical experience:

> It pleased the Lord that I should see this angel in the following way. . . .
> In his hands I saw a long golden spear and at the end of the iron tip I
> seemed to see a point of fire. With this he seemed to pierce my heart
> several times so that it penetrated to my entrails. When he drew it out,
> I thought he was drawing them out with it and he left me completely
> afire with a great love for God. The pain was so sharp that it made me
> utter several moans; and so excessive was the sweetness caused me by
> this intense pain that one can never wish to lose it, nor will one's soul
> be content with anything less than God. It is not bodily pain, but spiri-
> tual, though the body has a share in it – indeed, a great share. So sweet
> are the colloquies of love which pass between the soul and God that if
> anyone thinks I am lying I beseech God, in His goodness, to give him
> the same experience.

Sex acts are mystics' clichés for conveying the sublime nature of a spiritual climax. When St John of the Cross escaped from prison, his first thought was to read his *Dark Night of the Soul* to the nuns among whom he took refuge. The pious virgins and their superiors apparently had no difficulty in understanding or, at least, excusing the incandescently erotic language. Spiritual fulfilment is not, presumably, much like sexual satisfaction; but writers who try to express its mystical form have been driven to the farthest margins of metaphor in the effort to evoke the experience for those who have never had it. 'One makes these comparisons,' St Teresa said, 'because there are no suitable ones.' After the sublimities of the poets, analysis makes the whole subject seem ridiculous but it has to be attempted because mysticism plays such an important part in our story.

Alongside the Bible and the Church, it has been Christians' third great route to God – a source of direct communication, unmediated, unrefined. Mysticism in the strict sense is the practice of attempting to unite the individual soul with God but we use it here to cover every convincing apprehension of the presence of God, whether in vision or revelation, prayer or trance, whether in ecstatic fit or in the still, small voice of calm. In the Reformation era, mysticism was the Protestantism of Catholics – the means by which, without unorthodoxy, the faithful soul could cleave through the trivial round of good works and routine obligations, overleaping the active life of a Martha to Mary's 'better way'. Mystics dodged to God around the sacraments, ducking the hierarchy and bucking the authority of a mediatory Church. By comparison with the mystic's personal perception of God in the depths of his or her own soul, the Bible can seem like an opaque, ambiguous and self-contradictory guide to truth; the Church a cumbersome and unconvincing substitute. If it was in the nature of mainstream Protestantism to cultivate a personal relationship between the Christian and God, how much more did mysticism do so, by igniting the soul with the tongues of fire and fanning them with the rush of wind?

In the middle ages, the Devil had seemed so good at divine disguise, the pretended Spirit had whispered so many heresies and so many folk had been misled by phoney apparitions, that the checks and disciplines demanded of mystics in the sixteenth century were exacting. Almost all of them – even St Teresa herself – were subjected to searching inquisitions. The Church expected rigorous preparation of those who set out to contrive a mystical experience, and would only authenticate cases where the doctrines of the Church were confirmed and where approved forms of devotion, including receipt of the sacraments and the practice of conventional prayer, were part of the worshipper's tool box of holiness. Nevertheless, for those who used it, mysticism could be a liberating force, an outlet for spiritual energies which might otherwise have been unattainable in hidebound rites and institutions. Licensed mysticism kept great saints inside the Catholic church at a time when many ardent seekers after God could only feel freed for their quest by espousing Protestantism.

Yet it should not be supposed that this was an élite devotion, limited to privileged ranks. Mysticism was part of the active Christianity which evangelically minded propagandists tried to promote among ordinary people. St Teresa and St John of the Cross were genuine evangelists of mysticism. St Thomas of Villanueva devoted entire sermons to counselling his congregations in mystical techniques. Popular handbooks of Catholic devotion by

Diego de Estella and Luis de Granada included – albeit not at a sophisticated or adventurous pitch – some of the same advice. Though a soulless art-criticism has tried to demote El Greco from mystic to mannerist, he was saturated in mystical reading, and his works – especially the late paintings in which figures seem translated into flame or atomized in cloud-like blurs – are among the most vivid memorials of the Catholicism of the Reformation era.

Within the limits generally approved in Catholic tradition, there were three main kinds of approach to mystical union: the contemplative, the meditative and the affective. The last two were highly suitable for adaptation as aids to mass devotion, because people at every social and intellectual level can be uplifted by an intense experience of love – which is the essence of the affective technique – and can be taught to meditate on words, images or scenes outside themselves. Contemplation is more esoteric, because the mystic who practises it can have no congregation around him to stir a propitious atmosphere, and no external props to inspire him – only his own inner resources of prayerfulness. Mystical writers have monitored their own progress through stages of ascent to fusion with God: the affective approach, for instance, works by the emotional arousal conferred by love, starting – in St Bernard's classic analysis of the stages – with self-love, ascending to love of others and progressing to love of God. The meditative approach fastens on an external object: a devotional image, or a biblical text, or the beauty of some part of creation or an impassioning scene of Christian love or sacrifice; and, if the technique works, it penetrates, beyond reasoned meditation, the 'cloud of unknowing', in which the intellect is suspended and only apprehension of the creator remains. A favourite exercise in meditative mysticism in the sixteenth century was contemplation of a starry night: in an amusing poem, Fray Luis de León strives earnestly for the effect without achieving it and it must be admitted that nature-mysticism has had a poor record among Christians ever since – more often adulterating Christianity with feeble pantheism than directing the worshipper to an encounter with a personal God. The contemplative method – or 'recollection', to use the jargon of its great sixteenth-century practitioners – has inspired the most powerful mystical literature, but usually at a cost in dedicated self-preparation, painful mortification and demanding prayer of which few people are capable. It starts with mental prayer – 'the expression of friendship with God,' as St Teresa called it, which becomes purged of sense and turns into a wordless dialogue of the spirit. Whatever is not selfish in the soul is divine: released from self-reference it can realize its true nature.

All three approaches to mystical experience have features in common: obliteration of whatever distracts the soul from God; passage through a 'dark night' of sensory deprivation; oblivion of the flesh, so total, in St Teresa's case, that she likened it to death – that moment of the soul's final release.

There follows penetration of a unique state of consciousness – variously called trance, transport or ecstasy. Properly speaking, in the Christian tradition, a defining condition of a genuinely mystical transport is that it is induced by disciplined practice of individual prayer. Congregational disciplines – music, dance, emotional utterance, the sacrament of the altar – can help and can of themselves induce similar states; the effect of some drugs is practically alike; but the results are at best peri- or pseudo-mystical states, which, like every easily attained effect, are pallid by comparison with the true mystic's hard won reward. Mere absorption, distraction, intoxication, delusion or lack or morbid loss of self-control have often been mistaken for mystical states, but they are the issue of human weakness, not divine grace.

Protestants, at least early in the history of their churches, did not need mysticism as Catholics did: the Bible gave them their hot-line to God. Indeed, early in the course of the Reformation, Protestant mystics were relatively rare and Luther tended to behold them with suspicion. Nevertheless, every kind of attempt to get close to God is an ally of all others and it was natural that as time went on, Protestantism should develop a mystical tradition of its own – especially when it spawned its own moribund churches, sprouted its own institutional deadwood and spread its own quasi-priesthoods, from which the seeker after God had to escape. Especially in the affective kind of mysticism, Protestantism became very rich. The early conversion-descriptions of Quakers and Methodists are full of what read like accounts of mystical experiences – overwhelming convictions of grace in which all rational and sensory faculties are numbed. Indeed, in the eighteenth and early nineteenth centuries, the torch passed from Catholic to Protestant hands; the Catholic hierarchy largely ceased to encourage mysticism, partly because of the excesses of some disappointingly ill-disciplined Catholic mystics and partly because the development of eucharistic devotion and of new, emotionally satisfying cults within the Church seemed to distract the interest of potential practitioners.

Catholic mystics began their journey in the forested foothills of traditional devotion and, while not losing their affection for the easy landscape of the valley, sought to guide aspirants via crags and glaciers to the spiritual peaks. Their Protestant counterparts began the ascent from the scriptural plain on the other side of the mountain but pointed towards the same summit. They knew the enervating influence of the biblicist flatlands and yearned to draw 'nominal' Christians to the higher paths of spiritual experience. John Bunyan wrestled with the supposed truths of the Bible. 'Everyone doth think his own religion rightest, both Jews and Moors, and Pagans! And how if all our faith, and Christ, and Scriptures, should be but a think-so too?' So he recorded his own early doubts in *Grace Abounding to the Chief of Sinners*. Such difficulties could only be surmounted when the sacred text was regarded as the signpost indicating a mystical journey.

O what mists, what mountains, what clouds, what darkness! . . . But faith . . . taketh stomach and courage, fighteth and crieth, and by crying and fighting, by help from heaven, its way is made through all the opposition that appear so mighty . . . [until] it sweetly resteth after its marvellous tossings to and fro.

COMMUNITIES OF EXPERIENCE

Only those could be accepted into Count von Zinzendorf's community of Herrnhut 'who have a living experience of the Saviour in their souls and who are of the same spirit with us.' Such Pietists strove to restore health to Lutheran and Calvinist orthodoxies whose arteries had become hardened by a diet of theological correctness and religious controversy.

They were linked with Christians of all epochs who insisted, for the individual, on the primacy of experience and its manifestation in works – especially, evangelism – and who demanded, from the Church, continuing reformation and constant vigilance against empty formalism. They had much in common with St Francis and activist mystics like Catherine of Siena. They shared the core conviction of those radicals who were called Anabaptists because they would admit to membership only those who had undergone a conversion experience. They found God, like the Anglican mystic, William Law, inside the 'attentive heart', rather than in a book or on an altar. Individualism and subjectivism were close relatives of Pietism as they were of the philosophy of the Age of Reason and Enlightenment. Kant believed no less than Zinzendorf in the primacy of experience but it was a despiritualized experience: 'Man himself must make or have made himself into whatever, in a moral sense, whether good or evil, he is or is to become.'

When the fifty-year-old Philip Jakob Spener was appointed court chaplain to the Elector of Saxony in 1686, he was already known through his books and his correspondence with an ever-growing band of followers as a powerful advocate of personal and Church renewal. By bringing small groups of believers together for study and mutual exhortation he utilized that simple but effective technique which, over and again throughout Church history, has strengthened the faithful and provided them with a method of multiplying. It was a technique not approved by the Lutheran leadership because it provided for people's spiritual needs outside the structures. But it was appealing to victims forced into migration or disillusionment by rulers' changing confessional tastes.

Spener was instrumental in upgrading the academy at Halle into a university and it was here that his disciple, August Francke, turned Pietism into a movement. Still under thirty when he took the chair of oriental languages (he later became professor of theology) in 1692, Francke proved himself to be one of the great Christian visionaries and also a remarkable organizer. He devised a system of state education which had Pietist teaching on conversion and the cultivation of the interior life at its centre. He demonstrated in an extraordinary variety of ways how that life was to be expressed in service in the world. He turned the Halle press into one of the busiest in Europe, pouring out Bibles, tracts and theological books in several languages. He established a missionary society which sent workers to India. He founded a Bible institute, schools, teacher training colleges and a dispensary. His orphanage had places for three thousand people and was far and away the largest such institution in Europe. And to pay for these impressive social and charitable exercises, Francke set up trading companies which sent agents to Hungary, Russia, Italy and even Asia. Francke was one of the pioneers who, under the patronage of the King of Prussia, helped to make Halle a leading commercial and cultural centre. Here lived Telemann, regarded then as the finest living German composer, and Handel spent his early years in the city. But more importantly Halle became the cradle of a religious programme that was as practical as it was well-conceived in theoretical terms. From this centre devotees took Pietism to many parts of the old world and the new.

Pietism was only one manifestation of an interiorized spirtuality which was scandalized by the clash of post-Reformation orthodoxies. Just as in earlier tumultuous epochs men and women had sought in the cloister or ad-hoc communities to safeguard their own souls and demonstrate to the world the better way of charitable service and contemplation, so in the seventeenth century Christians on both sides of the confessional divide established communities to discover and demonstrate something of the Kingdom of God among the kingdoms of men.

3.1 Port-Royal Convent, Paris, engraving by Jean Marot.

Cornelius Jansen (1585–1638) was a Dutch Catholic who was incensed by the revival of scholasticism and the new Jesuit dialectic which fuelled religious conflict. Experience, not intellect, he insisted was the key to saving faith. Conversion was an essential first step for anyone who would find God. Without this, ceremonies and sacraments were quite useless. The spiritual aspect of Jansenism was centred on Port-Royal des Champs, near Paris, where a community of Benedictine nuns was strongly influenced by the new teaching. Also to Port-Royal came several lay men and priests to live as hermits, devoted to prayer and, later, teaching.

Blaise Pascal (1623–62) had already established his fame as a brilliant young mathmatician, inventor and physicist when, in 1654, he had a conversion experience which changed the rest of his short life. He was drawn into the intellectual-spiritual world of Port-Royal, where his sister was a nun, and devoted his remaining years almost entirely to religious reflection and writing. He found proofs of God illusory. Man could only come to an inner, saving experience of the divine through the mediation of Jesus Christ. 'It is the heart which perceives God and not the reason. That is what faith is: God perceived by the heart, not by the reason.' Indeed, intellectualism was positively dangerous, for there is a wide gulf between knowing God and loving him.

Quietism was a similar reaction against the prevailing rationalism but it led its adherents in a very different direction from that indicated by Pietism or Jansenism. Quietism took its Catholic form (it has similarities with some aspects of Quakerism) from the Spanish, Jesuit-trained priest, Miguel de Molinos. He taught that passivity was the only way to an inner experience of God, since all action, desire and thought must be expelled before divine inspiration can occur. It followed that all external stimuli should be shunned. Many medieval mystics had played down the value of images and other devotional aids but none, before Molinos, had suggested that they were positively harmful. He became the guru of the ageing ladies of Roman salons. His friends' friends included Innocent XI. Only after several years were Molinos's critics vindicated. The inspiring priest and confessor had fallen into the antinomian pit always yawning at the feet of those who shun the guiding hand of conventional morality. Having liberated their minds of all earthly thoughts, he and some of his followers had, so they believed, become perfect vehicles for divine stimuli. Molinos spent the last nine years of his life in prison.

Nicholas Ludwig, Count von Zinzendorf, explored both Jansenism and Quietism in the course of his erratic spiritual pilgrimage. His parents both belonged to Spener's circle but since his father died when Nicholas was only weeks old and his mother abandoned him to the care of his grandmother after her remarriage, there was little direct influence from that quarter. The boy had connections with the court of Eugene of Savoy, one of the most cultured and enlightened princes of the day, who was very sympathetic to

Jansenism. He was educated at Halle and Wittenberg and thus drank from both orthodox and radical Lutheran wells. His grand tour acquainted him with the religious thought of Port-Royal and Fénelon. He was a close friend of Cardinal de Noailles, Archbishop of Paris, one of the few leading churchmen to defend the Jansenists from papal attack. His wife belonged to a leading family of the Pietist nobility. Shortly after his marriage, in 1722, the young Zinzendorf acquired the estate of Berthelsdorf, close to the Polish border, convinced that God had called him to the vocation of a Christian landowner. Zinzendorf's religious beliefs continued developing throughout his lifetime and were, perhaps, never wholly coherent. However, it remained a basic conviction of his that confessional barriers were illusory. He built the village of Herrnhut as a philadelphian ideal; a place where Christians of all persuasions who shared an inner experience of salvation could live and work together in harmony.

The surprising fact about Herrnhut is not that it became a great gener-ator of evangelistic zeal and methodology, but that it survived at all. Bands of Protestant refugees (no Catholics were ever attracted to Zinzendorf's *Unitas Fratrum*), fleeing persecution in neighbouring lands, poured into Berthelsdorf. There were inevitable clashes between different bands of immigrants. There were clashes between the settlers and their patron. There were clashes with ecclesiastical and civil authorities. Yet, somehow, Herrnhut survived. It adopted a constitution based on that of its largest con-stituent, the exiles from Moravia who traced their spiritual descent back to Jan Hus. It offered a pattern which was employed by other Protestant landowners. It demonstrated the viability of a non-national Christian move-ment, which needed permission from no earthly leader to transplant itself. And interdenominationalism permitted Moravians to work with any Protestants who shared emphases on conversion and evangelism. The Moravian Brethren insisted that spreading the Gospel was a task incumbent on every Christian and not one reserved for clergy, evangelists or missionary societies.

By the time of Zinzendorf's death (1760) Moravian groups were propa-gating a simple, personal, evangelical faith in the Baltic lands, North America, Lapland, South America (primarily among black slaves), the West and East Indies, Greenland, Egypt and South Africa. The fact that the Moravian Brethren never grew to be a large denomination belies their influence. Their concern was always to win men and women for Christ, not for their own particular version of the faith. Their influence on the growth of other Protestant churches in the eighteenth century and on later revivals was enormous.

All these experience-based groups aroused suspicion, hostility, mis-understanding (often deliberate) and persecution. Zinzendorf was forced into exile for several years. More than once, Herrnhut came within an ace of being closed down. In 1710 Port-Royal was suppressed and its buildings razed to the ground. Archbishop Fénelon of Cambrai, who sympathized with Quietism, became involved in an acrimonious dispute with the polemicist, Bishop Bossuet, and some of his propositions were condemned in Rome. The reasons for the outlawing of those who stressed the interior aspect of religion were the same as they had always been. They ranged from popular dislike of those who appeared 'holier than thou' to establishment-arian outrage at those who challenged, implicitly or explicitly, traditional doctrines and practices. Contemporaries were fully aware that they were witnessing a continuation or recrudescence of the spiritual forces of the Reformation. Yet, as so often in the past, it was the reluctant rebels who set the agenda.

THE COMMON PURSUIT

Catherine Schütz was an early member of the reformed group in Strasbourg and one of the first to marry (in 1523) a renegade priest. When her husband was excommunicated by the local bishop, Catherine wrote a series of vigor-ously worded and Scripture-soaked pamphlets against Catholic leaders who attacked clerical marriage while frequenting whores and turning a blind eye to homosexuality among priests. She did not hesitate to criticize Protestant champions. She chided Luther and Zwingli because they failed to reach agreement on their understanding of the Lord's Supper. And she refused to countenance criticism of Anabaptists, whom she regarded as fellow evan-gelicals. In fact, she openly visited religious radicals in prison; she encouraged them to stand firm against their persecutors; and she urged Protestant leaders, by letter and pamphlet, to make common cause with them.

Such examples – and Catherine was far from unique – serve as a warning against the historian's tendency to categorize. There was a time when the Protestantism emerging from the Reformation was described under three convenient headings – Lutheran, Reformed and Anabaptist – though all these categories were acknowledged as being subdivisible. Closer scrutiny revealed that believer's baptism was not a universal badge worn by all those on the 'left wing' of the Reformation. So, 'Anabaptist' was not strictly accu-rate. Some scholars, determined to find a pigeonhole wide enough for all those movements which did not fit into other compartments, applied the term 'sectaries' to those they wished to discuss, thus begging such questions

3.2 The advent of Antichrist, a necessary precursor of the end of the world, as envisaged by Hartmann Schedel in *Liber Chronicarum*. People who did not live in expectation of the Apocalypse were reminded of it in church paintings and sculptures, sermons and printed books. Leaders of apocalyptic sects had a rich traditional imagery to draw upon.

as 'what is a sect?' and 'when does a sect become a Church or a denomination?' Others favoured the description 'radicals' but some of the movements thus dubbed were not at all extreme in their theological views; they consisted of people who simply wanted to separate themselves from society, as other groups of Christians had done for centuries, in order to get on with the business of living holy lives.

Those who were physically or verbally violent in rejecting contemporary society and setting up their own defiant communes were always a minority. Like many of their spiritual forbears who pursued an individualistic path, the new radicals tended to be indifferent rather than hostile to dogmas, devotional exercises and ecclesiastical directives which seemed not to further the cause of holiness. They accepted the resultant persecution. There was a world of difference between the militant rallying cries of the millenarian warrior-'king' Thomas Müntzer and the summons of Menno Simons, who called to 'battle; not with external weapon and armour as the bloody, mad world is wont to do, but only with firm confidence, a quiet patience, and a fervent prayer . . . The thorny crown must pierce your head and the nails your hands and feet. Your body must be scourged and your face spat upon . . . Be not dismayed, for God is your captain.'

Simons was the leader of a lower Rhineland band of believers. Once a Catholic priest, he left a church which had fallen into error and went into the wilderness with the 'true saints'. His preaching tours helped to keep the movement together during the early phase of persecution. The 'Mennonites' (as they were eventually called) tried at first to coexist with their neighbours. They met in secret for worship and instruction and maintained their identity by encouraging marriage 'within the faith'. They tried to win over their friends and relations by quiet persuasion. However, sporadic persecution obliged communities to move from time to time. When they did so, the emphasis of their religious beliefs subtly changed. Their evangelistic edge was blunted. They turned in on themselves and ceased to be a prophetic people living in the shadow of the parousia. They put survival before suffering and instead of being an irritant to society's conscience they sought a peaceful life on or beyond its borders. Mennonite communities fetched up in the American colonies and the Ukraine, many of them deliberately preserving their own customs and their Dutch or German language.

The religious enthusiasts who had set out to distance themselves from de-spiritualized conventions eventually became trapped within their own traditions. There could be no more dramatic evidence of the power of institutionalism than the present-day lifestyle of the Old Order Amish communities in Pennsylvania, Ohio and Indiana. In their closed villages they wear seventeenth-century dress, eschew motorized transport, speak an archaic form of German and are widely regarded by their neighbours as 'quaint'. Having said that, we must acknowledge that the Amish are not typical of the Mennonite movement as a whole which is well known for sacrificial social service and disaster relief work through and alongside such organizations as the Red Cross. The Hutterites (followers of the Tyrolean, Jacob Hutter) had a similar story. They found a home for many years in Moravia, where nobles welcomed settlers prepared to work their land but were scattered by seventeenth-century persecution and founded communities in the New World. Today there are over 400 Hutterite communities worldwide living a simple life in semi-isolation.

Human generation always creates problems for gathered churches. It is one thing for Christians to band together because they have shared spiritual experience and commitment to an agreed corpus of doctrine. They can preserve their purity by marrying within the community. But what about the children? They cannot travel on the parents' spiritual passports. They, too, must be nurtured, not only to accept the teaching of their elders, but also to undergo the same kind of conversion experience. This is what, above all, forces closed, authoritarian polity on such societies as the Hutterites. Communities based on evangelical, affective, experiential religion tend to develop tight, often oppressive, internal discipline.

The Restorationists who emerged in the mid–1960s present a contemporary example which can be closely observed. They bear all the hallmarks of earlier movements. They are ardently evangelistic and involved in worldwide mission. They major on apocalyptic and are biblical fundamentalists. They make much of dramatic manifestations of spiritual power and encourage emotional expression and experience. They are scornful of denominationalism and are fastidious about relations with other Churches. Yet they are trapped into the same compromises as those they condemn. While rejecting the materialistic baggage which weighs down older Churches they have built themselves expensive buildings for worship and administration. While proclaiming the imminent end of this world leaders make themselves very comfortable in it. They rediscover 'long lost' biblical truths and then split into rival groups over their understanding of them. They regard the local congregation as autonomous, but through mammoth conferences, literature crusades, video tapes, audio cassettes and nationwide supervision seek to ensure that all units are kept on the right lines. They emphasize freedom in the Spirit and end up imposing authoritarian systems which, in a few instances, have become exceedingly oppressive. The 1970s produced the scandal of 'heavy shepherding' – a system, of American origin, of control by elders and apostles which extended into the private lives of members. It was justified by the need to preserve internal purity:

> The spirit of this age is anarchy, independence, rebellion, and anti-authority and we must always guard that the Church is not affected by this. An essential element in the care and concern necessary in Church building is spiritual authority by God's delegated authority. Submitting

(3.3) Early sixteenth-century woodcuts indicate how prophecy could become self-fulfilling within the world of experiential religion: (opposite, top) cites signs in heaven and on earth to prove that the end is nigh; (above) exposes the blindness of the clergy to divine truth which is revealed to the simple and (opposite, below) Armegeddon seems close at hand when the lay estate, led by the emperor, take arms against ecclesiastical leaders and burn down churches.
(opposite, top) Joseph Grunpeck's *Eine neue Ausslegung*, 1507.
(above) Haug Marschalck, *Ein Spiegel der Plinden*, 1523.
(opposite, below) Joseph Grunpeck's *Spiegel*, 1522.

to spiritual authority in another person whom I can accept as appointed by God, is at the heart of restoration life and growth in Church.

Another danger inherent in a system based on personal, interiorized religion was untamed subjectivism. Here again, submission to authority was one means of protecting the community from spiritual anarchy. Yet it went hand-in-hand with the encouragement of even deeper experience. By stressing the importance of being totally yielded to God in passive surrender (*Gelassenheit*) it aimed to correct the tendency in all Spirit-based religion towards the exaltation of the individual who has received special revelation. Seclusion, obedience, spirituality – there was little to choose between the more moderate radical Protestant groups and the religious communities of the pre-Reformation era.

'Time brings roses. He who thinks that he has all the fruit when strawberries are ripe, forgets that grapes are still to come. We should always be looking eagerly for something better.' So wrote Christian Entfelden, one of the South German radicals. In 1620, John Robinson, pastor of an exiled English congregation at Leyden, bade farewell to those of his flock who were to be numbered among the Pilgrim Fathers. Prophesying a brave future for them, he assured them, 'The Lord has more truth yet to break forth out of his Holy Word.' The single most important concept to emerge from the radical wing of the Reformation was that of the dynamic relationship of Word and Spirit. It provides a genetic link between thinkers, revolutionary leaders and contemplatives whose cousinage is not immediately apparent. Acknowledging the Bible as a 'living' revelation through which God speaks to the faithful, and rejecting traditional interpretations as in any way binding gave rise, over the centuries, to a varied array of Christian sects whose chronicles make fascinating reading – richly varied, often amusing, sometimes frightening but always intriguing. Wayward though many of these movements were, they did evolve a new approach to truth which eventually became orthodoxy for most Churches.

Humanists and reformers had run into problems with the open-Bible policy. Catholic and Protestant leaders had hedged the Scriptures around with restrictions. For the dissenting Churches free access to the word of God was fundamental – but not unrestrained interpretation. Right understanding and application were guaranteed only by the inner testimony of the Holy Spirit. 'Let everyone weigh and test Scripture to see how it fits his own heart. If it be against his own conscience and the Word within his own soul, then let him be sure he has not found the right meaning.' So advised Sebastian Franck, one of the intellectual virtuosi of the Reformation, who began as a Catholic humanist, passed through Lutheranism, flirted with Anabaptism, eventually rejected all dogmas and ended up as a highly individualistic writer and preacher. To be sure, Luther, Calvin and other reformist theologians had made the same point but not with the same degree of emphasis. It was the radicals who successfully fused Protestant insistence on *sola scripturea* and the mystical experience of the direct action of God upon the soul.

This understanding of the interaction of Word and Spirit, capable, when necessary, of bypassing both intellect and tradition was of course, a dangerous concept. It did not rule out subjectivism. It did not prevent charlatans and deluded fanatics imposing their own bizarre interpretations of Scripture upon the gullible. But intelligent seekers could check the claims of 'Spirit-filled' prophets against the plain word of the Bible. When tradition was also considered, there existed a threefold system of checks and balances available to inform the deliberations of individuals, congregations and denominations. In practice, church members continued to be guided by their priests or ministers, the guardians of that version of Christian truth they had been brought up with or had decided to espouse.

Bible, Church (tradition), Experience (Spirit) – the Reformation did not invent any of them. But it did realign them. It did encourage a new kind of creative tension which would always exist in progressive churches thereafter, producing mini-reformations when old truths had been neglected or new truths were being suppressed. When Jansenism challenged the Roman communion, or Wesleyanism shamed a recumbent Church of England, or the New Connexion stirred up the Baptists, or the Salvation Army attacked the social conscience of conventional Christianity or Pentecostalism provoked a new awareness of the third person of the Trinity or liberation theologians called Western Christianity to rethink its attitudes towards the Third World, they were setting off that three-sided debate by which believers try to arrive at the truth.

Chapter Four

HERESY: SO WHAT?:
The Doctrinal Debate

DOCTRINE IN ITS PLACE

Every Lord's Day, John Betjeman's teddy bear, Archibald Ormsby-Gore, put on brown-paper wings and flapped across the valley until he came to the low, neat Strict Baptist Chapel. There he could thunder out his sermons for eight hours at a stretch, across the gas light, over the sparse and ageing congregation, between the aggressively unadorned walls, before returning to his work of converting Jumbo, the rather characterless friend who shared his toy-cupboard in the attic at home.

Perhaps there was never really a radical Protestant as austere, as indefatigable and as enterprising as Archie; but his religion was, in an extreme form, representative of the Protestant tradition, with its emphasis on sermons instead of sacraments, exhortations to living saints instead of prayers to dead ones, and honest resolution to make the house of God earnestly earthy, rather than imitatively glorious, as though a church which echoes heaven were a mockery of God. Archie even encapsulated two broader features commonly attributed to Protestant culture: those paper wings connoted the industrious inventiveness which, it has been claimed, made Protestant peoples precocious in modern economic development; and Archie was an amateur archaeologist, who believed that molehills were the graves of baby druids: he can therefore be presumed to have based his faith on a study of the evidence about primitive Christianity. The environment he went so far to find for worship is reduplicated in thousands of chapels, where the pulpit – huge and gleaming, polished by ladies alive with the ardour of the gospel of work – stands where an altar might otherwise be, and the ranks of pews are arrayed around, tall and hard and tightly enclosed, under big windows of bare panes. These are temples to unintrusive fellowship and unfiltered light.

The peculiarities of Catholic tradition are also encoded in décor and design. In the chapel of the Hospital de la Caridad in Seville the trends and tenets of post-Reformation Catholicism are comprehensively packed into a tiny space, like jewels in a watch-case. Some of the features are specific to the time and place of their making. The confraternity that endowed and kept the hospital in late seventeenth-century Seville was a rich and aristocratic club with a waiting-list for membership that could run into years. But the city in which it operated was an impoverished and decaying wen, plague-stricken, crime-ridden; a 'Thieves' Babylon' where the anti-heroes of picaresque novels took flesh, a Golgotha where the unburied dead stank in the streets, a sin-city where the theatres were shut in expiation of the citizens' cry for penance. The rich and noble members of the confraternity were obliged by their rules to carry sick paupers on their own shoulders and to tend, feed and bury them with their own fastidious hands, 'and when they arrive at the poor man, they will fall on their knees, and however wounded or disgusting he may be they will not turn their faces.'

Thus the sanctuary of the chapel is dominated by a grim and glorious altarpiece of the burial of Christ and the nave is decorated with saints who pre-figured the brothers' duties. St Elizabeth of Hungary, painted by Murillo, struggles against revulsion as she picks at the lice and dabs at the sores of her patients; St John of God enacts the rule of the confraternity: 'before putting the poor, sick man to bed, wash his feet and kiss them.'

Beyond the inmates and attendants of the Hospital, the universal Church is addressed by the scheme of the chapel, which makes a complete and moving statement of the means of salvation according to Catholic teaching. Entering at the west end, the worshipper is gripped by an irresistible summons to penance: on his right and left are two of the most beautiful and terrible paintings in Spain, the Hieroglyphs of the Four Last Things, of Juan de Valdés Leal. In one, in fierce, stabbing brush-strokes, a skeleton with a menacing scythe strides gloatingly, smothering the candle-light, among symbols of worldly vanity – books and arms, helms and mitre, globe and altar. In the other, the bodies of a bishop and a knight moulder and putrefy before the beholder's eyes under scales in which carnality and lust teeter alarmingly with the instruments of Christ's passion and the tools – hair-shirt and scourges – of mortification of the flesh.

After this summons to repentance, chastened and chilled, the worshipper approaches the altar, encouraged on either hand by paintings of works of mercy and charity – feeding the hungry, clothing the naked, welcoming the friendless, tending the sick, burying the dead, visiting the imprisoned. Though the experience cannot be perfectly recreated today, for the depredations of war have left the display incomplete, the promise of salvation by works is still unfolded to comfort and exhort the penitent. Before he reaches the sanctuary, the Catholic sees paradigms of the holy mass, painted by Murillo – the miracles of manna in the wilderness and of water sprung from the rock, figures of the eucharist traditional in the Church from some of the most ancient surviving Christian art and verse.

Ahead of him, Christ's sacrifice is commemorated in the altarpiece of the entombment by Pedro Roldán. Apart from its special resonance for a brotherhood of buriers of the dead, this subject is the supreme statement of the mystery of God Incarnate. For Christ was surely never more human than when He was dead – a pale, gaunt, broken sharer in our misery. Yet the stark image is surrounded with a blaze of gilding and a riot of ornament which transcends taste in a desire to affirm that even at His most abject the human Christ never ceased to be God, and no dirt or dimness of man can blot out the radiance of heaven. Today, in this place, you can watch the half-tanned tourists, from England or Scandinavia, secular-minded or Protestant-educated, twitch in embarrassment or blink in incomprehension, but in the Catholic tradition it makes transcendent sense to put images of bloody and tearful beings into effulgent frames and lavish niches.

After receiving the sacrament, the worshipper can raise his eyes to a figure of Charity above the altar. Reminded of the love that conquers death, he turns to go back to his place and sees, ahead and above him, on the face of the choir loft, a triumphant vision – poorly painted by comparison with the rest of the chapel, but of impressive scale and inspiring boldness – of the exaltation of the Cross. Admonished, reconciled and revitalized, he can return to his seat – and, perhaps, to his duties as a nurse or gravedigger or, if a patient, to the prospect of death.

The reader who dons paper wings to fly back from Seville to the English downs of Archie Ormsby-Gore will have seen divergent traditions embodied in chapels so different that an uninstructed onlooker would hardly recognize them as belonging to the same religion. The Catholic chapel is a celebration of the saving effects of charity; the Protestant chapel, by omitting such allusions, makes an implicit statement of the sufficiency of faith. The Catholic chapel is a theatre of priestly ritual; that of the Protestants is a sheepfold for the urgings of a pastor. The Catholic chapel provides a sanctuary for the enactment of a perpetual sacrifice; its Protestant counterpart a space for the commemoration of an unrepeatable event.

Four hundred years of mutual influence between the Protestant and Catholic traditions have not eliminated the differences or the unfraternal feelings they sometimes inspire. In 1986 the rich art-patron, Peter Palumbo, commissioned a new altar by Henry Moore for the Anglican parish church where he was a warden. The necessary planning consent for its installation was withheld not for aesthetic reasons – though haters of modern art deplored the intrusion of an innovative sculpture in a Carolean setting – but on the doctrinal grounds that Moore had provided a stone altar of sacrifice, which invited the onlooker to imagine it running with blood, rather than the common supper-table preferred by the Protestant element within the Church of England. The case had been almost exactly prefigured by another in Bedfordshire in 1636.

Yet the measuring-rods of heresy swell and shrink from time to time, according to the position of the measurer. No serious doctrine is original to Protestantism, but was formerly part of the doctrinal diversity enfolded in the medieval church. As doctrine develops, heresy and orthodoxy get re-formulated and redefined until they overlap or coincide, as they did in the earliest days of the Church when diversity was still unrefined and orthodoxy barely codified. After the scandal of numerous secessions from the Church in the sixteenth century, Protestants and Catholics defined their positions with reference to each other and in distinction from each other; for a while, in consequence, dogmatic squabbles were exacerbated and doctrinal differences were sharpened in mutual antagonism, like the heads of clashing arrows. Longer time, however, has blunted and rusted them and they seem fearsome no longer. It even became possible, from the generous perspective of the 1960s, for Catholic theologians to deny, without trapping themselves in unorthodoxy, that Luther was a heretic at all. Re-examining today doctrines once thought irreconcilable, as we gingerly finger their points, we can fit them back into the same quiver.

Doctrinal issues have subsided partly because they are hard to understand. There have been times when theology has made good popular entertainment. Gregory Nazianzenus was amused to find he could debate the nature of the Trinity over shop counters in fifth-century Constantinople; when the Jesuit Louis Coudret undertook a mission to Geneva in 1559, he was surprised to find that 'every Genevan artisan presumes to speak of predestination' and impressed at the reasonable level of debate in which he was engaged in the streets. Today, however, like so many once-interesting subjects now withered by academic desiccation, theology has lost its popular appeal. Theological *vulgarisateurs* can make an impact only by bludgeoning the public with the sledgehammer of apostasy – denying the divinity of Christ or the virginity of his mother or the reality of his resurrection. These crass ploys are easily recognized as attention-seeking and popular debate about them rarely rises above the level of the banal or the abusive. Not only has the queen of the sciences been dethroned in the republic of letters, now she is shunned in the gutter by her former subjects, in indifference or embarrassment.

Taken seriously, by the minority still willing to do so, theology is an elusive subject which demands a subtle intelligence, linguistic skill and years of study to master – and unusual humility and charity to teach. Even professional theologians seem unable – when their injudicious pronouncements are boiled down to sound-bites for public consumption – to mask their deficiencies of character, learning or thought. Exhibitionist-bishops and clever-clever dons, shying at Christian verities like fairground drunks, have helped to turn the public image of theology from discredit to disgrace. Dwindling popular patience with the niceties of doctrine in twentieth-century England was brilliantly captured by Robert Graves, who turned in disgust from the irrationality of a creed that insisted no man could be saved unless he believed that 'three incomprehensibles are not three incomprehensibles but one incomprehensible'; or by Alan Bennett, who depicted a headmaster in a catechism class replying to a boy who asked about the Trinity, 'Trinity? Three in One. One in Three. Any doubts about that – see your maths master.' Nowadays, indifference has deepened to the point where there are no longer even any jokes worth making. Most Christians take refuge from the demands of doctrine by reducing their religion to a rumble in the gut or a code of outward behaviour. The Christian's is usually a life of sensation, not of thought. But we still have to devote a chapter to the kind of Christianity that goes on in the mind, and is expressed in doctrines and attitudes, because it has meant so much to the élites who have defined the difference between Protestants and Catholics.

The Tridentine Power-house

Fortunately, to appreciate the depth of feeling generated by the doctrinal disputes of the Reformation, and the surprising extent of the common ground on which they rested, it is unnecessary to understand them intellectually. They are embodied in granite and blazoned in art in the Escorial, the great monastery-palace – 'a hovel for a king and a palace for God' as its founder called it – where the writers of this book began their exploration of the Protestant–Catholic clash in 1988. It is one of the world's biggest engines of prayer – 205 metres by 160, with 2,673 windows and, inside and out, 1,200 doors. Philip II built it to be the nerve-centre of his monarchy – the biggest empire, in terms of reach and breadth, the world had ever seen, the most widely spread around the globe. It was designed to be a mausoleum for his dynasty, a godly corrective to other Renaissance courts, and a school of Catholic missionaries. It was consciously planned to echo the Temple of Solomon and dwarf the palace of the popes. It was also intended to defy the Reformation and to proclaim the doctrines which, as the edifice was built, were being formulated at the Council of Trent in revulsion from the heresies of the Protestants.

It housed, for instance, a religious order who were custodians of the tradition of St Jerome, author of the translation of the Bible which Protestants had impugned. It was a power-house of prayer for the dead, where thirty thousand masses were ordered for the founder on the day of his death and where perpetual prayers were to be offered for the repose of his father and descendants. Their remains are stacked today, like the contents of a club sandwich, one above the other in gilded caskets, underneath the chapel. It was a repository of over seven thousand relics of the saints, anxiously garnered from battlegrounds of the the Reformation in northern Europe to protect them from profanation at derisive hands. You can still be amused, inspired or outraged by them today: a bone from the head of St Maurice is encased in a bust with a detachable head, from which globules of stylized blood drip onto the gilded breast-armour, while sad eyes stare under a brow crowned with an oriental helm. A relic of St Jerome is wittily enclosed in a window in his breast, opened where he pounds himself in penance with a fragment of rock; that of St Lawrence, the patron saint of the foundation, is to be found under his hinged pate, which opens just above his tonsure. The propriety of invoking the saints and angels is affirmed above the choir in the vast painting by Luca Cambasio, where they queue serenely in their hundreds before the heavenly throne. On the face of it, the entire scheme seems to put Protestants at arm's length and sword's point. Yet even here, where awareness of the doctrinal differences seems to inform the whole building, and where every image and adjunct is designed to proclaim them, underlying similarities with the cultures and thought of the reformers can be detected. Catholic verity and Protestant error are shouted aloud, but if one listens for the whispers and echoes, the distinctions blur.

The One Bread

Above all, the Escorial is a temple of the Blessed Sacrament of the altar, a statement of faith in the miracle and sacrifice of the mass. Those who think they can see a clean break between Protestant and Catholic doctrine some-times point to contrasting ways of understanding the eucharist – the thanksgiving with which Christians of both traditions share a meal in accord-ance with the orders Christ gave to the apostles at the Last Supper. In practice, divergence on this matter is an insurmountable obstacle to the fully restored Christian unity which inter-communion would signify, for, as St Paul said, 'although we are many, we are one body, because we share in the one bread.' While Protestants and Catholics can join happily in eucharistic celebrations today (see below, pp. 120–121), the Catholic hierarchy could never admit to Communion worshippers who did not offer the awe and reverence which the Catholic tradition demands; for again the apostolic ruling seems peremp-tory: 'anyone who eats the bread or drinks the cup of the Lord unworthily is answerable for the body and blood of the Lord.' These words can be variously understood; but they turn differences of perception of the eucharist into grounds of conflict. Of all the doctrinal clashes which date from the Reformation, that over the eucharist reverberates most loudly today.

From the earliest documented days of Christian worship, the eucharistic ritual has been its centrepiece. St Paul told the Christians of Corinth how to do it in words which, in one version or another, are still read in most churches as glosses of the actions of priest or minister as he or she goes through the motions: 'For the tradition I received from the Lord and also handed on to you is that on the night he was betrayed, the Lord Jesus took some bread, and after he had given thanks, he broke it, and he said, "This is my body, which is for you; do this in remembrance of me." And in the same way, with the cup after supper, saying, "This cup is the new covenant in my blood. Whenever you drink it, do this as a memorial of me."' The origins of the ceremony at the Last Supper are described by three of the gospel-writers, in words very similar to St Paul's, and alluded to by the fourth. 'The breaking of bread' is included in the book of Acts in a list of observances of faithful Christians; two disciples were said to have recognized the risen Christ at Emmaus when he repeated the ritual within the first few days of the history of the Church; and the letters of St Paul emphasize participation in the eucharist as a Christian duty – a common act which signifies the adhesion of individual Christians to one body, 'the Body of Christ'. Depictions of a congregational meal occur frequently in early Christian art, also commonly including fish – the fourth evangelist's addition to the sacred table d'hôte – with the bread and wine. A satirist of the second century lampooned what was recognizably the doctrine of the real presence of Christ in the eucharist: 'These Christians take a bit of bread and say it is their god. Then they eat him and crunch him with their teeth!'

The antiquity of the eucharist is therefore not in question. Its meaning is. The Last Supper was a passover meal in the Jewish tradition, enjoined in Jewish law as 'a feast-day for all generations . . . a decree for all time' – a memorial of God's promise to his people and a sacrificial feeding on 'an animal without blemish', eaten, after extraction of its blood, 'with unleavened bread and bitter herbs . . . hurriedly: it is a Passover in Yahweh's honour.' Christ revised the menu and created a new paradigm, in which the balance between supper and sacrifice, souvenir and sacrament have been doubted and debated.

During the middle ages the focus of the debate was on the curious divine chemistry by which bread became flesh and wine blood. A particular way of interpreting the eucharist grew in dominance, until in the thirteenth century it acquired the status and role of theological litmus, by which the orthodoxy of an opinion about this sacrament could be tested. This doctrine of 'transubstantiation' was formulated in the language of its time – which does not necessarily mean that it does not hold true for other times, any more than that the gospels should be held false in China for being written in Greek. The simplest way of understanding it is in the context of medieval ideas about physics, which drew a perfectly sensible distinction between two kinds of being. If for instance, I say of someone, 'She is a woman,' I am using the verb 'to be' in a sense relating to her essential nature. If I say, 'She is a student' or 'She is tanned' or 'She is unwell' or 'She is in London', I am speaking of a different kind of 'being', which is accidental and therefore mutable and fleeting. Some languages have different verbs to signify these distinct kinds of being and in modern Spanish, for instance, the contexts in which they are used correspond pretty exactly to medieval notions of the difference between 'essence' and 'accidence'. In a culture in which the distinction seemed lively and ubiquitous, like that of the middle ages in Western Christendom, it was a straightforward, though not uncontroversial, matter to understand the mystery of the eucharist in these terms. Christ was essentially present, under the accidental forms of bread and wine.

The very clarity of this doctrine made it an easy matter to classify as heretical other attempts to express the same truth. In the climate of mutual defiance in which Reformation theologians formulated their doctrines, paradigms which, in other circumstances, might have been seen as alternative or complementary were treated as mutually exclusive. Luther, whose cast of mind was old-fashioned, stuck to the language of medieval physics, but tried to make the mystery of the eucharist more conformable to sense-experience by reformulating it as 'consubstantiation', according to which both the bread of the offering and the body of Christ were 'really', essentially present after consecration. Calvin, who had great gifts of mental lucidity, acknowledged Christ's 'real presence' in a special sense, peculiar to this sacrament. This is hard to fault from a Catholic perspective and has the advantage of a strong appeal to common sense. Luther and Calvin both cursed reformers who went further and denied altogether that Christ was present in the eucharist except in a figurative sense. When Ulrich Zwingli uttered that heresy at a conference at Marburg, Luther chalked or carved, 'Hoc est Corpus Meum' on the table. The Protestant tradition seems today, for many of its adherents, to have developed away from the subtle teachings of its founders and though the pure doctrines of Luther and Calvin on the eucharist still have their guardians, most Protestants, if they think about it at all, leave the real presence out of their accounts, or diffuse it to the act of sharing, rather than concentrating it in what is shared.

The offence the early reformers gave to orthodoxy arose less from the novelty of their doctrines on the eucharist than from the acerbity of their denunciations of transubstantiation. Every bit as much as the formulators of the doctrine of transubstantiation, Luther was locked into the mental world of late-medieval philosophy. He belonged – he proclaimed it with pride – to a school which refused to distinguish between a name and the reality it signified; for 'nominalists' like him, the *term*, not the object it might be supposed to denote, was the only reality to which a statement could reliably refer. One widely espoused way of explaining transubstantiation was by analogy with

4.1 The Last Supper, 1523. Dürer's depiction owed much to Leonardo but his emphasis both on bread and wine reflected the practice of Protestant churches.

the way a term corresponded to some reality distinct from itself. Partly because he rejected the analogy, Luther condemned transubstantiation as a perversion of Christian tradition, rather than a valid part of it. Yet in another climate, like today's, the imperfections of rival formulae can be more charitably indulged, on the grounds that the realities which Christian doctrines try to express can only be approached, not attained; the formulae of theologians are approximations – reflections in the dark glass. The God worshipped by Christians is invisible to the eye, inaccessible to the intellect and irreducible in the words or images at our disposal.

One measure of the goodness of a doctrine is the depth and quality of the response it evokes in the worshipper. When Mass inspires Catholic worship at its most solemn and sincere, the host is a lens which focuses thoughts and senses on God; only a prejudiced eye could mistake this for idolatry. On a night of Maundy Thursday, in a Catholic church, to kneel in adoration of Christ, in the sacrament of the altar – a form in which he bequeathed his presence to the world in his own words; to follow him on his way to the tomb, as the sanctuary is stripped and the tabernacle emptied and the host carried in procession to an altar of repose; to share the sentiments which the same experience evoked in St Thomas Aquinas; to sing the stirringly simple and beautiful verses he wrote for the occasion; and to recall the hosts of saints who have done the same thing for hundreds of years and are doing the same thing at the same moment all over the world: this is to share in an act sanctified by devotion, whatever its historical origins, and to witness, with the conviction of faith, the workings of the Holy Spirit in the world. To abjure it would be a glaringly obvious impoverishment of Christian experience – just as bad, in its way, as the proscription and persecution of Protestant traditions of which the Church has been guilty in the past.

Still, this sense of presence at a sacrifice, in which the body of the divine victim is broken and his blood shed, could not be shared even by Protestants who acknowledge Christ's real presence in the sacrament. Aware of the immediacy with which the imagery of sacrifice is wielded in allusion to the eucharist in the epistles of Paul and Peter, they can admit the use of the word 'sacrifice' in this context in various senses: as an offering up of gifts brought to the table or altar; as a sacrifice, in words authorized by scripture, 'of praise and thanksgiving'; as a dedication of the worshippers' resolve; as a thanksgiving for grace; but further than that they decline to go. This reluctance had, among the early reformers, and continues to have, among their successors today, a sound emotional justification for those who reject a re-enactment of the events of the passion as detracting from the uniqueness and sufficiency of Christ's once-and-for-ever act of self-immolation on the cross.

There is also another reason for it, of a more partisan kind: the notion of the mass as sacrifice underlies the Catholic tradition of a priestly ministry with exclusive responsibility for offering the sacrifice. This made the most influential contemporary Protestant commentator on the decrees of the Council of Trent, who was usually a very mild and reasonable man, fulminate against the idea of sacrifice as 'the citadel, bulwark, strength, stay and stronghold of the reign of Antichrist'. On the doctrinal question of the nature of the eucharist, a political question about the balance of lay and clerical power therefore depends: without the sacrifice of the mass, the ministry of priests can be eliminated in favour of a 'presbytery' – such as the earliest Christian writing explicitly describe. In practice, of course, clergies can be tyrannous in both traditions and Protestant communities have been even more prone than Catholic ones to the vice of theocracy (see below, p. 122ff). In the period of the Reformation, Catholics and Protestants alike wanted to promote lay participation in the rites of the church. A Protestant way of achieving this was by questioning the uniqueness of the priesthood; for Catholics, part of the answer lay in making the sacrament more visible and accessible and by encouraging laymen to partake of it.

To share the passions inspired by sixteenth-century perceptions of the nature of the eucharist, an evocative place is a small oratory off King Philip II's bedroom in the Escorial, from where the king could look down on the sanctuary of the chapel to see the sacrifice of the Mass performed: 'the final purpose', according to the Escorial's contemporary historian, 'for which this whole foundation was designed'. It must not be supposed, however, that

4.2 To contemporaries it was obvious that Luther was either in league with the devil (above) or at war with him. The woodcut opposite depicts Satan issuing a challenge to the reformer, whose pose and surroundings are modelled on the traditional iconography of St Augustine.

Philip was distracted from adoration of the sacrament by hostile thoughts of Protestantism. For Philip the cult of the sacrament was not only a demonstration against the impieties of Protestants but also – and perhaps, for him, more importantly – a dynastic obligation. A thirteenth-century pope had confided guardianship of the cult to the founder of the house of Habsburg. Philip's Austrian cousins let this strenuous legacy go by default: Maximilian II declared himself 'neither Catholic nor Protestant but Christian'; Rudolf II found all formal religion unbearable and channelled his spirituality, such as it was, into the occultist and magical. The king of Spain, by contrast, shouldered the atavistic burden with enthusiasm.

After the Council of Trent had pronounced on the eucharist, Philip's

ANNO AETATIS EIVS XLVIII.

4.3 (Above) Martin Luther by Lucas Cranach the Elder, 1520. (Right) Ulrich Zwingli, 1539. At the colloquy of Marburg in 1529 attempts to bring the reformers together foundered on their incompatible doctrines of the Lord's Supper. Zwingli called Luther's insistence on a real presence a 'barrier of bran'.
(Top right) Luther's sermon The Blessed Sacrament, 1520. The title page depicts the miraculous delivery of the sacrament by angels, as in traditional Catholic discourse.

4.4 Depiction of printers by Jost Amman's *Das Ständebuch* (Frankfurt, 1568). An accompanying verse informs readers: 'Books have been written since olden times/ But the art of printing was practised first in Mainz.' Printing made it impossible to hush up doctrinal difference and criticisms of church leaders. Here printers set lines of type, but woodcuts were probably more important – and in an age of imperfect literacy – in communicating Reformation notions outside the élites.

obligation was even stronger. The time and space the council devoted to the subject left no doubt of its importance. The presence of Christ in the monstrance and tabernacle was a demonstration of priestly power strong enough to channel God's appearance in the world. Frequent communion could nourish the faithful in the strength which the struggle against heresy demanded. The Blessed Sacrament could be brandished as a banner – almost wielded as a weapon: 'the Eucharist should be borne in processions which represent the victory and triumph of Christ over death . . . And truth, victorious over heresy and lies, shall so celebrate that triumph that her adversaries, humbled before the vision of a magnificence so refulgent, and by the concerted joy of the Church, shall fall silent in meekness of spirit or conform to reason in their shame.'

As the eye travels up the aisle of the chapel of the Escorial, the glamour of the sanctuary – glowing marble after chilling granite – is immediately impressive. This is the throne-room of the 'palace for God' which Philip II conceived the Escorial to be. The tabernacle, where God is enthroned, forms the apex of an equilateral triangle, of which the chapel façade is the base. It is built of the gold and jasper with which Solomon adorned the Holy of Holies, and engraved with an acclamation of Christ, Priest and Victim. The room behind, which gives access to the tabernacle, is bathed in light and decorated with paintings of the Old Testament scenes which St Thomas Aquinas had identified as prefigurations of the Mass: the bestowal of manna, the bread and wine offered by Melchizadek, Elijah's angelic meal and the sacrifice of the paschal lamb.

Yet even in this holiest enclosure within the Escorial, a redoubt against the Reformation, the signs of battle are of civil war and Philip II is stamped as a contemporary of Calvin. Even in the sanctuary of the chapel, amid the aggressive rebuttals of Protestant eucharistic heresy, you could hear, in Philip II's day, the resonance of the reform in the music. Polyphony was banned from the regular services. The simplicity of the liturgy was not to be smothered by sumptuous settings and the king – echoing the preferences of the fathers of Trent, who shared in this respect the cultural bias of their Protestant adversaries – ordered plain chanting, slow speaking and distinct enunciation; the emphasis, as with the liturgical reforms of the Protestants, was on communicating the divine message. Philip had in his service some of the most skilful composers and performers of polyphonic music of the day, whose work adorned special and extra services: but even these were cautiously disciplined and made to sound austere and sober.

The same values of clarity and simplicity inform the Escorial as a whole – doric and gaunt, massive in monumentality but sparing in ornament – and the way of life lived there by the king and the religious community. The priorities of Protestants were echoed in the labour of biblical and patristic scholarship that went on in the library, the hours devoted to mental prayer and the Catholic puritanism that imposed punishing routines of work, austere standards in refreshment and dress and a rigid code of personal morality. When you enter the Escorial by what was designed as the main way in, the towering statues of six kings, lining the sky, confront you in the inner court and make the first and lasting impression on the visitor. They are Philip II's predecessors; yet they are not kings of Spain but kings of ancient Israel and Judah, reflecting Philip's self-perception as the leader of a chosen race through a trial of faith, by providential design, in a re-enactment of sacred history. They include Protestant heroes like Josiah, Jehosaphat and Hezekiah, who humbled the high priest and cleansed the temple of their filth. The same vision, expressed in the same terms, animated the self-evaluation of Protestant congregations and eclipsed the title-pages of Protestant books of martyrs. In England, Edward VI and Elizabeth I were hailed as reincarnations of the great reformist kings or judges of Israel.

Philip's propaganda image was as defender of the Church against infidels and heretics. In Titian's great allegory of the early 1570s, when the Escorial was nearing completion, religion is depicted wilting and downcast, assailed by serpents, with arms, cross and chalice fallen from her grasp: only the Spanish monarchy, entering, stage right, like a buxom Amazon, can save her. Philip's title of 'Catholic Monarch' was hereditary, but he was anxious to display its particular application to himself. His faith was deeply felt, not conveniently affected, after something like a religious conversion at the end of the 1560s – connected, perhaps, with the tragic end of his son and heir, Don Carlos, who died, imprisoned by his father's command, after showing signs of violent madness. Yet, at the same time, Philip's Catholic image concealed certain ironies. In his youth, Philip had been quite differently portrayed, as a prince of the pagan Renaissance, in gilded armour or even, perhaps, playing the organ in serenade to the goddess of love. After his conversion he continued to quarrel with popes, protect heretics when it suited, ally with them at need and cheerfully secularize Church property; his personal spirituality, with its liturgical austerity, its Old Testament allusions and its strenuous exercises in mental prayer, had in some ways more in common with the Reformation than with mainstream Catholic piety – echoing his severe tastes, his black garb and his erastian policies. His own choice of devotional reading – the forty-two books of piety he kept close at hand at all times – contained almost nothing that would have offended Luther, but was altogether in the tradition of late medieval personal piety, scriptural reflection, mystical devotion and critical self-examination which helped to inspire the Protestant reformers in their search for a direct and personal experience of God. Even the custodian of the Blessed Sacrament, the guardian of the sacrifice of the mass, was not far, in cultural terms, from his confessional enemies.

MEANS OF GRACE

The doctrinal conflicts with Protestantism displayed in the fabric or decoration of the Escorial are riven by what might be regarded as a deep – perhaps even a fundamental – difference between Catholicism and its Protestant critics. The invocation of saints, the orations for the dead, the hunger for the eucharist are habits of a community anxious about its members' need to work and strive to deserve God's mercy. So is the rite of penance – now called in the Catholic church the sacrament of reconciliation. This was also emphasized in the Council of Trent in conscious riposte to Protestant objections, though not made explicitly prominent in the Escorial. The increasing rigour of the Church's penitential discipline was one of the dynamic features of late medieval Catholicism from which Protestants were trying to escape – 'sheer tyranny,' Luther called it, 'a disease and a means to increase sins.' His advice to the troubled penitent, 'Cast yourself upon the grace of God,' could become a by-pass around all the sacraments as they were traditionally understood. Protestants – according to their tastes or proclivities – could be relaxed, indifferent or hostile in their attitudes towards these channels of God's grace because they perceived acutely other ways in which God could reach man and man God: that closeness, sought at full stretch, like the act of creation painted by Michaelangelo on the ceiling of the Sistine Chapel, was the object for which the devout in the sixteenth century strove on both sides of the confessional divide. In this context – like that of the mass and ministry – the quarrel was not over ends but means.

Most Protestants pare down the traditional seven sacraments to two; some avoid using the word; others have demoted it to mean merely an important ceremony rather than a means of transmission of grace. The flight from the sacramental life often starts with an assurance of salvation like Luther's: 'never doubt that you have come to grace.' From this follows, according to one of the first generation of Luther's followers, the conviction that 'the papal church and all its contrived practices are against Christ and disinherited by God.'

To this day there are thoughtful Protestants who regard the doctrine of justification by faith alone as the defining feature of their theology and as the starting-point of the Reformation. According to this doctrine, entry to heaven is not earned as a reward for good works, but is conferred by the unaided grace of God, signified by faith in the Lord Jesus. Its central significance was recognized by early Protestants. The leading Protestant commentator on the Council of Trent called it 'the chief point in Christian doctrine. For anxious and terrified minds which wrestle with sin and with the wrath of God seek this one haven: how they can have a reconciled and gracious God.' Luther depicted his first experience of revelation as the impact of the perception of the truth of this notion. Woebegone in awareness of his

4.5 Foxe's Book of Martyrs, 1563. Thomas Bilney, one of England's earliest Protestant martyrs gave offence to many who did not understand his doctrine but disliked his criticism of traditional practices.

own inadequacy, he suddenly felt liberated, while reading St Paul's Epistle to the Romans, by the realization that he had been saved in spite of himself. From the end of this thread, Luther unravelled the history of his own spiritual development and his followers have understandably treated it as the moment of inception of their movement. Felipe Fernández-Armesto remembers that when he was a schoolboy a teacher seeking to explain the Reformation began by chalking the words *FIDES SOLA JUSTIFICAT APUD DEUM* in huge letters on the blackboard. As a young man, he told a Welsh audience that he thought Protestantism was difficult to define. 'Not at all,' countered a redoubtable lady – who happened also to be a distinguished historian. 'It's a matter of justification by faith alone.'

Yet in Luther's day the doctrine was quite unshocking to orthodox ears. It was shared by some theologians whom we should unhesitatingly classify as Protestants and others who were unequivocally Catholic. Controversy is literally as old as the Church itself over the correct formulation of the conferment of grace; doubts have arisen and disputes raged over its compatibility with the Christian's obligation to perform works of mercy and with the doctrine of freedom of will – the option, that is, confided by God to accept or reject Him freely. Indeed, almost no other theological dispute disclosed by documents from apostolic times is more sharply delineated in Scripture. It can be detected in St Luke's attempt to suppress the discord of the apostles in the Council of Jerusalem; it is made explicit in the rival letters of Paul and James, each of whom attacks the other's doctrine. 'How does it help, my brothers,' asked James, 'when someone who has never done a single good act claims to have faith? . . . You see now that it is by deeds, and not only by believing, that someone is justified.' That he was replying directly to Paul is obvious. In vivid, jerky, disquietening prose – so different from James's smooth, pedantic manner – Paul put his convictions to the Romans, 'So what becomes of our boasts? There is no room for them. On what principle – that only actions count? No; that faith is what counts, since, as we see it, a person is justified by faith and not by doing what the Law tells him to do.'

This first conflict over justification arose in the course of Paul's mission to the gentiles: the 'works' from which he sought to exempt converts were, in particular, the exactions of Jewish laws. His campaign, however, was far more than a recruiting slogan: he was defending the very existence of Christianity, for unless Christ subverted the Old Dispensation and replaced it with a new means of access to heaven, the Incarnation was a superfluity. The unique and essential place of Christ in the salvation of Christians was at stake. This was explicitly the context of the next great convulsion in the peace of the Church to be caused by a dispute over justification. In the early fifth century, the issue was re-opened in a controversy which pitted against each other the Paul and James of their day: Augustine of Hippo – a self-tortured child of revelation whose awareness of his personal need of Christ's grace was absolute – and Pelagius, a priest from Britain, whose life was an unruffled pilgrimage towards a self-certainty that smacked of complacency. Pelagius, exulting in man's freedom to make or mar his own salvation, seemed to obviate his need of Christ. St Augustine was temperamentally incapable of self-reliance. Child of a dominant mother, victim of a guilt-ridden conscience, he wrote bewilderingly haunted *Confessions*, in which infantile peccadilloes like stealing apples and adolescent fumblings with instinctive sexuality are bewailed with all the anguish of a frustrated perfectionist. He needed God and he knew it. He was trapped between the humility of acknowledging his own dependence and the arrogance of insisting that everyone else was equally tainted by original sin, irredeemable but by the grace of God. His emphasis on the inefficacy of human goodness, combined with his unexcelled status as a doctor of the Church, made justification by faith part of the change every medieval theologian carried in his pouch. He made familiar the texts from St Paul which express the doctrine and passed, across the centuries to Luther's generation, the sense in which they were interpreted.

Among Luther's contemporaries, the doctrine of justification by faith alone was not only uncontroversial: it was fashionable at high levels of intellectual achievement and in lofty circles of theological debate. Throughout Luther's lifetime, and for a while afterwards, it was 'neutral country' linking the territory of Protestant and Catholic controversialists. Five years before Luther's *Ninety-five Theses,* Jacques Lefèvre d'Étaples published a commentary on St Paul in which he declared unequivocally that man was justified by faith, not works. Some of his followers became Protestants, others adhered to Catholicism without foregoing the doctrine. One of his pupils wrote the best brief evocation of the meaning of the doctrine in 1524: 'Faith is a grand and singular gift of God, which makes us sons of God. It is an affection, an experience and a true knowledge that God our father is good, perfect, powerful and wise, and that he in his self-love has chosen us to be his sons, saving and redeeming us by our saviour Jesus.'

The language of that profession of faith is strong and fresh, uninhibited by fear of a magisterial church: but it contains nothing to which a Catholic could not assent. Lefèvre d'Étaples himself died in 1536 without compromise of his personal Catholicism and without incurring serious censure at the time on doctrinal grounds. In 1541, the Protestants' doctrine of justification was conceded to them in the Compromise of Regensburg: the talks which produced that document broke down on other grounds. Cardinal Contarini, who nearly became pope and was the great patron of the first Jesuits, writing to a fellow-cardinal in 1542, regarded justification by faith alone as 'fundamental to the Christian religion'. His correspondent, Reginald Pole, who was notorious for presiding over the slaughter of Protestant martyrs in England, agreed with his victims about justification by faith and nourished a 'platoon of heretics' of the same persuasion in his house in Viterbo. Some continued to espouse the doctrine, suppressing only their proclamation of it, even after it was outlawed by the Council of Trent.

Contarini and Pole were leading lights of the Oratory of Divine Love, a circle of practitioners of demanding devotion among the higher clergy, which numbered popes in its ranks, and which made the doctrine of justification a subject of rational and unscandalized debate in Rome. And although the Council of Trent authorized formulations of doctrine which Protestants could not accept and which were, indeed, designed to shock them, it also proclaimed in Canon I of the Decree or its sixth session, 'If anyone says that a man can be justified before God through his works which are done either through the power of human nature or through the teaching of the Law, without divine grace through Jesus Christ, let him be anathema.' By declaring works to be dependent on prior grace, this captured the practical essence of the doctrine of justification by faith alone as a prescription for the Christian life. Once the conviction that man needs God has seeped into a believer's consciousness, the idea of self-contrived righteousness becomes revolting; good deeds seem to shred to 'filthy rags' and any compromise with the doctrine of justification by works seems to impugn the very holiness of God.

It seems extraordinary that a doctrine so ancient and current as that of justification by faith should have been proscribed by the hierarchy and become the exclusive property of dissidents who flourished it as a badge of their separateness. Before Luther made an issue of the difference, believers in justification by faith could happily cohabit the house of many mansions with those who put some of their trust in works. To change the metaphor – in the capacious penfold of traditional Catholicism, there was room for sheep dyed in the wool in many contrasting colours. The Christian religion has always exulted in glorious contradictions: of a God who is both three and one; of a Christ who is both God and Man; of a Virgin who gave birth to a son of flesh and blood without loss of her virginity; of wine made blood and bread made flesh; of substances, indeed, in Luther's interpretation of the eucharist, which were both bread and flesh, wine and blood simultaneously. Surely the resilient elastic of theology could be stretched – as it was, apparently, in the time of Paul and James – to enclose both traditions of justification.

The great Protestant critic of the Council of Trent, Martin Chemnitz, recognized the dispute as the result of a misunderstanding. 'The papalists', he pointed out, in a formula which remains influential with both Catholic and Protestant theologians today, 'understand the word "justify" as meaning "to make righteous". The Lutherans, however, accept the word "justify" as the absolution from sins. It is certainly not fitting in the Church to cause disturbances about words when the matters themselves are safe.' His formulation of what he called 'the real issue' was 'whether God forbears to condemn us' because of the sacrifice and merits of Christ or because of 'the renewal which has been begun in us.' In 1567 the Council of Trent defined solafideism as heretical in revulsion from Luther and in reaction to his advocacy of it. It was not the doctrine which made Protestants heretical, but Protestantism which made the doctrine seem unorthodox. We are still reaping the whirlwind. In 1987, a joint statement on justification worked out by Catholic and Anglican scholars over three years of discussions was shelved in Rome.

Even after Trent, the Protestant doctrine of justification could resurface in Catholic circles. Michel Bains, who taught it to successive cohorts of up-and-coming priests at the University of Louvain – one of the most fertile Catholic seminaries in Europe – died, without dishonour, in 1589. The tradition was continued by his successors at the same university and transmitted to Paris early in the new century. When the ablest of its advocates, Cornelius Jansen, who claimed to have read the works of St Augustine ten times over, returned to Louvain from Paris in 1617, he joined in the defence of a doctrine of justification strikingly similar to Luther's. None of this stopped him from earning the patronage of Philip IV of Spain – self-appointed guardian of Catholic orthodoxy – or becoming Bishop of Ypres. His *Augustinus,* his theological apologia, published posthumously in 1640, inverted some traditional language on redemption. Instead of 'freeing' man from sin, Christ's sacrifice 'enslaved' him to the attractions of heaven rather than of this world. He was not so much ransomed as auctioned. Grace was irresistible; election by God was a yoke, 'easy' but ineluctable. Messages of this sort proved almost as popular as when Luther uttered them more than a century before. Jansenism almost caused a schism in the Dutch Catholic church and became the most active movement in the French church for most of the rest of the seventeenth century and the next. Nuns at Port-Royal wished to be martyred for it; communities of Jansenists made it the basis of a rule of life; and hermits were inspired by it to flee from the 'damned mass' of their fellow-men.

It resembled Protestantism even in lifestyle – austere, censorious, self-reproachful and exclusivist; and in spirituality – prayerful, practical and sparing of the sacraments. Its political resonances were similar: suspicious of the papacy, abject before the prince, inimical to the Jesuits. In retrospect, its history casts a dazzling light on the Reformation. Jansenists were no less heretical than Lutherans: in a sense they were more so, or more clearly so, than Luther was when he launched his schism, for they were reverting to doctrines candidly condemned at Trent. Yet Jansenists were able to remain in the Church by arguing their case without disputing the Church's authority; when denounced, they dodged; when refuted, they reformulated; when condemned, they temporized. When they could not answer a charge without provoking a schism, they took refuge in the sanctuary of 'obsequious silence' – the theological equivalent of the Fifth Amendment.

It is probably true that, just as justification by faith alone has continued to be trusted by Catholics, so there have always been many – perhaps most *soi-disant* Protestants – who believe in justification by works: indeed, in parts of England Protestant clergy were still teaching it to their flocks, perhaps out of a sense of social prudence, well into the seventeenth century. In the eighteenth century, Protestant tradition developed the complementary doctrine of 'sanctification' and practitioners of good works formed 'holiness clubs'. Man's sinful determination to be self-sufficient is condemned by Protestant and Catholic teachers alike, but is so powerful that it influences behaviour almost universally and so insidious that it probably slips unnoticed into the faith of individuals in every kind of Christian congregation. Though some theologians profess to find it simple, justification by faith alone is a far harder doctrine to grasp than the prudent dogma, in its plain and obvious meaning, that God rewards the good and punishes the bad.

THE PREDESTINED SOUL

If the bestowal of grace is absolute, it must be predestined; if the individual soul can neither attract nor resist it, God must be supposed to have made up his mind about it independently of the behaviour of the person saved or condemned. The path of justification without works therefore leads across two pitfalls. First, it dispenses with the gift of free will, the loving concession of God to his children, without which the notion of a God of love seems to slip from the Christian's grasp. Secondly, if predestination is understood in a time-frame, it traps the believer in the same hell with his Pelagian enemies: Christ's sacrifice, occurring once and for all at a moment in history, is rendered superfluous if all the relevant decisions, saving or damning, had already been made.

There are ways around these traps. There is Erasmus's way, understanding God's omniscience as comprehending every possible contingency. There is Milton's way of absolving God from responsibility for human sin: 'if I foreknew,' he makes God say, 'Foreknowledge had no influence on their fault.' There is a Catholic way, which empowers God in his omnipotence to see you, today, make a free choice tomorrow. There is St Augustine's way, which pictures time as a journey, which God beholds from outside, as if from a cosmic height, so that all the halts which to a man, crawling along from place to place, seem strung out, one after another, are visible from on high in a single blinking. There is one Protestant tradition which conceives man's sin and God's self-sacrifice as happening outside time; and there is the preferred solution of Catholic tradition which admits that God is the unique source of human righteousness but includes, as part of his grace, the gift of freedom to accept or reject it. Rather terrifyingly, there is the solution of Luther and Calvin, who were happy to leave human will 'in bondage' and to admire in God a kind of justice which would seem capricious – even cruel – in man. The 'freedom' God confers is made clear by St Paul: that God should give man freedom to sin is, in Paul's favourite, peremptory phrase, 'out of the question'. Real freedom is thraldom to the will of his divine master by a slave who has been 'bought and paid for'.

The theologians who sparred around the ring of truth were fighting for the same prizes: our sense of the existence of a God of love and also of a God of holiness; our awareness of our need of Christ. In their different ways, pertinacious predestinarians and free-will fanatics have both had to struggle to keep their hold on those Christian insights. There was a time, which began in the sixteenth century, and which, for some people, has lasted to this day, when some of the combatants seemed, blinded by battle, to have lost sight of the prize. The debate turned indecent when Luther replied in 1525 to the mild-mannered criticisms of his one-time friend, Erasmus. As reformers, they shared so many opinions and attitudes that many contemporaries found it hard to distinguish between them. Indeed, Erasmus has been accused, in one of the most-quoted jokes of the Reformation era, of 'laying the egg which Luther hatched' and, like most jests, it holds a grain of truth, for Luther was launched on the path towards his own conversion by a textual insight transmitted by Erasmus from an earlier humanistic tradition: that, in the gospel accounts of John the Baptist, the cry, 'Repent!', usually translated as 'Do Penance!', really meant, in the original Greek, 'Change your minds!'

Erasmus was an enthusiast for primitive Christianity whose scholarship was dedicated to purging tradition of impurities. Like Luther, he disliked monasticism, despised relics and regarded priesthood as a gift inseparable from faith. Luther – his admirer and, at an early stage of his biblical studies, his self-professed disciple – expected him to join the revolt of the Protestants and was disillusioned to the point of bitterness when Erasmus held aloof. Erasmus, in turn, was made miserable by Luther's combativeness: he wanted the Church reformed from within, not wrecked by secession; but – at some risk to his own reputation – he postponed for years the compulsion to enter the arena of debate against the schismatics. His decision at last to join combat in defence of free will was the result of constant goading by friends (and even enemies) who wanted the great scholar to take sides publicly. His essay *On Free Will* was, characteristically, an affirmation of his overwhelming sense of God's loving indulgence of his human children. It was not received by Luther in the same spirit. The Protestant felt betrayed and suspected Erasmus of venal motives, dismissing him as the pimp of the whore of Babylon and exonerating him, if at all, only on the grounds of madness. The only merit of his 'vast, drunken follies' were that they were well expressed: 'ordure in gold pots'.

This first round of the debate was marked by the reluctance with which it was joined: reluctance betrayed in the hesitations of Erasmus and the splenetic anger Luther felt at being obliged to respond. Calvin's explanation of the doctrine of predestination was unflawed by hurry and almost unspotted by rancour. Occasionally, flashes of resentment show through, as when he denounces counter-arguments as the 'wantonness and prurience' of minds 'tickled with desire'; sometimes rhetoric intrudes, as when he explains traditional Christian emphasis on free will as a concession made by patristic writers 'to reconcile Scripture with the dogmas of philosophy.' Generally, however, Calvin proceeds with measured reflectiveness and winning confidence, unprising 'the dominion of sin' from the soul and building dykes against 'the immense flood of error with which the whole world is overflowed.'

His case for predestination is logical – starting from the premiss of justification by faith – and scriptural – based on the verses of blessing with which the so-called letter to the Ephesians begins: 'He chose us in Christ before the world was made . . . marking us out beforehand to be his adopted sons, through Jesus Christ.' Yet the saviour might have dropped out of Calvin's world altogether: in his great exposition of his faith, the *Institutes of the Christian Religion,* Christ is unmentioned through literally hundreds of pages of cosmogony and legalism and Old Testament texts. He is ignored until the twentieth of the hundred 'aphorisms' in which Calvin summed up his understanding of Christianity. The ferocity with which Calvin hated images of Christ argues a certain insensitivity before the mystery of the incarcaration, for the human Christ is, according to orthodox tradition, the ultimate icon – God made intelligible and emotionally communicable – whose worship is the pattern and precedent for the adoration of other holy images. (cf below p. 105f) Some of Calvin's followers even wanted to abolish Christmas. Calvin, who was a humanist and a lawyer before he became a theologian, was, in a sense a converted Pharisee, whose pharisaism shows through: rules inessential to salvation still had, in his view, to be observed.

There was no obvious way for Christ into his system, except through the wounds of sensibility and the pores of piety. Though hostile critics have accused Calvin of indifference to Christ, no objective reader could fail to acquit him, or to be moved by the depth of his love of his Lord. Even the *Institutes,* which were a designedly austere and systematic work, were written in 'hunger and thirst for Christ'; and Calvin, who had no mystical gifts, longed for a sense of union which seemed always to elude him, to be 'ingrafted into Christ and clothed in him'.

Catholics have a corresponding – almost, an equal and opposite – problem: how to fit the vital tradition of a God of grace into a prescriptive religion which demands so much in the way of formal observance. In the agony which this dilemma inspired in Catholic theologians and – more graphically – in Catholic artists and their patrons, a profound effect of the Reformation can be observed. The Protestant movements were a genuine crisis of conscience and of nerve for those who decided to remain Catholics. Why had God allowed the new schismatics a measure of success which, albeit limited, exceeded that of any heretics in the past? As a trial of faith? A scourge for sins? Or an exemplar for the correction of error? All those questions evoked positive answers, though the balance between them varied from time to time, group to group and individual to individual. We can return to the Escorial to see evidence of some of the haverings and self-doubts. Artists unnerved by the aesthetics of Protestantism filleted the humanity out of the denizens of heaven. Cambasio's saints are shapeless, characterless and eerily serene. St Maurice and the Theban legion are enjoying a Renaissance *conversazione* rather than enduring suffering. Cellini's naked Christ, with exposed phallus, was expelled to a side-chapel less, perhaps, for reasons of prudery, than because so lively a depiction of Christ's humanity was not to the taste of the court. In El Greco's exciting portrayal of Philip II, kneeling unruffled on the edge of hell's maw – depicted as the jaws of a huge Leviathan gulping twisted, bloody souls – the king adores the name of Jesus rather than a figural representation of God. These manifestations of taste were different in degree from the iconoclastic zeal of extreme Protestants, but similar in kind.

BACK TO THE FUTURE

What is true of the doctrine of justification by faith, is true of virtually every other doctrine that has come to be defined as Protestant. There can hardly be an utterance made by a Protestant on a matter of faith in self-awareness as a Protestant, which has not been echoed by a Catholic without ceasing to be Catholic. Luther was drawn or driven into schism not by heresy but by stubborness; not by condemning indulgences, for Catholics have done so; not by dissenting from Councils, for Catholics have done so; not by questioning the authority of the Pope, or challenging or subverting the priesthood, for Catholics have done so; not by denying transubstantiation, for Catholics have done so; not by advocating predestination or justification by faith, for Catholics have done so; not by docking sacraments or exalting scripture or tampering with the liturgy or marrying a nun, for Catholics have uttered equally flagrant heresies and committed worse abuses without separating from the faith. The grounds of Luther's secession from the Church was his unwillingness to stand corrected 'unless I am convicted by scripture and plain reason'. Though he was a humble man in laudable ways – in his forthright conviction of his sinfulness, in his awareness of bare, blemished dependence upon God – he yet lacked the special kind of humility that defines a Catholic: readiness, in spite of one's own convictions, reason, learning, or experience, to admit that the collective wisdom of the Church is likely to be superior to one's own. The Protestant says, as Luther said at Worms, 'Here I stand. I can do no other.' The Catholic shuffles his feet. Catholics today may share many of Luther's opinions; in Church, they imitate some of his practices and even sing some of his hymns; they may even expect, if they get to heaven themselves, to meet him there as one who sought God with a sincere heart; but, if they will not condemn him for error, they must indict him for pride. Most Catholics today see the wisdom of Erasmus's conclusion: 'we tolerate Jews and Bohemians. We might have tolerated Luther.'

The doctrinal difference between Protestants and Catholics cannot be boiled down to this heresy or that heresy but only to disagreement over how to identify an opinion as heretical. Despite the ferocity of the doctrinal disputes, the divisive issues of the Reformation were – to put it another way – historical rather than theological. The decisive question could be put thus: was the Church founded by the apostles, or had some disfiguring discontinuity set in? A Protestant opinion, in a moderate form, might answer that the Church had got deflected from the true path along her way; at a further extreme, she might be seen as the child of some diabolic intervention in the plans of Providence, the Church not of Christ but Antichrist. Luther denounced the see of Rome as the foundation not of an apostle, but of the devil.

While the Council of Trent enshrined the schism in doctrine, Cardinal Baronius tried to heal it by scholarship. He was a law student who fell under the influence of one of the great saints of the Catholic Reformation – the magnetic, energetic ex-Protestant Philip Neri. He set fire to his secular poems and his law diplomas and joined Neri's community of prayer and charity, where he found a role in the kitchens 'perpetually cooking' food unrecommended by his own health-destroying fasts. Neri gave him a sense of being preserved for some great work. In 1559, it was suddenly thrust upon him: the labour of writing the Catholic reply to the *Centuries of Magdeburg* – a Protestant version of Church history, begun in 1552, which, so far, Catholic scholarship had not matched. Baronius had shown no aptitude for history; the brilliance he now brought to it seemed miraculous to hagiographers. He made mistakes which became gleefully notorious to his Protestant adversaries; his version of the ecclesiastical past was dappled with blind spots. Yet for its time his *Annals* was a masterpiece and his integrity commanded universal admiration. By his death, he had taken the story up to 1198, but his earliest volumes, which tried to trace the links between Catholic tradition and apostolic origins, had the greatest impact on their own times. They deployed all the resources of scholarship except linguistic skill, which was never Baronius's forte; and they deployed all the sources known to antiquarianism, including, with the texts surviving from the past, the physical fragments of the demolished world of antiquity.

Early Christianity of the kind he unearthed can be sampled today in the underground tombs known as the Catacombs, scattered around the Appian Way out of Rome and, less thickly, beside other thoroughfares out of the city. In this dank and gloomy Avernus the living met the dead in secret worship. Here, and in private houses, the rites of unenfranchized Christianity were confined until, in the fourth century AD, it was safe to emerge into the light. The tunnels are honeycombed – or, as the Christians themselves said, 'pigeonholed' – with cramped tombs and open occasionally into low vaults, smeared with stucco, daubed with paint, spotted with candleblack and pitted with age. Some of the catacombs were shared by Christian dead with pagans and Mithraists. The good shepherd rescues errant sheep in vault paintings, while the war-god sacrifices a bull on the face of a nearby altar. Tellus and Oceanus recline not far from the apostles at the table of the Last Supper. Christ's image is blended with that of the sun-god as he drives his sacred chariot heavenwards in the mosaic decoration of a tomb under the Vatican itself.

Considered from one angle, this is an heroic young Christianity, struggling to define itself within the glutinous common culture it shared with its pagan environment. From another, it is an already corrupt Christianity, warped by syncretism, compromised by its underworld setting of evasion and decay. Here the sarcophagi of martyrs became transformed into eucharistic altars stuffed with relics. Before the end of the first century AD the author of the Revelation to John could experience a vision 'underneath the altar' of 'the souls of all the people who had been killed on account of the Word of God, for witnessing to it.' In the darkness of the catacombs the eucharistic feast shaded into the pagan 'refreshment-meal', eaten at the graveside in honour of the dead; here the constraints of space and the placing of tombs turned the priest's back to the congregation. Here prayers for the dead became an inescapable part of the devotion of the living, whom circumstances thrust into such close communion with them. According to one's sensibilties, it may seem proper to venerate such practices as hallowed by antiquity, or to reject them as 'accretions'.

Among the catacombs and on the Vatican hill are three shrines of Saints Peter and Paul, where the physical presence of those apostles in the city is commemorated. St Peter's passage through Rome, even if it could be proved to have happened, would not of itself validate the popes' claims to universal primacy; but the question of its authenticity is a critical test of the historical credentials of the Catholic tradition. If St Peter was indeed here, continuity with the apostolic church is demonstrated. If the link is missing, the tradition dangles in the néant, from a broken chain. In view of the many pious frauds perpetrated or tolerated in the name of the Church, Protestant critics at the time of the Reformation were justified in their scepticism. Nor was the Catholic defence of the Peter story very convincing at the time. Cardinal Baronius, for all his intellectual integrity, seemed to forfeit his critical sense when the credentials of the Church of Rome were under discussion.

Luther began the attack, without explicitly denying that the apostles had visited Rome, by impugning the story of their martyrdom and burial there. Seeking the strength of an a fortiori argument, other reformers pointed out the weakness of the evidence that Peter had ever been there at all. Local pride, pilgrimage rackets, the relics trade and popular demand had devised or encouraged so many mythical itineraries for improbably well-travelled apostles and early saints that critical minds – among Catholics as well as Protestants – were increasingly inclined thereafter to put all such legends on a par and to regard Peter's sojourn in Rome as no more likely than St Martial's in France or St James the Great's in Spain or even St Thomas's in Brazil, where his footprints were piously recorded in the 1540s. And yet the legend has refused to die: on the contrary, the evidence for it has grown under the ever closer scholarly scrutiny begun in the Reformation.

The biblical evidence rests on the dateline in 'Babylon' of one of the epistles attributed to St Peter. Luther was content to call Rome 'Babylon' for a joke, but his followers were reluctant to believe that the apostle could have shared his sense of humour. Yet examples of the use of 'Babylon' to mean Rome among Jewish and Christian writers, over a long period encompassing St Peter's lifetime, have accumulated in support of the traditional identification. Peter's martyrdom was mentioned towards the end of St John's gospel, without indication as to place. It was located in Rome by Dionysius, bishop of Corinth, writing in about 170 AD, who believed that, with St Paul, Peter had 'planted' the faith in Rome. By then, the shrine dedicated to St Peter, directly under the centre of the present dome of the Basilica of St Peter at the Vatican, was in place over an earlier grave. A casket of bones unearthed nearby – the near-complete skeleton of one old man – has even been acclaimed by critically minded scholars as the remains of the apostle himself: such an identification would not be inconsistent with the evidence, but would exceed it.

The Roman Church's search for apostolic credentials was not initiated in response to Protestant reforms: it was part of a tradition of pursuit of primitive models of Church life and doctrine in which Catholics were engaged from the remotest antiquity. The debates of Baronius and his critics were conducted with a shared aim – the retrieval of apostolic 'purity' – in the common discourse of early modern humanism, with respect for the same critical, textual, antiquarian and archaeological methods. The goal was to build a future directly on foundations unearthed from the remote past. In this goal both Catholic and Protestant reforms were comprehended.

The movement back to the future had been gathering pace in the late middle ages. Its conspicuous moments came in 1206 when St Francis tore off his clothes in the main square of Assisi in an effort to return to the apostolic Church's regime of poverty; and when St Brigid in the 1350s or St Catherine in the 1370s admonished popes with the examples of the apostles; and in 1405, when St Bernardino of Siena began to brandish his placard with the name of Jesus on it and to encourage congregations to see St Paul as their 'little friend'; or in 1494 when Savonarola turned Florence into a republic of the godly or in 1509 when Erasmus sat down to produce a new and more accurate edition of the New Testament from what he hoped were authentic texts. The recovery of the 'purity' of a 'primitive' church was an enterprise in which Protestant and Catholic reformers were engaged together.

ATTITUDES IN PRACTICE

Tunnelling under medieval 'accretions' was a way back to the early practice of the Church and also – some tunnellers hoped – a way of getting closer to God. Protestants and Catholics today, confronted with the narrowness of their doctrinal divisions, the similarity of their projects, the overlap of their traditions, will sometimes try to hold on to a sense of their differentness from one another by appealing to 'a matter of attitude'.

Attitudes are the shadows of doctrines: they hover in the background and sometimes loom large. Where attitudes are common, differences of doctrine can be bridged but differences of attitude open chasms of misunderstanding and can lead whole societies to develop in different ways. Protestantism, it is said, is the outgrowth of a concern for the establishment of a direct knowledge and awareness of God by the individual Christian, whereas a Catholic is dedicated to a collective and mediated relationship through the Church. This is not altogether false: Protestant history has been moulded by that very robust self-perception. Although, as we have seen,

Protestants and Catholics emerged from a common cultural background in the sixteenth century, distinctively 'Protestant' and 'Catholic' cultures have developed and grown apart since then. Protestant values have contributed, for instance, to the emergence of a tradition of civil liberties by exalting conscience as a guide to truth; and to the creation of welfare systems by shifting responsibility for works of mercy out of the hands of sinners into those of the state. Protestant philanthropy, in Catholic caricature, is personified in Edith Wharton's Mrs Cryce, who 'had a kind of impersonal benevolence: cases of individual need she regarded with suspicion, but she subscribed to Institutions when their annual reports showed an impressive surplus.' It is only in Catholic countries, or outside Catholic churches, that beggars gather at church doors. Richard Ford was surprised to find that beggars in Spain attracted deferential forms of address: he should have recalled the extent of their benefactors' obligation to creatures whose poverty was an opportunity to contribute to one's own salvation.

The strength of the common assumption that toleration and state welfare are essentially Protestant in origin is hardly diminished by the facts that can be cited in contradiction: the fact that the first welfare state can be said to have been founded in Medicean Florence; or that free consciences were initially admitted on neither side of the Reformation divide; or that Catholics, from as early a period as their Protestant counterparts, naturally advocated toleration wherever they were in a minority. On the whole, it remains true that Catholic societies have imitated Protestant 'attitudes' in these respects out of practical admiration rather than the inherent momentum of their own development.

Nevertheless, it must be doubted whether 'attitude' any more than 'doctrine' provides a key to understanding what keeps Catholics and Protestants apart. From a Catholic perspective, the Church is there to help, not impede, the strivings of the individual soul. As a means of by-passing the scaffolding of the sacraments, the ladder of the angels, the mediation of the priesthood and the intercession of the saints, no channel of access to God is more direct than mysticism (see above p. 50). In the Protestant churches believers have also been urged to personal holiness – through hearing sermons, engaging in daily meditation and Bible study, attending lectures, prayer meetings, Bible classes, 'holiness' clubs and fellowship groups, singing 'psalms and hymns and spiritual songs'. Both the Catholic and Protestant traditions have had their successes and failures – both have ignited souls and dampened them; both have communicated consciousness of God and both have garbled the message. Both have provided hot lines and cold douches.

Protestant and Catholic attitudes to transcendence are as far apart as the ends of a horseshoe: along one dimension, there is a long way between them; yet they almost touch. Faith healing and miracle cures show how much divides them and how much they have in common. The 'decline of magic', over which godly élites have presided in both traditions since the

Reformation, has never been able to exclude these barely spiritual practices from the popular substratum of religious life. The idea of seeking a bodily cure from God rather than a spiritual experience seems repugnantly worldly to elevated sensibilities. It belongs to the essence of 'popular' religion: concern for survival in this world rather than salvation in the next. At one level, it is a relic of pre-scientific diagnostics, which saw sickness as the wages of sin – a temporal penance or penalty imposed from on high. At another, it remains, like prayers for the sick, as a touching submission to God's omnipotence out of the mouths of babes and sucklings – the charming, innocent folly of holy fools. In the healing ministry of Morris Cerullo it is big business. In the world of holy hucksters depicted in *Golden Child* it is a sad scam, occasionally redeemed by real conversions. In Lourdes, the real miracle is the management by the Church of ill focused, ill disciplined devotion in the service of one of the great universal cults of the Church, where the Blessed Virgin, speaking in dialect, assured a little girl of the truth of the doctrine of the Immaculate Conception.

G.K. Chesterton once said that if the water of Lourdes were bottled and sold in chemists it would be hailed as a great scientific discovery. Yet the penitent pilgrims to Bernadette's grotto seem to be in the classic position of the Catholic worshipper, at the feet of a mediator, seeking the intercession of Mary in their plight. The rite they perform looks rather more like the baptism by total immersion favoured by some radical Protestant sects – wading out into the water in billowing smocks before being ducked by peremptory helpers. Some of the frippery is the silly spillover of folk religion: you must not take off the wet smock; you must not dry yourself before putting your clothes back on. The preacher at a Protestant faith-healing will claim to be doing something altogether different: reconstructing a biblical experience, reviving an apostolic ministry authenticated by the New Testament and bringing 'witnesses' directly to 'Jesus'; in practice, however, the experience of encounter with God is surrounded by the language of frank animism – the exorcism of spirits from their dominion inside the defiled temple of the body. The healing moment usually involves laying-on of hands – the priestly gesture by which the conferment of sacraments is signified in the Catholic tradition. The faith-healer who touches his patients with the paraclete and 'commands' spirits to leave their victims is a mediator *par excellence,* performing a more esoteric, more hieratic ministry than that of any Catholic priest.

Chapter Five

A GIFT WRAPPED:
The Externals of Catholicism and Protestantism

SERMONS IN STONE

The Église Sainte Jeanne d'Arc resembles a resurrected dinosaur. Its long, curved walkway lies like a tail across Rouen's Place du Vieux Marché and its globular body seems about to trample the stalls of the fishmongers, greengrocers and vendors of tourist *bijouterie*. It was built in the 1970s to commemorate the Maid of Orleans, burned in the market place in 1431, and to replace the war-shattered church which had previously stood on the site. Yet, despite these historic connections, it makes little concession to tradition. The interior is spacious, uncluttered and uncompromisingly 'modern'. Its only decoration is the wall of sixteenth-century stained glass preserved from the earlier building. There are no statues, no paintings, no carved or gilded woodwork. No crucifix or monstrance adorns the freestanding altar. The raked, curved, low-backed pews serve to emphasize the feeling of spaciousness in this sacred amphitheatre. Some people do not like it. That much is obvious from complaints written in the church's *livre d'or* by visitors who believe that such a prominent memorial to France's most famous saint should conform to their idea of what a 'real' church looks like. Yet the same source emphasizes the fact that, for the large majority of those who go there, the

Église Sainte Jeanne d'Arc 'works'. Many touching testimonials, by believers and unbelievers alike, speak of being 'inspired', of feeling 'at peace', of 'sensing the presence of God'.

Perhaps the most striking characteristic of this church (and the same holds true for many churches built during the postwar decades) is its denominational anonymity. It does not proclaim, 'This is a Roman Catholic building'. It could be Lutheran or Anglican and there are several American evangelical temples to which it bears a striking resemblance. To some extent, the same could be said of the worship which takes place in it. Liturgical reform no less than architectural innovation has helped to close the gap between the churches. In the Roman Catholic communion the movement towards vernacular services has been faster and more thorough than even the Vatican II fathers envisaged. At the same time, Anglicans, many free churches in the Reformed tradition and most new charismatic congregations have made Holy Communion, Eucharist or the Lord's Supper their central Sunday celebration. Increased lay participation and the desire to make worship more accessible to the unchurched has led to a considerable increase of less-structured services in places where formal liturgy was previously the norm. Church music has flowed even more easily across denominational barriers. Repetitive chant from the ecumenical community of Taizé is used as an aid to corporate meditation in Protestant and Catholic worship, and music generated by the charismatic renewal has found its way into congregations of all traditions.

Modern changes in liturgy have been more extensive than any that have occurred since the Reformation of the sixteenth century. They have aroused passions no less intense. There have been no burnings and few rampaging iconoclastic mobs but there have been schisms and defections, changes carried through with more enthusiasm than sensitivity, angry denunciations and zealous campaigns.

As in any age, the majority of modern churchgoers acquiesce in the decisions of their leaders, though sometimes with heavy hearts. 'I have not yet soaked myself in petrol, and gone up in flames, but I now cling to the Faith doggedly without joy. Church going is a pure duty parade,' wrote Evelyn Waugh, in 1966, about the changes in Roman Catholic worship. There are many in his and other communions who share his nostalgic longing for the old, familiar rites. Yet there are just as many frustrated souls in churches untouched by new movements. They watch their congregations dwindling and feel stifled by the weekly recitation of Caroline prayers and Victorian hymns in medieval buildings which are a constant drain on their financial resources. Others are less quiescent. Most activists simply vote with their feet. Some seek out priests who remain faithful to the ancient liturgies. Some cross denominational boundaries to join charismatic or evangelical Churches or to found new sects of their own. And there are those who simply give up 'irrelevant' churchgoing altogether.

Over the last forty years there have been many traditionalist campaigns. In Opus Dei houses directors were ordered to maintain the celebration of the Latin mass by a priest with his back to the congregation. Archbishop Lefebvre, declaring that 'the throne of Peter has been occupied by antichrists', led his followers into the wilderness (see below p. 250). Disaffected Anglicans formed Church in Danger, which identified the new Alternative Service Book as part of a conspiracy by liberals, charismatics, and 'trendies' to undermine the authority and purity of the Church of England. Conservative scholars pointed out the theological dangers of liturgical innovations.

> '. . . not only is the Church splintered, but the organic sacramentality of the Church as redeemed humanity standing worshipfully and in unity before God in Christ by the Holy Spirit falls away. Individualism flourishes, and the liturgy may almost become the plaything of the celebrants . . .'

Yet all the time, the reformers – clerical and lay – continued with their programmes. They reordered church interiors, installed music groups, introduced new service books and hymn books, set up worship committees and encouraged lay participation and greater freedom in worship.

It is easy for cynics outside the Church and opponents of change within it to accuse the reformers of pandering to fashion. Both insist on regarding the process of innovation as something new. Both are wrong. The practical, the spiritual and the aesthetic are in constant tension. No buildings are purely functional and church architects are prone to use their art to make symbolic statements or reflect secular influences. Cruciform churches are rather inconvenient for most of the functions they house. Big churches can be useful for processions but often their size is determined by a passion for conspicuous consumption or reckless emulation. Small, simple churches can be justified on the grounds that they echo the apostles' environment, but the *Dutch Catechism* recommends them on grounds of deference to a worldly society because 'the population as a whole no longer looks to these buildings for its worship'. The basilica shape suited the newly triumphant church of the fourth century AD because it resembled a vaulted catacomb – but it was a psychological as well as a functional success: it is hard to demonstrate, but easy to imagine, how the sensation of emerging from underground burrows into pillared halls must have seemed like a reenactment of the Resurrection and encouraged decorative audacity.

Nevertheless, every space for worship must be compatible, at least, with the functions it houses. Christians whose command of doctrine is shaky can be clapped to their Protestant or Catholic allegiance by perceptions of heaven projected from their experience of worship and their surroundings in church. Changes in church in the way spaces are enclosed and furniture disposed are often said to document and reflect the progress of the

Reformation: a trend towards broad spaces with a unique central focus, a pruning of the multi-focal clutter of the Catholic tradition. Yet some major trends in church design since the Reformation preceded Protestantism or spanned the Protestant–Catholic divide. Secluded pews, with their high backs and blinkered sides, such as one still encounters in survivals from the seventeenth and eighteenth centuries in Protestant countries, are often thought to evoke the very essence of Protestantism: individualism to the point of exclusivity, private devotion shuttered from the communion of fellow-worshippers in compartments encased but not cast down by the enveloping church. Yet the existence at Rycote Chapel in Oxfordshire of pre-Reformation pews of similar design shows that these furnishings represented a long-term trend towards greater privacy in the habits of the upper classes. They were paralleled in domestic settings where, in the same period, private dining-rooms and withdrawing-rooms were superseding communal halls as the foci of domestic life. In the 1520s, the cathedral of Granada was redesigned as a temple of 'humanist' worship: instead of the prevailing style of the time – an intimidating interior, with an altar barely glimpsed and space for the laity fended to the margins – the new church was white, airy and bathed in light with an altar positioned so as to be visible and accessible from all around. The 'inter-denominational' interiors which are becoming familiar today reflect, more than anything else, the increasing homogeneity of Western society but they also represent a convergence of old trends.

This movement towards common styles in ecclesiastical art and liturgy has emerged very slowly throughout centuries during which conflict has been the more readily observable phenomenon. That conflict has been within churches as well as between them. Most denominations have developed sub-groups whose preferences are for 'decorous' or 'extravagant' worship; 'simple' or 'exuberant' surroundings. The long and often bitter confrontation between the 'high' and 'low' segments of the Church of England was only the most dramatic example of a trend shared by most Christian communions.

Until this century, old churches were frequently pulled down to make way for new ones. Where this did not happen countless acts of 'cultural vandalism' were perpetrated. Buildings were added to in the prevailing style without reference to the artistic integrity of the whole. Pews, funeral monuments, organs, pulpits, parcloses and galleries were installed. Frescoes, stained-glass windows, reredoses and rood screens were replaced. In order to make room for the works of contemporary masters, old paintings, sculptures and carvings were sold off or simply scrapped. The motives behind these changes were the glory of God, the prestige of wealthy patrons, the desire to express new theological insights and the need to provide more effectively for the requirements of the worshipping community. Aesthetic considerations, if they were relevant at all, came a long way down the list.

Change was very often a feature of vigorous Catholicism. For example, a visitor must search the Catholic churches of southern Germany diligently to discover fine examples of pre-Renaissance painting and sculpture. Yet Nürnberg, the first imperial city to embrace the Lutheran reform, boasts places of worship (particularly St Sebaldskirche and St Lorenzkirche) rich in Gothic art. This is no paradox. Luther was not an image-hater. He regarded visual stimuli as things indifferent unless they clouded men's minds to the truths of the word of God. His followers, thus, had little incentive to iconoclasm but even less to the commissioning of new works of religious art. So, when Nürnberg's neighbours embraced the exuberance of ecclesiastical Baroque, the city of the mastersingers turned its back on the new movement and, in so doing, inadvertently conserved its medieval heritage. Certainly, in the early sixteenth century the idea of the 'work of art' as something of intrinsic worth to be preserved for posterity only existed in a small number of princely and episcopal courts. Painting, sculpture and architecture were utilitarian crafts. The products of carvers', gilders', painters', glaziers' and sculptors' workshops were there to serve the requirements of patrons, secular or religious.

For Protestant congregations, meanwhile, church became an essentially Sunday place. Since saints' days and festivals disappeared along with shrines, statues and private masses, there was little to draw worshippers at other times. Internal space was reorganized to accommodate the new kind of worship. Pulpits and lecterns were set up by law. Ironically, for an evangelical movement, the church rather than the market cross became the place for preaching. Empty naves were filled with pews so that congregations could listen in comfort to the exposition of the word. Altars became tables and, in some cases, were brought into the body of the church. The relative positioning of the furniture made a clear visual statement about the ascendancy of word over sacrament. There were instances of chancels being allowed to fall into disrepair in order to emphasize the demise of the Mass.

Sixteenth and seventeenth century preaching churches have now largely disappeared. Just as the 'holy clutter' of medieval buildings was swept away by the Reformation, so, too, the bibliocentric interiors created by the new Protestant orthodoxy have given way to later ideas about the balance of worship. Reference to contemporary documents shows us, not only how much church interiors had changed, but also that the worship offered in them was far from dry and cerebral. In 1636 the Bishop of Norwich made a visitation of Bury St Edmunds. He discovered 'a "mountainous reading desk", blocking the entrance to the chancel, the chancel itself full of seating which ran "all the waie under the east window", high pews in the middle aisle, a pulpit halfway down the nave.' And the preaching was heard with 'the deep, passionate, trembling, quavering, singultive twang, which crept into the brestes of the thirsty auditory.'

One reason for the disappearance of such Protestant furniture was that it never fitted comfortably into medieval churches built to express very different spiritual insights. The structures themselves exerted psychological pressure. Sporadic restorations over the last three hundred years, based on mixed motives of aesthetics, theology and convenience, have tended to simplify the interior arrangements of pre-Reformation churches. This has usually meant returning the altar to the only place where it really fits in a building with a chancel, and locating pulpit and lectern to right and left of the chancel arch. The end result is seldom ideal in that there are usually points in the church from which one or more of the three foci of devotion are invisible. Much more successful were the purpose-built new churches and dissenting chapels of the seventeenth and eighteenth centuries, such as those designed by Christopher Wren for London in the aftermath of the great fire. These were usually rectangular in shape with galleries running round three sides. Pulpit, table and lectern were grouped in such a way as to be easily seen by the congregation and also to make a theological point about the relative importance of word and sacrament.

The local church has to respond – visually – to changing community needs and theological emphases. To give an obvious example: a medieval European peasant entering his parish church can hardly have failed to be impressed by its splendour, immensity and sumptuousness when compared with his own cramped, verminous hovel. His late twentieth-century counterpart is more likely to notice the cold, the damp and the hardness of the pews and to hurry back to the centrally heated comfort of his three-bed semi-detached. The last thirty years have seen a growing willingness to grapple creatively with the problems of adapting ancient edifices to contemporary needs. Such activity always arouses the hostility of conservatives. The new vicar of St Nicholas's, Durham, was faced with large-scale revolt in the late 1970s when he made sweeping changes to the liturgy and laid plans for a £325,000 architectural 'revolution'. By the time he left in 1982, the city-centre church had been transformed. The 'worship area' was equipped with light-weight chairs. The communion table was central but movable, permitting varied arrangement of the space. The old sanctuary was screened off to make a chapel for private prayer and counselling. Wasted space was turned into meeting rooms. A former vestry became a shop, with one door opening on the market place and another into the church. Banners, posters, changing displays and an efficient heating system gave the building a warm, bright welcoming appearance. The complex was used by a variety of local organizations. St Nicholas's had become once more what its medieval builders had intended it to be – a seven-day-a-week church. Making changes to familiar, much-loved places of worship requires vision, courage and forcefulness. Those who dislike the process will see those qualities as bigotry, bloody-mindedness and dictatorship. Certainly, the sixteenth-century iconoclasts did not have things all their own way. Workmen taking down a rood in Exeter were forced to flee from a posse of enraged local women and there were examples of others carrying out royal policy narrowly escaping being lynched. That did not happen to the vicar of St Nicholas's, Durham. Within ten years he became Archbishop of Canterbury.

Reform by the Axe

It is as well that we keep such modern parallels in mind when we come to consider the most emotive aspect of the Reformation story – the destruction or defacing of thousands of objects of popular devotion.

Conrad Witz (c.1400–c.1445) may have been a significant figure in the development of landscape painting. We can say no more because only a handful of the many works he must have produced during a creative life of about thirty years have survived. In Geneva a few small panels remain of the altarpiece he made for St Peter's cathedral in 1444 – a gift from Bishop François de Metz. One depicts, in gemlike detail, Lake Geneva and its environs. In the distant fields, a farmer tills the soil and a hunting party seeks its quarry. The foreground presents a serene Christ looking from the water's edge towards the boat where his disciples are struggling to haul in the miraculous draught of fishes, while Peter wades towards him through the translucent water. It is an impressive example of early realism. Three generations of canons may well have drawn inspiration from it during their daily recitation of the liturgy. Until 1535.

5.1 Iconoclasm in the Netherlands, given an orderly and directed air, enhancing the fabric of the church.

Within a few summer days, bands of townsmen, urged by the preaching of Guillaume Farel and Antoine Fromment, broke up the altarpiece and the altar. They tore down the elaborate screen separating choir from nave. They made bonfires of carved stalls and statues. They whitewashed over the vivid frescoes covering almost every square centimetre of the walls. They trashed the altars lining the side aisles. They stripped the precious metal from crucifixes, reliquaries and shrines and melted it down for coin. They smashed almost all the stained-glass windows. They emptied the adjoining Maccabean Chapel of holy objects and turned it into a warehouse.

The final onslaught began on 8 August 1535. Defying an official ban, Farel went into the cathedral pulpit and there preached an inflammatory sermon to a large congregation. After the crowd had dispersed, a group of youths stayed to throw taunts at the canons who were preparing to say Vespers. Violent words gave way to vandalism. Others, hearing the commotion, rushed in and joined in an orgy of image-breaking. The authorities were now powerless to control the mob. When appealed to for aid, one of the syndics could only shrug his shoulders: 'If the images really are gods, then they can defend themselves if they want; we do not know what else to do.' The destruction did not long remain in the hands of mindless adolescents and the wilder elements of Geneva. Overnight a group of substantial citizens met to plan a scientific purge of the more prominent churches and convents. They paid particular attention to the chapel of Notre-Dame de Grave which was closely associated with the dukes of Savoy. The eagerness with which the mobs tore down objects provided by wealthy patrons suggests that elements of social protest and score settling were not absent from the demonstrations.

The council, desperately trying to uphold legal forms, summoned the offenders to account for their actions and called upon the Catholic clergy to defend their rites and devotional practices. In the meantime they suspended the celebration of Mass. Thus the municipal authorities usurped the spiritual authority of the bishops and they understood perfectly the momentousness of the step they were taking. This explains their desire to engage the protagonists in theological debate – they did not want to give the impression that decisions were forced upon them by unruly revolutionaries. In the event, the cowed and dispirited clergy declined to put up any arguments. Several of them, indeed, fled the city.

Financial considerations played a significant part in the council's deliberations. The conflict with the bishop and the hiring of Bernese mercenaries had left them short of cash. The possibilities of those confiscated church treasures which they had under lock and key 'for safe keeping' did not escape them. Within days they had begun melting down plate, crucifixes, reliquaries and other cultic objects and minting their own coins (another act of defiance against the bishop). As well as prohibiting the rioters from looting, they ordered the clergy and religious not to remove their precious objects to places of safety. On 12 October they authorized the public hospital to appropriate the goods of certain churches to augment its funds.

The city fathers maintained notional control but iconoclastic outbursts continued throughout the autumn. Protestant bands openly paraded their spoils through the streets. Pamphlets, songs and sermons exulted in their triumphs. The reformers were particularly cock-a-hoop at the exposure of certain frauds. The 'brain of St Peter', a relic proudly housed in the cathedral, was revealed to be a lump of pumice stone. 'Voices' believed to emanate from the tombs of long-buried saints were shown to be nothing more miraculous than the wind moaning through subterranean pipes. The exposure of such falsehoods further fuelled the righteous indignation of the mobs and added to their numbers. The denuding of churches and the abolition of mass spread out from Geneva through all the territory controlled by the city and did not stop until the purge was complete. The transformation was confirmed by a general gathering in the cathedral cloister the following May when, according to the minutes,

> It has been decided and agreed, by a show of hands and a unanimous declaration of vows before God, that, with God's help, we now live according to the holy, evangelical law and word of God in the way it has been preached, getting rid of all masses, ceremonies and papal errors, images and idols and any things which are similar . . .

This 'bag and baggage' expulsion of Catholicism left an ideological vacuum in Geneva. Despite the official determination to 'live according to the holy, evangelical law and word of God', the frenzied events of the past few months had been wholly negative, as Jean Calvin later recorded: 'When I first came to this church there was almost nothing . . . People were searching for idols and burning them when they found them, but there was no Reformation'. No new order had been established based on Protestant principles, nor, in the spring of 1536, was there any indication that this city would become the godly commonwealth *par excellence*. It was only Calvin's appearance 'in transit' and Farel's recognition that this man's incisive mind and forceful personality could transform the situation which made Geneva an exemplar of Protestant theocracy.

THE SINS OF THE IMAGES

Iconolatry and iconoclasm both sprang from that intensity of lay devotion we have already recognized. The proliferation of statues, paintings, guild chapels and chantries is one proof of the strong religious impulse which was a main feature of the life of the age. Most European churches around 1500 were stuffed with objects of devotion, each of which had its own group of 'fans' in the local community. It is difficult for us – except, perhaps in one of the Hindu temples which Vasco da Gama mistook for a church – to envisage the exuberant jumble of painted and gilded religious artefacts which would have met the eye of someone entering a church at the turn of the sixteenth century. It was natural that those seeking a deeper spiritual experience should turn first to the means traditionally offered. The hierarchy endorsed this dependence on material stimuli. By the time of the Council of Trent it had been generally recognized that the cult of the saints had generated many superstitious abuses and that several frauds had been perpetrated on gullible pilgrims. Yet the leaders gathered in conclave could still affirm, 'The nature of man is such that he cannot without external means be raised to meditate on divine things'.

Rejection of that principle linked a wide range of radicals from illiterate Lollards to highly educated humanists. Francisco Quiñones, the Cardinal General of the Observant Franciscans, issued in 1535 a reformed breviary for use throughout the order. He did so because the annual cycle of Scripture recitations had become disrupted by additional ceremonies and readings from other books and because various psalms had been omitted from the monthly performance. When Thomas Cranmer, fourteen years later, devised a new order of vernacular services for the English Church, he lifted passages from Quiñones's book for inclusion in his own preface. By 1552 the English Reformation had moved further and the Archbishop found it necessary to add another apologia to his second Prayer Book explaining why it had been necessary to prune traditional ceremonies so drastically:

> Some are put away because the great excess and multitude of them hath so encreased in these latter daies, that the burthen of them was intoler-able . . . This oure excessive multitude of Ceremonies was so great, and many of them so darke: that they did more confounde and darken, then declare and set forth Christes benefits unto us.

What cultured men, holy men and religious zealots expressed in writing, countless ordinary folk felt. Humanist reformers saw how the top-heavy cult of the saints was creating superstition on the one side and scepticism on the other. Erasmus pointed out in the *Enchiridion* that local saints performed the same functions as the old pagan gods. Writing to a friend in 1529 about the recent iconoclasm in Basel, he ridiculed the cult of the saints in language reminiscent of the taunts of uneducated critics: 'I am greatly surprised that the images performed no miracle to save themselves; formerly the saints worked frequent prodigies for much smaller offences.' And in *A Pilgrimage for the Sake of True Religion* (1526) he wrote:

> Seriously, I wonder sometimes what possible excuse there could be for those who spend so much money on building, decorating, and enriching

churches that there is no limit to it. Granted that the sacred vestments and vessels of the church must have a dignity appropriate to their liturgical use; and I want the building to have grandeur. But what is the use of so many baptistries, candelabra, gold statues? What is the good of the vastly expensive organs . . . What is the good of that costly musical neighing when meanwhile our brothers and sisters, Christ's living temples, waste away from hunger and thirst?

Scholars and artisans did not occupy hermetically sealed worlds. The thinking of radical commentators filtered down through universities, pamphlets, sermons and, indeed, through reform-minded friars and parish priests.

Clear-sighted Church leaders realized that when men abandon their respect for the peripherals of religion they may eventually come to reject core truths. Urging reform upon the Fifth Lateran Council, Egidio of Viterbo, General of the Augustinian Order, challenged his exalted congregation:

When has temerity in speaking, in arguing, in writing against piety been more common or more unafraid? When has there been among the people, not only a greater neglect, but a greater contempt for the sacred, for the sacraments, for the keys and for the holy commandments? When has our religion and faith been more open to the derision even of the lowest classes?

Over the centuries the Church had made a heavy ideological investment in holy places and things, the rituals attendant upon them and the priesthood which alone could validate those rituals. The patent absurdity of much that passed for routine devotion opened a breach through which the forces of heresy and atheism might advance.

While some reforming voices warned about excess, others were concerned about error. The portrayal of fictional saints and miraculous events for which there was no historical basis worried many Church leaders. If, as defenders of religious art contended, images and pictures were the 'books' of the illiterate faithful, it was important that what the people read in them was true. Representations of holy subjects were intended as vehicles of devotion but they also served a didactic purpose. When an artist was commissioned to make an altarpiece or a fresco or a design for a window he was charged with a responsibility, not only to portray his subject accurately, but to reflect the orthodox theological understanding of it. The Church was a famously hard task master in such matters. When Veronese painted a *Last Supper* for the church of SS Giovanni e Paolo, Venice, his sumptuous treatment of the subject and particularly his inclusion of black servants, buffoons, monkeys and dogs outraged the Holy Office. Did the artist, they enquired, really think the Last Supper looked like this? 'No,'

Veronese replied, 'but we painters are all a little mad.' Did he not realize that such exercise of licence provided fuel for Protestant critics? 'Yes,' Veronese admitted, 'but I feel obliged to follow my predecessors.' The Inquisition demanded major alterations. Veronese stood his ground. Rather than tamper with his work he changed the title to *Feast in the House of Levi*. After all, did not the Bible state that that event was attended by publicans and sinners?

Through a Glass Darkly

Most artists, certainly most pre-Renaissance artists, were more compliant but all patrons had to make allowance for the creative imagination. Good patrons recognized and encouraged genius, as long as it was partnered with piety. This meant that Christian truth was mediated through the interpretive vision of the craftsman – with all that that involved for good or ill. The typical Mérode altarpiece of Robert Campin is a sermon on Marian devotion which speaks to the viewer on several levels. It retells the well-known story of the Annunciation, representing the Virgin as a pious and scholarly woman surrounded by conventional symbols indicating her purity and the uniqueness of her role. It reminds us that Joseph was a carpenter by depicting him with the tools of his trade. It also portrays him – in keeping with tradition – as an old man. It locates the biblical event in a contemporary setting (Joseph's window looks out on what is, presumably, the local town square) to indicate that the coming of Christ is of timeless significance and should move us, as it moves the devout patrons on the left, to wonder and worship. The theological significance of the event is pointed by the infant descending on a sunbeam, bearing a cross, and also by the mousetrap offered for sale in Joseph's window. The Incarnation was the baited trap which successfully caught the devil.

A few months before Luther published his theses, an artist died who had taken preaching in paint about as far as it could go. Jeroen Anthoniszoon Van Aken, known to posterity as Hieronymus Bosch, gave the world a collection of bizarre allegorical and religious images. Many of them are crammed with his comments on contemporary life, by turns cynical and pious, witty and despairing, terrifying and whimsical. All sprang from the intensity of his own religious experience. It is significant that one of Bosch's most ardent devotees a couple of generations later was the highly introverted Philip II of Spain.

A painting such as the *Haywain* triptych goes infinitely further in its didacticism than the orthodox mind-elevating altarpieces of the High Gothic. It tells the story of man from creation to judgement but its centre panel is an elaboration, not of a biblical text, but of the popular contemporary aphorism 'The world is a haystack and everyone plucks from it what he can get.' A despairing Christ gazes down and a solitary angel prays while an oblivious world is obsessed with greed, avarice and lust. No-one is spared in Bosch's tumultuous catalogue of evil. Pope and emperor are as tainted as the meanest peasant. The Church certainly does not escape. We see a fat abbot laying aside his rosary, quaffing wine and watching nuns stuff hay (worldly treasure) into an already bulging sack.

Few ordinary citizens had the opportunity to meditate on works by great artists but everyone could find in his parish church some painting or image to lift his thoughts to the spiritual realm. There was much greater variety of Church art than we may realize. Some clergy took seriously the need to instruct their people about the Scriptures. Narrative paintings have survived, telling stories from both Old and New Testaments, with labels describing the salient points of each scene. They must have performed a similar function to the Bible picture books which were produced in growing numbers throughout the later Middle Ages and provided useful visual aids for diligent parish clerks who wished to raise their flock above the level of mere observers of sacramental acts.

There was much in all this that most reformers were happy to accept. It is, for example, difficult to imagine any zealot – Catholic or Protestant – dissenting from Bosch's moralizing. Luther certainly refused to join in the outcry against images. He attacked the superstitious misuse of sacred objects but feared the seditious disorder implicit in iconoclasm and regarded the demand for the wholesale destruction of images as an example of a new legalism. But amongst the multitude of objects of popular devotion there were those which did cause concern. Jean Gerson was dismayed to discover a statue of the Virgin whose stomach opened up to reveal the three persons of the Trinity. Savonarola condemned artists who hired as models men and women discovered in the brothel, the jail or the gutter and transformed them into saints: 'You paint their faces in the churches, which is a great profanation of divine things. You do very ill, and if you knew, as I know, the scandal you cause, you would certainly act differently . . . You fill the churches with vain things. Do you think that the Virgin should be painted as you paint her? I tell you that she went clothed as a beggar.'

INTO THE PIT

The greatest opposition to iconoclasm came, not from outraged clergy, but from lay people who wanted to stop the destruction of objects donated by themselves or their families. Recent scholarship has shown that, especially in newly prosperous countries like England, there was, in the early years of the sixteenth century, a considerable increase in donations of chantries, altars and windows as well as images and the jewels and coverings for them. To what extent this generosity was prompted by genuine fervour we can never know, but social emulation certainly played a part. Leading families jealously guarded their local pre-eminence and the church was the place where they could demonstrate it most effectively. They took prominent places in the processions, in which there was a well-defined (though by no means undisputed) pecking order. Their names and heraldic devices were displayed in paint or carved wood. The wealthy had themselves portrayed in suitably devout poses in the religious pictures they donated. This feature of church life survived in Protestant lands as well as Catholic long after the Reformation, as witness the grandiose tombs and memorials erected by the leaders of society until well into the present century. So, by the time religious images came to be called into question, the upper classes had a large investment in the status quo. Donors and their families frequently tried to stop the destruction of 'their' cultic objects. When that was impossible they removed them themselves or even tried to buy them back.

Theological reasons, however, also demanded that images be defended. Catholic doctrine on images rested on a declaration of the same fourth-century council that had formulated the creed: there was a difference between the worship offered to God alone and the veneration or honour directed towards the saints through their painted or carved replicas. If that was all there was to it, the controversy over images could never have inspired so much passion. In the perception of the fathers of Nicaea, however, icons were also holy objects, venerable in themselves. Their painters prepared by prayer and fasting. They were brought into the churches reverentially and blessed. They were not visual aids but channels of grace. Like relics, they conveyed to the worshipper something of the presence and persona of the person represented. The ultimate proof of their aptness was the Incarnation. If flesh and blood could be infused with the nature of God by the Holy Spirit, wood and paint and gold leaf could acquire worshipful properties, too.

In the West images could attract some of the same associations with holiness: many worked miracles; some, like the Holy Face of Lucca, were borne to their destinations by angels. Some were so beautiful, so powerful in their hold on the emotions, that their making was ascribed to angelic or divine hands. Woodcut-souvenirs from the shrine of the Virgin of Cesena show God completing her picture while the human artist falls asleep.

Though generations of priests and bishops enjoined their flocks to guard against any confusion of these different levels of adoration, the orthodox position was that most people were quite clear about the relationship between the Almighty, the honoured dead and material representations. Thomas More, in his controversy with Tyndale, boisterously asserted that even the simplest believer 'will tell you that our Lady herself is in heaven . . . will . . . call an image an image, and . . . tell you a difference between an image of an horse and an horse indeed.' This was precisely what reformers called in question.

Ulrich Zwingli was the first of the major Reformers to insist on the 'purification' of places of worship. By drawing several logical conclusions from humanist insistence on the supremacy of Scripture, he made an impact on the development of Protestantism which was out of all proportion to the brevity of his ministry. In 1519 he was simply an orthodox priest with evangelical convictions. A mere twelve years later he was hacked to pieces by Catholic troops; his body was burned and his ashes were mixed with dung. Zwingli was captivated by the Bible and his fresh, exegetical preaching captivated his Zürich congregations. He insisted that all Church teachings and ceremonies should be submitted to the judgement of holy writ. Veneration of images failed this ordeal by Scripture.

It did so, not just because it was a violation (in Zwingli's opinion) of the Mosaic prohibition. The existence of a host of heavenly intermediaries and their material representations obscured the central message of the New Testament in two important respects: it detracted from the uniqueness of Christ and it denied to God the complete and undivided worship he rightly demanded. This, in turn, posed serious pastoral questions. For Zwingli they were summed up in the word 'idolatry', to which he gave a new breadth of meaning. In *An Answer to Valentin Compar* (1525) he set out what he intended by it. He began from the double premiss that God is spirit and man is flesh. St Paul taught that these two stand in contradistinction and that natural man could not worship God without the indwelling of the Holy Spirit. But all men have a desire to worship and so they substitute other things for him who alone is worthy to be adored. They make images of men and women and even of the invisible God. They take bones and the material residue of holy lives and turn them into objects of veneration. But devotion to religious images does not constitute the only form of idolatry. Some men worship money, some power, some popularity. Anything that a person puts at the centre of his life is an idol. It was the Church's task to draw people away from all these things and enable them to worship God 'in spirit and in truth'. It followed that Christian magistrates were constrained, out of charity, to remove from churches all objects that did not serve this end.

Early sixteenth-century converts had come to a direct experience of God by reading or listening to the Bible. They enjoyed the heady shock of being certain of their salvation, a certainty which traditional religion had not given them. The bolder among them urged their neighbours to abandon practices which hindered rather than helped their access to the throne of grace. 'Christ promised to grant what was asked in his name, not in the name of SS Peter, Nicholas, Sebastian or any other,' wrote the Franciscan Michael Hug. Pamphlets written by evangelical laymen slid from the presses. By no means all of them were inflammatory but most of them stated or implied scriptural disapprobation of the use of religious images and intercession to the saints. Here is a son 'quoted' in one as supposedly writing to his mother:

> I am grateful to you for sending me the little Agnus Dei, to protect me against being shot, cut and from falling, but honestly, it won't do me any

good. I cannot set my faith in it because God's word teaches me to trust only in Jesus Christ. I am sending it back. We'll try it out on this letter and see whether it is protected from tampering. I don't thank you one bit less, but I pray God you won't believe any more in sacred salt and holy water and all this devil's tomfoolery.

When Hugh Latimer, who prided himself on being the son of a hard-working yeoman farmer, addressed the bishops gathered in convocation in 1536, he knew that he voiced the complaints uttered by many in alehouse and market place against preachers who urged that

dead images . . . not only ought to be covered with gold, but also ought of all faithful and Christian people, (yea, in this scarceness and penury of all things,) to be clad with silk garments, and those also laden with precious gems and jewels . . . as who should say, here no cost can be too great; whereas in the mean time we see Christ's faithful and lively images, bought with no less price than with his most precious blood, (alas! alas!) to be an hungered, a-thirst, a-cold, and to lie in darkness, wrapped in all wretchedness, yea, to lie there till death take away their miseries.

Martin Bucer, one of the more engaging characters of the Protestant reform, was not given to dogmatic extremism. Much of his active life was spent in trying to draw Catholics and various groups of Protestants to unite around an agreed programme for the renewal of Church life. Yet Bucer moved gradually to outright condemnation of images. He likened them to decoy birds which lured people away from true piety. Since 'bones are bones and not gods,' he declared, they cannot perform miracles. It followed logically from this premiss that where well-attested signs and wonders were associated with certain relics they must be the work of Satan, whose objective was always to deceive the faithful. Bucer urged godly rulers to order the total eradication of all objects of superstition, although he opposed zealots who wanted to take the law into their own hands.

Protestant suspicion of the visual arts as aids to worship enabled the campaigners for a revitalized Catholicism to commandeer them, lock, stock and barrel. More than ever before, the post-Tridentine church used painting, sculpture and architecture to reassert traditional teachings – especially those the Reformers rejected – and to assert new doctrinal emphases. Enthusiastic patronage of artists striking out new paths away from the Renaissance helped to create the Baroque, which has been called 'a militant civilization operating through the power of the image.' In the spate of newly commissioned works for church interiors worshippers' imaginations were roused by visions of angels releasing souls from purgatory, popes and bishops caught in spectacular attitudes of devotion, St Peter performing miracles, the sacred heart of Mary (a devotional motif widely promoted by the Jesuits) and radiant representations of *Corpus Christi*. The new wave of religious art made its impact not simply by dramatic emphasis of its chosen subject matter. Where new churches were built or substantially re-ordered, an exuberant, sensual combination of architecture, painting, sculpture, metalwork, carving and gilding wrought mightily on the emotions to create an impression of the Church militant, triumphant and united in heaven and earth.

The trouble with religious buildings is that they set in concrete ideas about God which are, or should be, constantly developing. More than any other type of material aid to faith a church fixes the attitudes of those who frequent it. It pours them into a cultural mould into which some fit better than others. The sixteenth- and seventeenth-century wars of religion were appalling but they did come to an end. By contract, the Catholic–Protestant confrontation in art left Europe (and the Americas) dotted with buildings which continued to scream defiance at each other. Baroque Catholicism's exuberant delight in colour and writhing forms, its reaffirmation of pomp and pageantry, the cult of the saints, the centrality of the mass and the permeation of the material by the holy contrasted sharply with Protestantism's treatment of the church building as merely a convenient auditorium where the elect could gather to hear the proclamation of the word. The tragedy

5.2 A seventeenth-century Calvinist church interior - Kirche in Stein, near Nürnberg.

was that there were devout Catholics who yearned for a simple expression of the faith and earnest Protestants who were tortured by being forced to deny their sensuality. Luther saw no reason why the devil should have all the best images. The last Jansenist synod in 1786 called for the removal of 'images in which it would seem that people have special faith.'

ALTAR AND TABLE

For most people in the sixteenth century mass was less important than it was for theologians. Its disappearance made less impact on the visual re-ordering of churches than the removal of statues, paintings, rood lofts and other foci of lay devotion. The layman was a passive participant mass. He probably received communion no more than twice a year (a situation which continued in both Catholic and Protestant churches after the Reformation). His relationship with the saints and their images was much closer, despite the marked growth of mass-centred lay activity from the mid-fifteenth century onwards. Wealthy patrons made provision in their wills for chantry priests, not only to say masses for their souls, but also to perform votive masses as contributions to the cycle of parish worship. Less affluent people banded together in guilds which were liturgical co-operatives for achieving the same purpose. Moreover, there were frequent moves to involve the laity more in these rites. The authorities, partly, no doubt, in response to popular demand, sponsored the production of mass books and other devotional literature. These largely comprised prayers and meditations tied to the movement of the liturgy. There were those among the literate minority who found such books valuable aids to devotion and they certainly sold in quite large numbers. Yet all attempts to involve the people meaningfully in the mass were hampered by the fact that it remained, in essence, a priestly activity.

Most worshippers were happy that it should be so. The majority of churchgoers have always been soulmates of Oliver Goldsmith, who observed to Dr Johnson, 'As I take my shoes from the shoemaker, and my coat from the tailor, so I take my religion from the priest.' The late Joseph Campbell, a leading world authority on mythology, explained this attitude as a compromise with spiritual reality:

> Religious experience demands, as its starting point, relinquishing control over our own lives. This goes against fundamental human freedom. So we tend, if we are at all religiously inclined, to settle for a halfway house. We carry out certain formal devotional functions and nominate certain persons as religious experts to be our intermediaries.

Worship has to do two things for the worshippers: it has to enhance the individual's experience of the divine and it has to bind together the Christian community. It has often been claimed that the Reformation emphasized the former at the expense of the latter. One Catholic commentator saw individualism as something which had been infiltrating the Church for over a century before the onslaught of the 1520s.

> The religion of the laity . . . came to consist more and more in their personal relations with God. A private prayer which seemed more effectively to bring the individual into conscious contact with God was more esteemed than communal prayer, whose psychological efficacy was less obvious. The faithful no longer understood that liturgical prayer comes first, as the prayer of the whole body of the Church united to Christ, nor did they see that the Church's intentions, in which every Christian should share, are there expressed. This led logically to a progressive depreciation of sacramental practice. What was sought in Holy Communion, which was still rare in any case, was chiefly a stimulant of interior religion. A paradoxical truth emerges from all this: on the one hand, the fifteenth century was excessively attached to those 'works' which Luther was soon to denounce as inefficacious for salvation: on the other, it was preparing the way for Protestantism, in the sense that salvation was thought of as a personal affair to be treated between God and the soul, without any attention being paid to the Church, its tradition, its hierarchy and its sacraments.

This certainly identifies one strand of late medieval spirituality. As we have seen, worshippers at mass were encouraged by clergy and printed manuals to do their own devotional thing while the priest celebrated. Wealthy people, families and guilds employed priests to serve their own altars and the multiplication of shrines and chapels created 'beaucoup de paroisses dans le paroisse'.

Against this we have to set the growth of Christian communities of all kinds. Men and women were seeking in the cloister, in beguinages, in the Oratory of Divine Love, in the Brethren of the Common Life and in hundreds of more transitory associations, to create the circumstances in which they could grow in holiness through communal worship and service. When Utraquists met in barns to celebrate communion and church guilds united in devotion to their patron saint they were both expressing, among other things, a desire for communal spirituality.

Individuality and communality were both vital to the Reformers. Having rejected the Catholic understanding of the Church, they had to develop their own. Protestant thinkers struggled to produce new definitions – 'the invisible Church', 'the community of the faithful', 'the Christian commonwealth', 'the elect'. The 'true' Church had to have liturgical expression. This is explicit in, for example, the definition (arguably the best and most concise of the period) Melanchthon gave of the Church as 'the community where there reigns the Word and the sacraments, love and discipline.' Congregations were lovingly disciplined to take an active part in the ministry of word and sacrament. The impact of vernacular worship must have been incalculable on the first generation of the untutored to encounter it. Apart from anything else, the degree of concentration required as lessons, psalms and hymns (canticles) were recited in their mother tongue must have been immense. Then there were the creeds and prayers to be repeated phrase-by-phrase after the clergy until they had been learned by heart. In addition, zealous ministers required their flocks to attend weekday Bible studies or lectures. The objectives were to advance individual believers in the faith and to bring into being a truly 'common' prayer. Worshippers were directed to channel the devotion hitherto expended in private or group endeavours into the communal liturgy. Sunday observance was enforced by the imposition of penalties (a twelve-pence fine in England) for absence.

Thomas Cranmer's dissertation *Of Ceremonies* in the 1552 Prayer Book has a very modern feel:

> . . . whereas in this our time, the minds of men are so diverse, that some think it a great matter of conscience to depart from a piece of the least of their ceremonies (they be so addicted to their old customs:) and again on the other side, some be so new fangled, that they would innovate all things, and so do despise the old, that nothing can like them, but that is new: it was thought expedient, not so much to have respect how to please and satisfy either of these parties, as how to please God, and profit them both.

In the event, it proved impossible to prevent factions and pressure groups developing. Just as under the old dispensation people gathered together to maintain devotion to a particular saint or to follow a common rule of life, so under the new, men and women came together in like-minded associations to emphasize a particular aspect of doctrine or campaign for further reforms. No Protestant state succeeded in devising a balance of authority and flexibility which would prevent breakaways. Calvin, who, more than any other reformer, imposed strict rules on both the form and content of worship, laid down guidelines in the *Institutes* that bordered on liberalism:

> We ought not to reject any assembly which entertains [the pure ministry of word and sacrament] even though it be defective in several ways . . . there may be some defect either in the doctrine or in the manner of administering of the sacraments, which ought not in any way to alienate us from the communion of a church.

As far as the liturgy was concerned individualism entailed a total change of

When post-Tridentine triumphalism produced vivid images such as the magnificent *Victory of Catholic Truth over Heresy* by Bernini in the Il Gesù church, Rome. Such vivid representation provided powerful and permanent icons of confrontation. *(Fratelli Alinari, Florence)*

The simplicity of the John Knox chapel in Geneva, a preaching auditorium for the proclamation of the word of God contrasts with the Baroque exuberance of Il Gesù church, Rome (ceiling shown here) which sought to draw the beholders from earth to heaven by visual stimuli.

A visitor from another culture would take some convincing that both buildings served the same faith. *(Pierre-Charles George; Fratelli Alinari, Florence)*

Holbein the Younger's (1497-1543) *Christ in Tomb*, 1521. Christ is never more obviously human than when depicted dead. When Holbein chose to represent the dead Christ in the utter isolation of the grave, he eschewed the sculptural and humanistic treatment which Mantegna gave this subject. In his uncompromising realism he was at one with contemporary reformers of doctrine who wanted to strip away post-New Testament accretions and reaffirm the core truths of Christianity. *(Öffentliche Kunstsammlung, Basel)*

Jörg Breu the Elder's (c.1475–1537) depiction of the Passion, painted for Melk Abbey around 1501 expresses and seeks to arouse intense emotions by overemphasizing the brutality and grotesqueness of the event. This effect is heightened by the way the arrangement of the tormentors mocks a fairground scene. *(Bundesdenkmalamt, Vienna)*

The vigour of much late medieval religion lives on in the heightened realism of such works of art as this 1493 altarpiece from Louvain Cathedral depicting scenes of martyrdom. *(A C L – Brussels)*

Of the thousands of decorative devotional objects presented to churches by kings, noble families, merchant guilds and other wealthy donors few were more splendid than Verrocchio's *Christ and St Thomas* presented to Florence's Or San Michele by the *mercanzia. (Fratelli Alinari, Florence)*

Dürer's *Four Apostles* indicates the 'Protestantization' of the visual arts. Emphasis is on the word God, and the inscription, supplied by the artist's friend Johann Neudörffer urges the leaders of Nuremburg society not to deviate from Lutheran truth. *(Bayer. Staatsgemäldesammlungen, Munich)*

Rome, the centre of pilgrimage. This engraving of 1575 indicates the principle centres of devotion and shows a long line of pilgrims and penitents making their tour of the sites. *(Instituto Nazionale per la Grafica, Rome)*

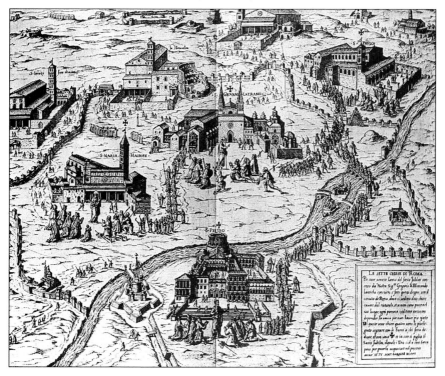

Hans Memling detail from the Donne altarpiece (1468). Devotion encouraged literacy among those who could afford books. Printing greatly increased this section of the community. *(National Gallery, London)*

In this book of hours (c.1452) the French court painter, Jean Fouquet, depicts the Holy Spirit illuminating a group of devout clergy and thus putting demons to flight. It may be thought of as an expression of the hierarchic concept of religious life which recognized clergy as possessing a closer contact with God than laity or as a reminder to Church leaders to live up to their spiritual calling. *(Metropolitan Museum of Art, Robert Lehman Collection (1975.1.2490 recto))*

Piero della Francesca's *Madonna della Misericordia* (c.1445–8) expresses one of the most powerful of medieval images; the Virgin as symbol of the Church spreads her protective mantle over the devout. *(Fratelli Alinari, Florence)*

Illustrations like this fifteenth-century
Netherlands example drawing parallels
between Old Testament heroes such as Moses
and Abraham and the apostles gathered at
Pentecost were designed as preaching aids
by a Church mindful both of its educational
responsibilities and of the inadequacies of
many parish priests. *(Bodleian Library,
Oxford)*

Images of death kept a summons to penitence before
all eyes. Such themes featured prominently in artistic
conventions like the *Dance of Death* and *Death and the Maiden*. This is an example
of the latter, created by Hans Schwartz, c.1520. *(Staatliche Museen Preussischer
Kulturbesitz, Berlin (photo Jorg P. Anders))*

Nothing depicts more powerfully the religious passion behind the reformation principle than the Eisenheim altarpiece of Mathis Neithardt-Gothardt (known as Grünewald), 1515. Grief, pain and the glory of the Resurrection are here represented with an intensity matched only by mystic writers and fiery preachers. *(Musée d'Unterlinden, Colmar (photo O. Zimmermann))*

Carpaccio's painting entitled *St Jerome in his study* (c.1507) is thought to be a portrait of the Venetian prelate, humanist and scholar Cardinal Bessarion. *(Fratelli Alinari, Florence)*

Lucas Cranach the Younger numbered Erasmus (4th from right) among Luther's supporters in this painting of Reformation leaders, c.1530. Melanchthon is on the extreme right. *(Lutherhalle, Wittenberg)*

Protestant radicals were far from being the only destroyers of religious art. This reconstruction of the Liesboner altarpiece shows how church authorities broke up the painting and sold it off in bits when they replaced it with a more modern focus of devotion. *(Westfälisches Landesmuseum für Kunst und Kulturgeschichte)*

The Reception of St Ignatius into Paradise – the church of St Ignatius, Rome. Ignatius of Loyola's fiery spirituality, total submission to papal obedience and founding of the educational Society of Jesus (Jesuits) made him a Catholic hero in the fight against heresy. Ironically, many of the enemies he made in his own church regarded him as a covert Protestant. *(Fratelli Alinari, Florence)*

Protestantism created a characteristic model of domestic lay devotion which was set forth as an ideal for three centuries and in many instances became the norm of middle-class family life. This Bruges merchant and his household were depicted (c.1585) saying grace before a meal by Anthonius Claeissius. *(The Shakespeare Birthplace Trust)*

Nürnberg escaped both Protestant iconoclasm and the rebuilding associated with baroque Catholic triumphalism. As a result many fine examples of High Gothic art survive. This Annunciation is in St Lorenzkirche and dates from 1517–18. *(Archiv für Kunst und Geschichte, Berlin)*

The Eglise St Jeanne d'Arc, Rouen. *(Editions Gaud, Moisenay-le-Petit)*

The miraculous draught of fishes, panel of an altarpiece painted by Conrad Witz c.1444 for Geneva cathedral. *(Musée d'art et d'histoire, Geneva)*

The Haywain Triptych, Hieronymus Bosch – centre panel. Like many contemporary artists, writers and preachers, Bosch did not spare religious leaders in his depictions of human sin and folly. *(Museo del Prado, Madrid)*

Mérode altarpiece of the Annunciation. Robert Campin. Flemish, c.1377–1444. *(Metropolitan Museum of Art, The Cloisters Collection (56.70))*

Savonarola, the moral and spiritual scourge of Florence made too many political enemies, including the pope, and perished at the stake in 1497. *(Fratelli Alinari, Florence)*

Robert Dudley, Earl of Leicester, was a prominent patron of Puritans. None of the virtues of humility and simplicity associated with that group were evidenced in the sumptous tomb he ordered to be erected in St Mary's church, Warwick, as a perpetual reminder of his earthly greatness. After the Reformation such very human memorials took much of the place that had hitherto been occupied by religious artefacts. *(A. F. Kersting)*

Demand for reform is a
continuing feature of church life.
It always involves calling leaders
back to the principles of the
Gospels and engaging in debate
about contemporary society. The
major *cause célèbre* of the 1970s
and 80s for Anglicans was the
ordination of women to the
priesthood. *(Hulton Getty)*

Henry VIII as Solomon receiving
the adulation of the English
church, in the guise of the Queen
of Sheba, c.1540. Holbein the
Younger probably devised this
drawing on vellum with the
support of Thomas Cromwell to
emphasize Henry's triumph over
Rome and the subservience of the
English church. *(The Royal
Collection © Her Majesty The
Queen (Elizabeth II))*

what worship was about. Lay participation was required. The intellect was to be engaged. The people were to hear, pray and sing in their own language. They were no longer mute participants in a transaction whereby the priest offered God to them and them to God.

The Reformation marked a significant stage of development in the perpetual tension between the universal, corporate and individual aspects of worship. The Protestant churches abandoned or, at the very least, narrowed the sense of the congregation as enwrapped in a timeless, infinite *mysterium* of praise, love and humble obeisance. It was more important that, in Cranmer's words, 'every country should use such ceremonies, as they shal think best to the settyng furth of Goddes honour or glory, and to the reducyng of people to a most perfecte and godly lyuyng, without errour or Supersticion'. But if liturgical practice may vary from nation to nation, why should it not do so from town to town, village to village? The end result of such an attitude is that worship ceases to be 'common'.

Naturally churches resisted this fragmentation. State churches were determined to preserve their identity. Later, as they grew into international denominations they abandoned the concept of liturgical self-determination. Just as the Catholic church retained the obligatory Tridentine Mass until Vatican II so the Anglican communion remained faithful for three hundred years to the Book of Common Prayer in its final, 1662, form, and exported it to Britain's overseas colonies. So, too, Lutheran, Baptist and other worship patterns duplicated themselves in other lands and remained largely unchanged for generations. But the quiet revolution of the last thirty years has led to a sweeping debasement or enrichment (according to one's point of view) of liturgical practice. Many Churches now contain separate, distinct congregations. For example, a not-untypical Anglican Sunday might begin with an 8 a.m. Holy Communion, according to the 1662 rite, have a mid-morning ASB Parish Communion, alternated with a loosely structured 'Family Service', and conclude in the evening with 'Youth Praise' or some other 'accessible' form of worship designed with outreach in mind. This flexibility, based more on the perceived requirements of the people than on any theology of worship, is evidenced nowadays in most Western-world denominations. One could argue that the churches have come full circle from the days when popular devotions were divided among various saints.

EVERYBODY SING

While the spiritual heirs of Calvin, Zwingli and (to a lesser extent) Luther have continued to look askance at the visual arts, they have made one enormous contribution to Christian worship – congregational singing. Reformers of all theological hues agreed with Erasmus that, 'Modern church music is so composed that the congregation cannot understand a word.' Iconoclasts who smashed organs and tore up service books were protesting about the separation between priests and people in worship and the obscuring of the plain word of Scripture by embellishments of the text. Vandals and philistines are always with us and frequently draw more attention to themselves than their numbers warrant. Most Protestants loved music. When Edward Winslow, with his fellow Pilgrim Fathers, took sorrowful leave of friends and loved ones in Leyden in 1620, he recorded, 'we refreshed ourselves after our tears with singing of psalms, making joyful melody in our hearts as well as with the voice, there being many of the congregation very expert in music; and it was the sweetest melody that mine ears ever heard.'

In both the great choral traditions which developed in Italy, Spain, England and other countries on both sides of the Reformation divide and in the worship in country churches we discern an overall desire for greater simplicity. The Council of Trent urged priests to intone the liturgy clearly and without unnecessary ornament. Luther provided detailed instructions for those singing divine service. Cranmer ordained that '(to thend the people may the better hear) in such places were thei do sing, there shal the lessons be song in a plain tune after the maner of distinct reading'. For the Reformers music was the servant of the word but Luther knew that it was much more:

> I have no use for cranks who despise music, because it is a gift of God. Music drives away the Devil and makes people gay; they forget thereby all wrath, unchastity, arrogance, and the like. Next after theology I give to music the highest place and the greatest honor . . . Experience proves that next to the Word of God only music deserves to be extolled as the mistress and governess of the feelings of the human heart.

Music that could be easily sung would enable illiterate people to commit scriptural concepts to memory and heighten their emotional response to those concepts. Luther's own *'Ein' feste Burg ist unser Gott'* (one of thirty-seven hymns he wrote for his followers), dubbed by Heine 'the Marseillaise of the Reformation', was metaphorically and sometimes literally a battle chant. The armies of Gustavus Adolphus and even of Bismarck sang it as they marched. Hymns enabled the untutored both to group and to express the whole range of Christian teaching and experience. John Wesley, in a preface to one of his brother's hymn books, spelled out its didactic purpose: 'The hymns are not carelessly jumbled together but carefully ranged under proper heads according to the experience of real Christians, so that this book is in effect, a little body of experimental and practical divinity.' It is no accident that every major evangelical revival over the last two hundred and fifty years has relied heavily on the impact of congregational singing. For those who had foresworn visual stimuli, hymns, songs, chorales and choruses became their oral icons.

Yet hymns did not establish themselves easily in all Protestant traditions as a regular ingredient of worship. While such groups as Lutherans, Moravians and Baptists were open to the fusing of music and religious poetry, those churches which drew their main inspiration from Geneva and Zürich remained suspicious of anything that added to the plain word of Scripture. In England, Scotland, France, Switzerland and the Low Countries the new assemblies turned to the age-old collection of religious songs, the Psalter. Thus was born the metrical psalm. It was not to everyone's taste. Queen Elizabeth referred to the new settings as 'Geneva jigs'. For the best part of two hundred years the separate traditions of congregational worship were the most obvious marks of difference between Protestant churches. Because people came to love their hymns and psalms (and it would be hard to exaggerate the cultural impact of religious tunes and lyrics) they guarded them against 'modern innovations' and championed them against those preferred by other denominations. Church music became one of those concentric walls the different groups of Christians built around themselves.

Because of the confessional gulf – widened by the religious wars of the seventeenth century – there were few meeting points between the Protestant and Catholic musical traditions. Most regular worshippers simply did not know what went on in the conventicles of the 'heretics' and the 'papists'. Discovery of the truth could be an overwhelming experience. When Joseph Haydn attended a service in the London Foundling Hospital in 1792 he was moved to record, 'I was more touched by their innocent and reverent music than by anything I had ever heard.' A few years earlier Sam Wesley, composer son of Charles the hymn-writer, was so overwhelmed by the chanting of mass in the chapel of the Portuguese Embassy that he – temporarily – converted to Catholicism, which caused much fluttering in Methodist dovecotes. In fact, there had been, in some Roman Catholic circles, a call for more lay participation in the music of worship. This was met in part by providing metrical plainsong settings of sections of the liturgy and of traditional lyrics.

Eighteenth-century revivalism brought together the different strands of Protestant hymnody in England. In 1819, the Reverend Thomas Cotterell, the new vicar of St Paul's Sheffield, introduced his own compilation, *A Selection of Psalms and Hymns* to his congregation. They rejected this invasion of 'enthusiasm' and took their priest to the ecclesiastical court. It was a test case and much depended on it. No legal provision had ever been made for the inclusion of hymns in Anglican worship. Archbishop Harcourt of York was quick to see the threat. If the hardliners won there would be fresh splits in his province. He summoned Cotterell to the palace and issued the following instructions 'Remove your book. That will stop the court action. Then compile a new edition and send it to me. I will vet it and give it my seal of approval.' From that moment there was nothing to stop the use of hymns in Church of England services.

Tractarians and others who wanted dignified, unemotional worship realized that if they could not beat the reformers they must join them. They wrote their own hymn books, drawing largely on pre-Reformation Christian verse. Across the border the Findlater sisters genteely attacked the Calvinist bastion by publishing *Hymns from the Land of Luther*. When the Roman Catholic hierarchy was re-established in England in 1850, the faithful began clamouring for hymns. Though musical style in church depends on the traditions of particular congregations, regions and countries, there is almost as good a chance today of hearing *'Ein' feste Burg'* in a Catholic church in Germany as in a Lutheran one, or of hearing hymns by Wesley or Milton in a Catholic church in England.

Meanwhile, the mainline Protestant denominations have returned to the centrality of the Eucharist. The Roman communion has established vernacular services. Trends in architecture and internal design are towards greater simplicity. Lay men and women play prominent roles in the conduct of public worship. The charismatic movement deluged all denominations with a torrent of new music. When Billy Graham led a crusade to Britain in 1984 a new hymn book – *Mission Praise* – was compiled for the meetings. It contained old and new hymns and songs from all traditions. Within a few years it had achieved something quite unique in the history of hymnody. It was being used, on a regular or occasional basis, by churches across the denominational spectrum. The music of Taizé has made a similar impact, and has been deliberately propagated as part of the community's commitment to reconciliation.

This drawing on a shared spiritual tradition and finding common ways of expressing religious feeling affects the visual arts as well as music. All congregations have images (even bare walls and an uncovered table constitute an image). Today, more than at any time in the last four hundred and fifty years, there are fewer religious objects that provoke division and more that make common statements of faith. According to a recent Catholic writer, after Vatican II,

> Images became less identifiably Catholic: sacred hearts and crowned virgins were on the decrease; golden sunsets, billowing waves, snow-clad mountain peaks and leafy glades took their place, usually with a short text in the corner and often in the form of a poster to stick on the wall rather than a card to slip in a missal.

What is true of individual devotional aids is true also of church fittings and fixtures. Differences of dogma remain and are profoundly felt by many but the posters, texts, pictures and banners one is likely to encounter in places of worship today are less likely to be making partisan statements than reflecting truths to which all Christians could assent.

In his charming book, *In Search of a Way*, a Catholic priest, Gerard

Hughes recounted a personal pilgrimage across Europe. The following incident occurred when he was staying at a French Franciscan community:

When the fifty American students arrived, we told them that we were having Mass after supper and that they were welcome to join us and contribute some prayers and songs in English. I had taken it for granted that they were a Catholic group and it was only after they had accepted the invitation that I learned they were, in fact, an intensely serious group of fundamentalist Protestant Evangelicals whose forefathers would be tossing around in their graves at the thought of their children attending Roman Catholic idolatrous worship. These children of the twentieth century seemed to have no scruple . . .

Most of them joined in the Mass; they chose some of the readings, commented on them, sang 'Amazing Grace', and when they joined in the prayers of intercession, I thought we would not finish Mass before dawn. It was a most Catholic Eucharist, in its literal sense, international and interdenominational. I said the Mass in French with an English commentary and we had prayers and songs in five languages, a great experience for all of us of Christ's power to unite us across the barriers of language and expression of belief. When Christ is our bond and our peace, then our differences are no longer barriers to communication, and we become grateful for our diversity in unity.

Chapter Six

SERVANTS AND SACRIFICERS:
Priesthood and the Reformation

THE REVENGE OF THE PHARISEES

For now I see the true old times are dead . . .
  now the whole ROUND TABLE is dissolved
Which was an image of the mighty world;
And I, the last, go forth companionless,
And the days darken round me, and the years,
Among new men, strange faces, other minds . . .

Tennyson, *The Passing of Arthur*

In response to that dismal prognostication by Sir Bedevere, the dying Arthur, in Tennyson's poem, told the distraught knight to pull himself together, stop harking back to a glorious past, and get on with life. 'The old order changeth', he insisted, because God ordains that it shall. When 'good custom' and revered traditions try to halt the process of death and renewal they become walking corpses and can only 'corrupt the world'. The poet was pointing out a truth no less important than that announced by Lord Acton. If power tends to corrupt so, too, do institutions.

It is of the nature of any human system to defend and preserve itself; to retain those structures which protect the beliefs and customs which it was founded to safeguard. Religious institutions are without doubt the most

stubborn. They rampart themselves with divine sanction. The clerical profession stands first in the dock to face Shaw's accusation of being a
'conspiracy against the laity' because it alone claims heavenly sanction for
indulging in such worldly failings as personality cults, social engineering,
ruthless exercise of power, élitism and exploitation. While 'old order' and
'good custom' become tainted by unworthy agents, the determination to
cling to them robs them of vigour. It is like trying, by climatic engineering,
to preserve a fine forest tree in the full splendour of its summer foilage.
Deprived of the necessary death and rebirth of the seasons it would become
a weakened and pitiful thing. That is why every religion needs its prophets,
its radicals and its heretics – to challenge the status quo and to make the
establishment re-examine its assumptions.

The usual fate of such outspoken critics underlines the tenacity with
which institutions cling to power and the traditions which support it. 'O
Jerusalem, Jerusalem, you who kill the prophets and stone those sent to you,
how often I have longed to gather your children together, as a hen gathers
her chicks under her wings, but you were not willing.' Jesus was condemned
by the leaders of first-century Jewry because he showed them scant respect,
and because he seemed to encourage anti-clerical sentiment. Specifically, he
clashed with the Pharisees, the most powerful contemporary sect in Judea.
If we were to look for a modern equivalent we might liken them to an
extremist Israeli group led by some of the best academics from the Hebrew
University. They were pious, puritanical, nationalistic and devoted to
personal holiness in themselves and others. They had striven to preserve the
purity of the faith at the time of the Maccabean revolt and proved with the
blood of martyrs their commitment to the faith once given to the patriarchs.
They were also intellectually respectable, numbering in their ranks scholars
of the stature of Gamaliel, Josephus and Saul of Tarsus. It must, therefore,
have been quite shocking to many of Jesus's hearers when he castigated
these pillars of the establishment as hypocrites, whited sepulchres and blind
guides, leading others along their own path to hell. Here was language as
extreme as any which passed between Reformation protagonists.

The central issue on which Christ and the Pharisees met head on was
the proper attitude towards the law, the source of all Jewish religious
authority. Jesus claimed that his enemies had added a vast corpus of oral
tradition to the Torah: they were so committed to pernickety details that they
had lost sight of the God of justice and mercy who had instigated the law;
finally, that very preoccupation with unattainable moral perfection had led
them into sophistry. Some Pharisees were challenged by such criticism (we
read of one who sought a secret, nocturnal interview with Jesus) but the
stock reaction was that of all establishments. When they could no longer
ignore him they ridiculed him, tried to undermine his popularity, engaged
him in public disputation and finally enlisted the aid of mob violence and
the secular arm.

Jesus's message in part echoed the ancient prophetic call to inwardness – 'Rend your heart and not your garments and return to the Lord your God'. It was a demand that believers should ascend above ceremonies and moral strictures and go for the greater spiritual realities towards which they point. His enemies could not argue with this and the gospels provide several instances of doctors of the law being outfaced by the carpenter's son from Nazareth. Theoretically they were in agreement with what he said. Practically they had become slaves to their own system: trapped in a symbiotic relationship in which they upheld tradition and tradition validated their authority. What was true of first-century Judaism has been true of all major world religions and of all the sects and churches into which those religions have become subdivided: they get incapacitated by sclerotic clericalism.

The dilemma, of course, is that institutions have to exist. Truth has to be protected. The life of the worshipping and witnessing community has to be regulated. Links have to be forged with secular authorities. Someone has to negotiate with them. Since this dilemma is persistent and inescapable we would expect it to form part of the Reformation debate. The nature, function and justification of ecclesiastical authority were among the more hotly contested issues of the sixteenth and seventeenth centuries. Ecclesiology was at the heart of the Reformation.

THE AUTHORITY TEST

Some time in the early 1980s there was a minor split in the British Restorationist or New Church movement. One of the 'apostles' summoned the leaders of a Surrey congregation under his 'guidance'. He instructed them to sever relationships with other New Church figureheads and physically move to a new location over a hundred miles away. Several families sold up their homes in obedience to the man God had placed in authority over them, suffering various degrees of hardship in the process. A time of tension, discord and mutual recrimination followed and eventually the fellowship disintegrated. Some of its members did not join another church of any denomination.

That is a relatively mild example of a pattern we are all familiar with in the life of modern extremist sects. More disturbing are stories of (usually young) people drawn into fervent religious groups whose leaders insist on their cutting family ties, surrendering their money and their independence and following slavishly the teaching and the instructions of their superiors. Occasionally, religious authoritarianism leads to even greater tragedies when bands of disciples follow their leaders into the wilderness with disastrous results. Christianity has never lacked the false messiahs prophesied by Jesus.

Even within the undemanding atmosphere of an English parish church, clergy have been known to make remarkable claims to spiritual authority and status. Some years ago a new vicar of Anglo-Catholic persuasion arrived in an East Anglian parish not used to this type of ministry. He had been in place for a week or so when one of the lay readers came to call on him. He brought a list of the church Bible study groups currently meeting and expressed the hope that 'Father Smith' would find time to visit them and familiarize himself with what they were doing. The elderly cleric's face darkened; his frame shook; he crumpled the piece of paper in a tightly clenched fist. 'Bible study?' he roared. 'Bible study? You don't need the Bible. You've got me!'

Problems of authority and structure in all churches are bound together. And in all churches the prevailing hierarchies look for their justification to the founding documents of the New Testament. Unfortunately, those documents are inadequate to bear such a heavy burden. They provide no blueprints for ecclesiastical organization and the principles they enunciate for the conduct of Church life are inevitably coloured by the cultures in which they were written and the attitudes of Christians living in daily expectation of the parousia.

According to the gospel records, the founder of Christianity left a group of eleven close friends (made up to twelve again after the traitor, Judas, had been replaced) who were entrusted with the mind-boggling task, 'Go and make disciples of all nations'. The apostles had an essentially missionary function. They were authorized to preach, teach, heal, forgive sins, cast out demons and baptize. Jesus had very little to say to them about their status and authority within that Church that would come into being as a result of their evangelism. What he *did* make clear was that the leaders of his movement would be characterized by service and not by the exercise of power: 'The kings of the Gentiles lord it over them; and those who exercise authority over them call themselves benefactors. But you are not to be like that. Instead, the greatest among you should be like the youngest, and the one who rules like the one who serves.'

But there were other occasions on which Jesus was more specific. When Peter became the first of the disciples to grasp and openly acknowledge that Jesus was Messiah, Christ responded:

> Good for you, Simon son of John! . . . For this truth . . . was given directly to you by my Father in heaven. And so I tell you, Peter, you are a rock, and on this rock foundation I will build my church, and not even death will be able to overcome it. I will give you the keys of the Kingdom of heaven; what you prohibit on earth will be prohibited in heaven, and what you permit on earth will be permitted in heaven.

And, according to John's version of the commissioning of the apostles, the risen Christ 'breathed' on some of his disciples (The number is not specified but Thomas was certainly absent) and said, 'Receive the Holy Spirit. If you forgive people's sins, they are forgiven; if you do not forgive them, they are not forgiven.'

So much is clear. What is not clear and what has been argued over for centuries is the application of such words. Does the authority Christ gives reside in the message and its faithful proclamation or in the apostles themselves? And who are the heirs of the apostles – the entire body of believers or a succession of leaders descended directly from the twelve? Does the message authenticate the ministry or vice-versa? The scattered churches of the New Testament provide no clear-cut pattern of authority. In the early days they depended for their sustenance on itinerant apostles and prophets and on local leaders appointed by them. The New Testament epistles and the small corpus of apocryphal writing are all that survive of what must have been an extensive correspondence by which teachers conveyed instruction on doctrine and conduct and by which Christian communities maintained contact with one another. With the passage of time the balance of authority shifted to the local *episcopoi* and *presbyteroi*. Each church or group of churches developed its own character – a process which can be discerned within the New Testament writings.

If we look to Paul's letter for some kind of authority model we find that he rested his own – often questioned – position on his divine call and the authenticity of his message. He supported his claims by appealing to his conduct (especially his sufferings). His summons to apostleship had about it, as he confessed, something of the appearance of an 'abnormal birth', as he was not one of the twelve and, indeed, had previously been a persecutor of the Christian community. Yet in the opening words of all but four of the thirteen surviving letters which bear his name, the writer insisted on Paul's divine commission. The epistle to the Galatians expresses this the most forcefully: 'From Paul, whose call to be an apostle did not come from man, but from Jesus Christ and God the Father, who raised him from death'. But he knew that it was not enough simply to make such an assertion. Believers, rightly require some evidence before submitting themselves to the authority of any human being. What Paul urged in validating his claim to be an apostle was his message and the quality of his life. And when he was obliged to defend his authority against critics in Corinth he clearly found himself in a dilemma: how can a Christian leader stick up for himself against rival teachers while, at the same time, maintaining that humility which Jesus enjoined on the twelve? Paul writes about his knowledge, his visions, his sufferings, his love for the brotherhood, but on none of these does he rest his authority. And he concludes: 'I will not boast, because I do not want anyone to have a higher opinion of me than he has as a result of what he has seen me do and heard me say'. He is less hesitant about condemning personality cults, false teachers and authoritarianism: 'You tolerate anyone who orders you about or takes advantage of you or traps you or looks down on you or slaps you in the face.'

All the New Testament writers used the same threefold test for recognizing legitimate leaders – call, message and conduct – and they urged believers to discern carefully those to whom they gave allegiance. Vocation, though largely subjective, could be tested: did the claimant live in the Spirit? Orthodox teaching was to be measured against the oral tradition and, increasingly, against the 'scriptures'. As for conduct – in many cases the most obvious touchstone – this involved, not just a high standard of personal morality, but also genuine love of the brotherhood. Anyone aspiring to oversight *(episcope)* in the Church should be motivated, not by ambition, pride or the love of power, but by a desire to serve. So, while Christians were called upon to submit themselves to those set in authority over them, they were also to use inspired intelligence in distinguishing between true and false shepherds.

The early scattered Christian communities were, thus, neither autocracies nor democracies. They combined elements of both, and each developed its own way of balancing the *exousia* (power, authority, rights) of leadership and the demands of ordinary believers. Since the Church's true Head would soon be returning to earth to take up his rightful rule, there was no need to develop elaborate hierarchies or an intricate theology of ministry. This had an inevitable influence upon what Christians actually believed and what marked them out as distinct from their Jewish and pagan contemporaries. As Professor Frend has pointed out, 'Wherever one looks, whether Asia, Syria, or Rome, one finds differing and indeed contrasting interpretations of the faith among those who were accepted as members of the Christian community.' This state of affairs persisted until well into the second century and no-one seems seriously to have questioned it.

As the Church defined heresy, it also established rules concerning order, authority and discipline. Regional and ecumenical councils frequently turned on the legitimacy of certain bishops. Disputants made furious attacks on their opponents; questioning their vocation, refuting their teaching and exposing their scandalous conduct - in order words, applying the tests advocated by the New Testament. So, for example, when Hippolytus denounced the heresies of Callistus I he did not confine himself to issues of doctrinal error. According to Hippolytus, Callistus was an imposter because, among other things, he used lax discipline to attract a personal following, 'he invented the device of conniving with men as to their pleasures, saying that sins were forgiven to everyone by himself.' According to Hippolytus (whose accusations need not be taken at face value), Callistus was permanently compromised by his earlier scandalous history. As a young slave he had embezzled money from his master and from members of the church in Rome. He ran away, was captured and punished. Unchastened, he stirred up a disturbance in the Jewish community, for which he served a term in the Sardinian mines.

However much truth there may have been in these allegations, it was

Callistus who had *exousia* on his side. It was Hippolytus who was the schismatic and it was Hippolytus who eventually had to make his peace with his rival's successor at Rome. The realities of power were asserting themselves. Faith and order were coming to be dominated by the leading bishoprics – Rome, Carthage, Ephesus, Alexandria and (to a lesser extent) Antioch. By the early fourth century it was commonly held that there was one, divinely appointed system for the governance of the whole Church. Jerome could appeal to Scripture and tradition in defence of this system against irregularities which had occurred at Rome:

> I hear that a certain person has broken out into so great madness as to place deacons before presbyters, that is, bishops . . . What happens to the server of tables and widows that he sets himself up arrogantly over those at whose prayers the body and blood of Christ are made? Do you ask for authority? Listen to the proof . . . that afterwards one was chosen to preside over the rest: this was done as a remedy for schism, and to prevent one individual from rending the Church of Christ by drawing it to himself. For even at Alexandria, from the time of Mark the Evangelist to the episcopates of Heraclas and Dionysius, the presbyters used always to appoint as bishop one chosen out of their number . . .
>
> The church of the city of Rome is not to be thought one church, and that of the whole world another. Gaul and Britain, and Africa and Persia, and the East and India, and all foreign nations worship one Christ, and observe one rule of truth.

THE CRITIQUE OF PRIESTHOOD

Over the ensuing millennium, which witnessed the development of the extensive ecclesiastical machinery of the Western Church, every reform movement and most heresies harked back to the purity and ardour of the apostolic age. The monastic life was seen as that which most closely resembled the holy communality described in the book of Acts.

> At Jerusalem the whole multitude of believers was of a kind which it is now difficult to find among the few who are in monasteries. But when by the preaching of the apostles the necks of all the peoples were subjugated to the yoke of the Lord, and the number of believers was infinite, and when the holy apostles had departed from the world in the glory of martyrdom, that holy fellowship and institution of the apostles began little by little to grow lukewarm. Seeing this, those whose minds were fervent in the doctrine which they had received from the apostles separated themselves and began to live together. They were called in

> Greek cenobites, that is 'Living communally'. From that monasteries took
> their origin.

So wrote the eleventh-century Bishop Pons of Marseille. Every revival of the religious life was, in part, an attempt to find a framework which would encourage and facilitate the recreation of New Testament Church life. Orthodox religious and heterodox holy men shared the same project. Among the Cathars the rigid distinction between the 'perfect' and ordinary believers seems to have been a mirror image of the orthodox differentiation between priesthood and laity, with the vital exception that the perfect were committed to a life of rigid austerity.

There were always those who distanced themselves from the sacred routine of parish life, acting on the conviction that the sinfulness of clergy invalidated the sacraments they administered. It is easy to understand the irritation of parishioners with priests who, in effect, told them 'do as I say, not as I do'. The rank and file of the Church continued to exercise the right enunciated in the gospels and epistles to assess the worthiness of their leaders. Chaucer's ideal parson emerged from his scrutiny with top marks because

> Cristes lore, and his apostles twelve
> He taughte, but first he folwed it him-selve

and, if the poet is to be believed, this made 'the goodman of religion' a rare bird indeed. It should scarcely need re-emphasizing at this point that denunciation of unworthy priests was not confined to those teetering on the edge of and falling into heresy. Let the eleventh-century reformist St Peter Damian prove the point:

> Why, o priest, when you should offer yourself sacred, that is as a sacrifice, to God, do you not first refuse to sacrifice yourself as a victim to an evil spirit? For when you fornicate you cut yourself off from Christ's members . . . What part . . . have you in the body of Christ, who by luxuriating in seductive flesh have made yourself a member of Antichrist?

No outraged Hussite or Lutheran could have made the point more forcibly.

The mainstream Protestant reformers tried to steer between the Catholic Scylla and the Anabaptist Charybdis. Both represented heinous error: the one in demanding submission to a hierarchy which had fallen into doctrinal falsehood and moral torpor; the other by challenging all authority, spiritual and temporal, save that exercised by its own appointed leaders. A common point of agreement was that, for the good of the Christian community, all corrupt clergy should be sacked. This, of course, had implications for the doctrine of priesthood and for relations between civil and ecclesiastical authorities (to both of which we shall return). But it had even more profound implications: that, either in the quest for a more scriptural pattern, or in response to purely current needs, the rule of bishops, priests and deacons, which had obtained since the age of the Fathers, could be set aside. Ecclesiastical polity was of the *bene esse* of the Church but not of its *esse*.

Luther's attitude can be seen in a set of instructions Melanchthon devised in 1525 for a programme of parish visitations and which carried a preface by his superior.

> We should have liked to erect again the genuine office of bishop and visitor, which is greatly needed. But as none of us was called, or had a clear commission thereto, and St Peter will have nothing done among Christians unless it be certain it is God's work, there was no one to undertake it rather than another. And so . . . we humbly and earnestly begged the serene, high-born, Prince John, Duke of Saxony, etc., our most gracious lord, ordained of God to be our country's prince and our earthly ruler, that . . . for the sake of God, the good of the gospel, and the benefit and salvation of the poor Christians in his dominions, he would graciously summon and appoint certain qualified persons to this office . . .

The visitations resulted in firm action (including expulsion) being taken against clergy deemed guilty of popish error, moral lapse, indolence or financial irregularity. Luther was exercised about discipline, sound doctrine and the maintenance of an effective ministry of word and sacrament. He was less concerned to establish a rigid pattern of church order. What emerged in the countries which 'went Lutheran' was the concept of the territorial church. Initially episcopacy was maintained, though only in Sweden was any importance attached to an apostolic succession linking the new order to the pre-Reformation heritage. When Lutheranism spread to America and other lands afar synodical structures and greater congregational autonomy became common features of church life. This variety of forms was not dissimilar to that pertaining among the scattered assemblies of the sub-apostolic age.

Those who regard Jean Calvin as an intellectual and spiritual superman, and also those who consider that he was a narrow and intolerant legalist, have commonly projected the image of the reformer as a systematic thinker who had the entire *schema* of Christian faith and order clearly thought out and rigidly expressed in his written works. In fact, Calvin's thought was in a process of continual development to the very end of his life. The fire in which he forged his theology was always being replenished by the coals of conflict – his own wrestling with the word of God and his clashes with opponents within and without Geneva. The *Ordonnances* (Calvin's regulations for the godly commonwealth of Geneva) like the *Institutes* went through several editions. It is important to grasp this when we come to consider 'Calvinist polity'.

'All we have attempted has been to renew the ancient face of the Church.' So Calvin explained the Genevan reform to Cardinal Sadoleto. What he meant, with reference to Church order, was that he had sought to apply to a sixteenth-century Swiss canton the principles contained in Scripture as understood by the Fathers (and he drew primarily on the works of Chrysostom, Cyprian and Augustine). What he discerned in the ancient writings was an insistence on certain *functions* essential for the good of the Church and not specific *offices* without which the Church could not exist. He recognized that the New Testament was very fluid in the language it used about these functions. For example, in Acts 6 certain 'deacons' were set apart for the practical tasks of day-to-day administration. Yet, in various epistles Paul referred to himself and some of his colleagues as *diakonoi* of the gospel. Calvin concluded that 'bishop', 'presbyter' and 'minister' were interchangeable terms. Thus it matters not what Church officers are called as long as they are fulfilling the correct functions. From his correspondence it is clear that he was no opponent of episcopacy *per se*. What mattered was that bishops did their job properly.

The functions Calvin identified were teaching, ministry of word and sacrament, pastoral oversight and administration. Translating this into a system for Geneva led not to a threefold, but a fourfold order:

> There are four orders that our Lord instituted for the government of his Church: first the pastors, then the teachers, after them the elders and fourthly deacons. Therefore if we would have the Church well ordered and maintain it in its entirety we must observe that form of rule.

The disciplinary teeth of Calvin's system were provided by the godly magistracy. Just as the pope called on kings and emperors to undergird the spiritual endeavours of Christendom and Luther looked to German princes to enforce his reforms, so Calvin regarded the civil power as an essential ingredient in his system. This was the sandbank upon which most claims to the rediscovery of New Testament Church life ran aground. Only radical sects which dissociated themselves from the political structures and groups which remained persecuted minorities could claim to have much in common with the vulnerable Christian communities of the first century. The major Protestant leaders accepted the political realities of their day. Having jettisoned the temporal authority of the Church, they needed the support of the secular arm.

That is why Calvin made no claim that the Genevan system was *the* system by which any reformed church must be governed. What he did believe was that the *schema* laid down in the *Ordonnances* was in accord with Scripture and that it would safeguard the two essentials of doctrinal purity and holy living. Doctors, like himself, were there to ensure that, both in major doctrine and day-to-day disputes, the assemblies were kept on the biblical straight and narrow. Pastors or presbyters were to administer word and sacrament – and for Calvin both were important. So far from subordinating the Lord's Supper to preaching, he regarded it as the central feature of the Church's life and wanted to see it celebrated every week, but in this the Genevans would not follow him. The consistory of elders existed not just to admonish and punish doctrinal and moral lapse. It exercised a much more positive support role for the Christian community – helping members to sort out personal, family and neighbourhood problems, to settle disputes and generally to live in brotherhood. The diaconate was a biblical institution Calvin claimed to have rescued from more than a millennium of misuse. It had become a minor order with no clearly defined function save that of being a stepping stone to the priesthood. In Geneva the deacons were entrusted with the Church's works of compassion – distribution of alms, sick-visiting, comforting and counselling the distressed. Apart from the presbyterate Calvin envisaged that all other orders could, and perhaps should, be made up of laymen. Clergy derived their authority from their call by God and the people and could exercise it only in the congregation to which they were appointed. However, the laity, once having endorsed their presbyters' elections, were to regard them as 'messengers and ambassadors of God, who must be heard as we would hear God himself, and . . . to hold their ministry to be a commission from God necessary to the Church.'

THE UNCOMFORTABLE FENCE

It has often been observed that the English Church which emerged from the Reformation had a Catholic hierarchy and a Calvinist theology – an uncomfortable marriage. For the first generation of reformers church order was not a burning issue. The preface to the Edwardine ordinal affirmed simply, 'It is evident unto all men, diligently reading holy Scripture and ancient authors that from the Apostles' time there have been these orders of ministers in Christ's Church: bishops, priests and deacons.' Though in some of Cranmer's writings he agreed with his continental counterparts that in the New Testament *episcopoi* and *presbyteroi* are synonymous terms, he was content to abolish the minor orders, reject the sacramental nature of ordination and sanction clerical marriage, while otherwise leaving the governance of the church unchanged. The Henrician and Edwardine divines developed no detailed theology of Church order. They were concerned about practicalities and they shared with Lutheran leaders a disinclination for (perhaps a mistrust of) systematic theology. They did not regard episcopacy as the only valid framework for the maintenance of true doctrine and proper authority. Each territorial Church was free to develop its own system, as long as that system was in accord with Scripture. They debated on a basis of happy equality with the leaders of other reformed Churches. While affirming their adherence to the faith passed down from the apostles they set no great store by a physical succession from the episcopate of the undivided Church. Cranmer stated quite unequivocally that where a reformed ministry did not exist it was the right or duty of the lay authorities to preach the Gospel and even to ordain pastors. The Thirty-Nine Articles were clear that any regional church had the freedom to change rites and ceremonies from time to time. By implication, at least, the same freedom pertained in matters of ecclesiastical polity.

This theological pragmatism left the door open for dispute between partisans of different kinds of Church order. 'Whether boys of sixteen years of age might put on their hats in the church': such was an agenda item at one of the monthly meetings held by ministers in the tranquil valley of the Stour (later to be made famous by the brush of John Constable). The Dedham Conference met between 1582 and 1589. It was one of many *ad hoc* presbyterian gatherings which existed in various parts of the country and exercised real authority independently and often in defiance of the ecclesiastical structures. It consisted of between thirteen and twenty earnest ministers (parish clergy, tutors maintained by Protestant gentry and lecturers appointed by town corporations) intent upon the establishment of truth and holiness in their locality. They believed, with some justification, that the existing system of spiritual husbandry did not plough deeply enough into the social soil. Several attempts to inaugurate further reform by statute had attracted the royal veto. Marian clerics continued to hold office at all levels of the church. Bishops, even 'sound' industrious bishops, were too far removed from parish life to exercise really effective discipline.

The Dedham Conference was much more than a fraternal assembly where clergy met for Bible study, exhortation and sharing of problems. It campaigned against the traditional Manningtree morality plays and against clothiers who operated their dyeworks on Sundays. It used its influence to achieve the appointment of approved men to vacant livings. More than that, it exerted strong discipline over its members and, through them, over the churches which some of them served. The dictates of the conference covered practical pastoral matters, the 'correction' of parishioners guilty of moral lapse, and major doctrinal issues. So, for example, it issued a new catechism, ordered certain parts of the Prayer Book services to be omitted, decided the issue of baptism of bastard children and chastised members guilty of preaching substandard sermons. Those who failed to carry out the injunctions of the conference were expelled or suspended.

The Dedham Conference was a power throughout the vale – an institution within an institution. It was linked to similar organizations in other parts of the country and to 'Puritan HQ' in London, where most of the reformist leaders were active. Puritans (clergy and lay) constituted another

6.1 Hogart satirized Sermon-centred worship in which the proceedings were conducted from two- or three-decker pulpits.

of those holiness networks, of which we have already noted many examples in pre- and post-Reformation Europe which worked inside or outside the structures of the Church to do what the Church (in the opinion of members) was failing to do. But eager reformists were as fallible as the 'papistical' clergy they opposed. The Dedham Conference collapsed in scandal, doubt-less much to the delight of its enemies. In 1589 Richard Parker, Vicar of Dedham, was accused of adultery with the wife of a parishioner and the following year the consistory court ordered him to resign his living.

Creeping institutionalism turned the presbyterian wing of this puritan movement into a political pressure group and, ultimately, into a denomi-nation. Many of the second generation of Calvinists had moved away from the position of their founder. In France, the Low Countries, England and Scotland they were striving for a system of government derived from the Genevan model; a system for which they claimed divine approval; a system which involved the overthrow of episcopacy – by force of arms if necessary. Like most of the so-called 'religious' or 'politico-religious' conflicts of the seventeenth century, the English Civil War was not about central Christian doctrine. It was about authority and power and the institutions through which they were exercised. The medieval, hierarchical model of top-down authority was challenged by the presbyterian bottom-up concept of *exousia* given to the people of God and exercised by those they elected to positions of leadership.

Questions of order became important again in the second half of the nineteenth century when a new reforming party emerged in Britain which asserted that the Church of England was not really Protestant at all but part of the Catholic Church. It shared in the gifts of priesthood and episcopal order with the larger Roman and Orthodox communions. It was doctrinally at one with Rome from which it was distinguished only by its rejection of certain papal claims. This led to an often bitter, ongoing debate on the nature of Anglicanism (a word first coined in 1846). There were several reasons why this issue arose at this particular time. The Anglican church, thanks to colonial expansion, was becoming a worldwide communion. The com-petition for souls in 'heathen lands afar' led to many conflicts between Church of England and Roman Catholic missionaries. The Revolutionary and Napoleonic wars had effectively signalled the end of the papacy as a temporal power and the political authority of the Vatican rapidly declined in the ensuing half century. At home, Catholic emancipation in 1829 had accorded a new respectability to what had been a persecuted minority community for two hundred and seventy years. Given all these changes it was almost inevitable that the next spiritual revolt against the institution should take the form of an assertion of pre-Reformation traditions.

One modern historian of the movement subtitled his book, 'A study in religious ambiguity'. Many Anglo-Catholic clergy found their position uncomfortable even during the interwar years when their party was a powerful force within Anglicanism. While regarding themselves as the 'real' Anglicans they were involved in an unremitting war within their Church. They were reformers in the mould of their sixteenth-century ancestors, fighting against apathy, declining moral standards and heresy (largely represented in the nineteenth century by theological liberalism). At the same time they were at odds with the ways the Anglican reformers had dealt with their problems – breaking away from Rome, abolishing the mass and the sacerdotal priesthood, minimizing ritual, outlawing Marian devotion, invocation of saints and prayers for the dead. They could not subscribe without reservations to the Thirty-Nine Articles. They found obedience difficult to bishops not of their own persuasion. They resented 'interference' by the laity. Like the Elizabethan puritans, they could be seen as an institution within an institution, a network, a pressure group seeking to nudge *ecclesia Anglicana* across the Channel, not to Geneva, but Rome. Their determination to identify themselves with historic Catholicity suffered a major setback in 1896 when Leo XIII (ironically one of the more ecumenically-minded popes) declared that Anglican orders were invalid and that the English episcopate did not share in the apostolic succession.

Over the years there was a regular exodus to Rome of Anglicans, for whom the tensions had become intolerable. Some would eventually return when they discovered that the ethos of their adopted Church was very different from what they had supposed it would be. For Anglo-Catholics remaining the situation grew progressively worse. True to its tradition of governing its own affairs in its own way the Anglican communion introduced various changes more or less inimical to traditionalists. Synodical government gave the laity a greater say in the Church's life. Ecumenical overtures to other Protestant denominations called in question the Catholic doctrine of the Church. The adoption of new liturgies did not find universal favour within High Church ranks. More and more liberal and evangelical bishops were appointed to the bench. At the same time the Anglo-Catholic position was threatened by one of its major successes. As Holy Communion became the centre point of Sunday worship in most parishes the party lost one of its distinguishing marks. After Vatican II Anglo-Catholics looked to Rome with growing uncertainty. The 'mother church' seemed to be moving rapidly away from its old, unassailable doctrinal and liturgical heights. An English parish priest might be celebrating in his traditional eastward-facing position at mass when, down the road, his Roman counterpart was facing west.

The issue of women priests provided the Anglo-Catholic minority with a platform for its swan song. After the first ordination of a woman in 1944, province after province of the Anglican communion faced the issue and accepted the principle. In 1994 the first women priests were ordained in England after a quarter of a century of agonizing disputation. During the course of the debate Anglo-Catholic thinkers desperately produced new justifications for their doctrines of the Church and the priesthood. They argued against the proposed innovation on pastoral and ecumenical grounds. But the central point at issue was whether or not the Anglican Church or parts of it had the authority to decide on something which, to Catholic thinking, profoundly affected faith and order without the agreement of the 'other two' branches of the Catholic Church.

As reform movements make the – seemingly inevitable – transition from progressiveness to reaction, so the negative aspects of their message come to dominate the positive ones. Yesterday's standard-bearer of a triumphant, forward-marching faith is replaced by today's waver of placards on which the word 'No' appears in heavy black. Luther offered the open Bible. Calvin presented the vision of a godly commonwealth. Wesley proclaimed assurance reinforced by stirring hymnody. The Tractarians gave men colourful worship and challenged the secular state. Those who saw themselves as maintaining these noble traditions all too often became uncreative Bedeveres clinging to the forms and thought patterns of the 'true old times' instead of facing the challenge of 'new men, strange faces, other minds'.

RIVAL KINGDOMS

Every year on the Sunday of Pentecost between 1744 and 1748, Patriarch Païsios of Constantinople exchanged ominous oaths with his metropolitans in the church of St George in Istanbul. They swore on the gospels that they would not overthrow him; he responded that he would not persecute them. On leaving the church, the bishops 'gobbled up their oaths like donkeys gobbling up cabbages.' This sinister and insincere compact, among brethren who should have been united by love and common purpose, can be understood, and perhaps pardoned, against the background of the history of a church in captivity to a hostile state. Since the late middle ages, most of the Greek-speaking Orthodox world had been ruled by Turkish masters. Patriarchs were appointed by sultans; the supreme ordinary of the Church was a Muslim. Païsios was enjoying or enduring his fourth patriarchate – a typical experience of the whirligig of office in which church leaders whizzed at speed, flung off and reinstated with dizzying frequency by a state which liked to keep Christians spinning. Of 159 patriarchs who owed their position to the Turks, only twenty-one died peacefully in office. The revolutions of leadership kept the Church weak, divided and submissive. At every installation of a new bishop, secular approval had to be bought with tribute; every appointee had to be eased into office with bribes. The sultans mulcted the system with glee. For most of the seventeenth century, patriarchs lasted in office for an average of less than eighteen months each. While sister-churches further west grew rich and recovered from the periodic bouts of confiscatory secularism which afflict all Christian societies, the Orthodox church slipped into a condition of permanent indebtedness to the state, from which it was liberated only by the decline and fall of the Turkish empire.

Yet by the standards of some other Babylons, Ottoman rule was not particularly onerous. A Western eye, like that of Sir Paul Rycaut in the seventeenth century, might weep at the evidence of oppression: the churches seemed to shrink into the ground, 'having their roofs almost levelled with the superficies of the earth, lest the most ordinary exsurgency of structure should be accused for triumph of religion.' Worship seemed to cower in the darkness, 'the Mysteries of the Altar conceal'd in secret and dark places.' Divided and demoralized, Christians seemed submissive to the point of self-sacrifice, rending – in Rycaut's image – their bowels to 'give them for food to Vultures and Ravens, and to the wild and fierce Creatures of the World.' The oppression, however, was hardly ever bloody; Christians bore humdrum deprivations – fiscal exactions and legal disabilities – but were denied the satisfaction of martyrdom.

There is a threshold on the path of persecution, up to which churches thrive. The blood of martyrs, in unswamping quantities, fertilizes the mission field. The church in its infancy was suckled by wolves – glamorized and glorified by Roman and Jewish persecutors. Over the centuries since the Reformation, the English Catholic community has derived great strength of mind and sense of purpose from making its pilgrimage inside a hostile band; the persecution has been bad enough to enhance Catholic identity but not bad enough to imperil its survival. The seven centuries of Waldensian history in the Alps show how sects can survive massacres, provided they are infrequent enough.

Ottoman persecution of the Greek Church fell well short of the critical threshold. The credal map of modern Europe shows only small and isolated pools of converts to Islam, left in Bosnia and Albania by the ebb of the Turkish tide. The church under Turkish rule got an evil reputation for spirituality sloughed, evangelism arrested and revenues reduced. State hostility bears some of the blame: schools were stifled, presses suppressed, wealth appropriated; but in some ways the church was more thoroughly corrupted by the favours of the State than bludgeoned by its blows. In return for the Christians' taxes and obedience, the sultans devolved to the patriarchs secular jurisdiction over their flock. The Greek church in the Turkish empire was a state-within-the-state and the patriarchs wielded devolved power over a huge underclass, who, as far as their disputes with each other were concerned, were exempted from Muslim justice.

Except, perhaps, within the small compass of a prince-bishop with a city-see, the modern history of Christendom suggests that Christian theocracy does not work well. When the Roman Empire dissolved, holy men replaced the vanishing institutions of the State as sources of jurisdiction; bishops could step in to replace organs of broken-down administration. In the new territorial states that replaced Rome in the West, or the kingdoms founded in imitation of them in the middle ages beyond the former Roman frontiers, clerical influence was a vital civilizing force and the clergy a necessary source of organizing manpower. But secular roles, once espoused, tend to take over. It is a law of prelatical economy that bad demons drive out good spirits. Priesthood is profaned by politics.

The vast secular patrimony the popes acquired was useful in preserving their independence in the middle ages; but its defence was at best a distraction and at worst a scandal. Remunerative positions in the Church became rewards for service to the State. Cardinal Wolsey confessed at the approach of death that he had served his king better than God; Cardinal Richelieu frankly saw ecclesiastical responsibilities as salaried sinecures. To purge the Church of this sort of worldliness was part of the aim of every movement of reform. Yet no proposed solution met the case. The Gregorian reformers, in the late eleventh century, expelled lay power from the Church without withdrawing clerical personnel from the service of the State: this was like driving money-lenders from the temple while putting priests into the market-place. Innocent III in the early thirteenth century advocated the unreserved submission of secular authority to the Church: this was a noble ideal, by which, in practice, only churchmen of impossible sanctity could be uncorrupted. St Francis advocated forfeiture of all the temporalities of the Church and resumption of apostolic poverty: this holy aim got smothered by the lavish endowments with which it was rewarded. Most Protestant reformers, including Luther, followed earlier theorists, Catholic and heretical, by opting to abdicate power over the Church to secular rulers: this helped to create state-churches staffed by vicars of Bray, whose dependence on secular patronage was a poor guarantee of vocation. Some radical Protestants installed godly tyrannies where they could: in some German, Swiss and Dutch towns these could develop into benevolent plutocracies; but they were easily warped into monstrous deformities: Puritan commonwealths of fear, like those imagined in *The Scarlet Letter,* or realized in practice in seventeenth-century North America; or despotisms of excess, like the antinomian kingdom Jan of Leyden set up in Münster in 1525, where women were enslaved and men massacred at the whim of a messianic megalomaniac.

Today, priests still make useful forays into the arena of secular politics. Under some dictatorships, the Church is the most effective organizer of dissent. It can be helpful to have a Makarios or an Aristide at hand to be a head of State. The pope can be an international mediator where others fail. In some democracies, priests are given status as popular spokesmen by the constitution; in the United Kingdom, some bishops are ex officio members of the legislature. These privileges help to ensure that statesmen feel the prick of conscience as well as the prod of the pitchfork. But they are the relics of largely vanished systems. Church and State have been separated, not by the efforts of reformers but by the grinding structures of slow, impersonal change. Rich societies can afford to split the functions of priest and politician because they can pay specialists in both. Economic growth has squeezed churchmen out of power. Clergies make unappealing élites in societies composed of religious minorities or irreligious majorities. Secularization and multi-culturalism have undermined state-churches. The Church of England is, as ever, an engaging anomaly in this world. In a land which abhors revolutions, it is hard to imagine that it will be turned out of its established status involuntarily; but its clergy have lost or are losing the will to minister to the phantom congregations, indifferent or hostile, who insult or evade the vicar on the doorstep. If they were allowed to take the property of the state-church with them, most of them would probably be happy to join the rest of modern Christendom in secession or extrusion from the State.

DRIVER AND PASSENGERS

The General Synod of the Church of England is not a demonstrative body. Displays of spontaneous emotion are, on the whole, frowned on. What was it, then, that drew a warm buzz of approval and a chorus of 'hear, hears' in response to an archiepiscopal speech in February 1989?

> . . . if the parochial principle is at root not a statement about boundaries and residential neighbourhoods, and instead about God's reign over the whole of society, we ought not to let it go merely because it is facing challenges from the way society is developing. One solution to maintain the parochial principle is thought to be or to lie in shared ministry. I have often sat and nodded in approval. But it may have the opposite effect to that intended.
>
> The mood of 'let's pile in and share the poor vicar's over-burdened ministry' has not only obscured his role, but often withdrawn the laity from their proper sphere of witness and influence. There is a danger that current talk about shared ministry, if it does not lead to the extension of ministry, can lead to the dissipation of ministry.

The answer is that Archbishop Runcie was telling a substantial section of his audience what they wanted to hear. The clerical manpower crisis of the late twentieth century has forced all Christian denominations to re-examine what they mean by ministry and to look afresh at the traditional roles of clergy and laity. In the Seventies and Eighties 'shared ministry' were buzz words increasingly assumed to express a vital new truth for a Church seeking, not only to find answers to its own internal problems, but also to come to terms with democratized, deregulated Western society. There were many who found the implied challenges to traditional assumptions too disturbing. It was to appeal to this constituency within his own Church that Runcie performed his public back-pedalling.

Conservatives saw in the rapidly shifting emphases a conspiracy of radicals, trendies and anti-clericalists. They were wrong. The ploughshare of new thinking was cutting much deeper into the tilth of traditional doctrine. In 1982 the Faith and Order Commission of the World Council of Churches produced a seminal report, *Baptism, Eucharist and Ministry*. Commonly known as the 'Lima Statement', it was the work of over a hundred theologians from every major denomination from the Orthodox and Roman Catholic to the Pentecostal Churches. This is part of what the report had to say about the 'Calling of the whole people of God':

> The Holy Spirit bestows on the community diverse and complementary gifts. These are for the common good of the whole people and are manifested in acts of service within the community and to the world. They may be gifts of communicating the Gospel in word and deed, gifts of healing, gifts of praying, gifts of teaching and learning, gifts of serving, gifts of guiding and following, gifts of inspiration and vision. All members are called to discover, with the help of the community, the gifts they have received and to use them for the building up of the Church and for the service of the world to which the Church is sent.

Lima was one of the major seismic vibrations that had been shaking the ecclesiological landscape since Vatican II. By 1982 it had become customary among the theological intelligentsia to think of clergy as part of the *laos*, the 'people of God', as man-managers or 'enablers' of their church membership rather than as controllers or mediators. Active ministry was a state to which baptism, not ordination, was the initiation.

This, of course, was a reflection of what was happening in Western society as a whole. Empires had crumbled. Ancient dynasties had fallen. Democracy and socialism had spread. More important, ghastly wars and economic dislocation had shaken public confidence in authority figures. 'Power to the people' was a slogan every political party had to espouse. It might have little actual meaning in the realities of government but it was an ideal that no contender for public office could afford to ignore. In Church life it could be said that, for the first time in four hundred years, the circumstances existed for Luther's doctrine of the priesthood of all believers to become a reality.

Not that Luther was a proto-democrat. When he proposed his radical understanding of priesthood in his *Open Letter to the Christian Nobility of the German Nation* (1520) it was couched not in terms of the rights and freedoms of ordinary lay folk, but rather in terms of their responsibilities and particularly of the responsibilities of temporal rulers. His rejection of the medieval notion of two swords – spiritual and temporal placed the task of regulating the material aspects of Church life in the hands of lay authorities.

6.2 Civil unrest was feared by all church leaders, Catholic and Protestant alike. The Peasants' War of 1524-5 was a double blow to Luther: it threatened to undermine his influence with German princes and it provided ammunition for his enemies. In 1525 he published a tract *Against the Murderous and Thieving Hordes of Peasants*. He stated unequivocally, 'If the peasant is in open rebellion, then he is outside the law of God'.

But there was much more than that to Luther's vision. Expounding the passage in I Peter 2 about the royal priesthood of the new Israel, he wrote

> . . . we are priests, which is a far greater thing than being Kings, for priesthood makes us worthy to stand before God and pray for others. For to stand before God's face is the prerogative of none except priests. Christ has so operated on us that we are able spiritually to act and pray on behalf of one another, just as the priest acts and prays bodily on behalf of the people.

That last clause is important. Luther had no intention of abolishing the clerical office or the hierarchy. That would have involved the disintegration of all order. He was not giving lay people the right to exercise ministerial priesthood. He was asserting that clergy exercised on behalf of the whole *laos* certain priestly functions which belonged to the whole. The well-known analogy employed to explain this was that of ten princes, joint-heirs to a kingdom, who elected one of their number to exercise sovereignty. The parish priest is a functionary, ideally elected by the local church and under the authority of the local magnate and the local bishop. If he resigned or was deposed from his office he reverted to being a peasant or farmer or burgher. He possessed no *character indelibilis* which set him apart from ordinary mortals, as Catholic tradition taught. Luther regarded it as scandalous that clergy should exercise any sanctions over the laity. The only exception he allowed was excommunication and that should be exercised with great care along lines strictly laid down in the New Testament. Luther, in effect, sought to combine the top-down and bottom-up concepts of authority. *Potestas* was a gift to God's people bestowed on all for the exercise of their earthly mission and deputed by them to chosen representatives.

Luther did not dissent from his Catholic opponents over the basic concept of social order as a gift from God. The systems and hierarchies which pertain in every Church and State should make – and, where necessary, must be reformed so as to make more clearly – what Runcie called 'a statement about God's reign over the whole of society'. This paramount concern to underpin the social status quo transmuted the priesthood of all believers into an endorsement of secular authority. In many regions, beyond removing the sacerdotal power of the clergy, it changed little. The leading local families still played a prominent part in Church life. They had their special pews, appointed the pastors and paid their stipends, maintained the fabric, commemorated their dead extravagantly in chancel monuments and exercised a listening brief over the doctrine preached from the pulpit.

This state of affairs gave rise to many bizarre anomalies. Francis Dashwood, Lord Le Despencer, was probably the most notorious English rake of the eighteenth century. His Order of St Francis of Medmenham (commonly known as the Hellfire Club) parodied Christian ceremonies in

6.3 Charles I, king and martyr. The frontispiece of *Eikon Basilike*, 1648–9, marks the summit of Erastianism, the linking of secular and religious authority.

their hedonistic revels and, many suspected, dabbled in Satanism. Yet Dashwood saw nothing at all inappropriate in building a new church at West Wycombe close by the scene of his debaucheries. According to John Wilkes, he even met with friends inside the large gilded globe which topped the edifice to partake of 'divine milk punch'. Small wonder that the satirist, Charles Churchill (another of Dashwood's drinking companions), in mocking 'Fancy' accused her of making

> . . . lordly temples rise
> Before the pious Dashwood's eyes,
> Temples which built aloft in air,
> May serve for show, if not for pray'r
>
> (The Ghost)

But St Lawrence's West Wycombe was not this 'pious' man's only contribution to English church life. He undertook, with his friend Benjamin Franklin, to rewrite the *Book of Common Prayer*. The new manual – greeted with unanimous apathy on its publication in 1773 – drastically shortened services and excised any surviving vestiges of Catholicism. Though the book made no impact in England, it did influence the framers of liturgy for the Episcopal church in America a few years later.

Was this profanation of the Church by lay power or influence, one wonders, quite what Luther had in mind? Certainly it was a state of affairs which persisted long into the present century in rural areas. It is still possible to find churches where a certain pew is unofficially reserved for the family from the 'big house' and where it is the lord or lady of the manor who shakes the hands of departing congregation, rather than the vicar. But such a watered-down priesthood of all believers did not agree with the vision of some of Luther's contemporaries. Certainly not to the man who emerges as one of the saddest figures in the Reformation story.

The Most Reverend Lord Professor, Doctor Andreas Rudolff-Bodenstein von Karlstadt, Doctor of Theology, Doctor of Canon and Secular Law, Archdeacon and Canon of All Saints Wittenberg, dressed as a peasant and insisted on being known as 'Brother Andy'. He determined to eradicate as far as possible all 'lay' and 'clerical' stereotyping and in the church he took over at Orlamünde he tried to establish a democratic form of government. Karlstadt, for all that he was ridiculed in his own time and by many later historians, was a man of intellectual and spiritual stature. His tragedy was that everything he might have been and achieved was marred by serious personality defects. He was a biblicist, anticlerical, and considerably influenced by mystics such as Tauler: it is much easier to trace a direct line from certain strains of medieval dissent to Karlstadt than to Luther. He was Brother Martin's superior in the university at Wittenberg but fell under the influence of the stronger personality. Once Karlstadt's radical momentum had been set in motion there was no stopping it. He soon moved beyond the gradualism of Luther and Melanchthon. Somewhat like Toad of Toad Hall, his irresponsible outbursts and doctrinal excesses embarrassed his friends who initially tolerated him out of affectionate loyalty but were eventually obliged to take him in hand. Again like Toad, Karlstadt refused to be restrained and went off, 'poop-pooping' his way into chaos and near-destruction.

It was actually Karlstadt who, during Luther's enforced absence from Wittenberg in 1521, inaugurated those defiant changes in church life which made clear that the Reformation was more than a clash of personalities, a dispute between theologians or a disciplinary problem caused by a troublesome monk. Karlstadt announced his intention, in contravention of an express order from the elector, of communicating the laity in both kinds at the Christmas Day mass. He was supported by many students and radical townsmen, some of whom wandered the streets in the days leading up to the festival, taunting priests and singing ribald songs. When the crucial moment arrived, a packed All Saints' church saw Dr Karlstadt climb into the pulpit in ordinary lay attire and invite all to come to the altar, whether shriven or not. Afterwards the members of the congregation were either elated or outraged to see him celebrate using a simplified liturgy without elevation, with a minimum of manual acts and omitting all reference to sacrifice. They heard him shout the consecration prayer in German. The following day Karlstadt announced his engagement to a sixteen-year-old peasant girl.

This demonstration has to be seen against the background of academic controversy aroused by Luther's early writings. The comparative status of clergy and laity had become a matter for very serious debate. The first to leap into print (in 1521) in defence of the Catholic understanding of priesthood were the humanists Thomas Murner and Hieronymus Emser. They attacked the reformer's arguments from Scripture, tradition and reason and went on to stake out the highest possible claims for the *sacerdotium*. In his reply to Luther's *Open Letter to the Christian Nobility,* Emser asserted that the humblest priest is superior to the most exalted layman and even to the heavenly powers, for it was to the clergy, and not to angels, that Christ had given the authority to bind and loose. Such an assertion may not have elicited wholehearted approval from the German aristocracy to whom it was addressed. The core of Murner's argument was more calculated to appeal to the powerful in this world. He insisted that Luther's intention in denying the distinction between clergy and laity was the breaking down of all social barriers. It was an effective debating point but, of course, quite untrue. Luther was acutely conscious of the need for temporal rulers to maintain peace and stability. There would, he acknowledged, always be distinctions of *function* in Church and State. What he rejected was any idea that God distinguished between men on the grounds of *status*. That is why Luther's exposition of the priesthood of all believers, although it fuelled all manner of egalitarian ambitions, was never intended by him as the basis for a programme of organizational reform.

Karlstadt could not accept this distinction between function and status. It seemed to him to be prevarication. If the word of God judged all men and if all men had access to the word of God then no man could base notions of superiority, authority or power on anything else. Indeed, Karlstadt went further: since a simple layman came to the Bible without any institutional baggage he was better able to apprehend its truth than any educated cleric.

> From the same blossom . . . the spider transforms what it has savoured into venom while the bee changes it into honey. This also applies to the law of God. Turning to the law, the naïve and plain soul is sprinkled solely with faith. When a mind filled with human doctrine (and of course with wisdom and good sense) reads and appropriates the same law, however, it turns all the claims of Scripture into something else.

It was ideas such as this which separated the extremist from his erstwhile colleagues. In 1523 he went off to Orlamünde to become Karlstadt *contra mundum*. There, he sought to embrace failure, rejection and persecution in a personal quest for *Gelassenheit*. He described his inner pilgrimage in rambling tracts which – however imperfectly – look back to St Mechtilde and St Gertrude and forward to the seventeenth-century quietists. To say that Karlstadt 'developed' his ideas about lay priesthood at Orlamünde is to use the wrong word, for it is impossible to distinguish any very clear pattern in his theological progress:

> Every man is bound to preach God's Word in house or at table, morning or evening, in field or barn, whether at leisure or at work, and he is to study God's Word and treat of it to those who are round him, or who belong to him. This is a universal command addressed to all who understand God's Word and God has made them all through this commandment to be priests, all men to whom he has universally revealed it. For nobody is excluded, because God's commands pertain to all men, and touch the love and honour of God and his neighbour.

Karlstadt wanted to urge on ordinary believers a more active, intense religion. It may be that he was the earliest advocate of the ideal Christian household gathered round the big family Bible for their daily (or, at least, weekly) devotions, a custom which became an important distinguishing mark of middle-class Protestant homes in ensuing centuries. In his disorganized, and sometimes ridiculous, writings Karlstadt was wrestling not only with biblical and mystical themes but also with the incipient egalitarianism which was certainly not new but which surfaced during the 1520s in such diverse ways as the Peasants' War and Holbein's magnificent *Dance of Death* woodcuts.

Puritans, Baptists, Congregationalists, Levellers, Quakers and other later Christian groups drew much, directly or indirectly, from Brother Andy. Not the smallest part of his legacy was the encouragement of lay initiative. The man himself spent several troubled years wandering from one centre of the Reform to another, always seeking a spiritual home, always eventually falling out with his Christian brothers, until, at last, he died of the plague in Basel, on Christmas Eve 1541 – twenty years, almost to the hour, after his aggressive assertion of lay spirituality in All Saints church, Wittenberg.

In every church possessing a professional clergy there is a tendency for all ministerial functions to be located in the person who is 'paid to do the job'. 'Church' is widely identified in the common mind with the ecclesiastical hierarchy. The phrase 'going into the Church' is often used to describe a man or woman seeking ordination. Even lay preachers, lay readers and Catholic lay orders have a tendency to become clericalized because their training and, in some cases, their styles of dress make them more akin to

1545 : HANS . SACHSN. ALTER 5 I. IAR

Ein Dialogus/des inhalt/ein argument
der Römischen/wider das Christlich heüflein/den
Geytz/auch ander offenlich laster ꝛc. betreffend.

Ephesios.v.
Hůrerey vnd vnrainigkait/oder geytz/laßt nit von
euch gesagt werden/wie den heyligen zů steet.

6.4 Lay theology, which had long struggled to find expression in practical and theoretical terms, was provided with a powerful medium in the printing press. One of the many protagonists who grasped the opportunity was Hans Sachs (1494-1576) the shoemaker, poet and Meistersinger. Before the Nürnberg council forbade him to publish in 1527, he produced several books including the *Dialogue on the Argument of the Romanists Against the Christian Community*, (1524) in which he countered Catholic attacks on the doctrine and ethics espoused by the Protestant city.

the stipendiary ministers from whom they are meant to be distinct. This state of affairs owes as much to the inertia of the laity as to the self-importance of the clergy. It is another example of the institution as a corruptive influence.

Only when and where the Church breaks out of its cosy complacency and motivates its lay members to discover and exercise their ministry does Christianity make significant forward strides. This can be seen in the twelfth-century apogee of Western monasticism, in the heyday of primitive Methodism and in the current dramatic spread of evangelical Christianity in Korea, to take just three examples. If we look at the post-Reformation era in Europe we can discern two, frequently interrelated, causes for the release of lay initiative: vigorous preaching and a manpower crisis.

An example of the former is to be found in the teaching of Philipp Jakob Spener. By 1666, a hundred and twenty years after the death of Luther, the priesthood of all believers had ceased to have any effect on lay spirituality in the Church he had founded. This was the year that Spener became a senior pastor in Frankfurt. Over the next twenty years the 'father of Pietism' urged all Church members to more active faith in sermons and pamphlets. He held up the ideal of the 'spiritual priesthood', set up meetings for Bible study and discussion and criticized the upper classes for usurping the rights which belonged to every believer. In *Das geistliche Priestertum* (1677) he defined these rights:

> What is the spiritual priesthood? It is the right which our Saviour Jesus Christ earned for all men, to which he anointed all his faithful through the Holy Spirit, by virtue of which they may and they ought to bring suitable sacrifices to God, to pray for themselves and others, and edify each other and their neighbours . . . From whom comes this spiritual priesthood? From Jesus Christ, the true high-priesthood according to the order of Melchizedek 1) which as he has no successor in his priesthood, but remains eternally the sole high-priest; also has 2) made his Christians to be priests 3) before his father to whom sacrifices have their sanctity solely from his son and are made acceptable to God.

This challenge to institutionalized authority brought the inevitable results – opposition from traditionalists and separation by those who were impatient to exercise their priesthood.

Pietism's importance lies not in its creation of schism within German Lutheranism but in its encouragement of an active, largely lay spirituality which infused several Protestant denominations, brought new ones into being, revitalized the Moravian Church, contributed massively to eighteenth- and nineteenth-century revivalism and missionary endeavour and was a major ingredient of the Great Awakening. Yet, we cannot ignore the schismatic tendency of many of Spener's disciples. When the laity get the bit between their teeth there is often no stopping them. Where the Church is at its most vigorous it is often at its most fissiparous – in for example, the multi-tudinous evangelical churches in the USA, Africa and the Caribbean. The threat of schism seems to be the inevitable price to be paid for mass movements of lay spiritual renewal.

However, there is another side to the coin. If lay initiatives sometimes challenge clerical leadership, there are times when clergy deliberately encourage the unordained to share in the government of churches.

The brilliant civilization of the seventeenth-century Dutch Republic owed much of its success to an official policy of partial religious toleration, which created a pool of indigenous and refugee talent.

> Hence Amsterdam, Turk, Christian, Pagan, Jew,
> Staple of sects and mint of schism grew:
> That bank of conscience, where not one so strange
> Opinion but finds credit and exchange

So Andrew Marvell described disapprovingly the great cosmopolitan entrepôt. With toleration and increased bourgeois prosperity went secularism. The Provinces were nominally Calvinist, and Reformed cartels maintained control of all public offices. However, Roman Catholics and members of all mainstream Protestant churches enjoyed freedom of worship which, though limited and always at the discretion of the local magistrate, was in advance of anything operating anywhere else in Europe. No Christian community was in very good shape for much of the century. Calvinism was split by the controversy with Arminius and his followers. All religious enthusiasts were faced by widespread scepticism and apathy. All churches suffered from a lack of clerical manpower.

The problem was particularly acute for the scattered Catholic communities. Only slowly did the hierarchy become reconciled to the church's changed role. There were always some who hoped for the restoration of Catholic authority by Spanish or, later French, arms. But the majority of clergy who were in or familiar with the situation realized that the northern Netherlands had become a mission field. Priests were specially trained for work in this region at various seminaries, particularly at the College of the Virgin Mary at Louvain and the College of SS Willibrand and Boniface in Cologne. Their increasing activities provoked an inevitable response from the Calvinist establishment. While quiet survivalism was permitted, aggressive revivalism was something different. Harsh fines were imposed on all caught attending masses and instruction classes conducted by the itinerant priests. Like the wandering heretics of old (and in this situation they were the new heretics – peddlers of a faith alien to the new orthodoxy) they had to gather the faithful together at night and in out-of-the-way places far from the gaze of informers. By the middle of the century a clear distinction had become apparent between the congregations led by regular priests eager to preserve their meagre privileges and the more committed groups drawing inspiration from their secret conventicles.

The success of missionary activity depended heavily on lay people filling leadership roles the hidden clergy could not take up. Some were commissioned to conduct worship when no priest was available by reading litanies or homilies.

This activist corps soon became the heart of the mission. They looked after priests, arranged meetings and services, oversaw the religious education of children, administered the collection and distribution of alms. It was this inner ring which took the greatest risks and, not unnaturally, it arrogated considerable authority to itself. In effect it discriminated between the 'faithful' who could safely be included in the clandestine community and the 'nominal Catholics' whose devotion and loyalty could not be relied upon. Local organizers also expected to have a say in the appointment of new missionary priests.

While their menfolk were organizing the secret church many dedicated spinsters and widows were performing another valuable function. Motivated by the same impulses that had earlier created the beguinages and unable to join convents which were forbidden to take in novices, these Catholic women banded together into communities under the spiritual guidance of confessors. Initially ridiculed and called 'klopjes' (a term implying bossiness, unfemininity – viragos) by their Calvinist neighbours, many of these little groups earned respect by their simplicity of life and their valuable service to the wider community. Klopjes frequently worked as nurses or teachers. Though their schools were often accused of being indoctrination centres, several achieved excellent reputations. Klopje houses often served as meeting places for the underground church and the sisters took a prominent part in singing the offices, in reading lessons and in catechesis. All this lay activity which, for more than a century, was crucial in maintaining a vigorous Catholic church life ensured that, when an easier age dawned, the lay voice would remain strong in the Dutch church.

Most of the evidence of the last four hundred years suggests that circumstance is a stronger force than principle in liberating lay ministry. An urgent necessity that all sixteenth-century reformers agreed on was that of improving the quality of the parish clergy. Attempts to achieve this led, over the generations, to the emergence of a distinct clerical caste set apart from the rest of mankind, or certainly from the lower orders, by education and social status. The Council of Trent inaugurated the system of seminary education which, theoretically at least, ensured that ordinands spent the greater part of the period between their twelfth and twenty-fourth birthdays in semi-monastic seclusion preparing for their solemn vocation as Christ's representatives. In Protestant countries systems of professional training were, generally, slower to emerge, though a university education was officially regarded as essential. However, there were countless examples of official and unofficial gatherings of brother clergy for mutual exhortation and encouragement. In national churches the patronage system created great inequalities of wealth which tempted incumbents to be blinkered by ambition from obtaining a vision of selfless dedication to their people. Thus, even in the more democratic sects, the two-tier church became a reality.

The spread of Western-style democratic ideas over much of the world's surface has involved the questioning and undermining of many traditional authorities, including religious authorities. In countless communities the local priest, vicar or minister no longer has the status enjoyed by his predecessors. However he may view his role in the divine order of things, he is viewed by most outside, and many inside, the Church as a functionary, a person who performs certain rituals and who has ceded to other experts such as social workers, psychoanalysts and marriage guidance counsellors many of his traditional activities. This is one factor which has led to low clergy morale, identity crisis and a drastic falling off in the number of ordinands.

Vatican II tried to equip the Catholic church with new concepts of ministry relevant to a vastly changed world. The very title of its *Decree on the Apostolate of the Laity* pointed very firmly at a new style of relationship between priest and people. In the wake of the council lay consultative bodies were set up in most provinces. At the local level clergy were encouraged to establish parish councils and deanery structures which would bring all church members into the decision-making process. For many priests the 'about face' demanded by the conciliar directives was painful and difficult. For some, it was impossible. They had been trained to think of themselves as intermediaries between God and man, overseers of the flock, not partners in a collaborative ministry. The Council of European Conferences of Priests meeting in May 1989 recognized that this was still a major problem. It urged that lay people should be involved in the selection of ordinands and that men should only accept if they were in agreement with the new ideas about the priestly function.

But if lay people participate in the apostolate as of right it is very difficult for them meekly to accept small parcels of authority graciously presented by a clerical hierarchy. This is what the Catholic Church in England discovered when it convened a National Pastoral Congress in Liverpool in 1980. Two thousand lay delegates assembled excited at the prospect of helping to shape the future of their Church. That was all very well as long as the people and the leadership were of a common mind and as long as the decisions of the congress could be squared with the stance being taken by Rome. But there were issues about which some of the rank and file felt passionately and which were not in line with Vatican decrees: contraception, married priests, the ordination of women, closer relationships with other Christians, Communion in both kinds and further extension of lay ministry. Many congress proposals were shelved.

John Paul II tried to channel and control lay ambitions when he addressed a congress of Roman Catholic laity in 1988. He spoke (*Christifideles Laici*) of the growing need for participation as one of the most striking aspects of the new humanity and called on Christians to be in the forefront of all moves to create a more humane society. But the pope was not underlining the message of Vatican II about greater lay involvement in church life: his concern was much more for the working out of lay ministry *in the world*. He was expressing a by now familiar conservative reaction to the vigorous wave of lay activity which had manifested itself in several countries in response to the liberating ideas of the Sixties. His concern, like Archbishop Runcie's, was about confusion of roles.

Yet no-one could be more aware than the pope that in large areas of his own communion Church life is only kept going by the laity. In Latin America 53 per cent of parishes are run by nuns. In France 40 per cent are under the day-to-day control of lay committees. In North America the permanent diaconate has been rediscovered so that parochial responsibilities do not go by default (1985 figures).

If the modern situation is confused – and it is – the churches' leaders and theologians are largely to blame. Worldly society, on which the *civitas Dei* is superimposed, is one in which law expresses not the mind of God, but the will of the people. Governments derive authority not from the Almighty, but from the consent of the governed. Active lay people, who are, on the whole well-equipped theologically as well as possessing organizational, educational, caring and other skills, are intent on a degree of participation which comes very close to realizing the priesthood of all believers. It is commonplace for churches of all denominations to have lay-led house groups, pastoral teams, worship committees and even eldership schemes on which clergy and laity share oversight as equals. The people in the pew are making their views known through both formal and *ad hoc* assemblies on a variety of major issues. The underlying theological conviction is that the priestly mission is the responsibility of the whole Church, to be developed and expressed in terms of the prevailing culture. The traditionalist view, by contrast, is that the Church has to stand over against the world, expressing theocentricity and divine order through its own structures. Realignment of responsibility between ordained and unordained members might become necessary from time to time but it can only be temporary – an application of lay patches to cover clerical holes. Secular fashion must, at all costs, be eschewed. To paraphrase Runcie, the types of order that the churches have inherited – diverse though they may be – make a statement about God's reign over the whole of society and ought not to be abandoned because we are facing challenges from the way society is developing. Change is always resisted in the name of tradition – that much history teaches us plainly. What it reveals with equal clarity is that change is part of every surviving tradition.

Writ Large?

In 1857 John Keble asserted

> The true oblation in the Eucharist is . . . that which our Lord by the hands
> of the priest offers to His Father in the Holy Eucharist, in His own Body
> and Blood, the very same which he offers and presents to him – with
> which, as St Paul says, He appears before Him *now,* night and day contin-
> ually – in heaven, in commemoration of His having offered it once for
> all in His Passion and Death on the Cross. It is the one great reality,
> summing up in itself all the memorial sacrifices of old.

Twelve years later Bishop Lightfoot of Durham insisted

> The kingdom of Christ . . . has no sacerdotal system. It interposes no
> sacrificial tribe or class between God and man, by whose intervention
> alone God is reconciled and man forgiven. Each individual member
> holds personal communion with the Divine Head. To Him immediately
> he is responsible, and from Him directly he obtains pardon and draws
> strength.

Such diametrically opposed statements by two leading Church of
England spokesmen might be regarded by some as demonstrating the
glorious comprehensiveness of Catholic and reformed Anglicanism. To those
of a more sceptical turn of mind they provide an example of that fundamental discord which renders absurd, if not dishonest, any claim that there
is such a thing as Anglican theology. These opposed views make a useful
starting point for our debate because both claims can be traced back to the
unfinished business of the English Reformation.

One of the ambiguities of the time concerned the status and function of
the ordained ministry. The ordinal of 1549 replaced the Catholic rite, which
included anointing and specific reference to the eucharistic sacrifice. Such
references were expunged and the newly-ordained priest was presented
with a Bible, a chalice and bread as symbols of his authority to administer
word and sacrament. By the time the Prayer Book was revised in 1552 the
ceremony had been significantly changed: now only the Bible was given.
Throughout the new liturgies the words 'priest' and 'minister' were interchangeable. Elizabethan Puritans campaigned for the removal of the former,
only to be told that 'priest' was an anglicizing of *presbyteros* and had pastoral,
not sacerdotal, connotations. That did not stop, and has never stopped,
Anglicans so inclined from seeing the priestly role in terms of sacrifice and
mediation.

If the sixteenth-century protagonists were right, they had identified two mutually exclusive religious systems. One was dependent upon a special order of men drawing heaven and earth together through the regular re-enactment of the sacrifice of Calvary. The other was an association of individuals redeemed by personal faith, led by functionaries appointed to proclaim the word of God and instruct people in the way of holiness. If, on the other hand, they were wrongly forced into confrontational definitions in the heat of bitter controversy (as was certainly the case in other areas) then the two systems become different vantage points from which to observe the same truth.

The essence of leadership in any religious community consists in bringing people closer to the deity worshipped. In a Christian context this involves three main areas of activity. Prophetic ministry (preaching and teaching) enlarges people's understanding of God and his requirements. Pastoral ministry expresses God's love for his people. Priestly ministry focuses the cultic activity of the people's worship.

In ancient Israel most prophets, certainly in the pre-exilic period, were attached to shrines or the temple but, unlike the priests, their office was not hereditary. The prophet was always a man especially chosen by Yahweh and recognized by his 'enthusiastic' or ecstatic activities. The calling demanded a degree of commitment which many found impossible to attain. It was too easy to become smeared with the establishment brush and to tell the people what they wanted to hear. 'The prophets are telling lies in my name . . . The visions they talk about have not come from me; their predictions are worthless things that they have imagined.' So the Lord denounced temple officials through the mouth of Jeremiah. The great prophets of Israel's history were members of God's awkward squad, many of whom came to a sticky end. But their testimony, gathered by disciples and preserved in written form, made up a corpus unsurpassed in the literature of any religion. As Judaism became more and more a faith anchored in the written word so the rabbinic schools developed. These produced Israel's religious intelligentsia, men versed in the law and the prophets (and, later, the Talmud), guardians of received wisdom, who defined religious orthodoxy. But, like all scholarly communities, the Jewish one frequently split into factions. The prominent schools at the time of Jesus were the Pharisees and the Sadducees (and, perhaps, the shadowy Essenes), who were divided in their attitudes towards written and oral tradition.

The priesthood was much more formalized in its personnel and functions. Its members were all, theoretically at least, descendants of Levi. The cultic life of ancient Israel is notoriously difficult to reconstruct and varied greatly with the changing fortunes of the people. Activities took place at various shrines but the ritual of temple sacrifice in Jerusalem runs as a scarlet thread through the history of the nation from the time of the settlement in Canaan to the great dispersion. Yahweh had fixed his dwelling in the temple and into his presence only the high priest was admitted. He and the two other orders of priests were responsible, not only for overseeing the ritual of major festivals, but for the day-to-day activities of the shrine. The priests made offerings on behalf of the nation as a whole and for individuals who thronged the precincts seeking expiation for their own sins. Although the temptation to a mechanistic religion relying on the performance of precisely detailed rituals was ever present, Judaism never regarded sacrifice for divine favour as a quid pro quo. When the writer of the Epistle to the Hebrews declared 'the blood of bulls and goats can never take away sins' he was enunciating a principle that had long been recognized. Israel's poets, teachers and prophets had always made clear that repentance must be heart-felt and that forgiveness is a gift from God.

The pastoral needs of the people were served by the synagogues. When the exiles in Babylon met together to 'sing the Lord's song in a strange land' they were doing something which may seem obvious but which was rev-olutionary in its implications. Under no formalized leadership house groups gathered to recite psalms, to pray, to read portions of Scripture – for the exile was a formative period in the assembling and defining of the Jews' written records – to ensure that the moral precepts of the Law were upheld in their community and to support one another in practical ways. After the return, synagogue life continued alongside that of the temple. By the first century special buildings serving as places for education, justice, worship and other communal activities existed wherever Jewish communities dwelt throughout the civilized world. The synagogue – and thus the life of the community – was overseen by a 'ruler' and a group of elders who appointed those who took leading roles in worship (including suitably equipped visitors) and those who distributed alms and generally cared for those in need. These were all lay officers and tended to be drawn from wealthy, respectable local families. The destruction of the temple in AD70, and, with it, the elimination of the sacrificial system was a traumatic event for the Jews but there was in place another religious system which was probably a greater reality for the majority and certainly for those who lived far away from the Holy Land. Zion would remain a powerful magnet for nineteen centuries but it was the syna-gogue more than anything else which preserved the identity of the diaspora people.

The synagogue was inevitably the pattern for the first Christian as-semblies. The well-known picture of the Jerusalem church in Acts 2, 42–47 depicts the members as worshipping in the temple but also living the life of a distinct community based on the apostles' teaching, with fellowship meals, prayer, praise and works of charity. This is the only type of Church life that can be discerned from the pages of the New Testament. Christian com-munities were governed by *episcopoi* or *presbyteroi*, the equivalents of the Jewish *archesynogogoi*, assisted by elders. When the apostles decided to appoint deacons to collect and distribute alms they were doing no more than their Jewish counterparts had done for generations. The instructions given to Timothy and Titus about the appointment of leaders might have been echoed by any synagogue ruler: Christian shepherds are to be respectable members of the community, faithful to the received tradition, apt to teach and to be ethical role models.

The Christian foundation documents were written during the long and painful emergence of the Jesus faith from the Mosaic matrix and its writers wrestled with the problems of what aspects of old Israel should be retained and what jettisoned. The leaders of the new Israel were not seen at first as successors to the temple priesthood. The writer of the Epistle to the Hebrews was at pains to point out the distinction. The sacrifices of the tabernacle, he insists, were pale shadows of Christ's self-offering. Jesus was a superior high-priest, not in the Levitical pattern but 'after the order of Melchizadek', which, in the writer's interpretation, implies a type of priesthood which long ante-dated that established by Moses and was, of itself, timeless. The role of Christ as priest (*hiereus*) continues in heaven, where he intercedes for God's people. It seems to be part of the writer's intention to dissuade Christians who hankered after some kind of priestly ritual. This was a very natural re-action for believers converted either from Judaism or paganism, both of which provided sacerdotal specialists who could directly link devotees to the relevant deity. It was difficult to hold to a purely spiritual religion in a world of other cults rich in temples, shrines, statues, colourful rituals, priests, priestesses, acolytes and other tangible conduits of the supernatural. Yet that is precisely what the anonymous author urges: the Christian is to run the race of faith, under the watchful eyes of all the heroes and heroines of faith who have preceded him, keeping his own gaze fixed on Jesus. For the New Testament writers christianity has no priestly office. The word *hiereus* is used only of Christ and metaphorically of the whole Christian community in its task of mediating divine grace to the world.

Much more research has yet to be done on the process by which a cultic priesthood developed in Christianity. The earliest Christian leaders were ambivalent about Jewish tradition. Christ himself both hallowed and chal-lenged it. Judaism was a model to be imitated, a rival to be emulated. The battle for converts was at its fiercest in the major commercial centres of the Roman empire and one of the earliest pieces of evidence to claim a Jewish origin for the Christian priesthood comes from Rome itself. In the *Epistle of Clement of Rome to the Corinthians,* written around the end of the first century, the Levitical hierarchy is seen as prefiguring Christian leadership in its role of 'making offerings' for the people. The writer's argument seems to be that the destruction of the temple transferred the ancient cultic responsi-bilities to the priests of the new dispensation. If this interpretation is correct, Clement was aware that the priestly ministry was not instituted by Christ.

The notion, however, of the love-feast as sacrifice grew out of Christ's own language at the Last Supper – language infused with the Jewish para-digm of the passover. The *Apocalypse,* though probably not written much earlier than the *Epistle of Clement,* is firmly entrenched as a canonical book of the Bible: it presents a vivid vision of the worship of heaven taking place around an altar, above the souls of the martyrs, surrounded by angels who swing censers and pour libations. References to the 'fire' of the altar place the visionary's image of the worship of heaven in the tradition of Jewish burnt offerings and suggest a link in the writer's mind between the communion meal of the Church and the 'communion sacrifices' of ancient Israel, in which the choicest fat would be stripped out of the carcase and 'the priests descended from Aaron will then burn this on the altar, in addition to the burnt offering, on the wood of the fire, food burnt as a smell pleasing to Yahweh.' The rest of the flesh would then be shared between priests and people. Powerful memories of these ceremonies tugged at early Christian minds. St Paul compared the eucharist with the sacrificial meals of the Old Testament. Warning Christians against participating against sacrifices to idols, he legitimized, for some readers, a sacrificial paradigm of the eucharist, comparing Christians, in their shared experience of the meal of Christ's body and blood, with 'the natural people of Israel: is it not true that those who eat the sacrifices share the altar?'

As well as by past example, Christians were driven to a hieratic ministry by present need: the ever-present need to maintain discipline and order. The occasion of Clement's letter seems to have been the deposing of some presbyters in Corinth. Such behaviour is denounced as scandalous because it is not the layman's place to exercise authority over ministers appointed by the successors of the apostles and who have 'in blameless and holy wise offered the gifts'.

Christian communities under repeated attacks from various directions and struggling to define the essentials of the faith in a multicultural environment needed to hold fast to their leaders. By the same token, leaders needed to exercise authority firmly but graciously, maintain unity and orthodoxy, deepen the spiritual lives of the faithful and maintain a commitment to mission. Prophetic, pastoral and – increasingly – priestly functions coalesced in the persons of presbyters and bishops. What emerged did so as a result of trial and error. Ministry was understood differently in different places and we search the few extant records in vain for theological consistency. Take, for example, the *Didache,* a document reputedly setting out the teaching of the apostles and variously dated between the first and third centuries. It accords highest honour to prophets and teachers (both settled and itinerant) and urges believers to provide for their needs, 'for they are your high priests'. It urges the churches to elect bishops and deacons 'worthy of the Lord', 'for they also minister unto you the ministry of the prophets and teachers'.

'The Church used to have chalices of wood and bishops of gold. Now she has chalices of gold and bishops of wood,' thundered Savonarola. Most reformers were agreed on the need to eradicate abuses of clerical conduct which had arisen because of an imbalance of function. They complained that prophetic and pastoral responsibilities were being neglected and that many priests were concerned only with the sacerdotal activities which undergirded their power in the community and, in many cases, were exploited for profit. Catholic and Protestant reformers were scandalized by priests who made a living out of private masses and parish clergy who did little more to earn their keep than stumble their way through the Latin offices. Cardinal Cisneros encouraged the study of the Bible and mystical writers and laid down for his clergy regulations concerning preaching, pastoral care and personal devotion every bit as demanding as the requirements outlined by Calvin.

Where Catholics and Protestants parted company was in their definitions of priesthood and ministry. Despite the divisions in the Protestant ranks about Holy Communion, what it is and what it signifies, Thomas Cranmer spoke for all on the subject of the administration of the sacrament:

> Christ made no such difference between the priest and the layman, that the priest should make oblation and sacrifice of Christ for the layman and eat the Lord's Supper for him all alone, and distribute and apply it as him liketh. Christ made no such difference, but the difference that is between the priest and the layman in this matter is only in the ministration; that the priest as a common minister of the Church, doth minister and distribute the Lord's Supper unto other, and other receive it at his hands. But the very supper itself was by Christ instituted and given to the whole Church, not to be offered and eaten of the priest for other men, but by him delivered to all that would duly ask it.

Cranmer was happy to retain the word 'priest' but he understood it to imply the mediation of grace through word and sacrament and not the offering or pleading of Christ's sacrifice to God. The only sacrifice made by minister and people was that of praise and thanksgiving.

In theory the result of this divergence was to create two distinct orders of being; the Catholic or Orthodox priest and the Protestant minister. Certainly it is true that the celebration of mass remained the ground of being for the former while for the latter the declaration of the lively oracles of God was his primary function. Yet, in reality, one has to make so many qualifications to this simple proposition as to rob it of most of its value. There would always be Protestant exponents of inward religion who championed Holy Communion as the principle vehicle for self-offering. John Wesley, for example, described the sacrament as 'a kind of sacrifice, whereby we present before God the Father that precious Oblation of His Son once offered.' Catholic counterparts, such as the Jansenists, advocated the necessity for conversion through hearing the Word of God and warned against reliance on attendance at mass. Luther, Calvin and most other Protestant leaders wanted the Lord's Supper to be returned to the people. They advocated more frequent reception and, thus, emphasized the role of the minister as president.

The early Church revelled in the diversity of its members' gifts; it used a bewildering variety of terms to reflect the spread of office and responsibility: apostles, bishops, presbyters, deacons, prophets, presidents, miracle-workers, interpreters; and Paul's list of specialized ministries shows that some responsibilities were exclusive to those with particular gifts. 'Are all apostles? Or all prophets? Or all teachers? Or all miracle-workers? Do all have gifts of healing? Do all of them speak in tongues and all interpret them?' It should not, therefore, be a cause of scandal that there is a diversity of ministry in the post-Reformation church: a cultic priesthood and a pastoral presbyterate are both deep veins in the body of Christ. Catholic and Orthodox priests – or those ministers in reformed or Old-Catholic or Anglo-Catholic communions who consider themselves to be priests – need not be fearful or jealous of pastors who aspire to no priestly power; Protestants who do not want sacrifices offered on their behalf have no grounds of intoler-ance of those who do. Sharers in the mass naturally lament the deprivation of those who stay outside their communion, but they can and do recognize that the deprivation is not all one way. Gradually, increasingly since the Reformation, and especially in recent years, Catholics and Orthodox have learned a lot from the examples both of the Protestant understanding of the eucharistic and of the Protestant tradition of a non-priestly pastorate. The first is a reminder that it is not enough to reverence the Body and Blood upon the altar without recognizing it in the fellowship of ordinary people; the second a proof that the priest's ministry can be shared, without derogation of his status or adulteration of the unique powers to which he is ordained.

THE CLERICALIST TRAP

As we have seen over and over again, questions of faith and doctrine were bound up with issues of order in Church and State. However clergy explained their power base in theological terms it remained just that, a power base. Catholics spoke of the priest as God's appointee, possessed of an indelible character which was demonstrated in his presence at the altar and his right to absolve penitents. Protestants invested in their ministers no less authority. By expounding Scripture they were making Christ available to people just as the priests were at their altars. Their knowledge of the Bible and their spiritual standing (notwithstanding the checks and balances inherent in the Reformed tradition) put them, in effect, above contradiction. In Calvin's Geneva the alliance between ministry and magistracy resulted in an onslaught on public morality. Dancing, bawdy songs, bad language,

Sunday games and unlicensed books were all prohibited by law and citizens were obliged to attend sermons and to see to the religious education of their children and servants. The same pattern was duplicated wherever the Genevan model was replicated. Small wonder that Milton could complain that new presbyter was but old priest writ large.

The necessity for authority, unity, leadership, guidance, discipline was urged in support of every type of ecclesiastical polity, as it always had been, but what most arguments came down to was power and the legitimizing of power. Richard Hooker was quite open about this in his defence of the Elizabethan settlement against Catholic and Puritan critics:

> To whom Christ hath imparted power both over that mystical body which is the society of souls, and over that natural which is himself for the knitting of both in one; (a work which antiquity doth call the making of Christ's body;) the same power is in such not amiss both termed a kind of mark or character and acknowledged to be indelible. Ministerial power is a mark of separation, because it severeth them that have it from other men, and maketh them a special *order* consecrated under the service of the Most High in things wherewith others may not meddle.

Three hundred years later Cardinal Manning wrote of the priest enjoying a special relationship with Christ than which none 'more intimate, close and ceaseless can be conceived'. This relationship gave him an unassailable power over lay Christians. It made him a co-worker with God in building up the body of Christ.

The same principle manifested itself in the churches of the New World. Thousands of emigrants, fleeing from political and ecclesiastical tyranny, established congregations which were lay-led or in which the laity exercised a degree of control over the ministers. In many places this democratic polity did not long survive. The clergy here, as in Europe, emerged as an élite body who jealously guarded their privileges and armed themselves with excellent theological reasons for the exercise of a power derived, not from the people, but from God. Protagonists for various systems bore in mind Jesus's exhortations to humility but, just as today the use of the word 'minister' in a political context to suggest 'servant' (either of the people or the crown) has a hollow ring, so, in earlier centuries, the *servus servorum dei,* whether priest, pastor or bishop, was essentially regarded as an authority figure. He was interposed between man and God and derived his power therefrom. A presbyterian controversialist could write, 'Whosoever doth despise the minister (which is the Ambassador of God) despiseth and contemneth God himself and Jesus Christ, which is a fearful and execrable thing'. A nineteenth-century Roman Catholic bishop could claim, 'Because of his ordination the Catholic priest and only he, and not the Protestant pastor, has . . . the power to consecrate, to make present the Body of the Lord with the precious Blood, with his entire holy Manhood and Godhead under the forms of bread and wine . . . what a high, sublime, altogether wonderful power! Where in heaven is there such power as that of the Catholic priest?' It really is six of one and half a dozen of the other.

Clergy are still expected to play their part in holding together the fabric of society. After the sixteenth-century turmoil, both Catholic and Protestant, they emerged as a professional class able to stand with landlords and mill owners as respected leaders of society. Many, perhaps most, dedicated themselves to discharging their responsibilities as prophets, priests and pastors diligently, faithfully and lovingly – and their names have passed into obscurity for that very reason. There were, of course, others who failed. There always had been and always would be. At the end of the seventeenth century the Presbyterian divine, Richard Baxter, recalled angrily the rural clergy he had known in his youth: they 'read Common Prayer on Sundays and Holy Days and taught School and tipled on the Week-days, and whipt the Boys when they were drunk. Within a few miles about us were near a dozen more Ministers that were near Eighty years old apiece, and never preached; poor ignorant Readers, and most of them of Scandalous Lives.'

We certainly do not belong to that school of historians who play down the religious content of the Reformation and claim that it did little to change common perceptions. What was said and done in the local church Sunday after Sunday after Sunday had a drip-feed on the way people thought about God, about themselves and about their 'heretical' or 'papistical' neighbours. Yet there is a sense in which the principle *'Plus ça change'* can be argued. In 1624 an English countrywoman commented nonchalantly that when her minister began to preach she knew that she was in for 'such a deal of bibble-babble that I am weary to hear it and I can then sit down in my seat and take a good nap.' A hundred and fifty years earlier Catholic reformists were condemning just such irreverence and inattentiveness among people attending Mass. At the local level, after the turmoil of church interiors being whitewashed, scrubbed and whitewashed again, altars broken up and re-instated, side chapels dismantled and pews installed, most ordinary people settled back into their old ways. As for the clergy, though they were progressively better educated and more of them took the trouble to preach, their core tasks of administering sacraments, presiding over rites of passage and helping the needy remained unchanged.

In all this it is institutionalism which is the real culprit. The Church began with a pastoral, prophetic and priestly ministry in which all shared by exercising the charisms each had been granted. As all ministry coalesced in the persons of those ordained, so the Church became impoverished. Exercise of spiritual gifts (preaching, ecstatic utterance, mystical experience) by the unauthorized tended to be associated and to associate itself with dissent. Worse still, the leaders of the flock were expected to possess the plenitude of Christian ministry. Few men were equal to the task. Few could excel at inspired preaching, sacrificial care of the needy *and* reverent, meaningful administration of the sacraments. The tendency was to associate the *essence* of ministry with one of its basic functions – the priestly or prophetic. The Reformation tried to put an end to the sacerdotalism underlying the late medieval Church. It succeeded only in setting alongside the Catholic institution rival institutions based on a preaching and teaching ministry.

Chapter Seven

THE EVANGELICAL IMPULSE:
Reformation as Mission

THE PENUMBRA OF CHRISTENDOM

In November 1594, a young Jesuit described a moment of peril on the wooded slopes of the Andes, a few days' trek out of the remote mountain mission station at Andamarca. Nicolás de Mastrillo had a great career before him, which would bring him the responsibility of leadership over all the Jesuits of Peru, but this was his first mission. His account of it is preserved in a letter sent with greetings and love to the parent-house in Spain from which he had recently arrived, fresh from training. With a senior Jesuit, he was sent into little-known country to make contact with a friendly chief called Bellunti and to find unevangelized tribes to convert. Revelling in the hardships of the journey, delighting in the company of every friendly Indian he met, he at last found himself in Bellunti's camp, communicating only by smiles, when an armed band under a chief called Liquiti suddenly appeared

> and this I understand was by God's leave, because that Indian lives some sixteen leagues from here and because of this it will make the news of our arrival spread greatly. We embraced the chiefs and they presented us with some turtle-doves and a monkey for Father. Here your Reverence

can consider the contentment we felt at seeing thirty Indians seated
before us with so much happiness when we had only just arrived.

The moment of unease occurred during the dinner of beans and herbs,
cassava and chillies, when Liquiti uttered a potentially fatal suspicion: 'These
are not Fathers but Spaniards in disguise.' The Indians were so aware of the
different treatment they got from Jesuits and secular Spaniards that they
assumed they belonged to different races. Mastrillo and his colleague
awaited with apprehension the resolution of Liquiti's doubt. 'Then Liquiti
looked at us and seeing that we ate of their food, said, "Now I believe that
they are Fathers because they eat what we give them."' The following day
the whole community began to build a chapel of staves and palms, while
Mastrillo settled to the work of learning the language, 'which,' he confessed,
'I am finding very hard.'

This typical episode – small-scale, strenuous, touchingly charitable –
reveals essential characteristics of the Christianity of the sixteenth century,
which stretch, from the distant frontiers where Mastrillo was at work, across
the Reformation divide and over the older schisms which separated Eastern
from Western Christendom. Clergy in the early modern period, of whatever
denomination, included, for instance, élites anxious to sharpen their self-
differentiation from the profane world around them, like Mastrillo distancing
himself from lay Spaniards. Like the Peruvian Jesuits in their preference for
a native diet, these self-consciously godly divines made cults of simplicity
and of ecclesiastical primitivism, such as exulted in churches of wood and
palms. Above all, they shared a commitment to evangelization – to pen-
etrating the parts which other evangelists had not reached and to enhancing
the Christian awareness of congregations whose lives and perceptions had
been left unreformed by a partial or conventional assimilation of the gospel.

Mastrillo happened to work on a distant frontier, where some of the most
challenging missions beckoned. But there were frontiers of evangelization
at home in Europe, too: in the godless wens thrown up by urban growth;
in the pagan countryside ill served by earlier clergy; among pockets of
heretics and infidels; among educated laities craving a more active and
fulfilling religion – or a more personal relationship with God – than established churches had formerly provided. There were needs and opportunities
among children, and among the worldly distractions that arose, at high levels
of education and society, from an excess of sophistication, or, among the
dregs, from the very need to survive. Wherever the critical eye sought to
detect them, there were practices – recreational, therapeutic, celebratory,
commemorative, social and sexual – which could be condemned as survivals
from a pagan past. Work in the mission field on the global frontiers of
European expansion was an outward projection of work also in hand at
home.

Our image of sixteenth-century Christendom is so dominated by the

Reformation that we have failed to see what else was going on or how the Reformation fitted into a broader picture. The Christianity of the time was divisive and conflictive but it was also expansive – burgeoning and spreading in a vast movement of which the Reformation was only part. Competition for souls between Protestant, Catholic and Orthodox apostles was the overlap of mighty works of missionizing to which each tradition allotted enormous resources in discrete spheres. They addressed unevangelized communities outside Europe, where the Catholic Church won the allegiance of so many millions of souls that the secession of some European communities seemed like a little local difficulty; but they also assiduously cultivated the pagans who still dwelt on the fringes of their home societies and such Jews and Muslims as lived in their midst; they took the Gospel to the rootless masses of new or growing towns; they zealously invaded neglected parts of the countryside. In these recesses of Christendom local religion was subverted in favour of universal cults; peasants' priorities – worldly or superstitious in clerical eyes – were punished by divines who rated the ethereal above the earthy; and above all, the godly élites made it their business to enhance the Christianity of their unsatisfactory co-religionists: to blow the bellows among the Laodiceans, to eradicate pre-Christian customs from the culture; to suppress non-Christian thoughts and tastes.

This great enterprise involved the Protestant reformers and their Catholic and Orthodox counterparts, with only nuances of difference; it began in the late middle ages, continued throughout the early modern period and has been revived at intervals ever since. Historians in the future will see the Reformation as part – in some respects, a small part – of this dominant theme in the history of the Church. Protestantism will appear not as a schism from the Church but as a movement within it subscribing to a common end: the spreading of the good news and the sharpening of Christian consciousness.

Indeed the early modern period was an age of evangelism in more than just a Christian sense. More or less simultaneously with the great dilation of Christianity, Islam and Buddhism experienced moods of intensely committed proselytizing which widened their own frontiers. In terms of territory and souls, the expansion of Islam was almost as dramatic as that of Christianity. Where the two systems were in direct competition, in the archipelagoes of south-east Asia, Islam scored the greater successes. Here and in Africa Islam experienced, from the fifteenth century to the seventeenth, the most copious spiritual conquests since the century that followed the death of Muhammad. A new wave of Buddhist expansion began not much later. Reformed into a popular force in south-east Asian mainland states in the fifteenth and sixteenth centuries it was carried north from Tibet over central Asian steppelands from the time of the Third Dalai Lama's mission to the Mongols in 1576.

The expansion of all three religions got confused with imperialism and muddled by syncretism. Like the Catholic missions in the New World and

Muslim jihads in west Africa, even the forays of Lamaists among the Mongols were shadowed by political conquistadores and heralded by torchbearers vigorous in the selective use of violence. The noble Mongol promoter of Buddhism, Neyici Toyin (1557–1653), burned before his tent a pile of shamanist gods four tent-frames high. The advice to missionaries on the farthest front, among the Ili of the extreme west of Mongolia in the mid-seventeenth century was, 'Whoever among those you see has worshipped ancestral idols, burn them and take his horses and sheep. From those who let the shamans perform fumigations, take horses. Fumigate the shamans, however, with dog-dung.' In practice, of course, the old gods did not altogether disappear, re-emerging as Buddhist deities, just as in Christian America they survived as saints and advocations of the Virgin. They continued to mediate between man and nature while the lamas did the same job between man and God. In parallel with official Islam, Christianity and Buddhism, 'popular' religions continued to confront the transcendent, or apparently transcendent, forces of this world.

While the proselytizing successes of Christianity belong in a worldwide context of the expansion of major religions, their extent has been singularly spectacular in some respects. Some early modern Christian successes could be reversed by vigorous counter-persecution, in Japan, for instance and Vietnam. In China a promising start was squandered in rivalries between religious orders and disputes over techniques of evangelization. And just as Islam could make no headway where Hinduism was entrenched – in parts of India and in Bali – so Christianity could not displace well-rooted Islam. The heroic Carmelite missionaries in Persia in the sixteenth and seventeenth centuries chronicled their own frustrations – by a lack of manpower in a country where ancient Christian minorities seemed 'a prey to Muhammadan wolves' and by a hostile culture where people would immediately remove and wash a garment touched by a Christian 'as if they were a foul race'. To the Jesuits who worked at the court of the Great Mughal, Muslims were 'as hard as diamonds' to work on.

Yet the New World was there to redress the balance of the old and, if measured in numbers of formal adherents or in volume of tithes, the missionary experience in the Americas was astonishingly gratifying. The pioneer in Mexico, Peter of Ghent, is supposed to have administered an average of fourteen thousand baptisms a day at the height of his ministry. Within a generation's span of the military conquest, the 'spiritual conquest' – according to the reckoning of the friars – had won a million souls. On the shores of Lake Titicaca, the huge mission-churches built in the sixteenth and early seventeenth centuries are impressive witnesses of the scale and power of the self-sacrificing devotion aroused by a handful of Dominicans. Protestant evangelization in the Americas was less committed in the early centuries. Though nowadays it is at work with an avenging intensity in part of the New World, even in the 1940s only a quarter of the Indians of the

United States belonged to Protestant churches. Still, a missionary enterprise like that of John Eliot in late sixteenth-century New England was as impressive, on its smaller scale, as most Catholic missions. Inspired by the conviction that the Algonquin were a lost tribe of Israel, this Puritan preacher began his campaign to convert them in the intense charity of fellow-feeling. His translations into Algonquin began with the catechism and ended with the complete Bible. His Christian communities, led by native pastors in 'praying towns', were exemplary essays in reorganising Indian societies in the image of those of European colonists. Twice on Sundays they met to 'praise God in singing, in which many of them are excelling' and to hear a reading and sermon 'after the manner of the English'.

In the end it was a heroic failure. Lay enemies doomed the experiment in wars of extermination; conflict ingrained the Indians' image as unassimilable heathen in most settlers' minds. There is a serpent in every garden and the fate of Eliot's Indians is a reminder of the limitations of even the most spectacular missionary successes of the time. In Catholic America, it had a sad parallel in the undoing of the Indian 'republics' – autonomous missions housing hundreds of thousands of Guarani – established by Jesuits in Paraguay, Uruguay and Brazil in the seventeenth century. They were decimated in wars against slavers from Brazil and wrecked or overrun when the Jesuits lost the favour and protection of the Spanish crown. Non-human adversaries were even more insidious. One reason for the frantic rate at which the early Franciscan missionaries laboured to multiply baptisms was the intensity of their apocalyptic forebodings, fed by the terrible mortality and withered fertility of indigenous populations in the early colonial New World. The statistics are too unreliable to give more than an inkling but however the figures are sliced the conclusions are catastrophic, with overall losses of not much below 90 per cent in the first hundred years of Spanish occupation in the Antilles, Mexico and Peru.

The depth of the survivors' conversion – which inspired the earliest friars to paeans of self-congratulation – soon aroused doubts. As early as 1539 clergy in Mexico were worried about the proliferation of small chapels 'just like those the Indians once had for their particular gods'. In 1562 Diego de Landa, a dedicated and sensitive missionary leader in Yucatán, began to suspect that his flock had deceived him by worshipping idols in secret. He unleashed a ferocious inquisition, in which 4,500 Indians were tortured – 158 to death – in three months. A witness at the ensuing inquiry claimed that 'the friars ordered great stones attached to their feet, and so they were left to hang for a space, and if they still did not admit to a greater quantity of idols they were flogged as they hung there and had burning wax splashed on their bodies.' This should be seen less as evidence of perverted missionary sensibilities than as proof of the depth of the friars' disillusionment.

Disillusionment can arise from unrealistic expectations as well as from poor results. The early missionaries, gripped by millenarian fever, convinced that God's work must be quickly accomplished in preparation for the end of the world, had no time for sophisticated catechism classes. Their manpower was too thinly spread to do more than make a start. Peter of Ghent aimed only to get four points across to his flocks: a single creator God of wisdom and goodness; the Blessed Virgin: the immortality of the soul; and the menace posed by diabolic temptations. Christ was included only by implication. The traditions established in these early days came from an unreformed old-world Catholicism, before the Protestant challenge had shaken up standards of evangelization and before the Council of Trent had set new benchmarks of doctrinal purity and dogmatic awareness.

As the missionaries' own standards of expectation rose, they seemed never to get much further with their flocks. It was like aiming at a receding target. An early eighteenth-century parish priest like Fr Francisco Jiménez in what is now Chichicastenango in the Guatemalan highlands, made the same complaints of the imperfections of his people's grasp of their faith as his predecessors uttered nearly two hundred years before: they were tenaciously attached to 'idols' and to their own healers and seers; they warped the saints into pagan deities; only with extreme caution could they be trusted to reverence images without idolatry. Jiménez would have found it hard to challenge the complaint of an English observer in 1655 that 'not all the teaching and preaching of those Priests hath yet well grounded them in principles of faith' for the Indians were 'inwardly hard to believe that which is above sense, nature and the visible sight of the eye.' A series of cases in early eighteenth-century Peru revealed how ready hag-ridden persecutors and jealous neighbours were to raise allegations of 'superstition' and demonic delusion. In 1701 a 'good Christian' of twenty years' standing was gaoled on evidence solely of unorthodox medical prognoses; in 1723 an Indian's private chapel containing six Christian images was condemned as a shell for idolatory; in 1710 a cause célèbre arraigned Juan Básquez, a button-maker with a miraculous reputation in the streets of Lima, who relied on Christian creeds, confessions and acts of contrition in a healing ministry which, he claimed, had been inspired by St John: he made no charge for his services but dissatisfied patients still accused him of collusion with demons and worship of pagan gods.

Periodic official investigations into the Church's penetration of the native world, throughout the colonial period, have left plenty of evidence for anthropologists and sceptics who regard the post-conversion religion of the Indians as pagan or 'syncretic', in which the old ways were influenced but unsupplanted. In the 1920s, the anticlericalism of Mexican revolutionaries was nourished by the works of Manuel Gamió, who traced saints' cults back to before the conquest and represented the Virgin of Guadalupe as a front for the worship of the sanguinary pagan deity, Tonantzin. In Bolivia and Peru, our Lady was identified with Pacha-mama. In Haiti, where the indigenous population has effectively been replaced by imported labour of African origins, the Church is said to have tried to suppress the cult of the Virgin of Saut d'Eau because of her identification or confusion with a pagan deity; in the Voodoo of the island, the appropriation of Christian images is a familiar part of pagan worship in practice. In Guatemala, on the shores of Lake Atitlán, the Church is still struggling against the cult of Má Ximón – that cigar-smoking, rum-swilling effigy who, in some drunkenly, smokily obnubilated sense, represents Simon Magus. In Tenerife in the Canary Islands, devotion to the image of Our Lady of Candelaria pre-dated the conquest: indeed, missionaries maintained with some pride that it was proof of the partial divine revelation with which the natives had been favoured in the time of their paganism. After the conquest, the cult remained popular with the natives, whose surviving wills from the early sixteenth century show an almost exclusive partiality to this Virgin. In these circumstances, it is hard to resist suspicions that she is, or was, as much a pagan goddess as a Christian symbol.

THE INDIES WITHIN

Yet the missionaries' labour was like that of a dog walking on its hind legs. As Dr Johnson said, one should not expect it to be well done; it was remarkable enough to see it done at all. If native American peoples' Christianity remained idiosyncratic, that made it no worse than the religion of rural communities in Europe in the same period, where simple people still lived in worlds full of spirits and demons, and where natural forces were personified and placated. St Teresa of Avila had her first vision of Christ after hearing a Franciscan preach about his order's mission to the Indies. 'There is another Indies waiting to be evangelised here in Spain,' said her celestial voice. It was a common saying of the late sixteenth century that 'within Spain there are Indies and mountains of ignorance' and as the clergy made increasing spiritual demands of their flocks, so the oceans seemed to narrow. 'I don't know why the fathers of the company go to Japan and the Philippines to look for lost souls,' wrote a Jesuit correspondent in 1615, 'when we have so many here in the same condition who do not know whether they believe in God.' According to a speaker in the English House of Commons in 1628, there were places in northern England and Wales 'which were scarce in Christendom, where God was little better known than among the Indian.'

The Christianity of Christendom simply failed to meet the high standards of the godly of the early modern era. The Council of Trent alerted Catholic clergy to their unfulfilled mission and to the huge gaps in evangelization caused by the uneven distribution of the clergy. In 1553 the Jesuit Robert Claysson was outraged by the neglect of forest regions near Bordeaux 'whose inhabitants live like beasts of the field. One can find people over fifty years old and more who have never heard of mass nor heard a single word of faith.' In rural Gascony in the early seventeenth century, St Vincent de Paul organized missions among 'people, aged sixty and more, who told us freely that they had never confessed; and when we spoke to them about God, and the most holy Trinity, and the nativity, passion and death of Jesus Christ and other mysteries, it was a language they did not understand at all.' A miller in northern Italy in the early sixteenth century could formulate a remarkably comprehensive cosmology of 'cheese and worms' from which Christian traditions about the creation of the world were entirely absent. A novel purportedly written in Rome in the 1520s could plausibly depict whole streets of the pope's own city as innocent of Christianity. Ignorance among the poor on the pope's threshold was compounded – it was feared – by doubts among the rich.

In the Europe of the Reformation era, more conspicuous than the distinction between Protestantism and Catholicism was that between godliness and worldliness: on the one hand a committed and critical kind of Christianity, a life-changing religion of conversion, which was shared by élites in all three communions, and on the other the Christianity of ordinary people – part-time Christianity which is content to leave some areas of life unaffected. In this latter kind of religion, ignorance, indifference, addiction to non-Christian or pre-Christian values, superstition, paganism and 'popular religion' all played various parts at different times and places. Protestants and Catholics were divided, in some particulars, about how to reform religion, but they were united in a common project for the reformation of culture – not just of 'popular culture' but of the life of society at every level.

A startling example was the Catholic debate over 'Chinese rites' provoked by the missionary methods of the Jesuit Matteo Ricci in the early seventeenth century. He had penetrated the interior of the country by cautious degrees and won the respect of his hosts by showing respect for them in his turn. His approach belonged in a long tradition, going back at least to the great mission-theorist of the late thirteenth and early fourteenth centuries, Ramón Llull, who stressed the importance of a thorough knowledge of and sympathy with the existing culture in the mission field. He allowed his converts to continue Confucian rites of ancestor-veneration, as a secular practice which need not necessarily conflict with Christianity. But he reckoned without the radicalism of the missionary culture of his age. The opponents of Chinese rites assembled a diverse armoury of theological and pastoral weapons: uniform worship befitted the universal church; the rites were specifically pagan and incompatible with rebirth in Christ; the Jesuits were teachers of an adulterated faith. Underlying all the opponents' arguments, however, was commitment to a programme of the reformation of culture essentially similar in every clime: nothing in a Christian's life could be untransformed by his faith.

The conflict of Protestants and Catholics has dominated the history

7.1 Matteo Ricci (1551-1610), who is shown on the left in this seventeenth-century engraving, established the first Jesuit mission in Ming dynasty China and owed his success largely to the 'accommodation method' of accepting local dress and customs.

books, but the assault of the godly on the world was the occasion of a much wider and deeper conflict. The first form it took was what might be called a catechetical offensive. The proliferation of catechisms is a sure sign of an era of evangelism and no age exceeded the sixteenth century in the production of material of this type. The propagandists' campaigns were not addressed only to children; as Luther observed, catechism was a form of what would now be called continuing education, the purpose of which was to impress the word of God 'as a seal' upon the hearts of men to allow the divine spirit to do its work. 'Speaking for myself,' he said, 'I stay forever a child and a student of the catechism.'

With children, however, the process began. Protestant catechists observed the popular German maxim, *Jung gewonet, alt getan':* the Catholic equivalent was the Jesuit slogan, 'Give me the child until he is seven and I will give you the man.' Anxiety to 'habituate' children in knowledge of the faith was a great stimulus to the boom in catechetical literature. The public, however, for which most of it was written, was composed of clergy and the function of the manuals was to focus instruction face to face. The revolutionary impact of Luther's own *Short Catechism* of 1529 was owed in part to its direct accessibility to lay readers. In the following half-century or so 'something like every third pastor drew up a catechism of his own.' In Hamburg alone, more than fifty different catechisms were in circulation.

These reformers' catechisms were not, however, a new departure but an aspect of a communications revolution already gathering pace within the Catholic church. The late fifteenth century was the great age of 'picture catechisms' and manuals on confession, illustrated with woodcuts of the inmates of hell feeding on each other's flesh, or of the devil whisking unworthy worshippers from church. The catechism drawn up in about 1470 by the Augustinian Dietrich Coelde was a bestseller of its time, and though its emphasis on the anatomization of sin would soon come to seem old-fashioned, it anticipated the reach of the catechetical revolution of the next century by addressing, in specially adjusted editions, young and old, clergy and laymen, beginners in piety and advanced practitioners. By the time Sebastian Brandt wrote the *Ship of Fools,* the world seemed to the author already 'full of the gospel.'

The huge Catholic output of sixteenth-century catechisms belongs obviously to the same project as the Protestants'; an idea of its scale is suggested by the scores of catechisms of the previous hundred years synthesized by the Jesuits Ripalda and Astete in the 1590s. Those of St John of Avila, Diego de Estella and Luis de Granada, for instance, all emphasize personal devotion, private prayer and the cultivation of an individual relationship with God as well as rote-learning of traditional formulae and the practice of traditional works of charity. Even in matters of doctrine normally thought to separate the reformed Churches from Rome, Protestant and Catholic catechetical works could be strikingly similar. Luther's *Short*

Catechism, for instance, repeatedly intones, 'We should fear God because of his threat to those who transgress his law and love him for his promise of grace to those who keep it.' This was doctrine a Catholic could fault only by appealing to St Paul, and bemoaning pharisaic rigidity.

Secondly came the reformation of customs. In one of the crime stories of G.K. Chesterton, his priest-detective, Father Brown, unmasks a criminal posing as a Church of England vicar because 'he talked like a Puritan about the Sabbath and had a crucifix in his room. He evidently had no notion of what a very pious parson ought to be, except that he ought to be very solemn and venerable and frown upon the pleasures of the world.' Father Brown's adversary betrayed himself by refusing to meet an actress. Three hundred years before, however, when there were Catholic as well as Protestant puritans, his queer blend of censorious devotion would not have seemed out of place. In the early modern period, the clergy's assault on unholy living was conducted without much difference between denominations. The attack was concentrated on popular fairs and festivals which combined – as Erasmus said of carnivals – 'traces of ancient paganism' with 'over-indulgence in licence'. To an Elizabethan Puritan dancing was 'a horrible vice, an introduction to whoredom, a preparative to wantonness, a provocative to uncleanness and an introit to all kinds of lewdness.' Catholic divines agreed with him: dances were everywhere driven from church and, in some dioceses, banned or restricted outside it. Bear-baiting was denounced by the same Puritan on the ground that 'God is abused when his creatures are misused'. The seventeenth-century Russian Archpriest Avvakum, the leader of the 'Old Believers', freed a dancing bear and drove the troupe that brought it from the village. His edict 'on the righting of morals and the abolition of superstition' included dancing, fiddlers, magic, masks and minstrels in a widely spattered anathema. Bull-fighting, too, was banned or, at least, proscribed on holy days after a papal pronouncement in 1565, not because it was cruel to animals but because it was corrupting of men.

Customs too entrenched to change could be sacralized. One common endeavour of Catholic and Protestant divines was the appropriation of social rituals. Marriage is the most obvious example: in the sixteenth and seventeenth centuries in most of Europe it was revolutionized by successful campaigns to suppress clandestine marriages and to bring all sexual unions under clerical bans. Ostensibly, for instance, the Spanish Inquisition was a tribunal of faith. In practice, most of its efforts in the second half of the sixteenth century were devoted to getting laymen's sex lives under priestly control. Bigamy became one of the most frequent causes in the Inquisition's courts in the 1560s and 1570s; fornication was the tribunal's major preoccupation from the 1570s to the 1590s. Sex had never been something of which Church leaders had unequivocally approved; but they were united in thinking it did least harm when licensed by themselves. Their campaigns were motivated by charity as well as power-lust. It seemed vital, as a saintly lobbyist claimed in 1551, 'to invalidate all marriages where there is no witness' because 'an infinite number of maidens have been deceived and undone, sinning with men and trusting in the promise of marriage made to them; and some have left their parents' house and gone to their perdition'.

Good intentions, however, can be joylessly enforced and the reformation of marriage was part of a more general clerical enforcement of a monopoly of ritual. In Protestant communities, it covered rituals of misrule, sacred dramas performed by lay groups and the more overt forms of lay competition in the clergy's proper fields, like fortune-telling, folk-healing and magic. The result was one of the most beguiling ironies of the Reformation era: belief in 'the priesthood of all believers' was a powerful source of reformers' inspiration; Catholics and Protestants worked hard at devising means to involve laypeople more deeply in the life of the Church. Yet, at the same time, vast areas of secular life were made subject to the arbitration or tyranny of a godly élite.

A third theme common to the early modern churches was the subversion of local religion. Cults specific to a particular place or community were – slowly, often unsuccessfully – eroded or displaced by the universal cults of the Catholic church or by Christ-centred or Bible-centred forms of devotion. Dethronement of saints and debunking of apparitions were not exclusively Protestant practices: in the campaign to make Christianity uniform, Catholics could be equally zealous in the same causes. The Fathers of Trent were anxious to keep in their kitbag the traditional spiritual paraphernalia: the invocation of saints, the veneration of relics and the sacred use of images; but they made space for Protestant criticisms of some excesses. 'All superstition,' they decreed,

> shall be removed, all filthy quest for gain eliminated, and all lasciviousness avoided, so that images shall not be painted or adorned with seductive charm, or the celebration of saints and the visitation of relics be perverted by the people into boisterous festivities and drunkenness.

Where the strength of local cults occluded people's sense of belonging to a universal Church, the saints of a spiritual *patria chica* did demons' work for them. Local religion was the patch on Christ's seamless robe, the boil on his perfect body. This was why, for instance, in Spain generally, official attitudes to apparitions changed with the pace of reform. The devotion apparitions attracted was concentrated at most, within a hundred kilometres of the epicentres. Whereas in the fifteenth century, local clergy and diocesan investigators were usually happy to validate the seers' claims and share the local benefits, from the early sixteenth century the posture of the authorities changed. No more visions were endorsed by the Church.

The same unease was directed against the deities of local religion. In Catalonia, priests struggled against pari-coloured local piety in a country where there were 'more advocations of the Virgin than kinds of sausage'. In Castile, when 'Our Lady of Riansares or the Christ of Urda . . . are valued above other Marys and Christs,'

> there is a tension built into relations between the idea and the example, between the Church Universal . . . and the churches of Toledo, Tarancón, and Las Mesas.

This sort of diversity was ineradicable in most of Europe, though reformers everywhere had at least some impact on the excesses which turned patron saints or images into the tutelary gods of their dwellingplaces. One aspect of local religion which was successfully eliminated, according to its most assiduous student, was

> the sense of divine participation in the landscape, the search for signs in anomalous events or coincidences, the idea that the saints are always searching for their chosen towns. No longer is nature invested with the kind of sensitivity to the sacred that made the dove come and land in the transept during the penitentiary mass to Saint Sebastián in Castillo de Garcí Muñoz, . . . that led the eagle to roost with the image of Mary in Ventas con Peña Aguilera, or the bird to clean a street statue of Mary in Almonacid de Zorita; that made a certain cow separate from her herd and kneel each time she passed the chapel of Our Lady of the Vega in Morata. Or is it that these things still happen, and nobody, no devout and curious monarch, wants to know?

In the ranks of moderate reformers, Protestant distaste for saints' cults was different, in degree, rather than kind, from that of Catholics, if at all. Like the Catholics, they had their own cults to promote: those of the heroes of Foxe's *Book of Martyrs* or of the 'slaughtered saints' of Milton's poem, or of Luther himself, whose woodcut image was revered, according to Erasmus, in the hovel of every rebellious peasant in the 1520s. Over the following two centuries Luther was often portrayed, sometimes complete with nimbus and dove, in quasi-icons which attracted miraculous renown as incombustible, thaumaturgic or oracular. A picture of him commissioned by a Duke of Saxony in the late sixteenth-century bears an inscription which echoes the scruples of Trent: *'non cultus est, sed memoriae gratia'*.

The camps armed against local religion were laying siege to 'superstition'. This was a war of the godly against popular religion an attempt to wean lives permanently threatened by natural disaster from a religion of survival in this world to one of salvation in the next. Trials of rats and exorcisms of locusts, appeals to folk-healers and wise women, vows to saints for worldly purposes, charms to master nature and spells to conjure the occult – these were the common enemies whom the clergy of all Christian traditions strove to control or curtail. The sort of range of activities attacked is represented in a Westphalian ordinance of 1669 against

> putting leaves in the water on St Matthew's eve, putting pigs' hair on the fire, binding trees on New Year's day, driving out spirits by putting St John's wort on the walls, Easter bonfires accompanied by all sorts of songs that take the name of the Lord in vain while a great deal of devilry goes on, soaking meat in water tied up with bread, butter, lard and the like, hanging up St John's wreaths or crowns, making sacrifices.

The frontier between religion and superstition was, of course, undefined, and Protestants and Catholics may have differed about where to fix it but their common ground, in this as in so many contexts, was more substantial and, in the long-term perspective, seems more significant than the grounds of difference.

Only a Protestant, for instance, could dismiss the rite of mass as such as magical, but Catholic reformers were equally keen to purge it of mumbo-jumbo and to purify congregations' understanding of its significance. Eucharistic processions were restricted by repeated decrees in German synods in the fifteenth and sixteenth centuries; bans were decreed on traditional ceremonies abusing the host as a talismanic object to influence the weather or other forces of nature. Catholics were more tolerant than Protestants of hopes invested in relics or holy water or blessed candles or incense as aids in healing or props to prayer but Catholic reformers were also alert to the threat of impropriety which such practices carried. By the end of the sixteenth century in Salzburg traditionally minded laymen had to plead with the clergy to get their blessed bread and salt for the Sunday table. The efficacy of 'sacramentals' – objects of apotropaic power hallowed by blessing or by use in church – was denied altogether by Protestants; but in Catholic circles their number and nature were progressively limited and controlled. Catholic and Protestant divines were as one in outlawing parish wakes and the traditionally lighthearted vowed vigils which so often degenerated into lewdness: these activities largely disappeared from early modern Europe. Catholics and Protestants also agreed, on the whole, about the necessity of persecuting witchcraft, though they could get involved in characteristic disputes over means: in Urach in 1529, for instance, the Catholic bailiff proposed to counter the alleged malevolence with 'Easter candles, baptismal water, stoles, albs etc as though they were about to baptise the witches' souls once more,' whereas the Protestant-inclined priest recommended that 'it would be better to drop the witches in the water in which the sheep had been washed.' In the seventeenth century, Catholic scrutineers were prominent in the reclassification of witchcraft as a psychological delusion; but all kinds of Christian communities remained subject, with diminishing frequency, to the fear of it, and inclined to persecute it.

Like the Christian missions to the wider world, the evangelization of Europe encountered mixed success. Where Protestantism was triumphant, it coexisted with survivals from before the Reformation: with the need for saints and angels, sometimes supplied by images of Luther; with an antiquated popular theology that went on stressing the necessity of good works (above pp. 87,175); in parts of England, with demand for prayers for the dead; in parts of Norway, with magical awe of the eucharist; in parts of the Calvinist Low Countries, with an indelible intellectual attachment to free will; in Lutheran congregations, with the Kyrie in Greek. Similarly, the reformed Catholicism of the 'Counter-Reformation' could not eliminate pre-Tridentine Catholicism altogether – or, in some places, hardly at all. The bull-fights persisted in Spain. Many of the ceremonies still enacted today in expiation of parish and municipal vows, from Oberammergau to Barcelona, originated in the seventeenth century. Even exorcisms of locusts turned up again in a Jesuit mission in twentieth-century Africa. Without looking so far afield, the observer must be astonished at how many irrational bumps in the spiritual landscape survived the epoch of reform. In Catalonia, religion 'stayed where it had always been – in the community, rather than the church'. Everywhere, devotion ticked away to the traditional rhythms of the countryside, with feasts and fasts adjusted to the oscillations of dearth and glut. The god of rural Christians still looked like a demiurge, personifying a Nature who was not always benign. In southern Germany in the late eighteenth century, the Blessed Sacrament was still being used to ward off fire and flood; magic was exorcized by sprinklings of water blessed on certain holy days and bewitched cows were fumigated with holy smoke. The last witch burned in Switzerland was the victim of Protestants in 1781; Catholics burned the last in Poland in 1793. When the Quaker anthropologist William Christian studied the religion of a Cantabrian valley in the 1960s, he found priests still struggling to mop up the excesses of local religion left undisturbed in the aftermath of Trent. There is still a circle of ladies in Écija who put the image of their patron, Saint Pancras, in the fridge when he disappoints their hopes of a win in the lottery. They mean it, no doubt, as a joke; but pre-Reformation rites of misrule were also celebrated in jest and the best jokes, to be funny, must have a grain of truth.

THE OUTSIDERS AT HOME

As well as the mission to the pagans of new worlds and the under-evangelized Christians of an old one, the Churches of early modern Europe faced the responsibility of communicating the Gospel to unassimilated outsiders at home. These fell into three categories: Jews, Muslims and adherents of pre-Reformation heresies. By the time of the Reformation expulsions had winnowed the Jews of Western Europe and shifted their settlement eastward, into the central and eastern Mediterranean, Poland and the region of the lower Danube. Missions were rarely mounted among them in any systematic way; mass conversions could be achieved only by persecution, which was widely applied; by bribery – which proved useful in Venice where Jews were relatively numerous and where 5,000 were said to have converted in 1724 for a hundred scudi each; and by encouraging movements of desertion of their own traditions within Jewish communities.

A spectacular example was that associated with Jacob Frank in eighteenth-century Poland. Even before he was exiled in 1756 as a breaker of the peace, Frank had a dubious reputation. Despite self-avowed ignorance, he became the seer of a sect of worshippers of Shabbetai Zevi, a self-proclaimed 'Messiah' who had defected to Islam in 1666; Frank was a lithe chameleon, who professed Islam in Turkey and Christianity in Poland, where the cult he founded was accused of conducting orgiastic revels with select female novices. His triumphant return in 1759 was marked by a successful disputation with the rabbis of L'viv and a mass baptism of Jewish citizens. After confessing to having impersonated the Messiah he was exiled again to a luxurious retirement near Frankfurt, where he was maintained, by the subscriptions of thousands of devotees, with an income reputedly greater than that of the Polish state. His guard of a thousand hussars wore diamond-studded uniforms and he went to mass in a gilded coach. Outside such unrepresentative episodes, Christian missions among Jews had little success until the nineteenth century, when social emancipation eased Jews out of their ghettos and into the ways of life and thought, both Christian and secular, of the societies which surrounded them.

Until the Turkish empire receded in the nineteenth century, the only pockets of Islam in Christian Europe were in Spain and the Russian empire. The Russian conquest of Khazan in 1552 was followed by intensive evangelization of limited success and a much longer era of persecution; by the mid-eighteenth century the Tatars were no longer considered a political threat and Catherine II began a policy of favouring the preservation of Islam. In early sixteenth-century Spain the mission to the conquered Moors of Granada was something of a dress rehearsal for the evangelization of the New World. It had some exemplary features. By the mastermind of its earliest phase, Archbishop Hernando de Talavera, it was conceived as a slow and careful enterprise, typical of the culturally transforming ambitions of the clergy. He would nurture Christianity by changing the dress and language of the converts, who would be spared from the scrutiny of the Inquisition for forty years. In practice, evangelical impatience wrecked the effort. 'Conversions' were imposed by force and rebellions provoked. Acculturation was rendered impossible by the ghetto-like structures of 'Moorish' communities – not only in Granada but in other areas where Moorish populations were concentrated, in Valencia and Murcia. In 1578, the Granadine communities were split up and spread around the kingdom by a policy of forcible deportations. In 1609, most of the remaining populations were expelled.

The only large and concentrated heretical churches to survive the Middle Ages in the West were those of the Hussites in Bohemia and the Waldenses of the Alps. Both in their different ways were swamped by the eddies of the Reformation.

Hussites was a catch-all name for followers of the doctrines of Jan Hus, the Czech advocate of an invisible 'church of the predestined' who had been burned at the Council of Constance (see below p. 231). They included bourgeois congregations, whose worst excesses were communion in two kinds or vernacular services, and menacing practitioners of peasant communism. When Luther read the works of Hus in 1519 he declared that all his doctrines had been anticipated by the earlier reformer. From 1521 he called Hus a saint. Yet a drift of moderate Hussites back to the fold of Rome was already under way. The election of a Habsburg as King of Bohemia in 1526 stimulated it. The establishment of a Jesuit College in Prague in 1547 speeded it. In 1564 it was confirmed by the pope's decision to concede the Hussites' main demand – admission of the laity to the use of the chalice in the eucharist. Meanwhile, overtly Protestant evangelization was not permitted in Bohemia but the more radical Hussites, especially among the pious movement known as the Unitas Fratrum, were in touch with German reformers and influenced by them. Thus between the twin fires of reformist Protestantism and resurgent Catholicism the Hussite tradition melted away.

The nature of the Waldensian heresy is much harder to pin down. Unlike the Hussites, the Waldenses had no coherent body of writings in which their beliefs were defined and differentiated from mainstream Christian tradition. They had their own collective Christian life in parallel with that of the Church, which they never utterly repudiated. The ministry of their *barbes* was preferred to, but not exclusive of, that of Catholic priests; their morality was particularly tough – or, at least, expressed with particular toughness, but not fundamentally different from that of the rest of Western Christendom. Riddled with contradictions, none of the surviving evidence from before the sixteenth century discloses a belief-system which is unequivocally heretical. The Waldenses were distinguished only by their sense of their own distinctiveness and by the harassment, occasionally overflowing into active persecution, with which the Church responded.

This was enough for reformers in Geneva, not far from the Waldenses' valleys, to see them as kindred spirits, potential allies and conscripts to the cause. In Provence, a group similar to the Waldenses initiated contacts with Protestants in the 1530s and received Calvinist writings and preachers with apparent enthusiasm. The Alpine communities have traditionally been seen as similar converts to Protestantism in a rapid mission, launched at their own invitation, at about the same time. In reality, the process was much slower and patchier. Missionary pastors from Geneva began to appear as permanent residents of the valleys in the 1550s; former *barbes* participated in Calvinist synods in the 1560s. In some ways the missionaries themselves were converted at least to Waldensian 'style'; the pithy, jokey preaching of the tradition of the *barbes* persisted in the communities converted to Protestantism. Here as in much of Europe, 'reformed' religion was really syncretic – a blend of the reformers' doctrines with many of the habits and much of the language of pre-Reformation Christianity.

The Arenas of the Gladiators

The evangelical vocations of Protestants, Catholics and Orthodox were most severely tested in the relatively few places where they were trying to convert one another. By repute, the most teeming of these arenas was Poland. In 1838 Count Valerian Krasinski dedicated a history of the Reformation in his native Poland 'to the Protestants of the British Empire and of the United States of America'. He set himself the task of explaining to his co-religionists how, after a promising start, Protestantism had withered in his country. His implicit agenda was even more ambitious. The Protestant in him was fascinated by a tale of subverted Providence, the patriot by a spectacle of national decline; the historian in him wanted to explain both. He beheld the Poland of his day, divided, crushed and oppressed, and recalled the Poland of the middle ages, strong, conquering and unconquerable. The defeat of the Reformation was, for Krasinski, the cause of the decline. 'No country in the world affords', he thought, 'a more striking illustration of the blessings which a political community derives from the introduction of a scriptural religion, and of the calamities which are entailed by its extinction.' Catholicism was 'the incubus which paralysed the energies of the nation.'

It was not altogether a contemptible theory: similar views have been popular among historians of the decline of Spain, and the power of Protestantism to enhance the liberties of a polity, the achievements of a culture and the performance of an economy is an old theme of Protestant historiography. In the case of Poland, the chronology did not fit: one of the country's most glorious periods, measured by military effectiveness, followed the triumph of Catholicism and during the seventeenth century Polish power was as remarkable for its durability as for its decline. Yet Krasinski's version of events was typical of its time and influential until ours.

With embarrassed abjurations of rancour, with warm protestations of friendly sentiments towards Catholics, he blamed the reformers' frustrations on the efficiency with which they were repressed. The Jesuits, 'a bigoted and unprincipled faction', incited rioters to break up evangelical congregations and destroy their property, while legal counter-measures 'were rendered nugatory by the influence of their order'. By this single cause an 'extraordinary reaction' was effected, which overturned a previously triumphant reformation, and 'the free institutions of Poland were afterwards rendered subservient to the persecution of its disciples.'

The Jesuits might have been flattered to be credited with so much; in fact, however, Krasinski glaringly exaggerated the early progress of the reformers in Poland and, therefore, the impact of the Catholic counter-measures. The contradictions of his arguments are obvious: had Protestantism really been triumphant at a popular level, the Jesuits would not have found mobs to incite. Had it really captured the allegiance of the élite, the members of the order could not have bent the courts to their will. For Krasinski, Protestantism and Catholicism seemed like contenders in a cosmic struggle; to us, they look like fighters on the same side, prone to squabble among themselves. In Poland, as in most of Western Christendom, they were phases of a single movement – an evangelical movement, aiming to heighten the volume and clarity with which the good news was broadcast. The peculiarity of Poland was that it was a marchland of the Latin west, and the competition of Rome and Reform was complicated in some parts of the kingdom by the presence of a third force: evangelically committed Orthodoxy.

The first big breakthrough of resurgent Catholicism in the Polish dominions came at the expense of Orthodoxy, not Protestantism. In 1596, Catholics and Orthodox met to counter the Protestant threat together, but the Synod of Brest ended in mutual excommunications and squabbles over property. Nonetheless, the adhesion of a large Uniate communion to Roman allegiance was the biggest single coup for Catholicism in Poland since the conversion of the kingdom in 987. The unrepentant Orthodox fought back and in the early seventeenth century seemed in some instances more susceptible to Protestant than Catholic overtures. Cyril Lucaris, who became Patriarch of Constantinople in 1621, broke out of his 'bewitchment' by reading the 'writings of the Evangelical Doctors. . . . I left the Fathers, and took for my guide Scripture and the Analogy of Faith alone. . . . I can no longer endure to hear men say that the comments of human tradition are of equal weight with Holy Scripture.'

Increasingly, however, competition with Catholics and Protestants sharpened Orthodox self-assertion in Poland. In 1632, the Mohyla Academy was founded as a centre of orthodox teaching; in 1633 the Orthodox hierarchy – in effective abeyance since the Synod of Brest – was reinstated; by the mid-century, Orthodox reconversions from Protestantism matched or exceeded those made by the Catholics in the Ruthenian and Ukrainian provinces. Over a longer period, however, the general outcome favoured Catholicism where the contest was three-cornered. Noble families lost by Orthodoxy to Calvinism in the sixteenth century tended to become Catholic in the seventeenth.

Because of the three-way competition, southern and eastern Poland was a particularly interesting zone of missionary competition; it was also highly exceptional. The fervour the missionaries of the different branches of the Church turned outward on the wider world or inward on their own flocks was sparingly expended on rivalry on each others' frontiers. Usually, where territory was in dispute and souls were wavering – in the Low Countries and across Germany, in the eastern Alps and along the Danube – the limits of the Reformation were set by persecutions, expulsions and war. The spiritual Reconquista achieved by the 'Counter-Reformation' and especially by its conquistador-vanguard, the Jesuits, worked best in under-evangelized terrain, as in Ireland, or where a non-Protestant 'third force' could be galvanized on its behalf, as in Poland.

The missionary impulse inside Europe, despite its limitations, was not without effects. There was no revolution in the spirituality of ordinary men, but there was a genuine transformation in the language and imagery – the total communication – of the Christian faith. For Protestant divines, vernacular services and the promotion of the Bible in translation were ways of helping the laity to a more active involvement in their faith; for Catholics the same purposes came to be represented by frequent communion and, for the particular involvement of women, the extension of the cults of Mary. 'You seem to think Christ was drunk,' Luther thundered against sophisticated doctrines of the eucharist, 'having imbibed too much at supper, and wearied his disciples with meaningless words!' This daring joke had a scandalous whiff of blasphemy about it when it was uttered. But it had the great virtue of treating Christ's humanity as literal and of picturing him, if only for our reproof, in the flesh of characteristically human weakness. Whereas Veronese could not be allowed to put ribald scenes into a version of the Last Supper (see above pp. 107–8). Caravaggio, at the end of the sixteenth century, was able to depict the same event as an episode of tavern low-life, without irreverence. Mathias Grünewald locked away his drawing of Christ as a coarse and low-browed picaroon; but after more than a century Murillo could paint the Christ-child as a naughty boy without fear of correction. As a result of the churches' early modern mission to bring Christianity to the people, sacred subjects were hallowed precisely by their relevance to the lives of ordinary people. On the ascent to heaven, Martha had caught up with Mary.

The Reformation is often understood as a movement to purge the sacred world of profanities; to some of its critics, it was almost the opposite: a step on the road to a secular society, a transference of sacred responsibilities into profane hands. The total effect of the changes made by early modern developments in Christianity seems rather to have been to redefine the relationship between the holy and the secular – to reknit the two kinds of stitching in a new pattern.

What Catholics could do with uninhibited freedom in the visual arts, Protestant propagandists could do in hymns: bringing the denizens of heaven down from the clouds to us as companions in our sufferings, sharers in our woes. The cults of a human Christ – wounded or dead – and of suffering saints, writhing in martyrdom, are most vivid in the tearful and bloody representations of baroque art. But in Protestant hymnody some of the images are just as clear, just as poignant, and just as powerful in bringing heaven home to earth. The vulnerability of a baby asleep on the hay was perfectly captured by Luther. The love gaping from Christ's wounded heart is as touching in Moravian hymns as in the visions described by St Margaret Mary Alacocque and depicted on Catholic altars. Contemplation of a sanguinary Ecce Homo can only be helped by Bach's setting of *O Sacred Head*.

EVANGELIZATION BY EVANGELICALS

In eighteenth- and nineteenth-century Europe, unredeemed places and classes were still waiting to feel the impact of the Reformation. Terrains beyond the Churches' reach were being opened up by the extension of settlement to lands made exploitable by new techniques and, by the end of the period, the impact of early industrialization on new towns. These last frontiers of early modern evangelization were conquered by the kind of Christianity loosely called 'evangelical'.

One of the authors once pressed a lawyer friend to explain exactly what the word 'curtilage' meant. 'You show me one and I'll tell you whether it is or it isn't,' was the only reply he would offer. We face much the same problem with a clutch of words hatched by the Reformation: 'evangelical', 'evangelicalism', 'evangelistic'. Secular commentators, and not a few churchmen, have difficulties with these terms, and not only because they have often been used in a pejorative sense. Definitions lack precision. An 'Evangelical' may be a German Protestant, a member of a particular party in the Church of England or a Christian who identifies himself with a certain set of religious priorities. The situation is made even more complicated by the addition of qualifying adjectives in such expressions as 'Catholic Evangelical', 'Liberal Evangelical' and 'Conservative Evangelical'. Yet, like the lawyer, we can usually identify evangelicalism when we encounter it.

When ordinary men and women were brought into that intensity of experience of the crucified Christ, as revealed in Scripture, to which the saints of old had testified they could not keep it to themselves.

> I prayed God with sighs and tears that he would give me, a troubled sinner, the gift of his grace and create a clean heart in me, that through the merits of the crimson blood of Christ he would graciously forgive my unclean walk and ease-seeking life . . . Behold, thus, the God of mercy . . . has first touched my heart, given me a new mind, humbled me in his fear, taught me in part to know myself, turned me from the

way of death and graciously called me into the narrow path of life, into the communion of his saints. To him be praise for evermore.

Thus Menno Simons described the enlightenment that set him firmly on the path from Catholic priest to Anabaptist leader but his conversion experience contained all the classic elements which devoted souls before and after his time have recorded.

François d'Andelot, converted as a result of reading Protestant books while in prison in Milan in the mid sixteenth century, launched Calvinist preachers on a mission to his Brittany estates where, according to one partisan, 'they were greeted like angels'. Anne Askew was the daughter of a prominent Lincolnshire gentleman with court connections, who gave impromptu Bible readings around the locality to illiterate farm workers in the reign of Henry VIII. She even went up to Lincoln cathedral, positioned herself by the chained copy of the Great Bible and challenged the clergy there to debate points of theology. Pert and defiant throughout frequent interrogations and bouts of torture, she went to the stake, the only English gentlewoman to be burned for her religious beliefs.

A personal experience of the Cross was the essential hallmark of an evangelical Christian. That is why believers' baptism was essential to many radicals; the sacrament could not be divorced from the individual's response or debased by being offered to infants. Anyone so stamped was a vessel for use in the work of the Gospel. The devotion which had once led to the cloister and the hermitage or into those religious communities which were in the world but not of it, was, for evangelicals, meant to be lived out in the home, the farmyard and the marketplace. Nor was the layman's role simply that of producing the fruit of good works, important though that was. German pamphleteers were quick to spot the gap which existed in Luther's theology between the theory and practice of the priesthood of all believers. They campaigned for the lay apostolate as a vital, everyday reality. The Christian was called upon to study Scripture, expound it to his household, admonish his neighbour to holy living and even to preach in church or the open air. The vivid eschatology espoused by most evangelicals added an urgency to this hortatory ministry. Hans Sachs, the semi-educated cobbler and poet of Nürnberg, would have no truck with the idea that *kerygma* and *didache* were exclusively the responsibilities of the professional ministry: 'Vocation is not something external, but internal; for externally we are all called to preach, the evil as well as the righteous.' To the argument that lay people are too ignorant to understand the Gospel Sachs has a ready reply: what university did the apostles attend? Their qualification was that they had been with Jesus.

The primacy of personal experience and the responsibility placed on the shoulders of the individual believer were the strength and weakness of evangelicalism. It called for intellectual discipline in attendance to the Bible, to sermons and class instruction. It called for moral discipline in progress in holiness. In rejecting reliance on priestly mediation and all other externals, it left the sin-burdened soul, in the last resort, alone. The pressures on reformed theologians to stress in reply the corporate aspects of the faith against the individualism of the radicals were as much political and social as theological. Hemmed about by powerful Catholic states, the cantons, principalities and kingdoms which accepted the reform needed internal cohesion. Religious divisions in a nation were disastrous, as was demonstrated over and again in France, Bohemia, Poland and elsewhere. Concern for unity became a barrier to conversionism. When John de Stogumber protested, in Shaw's *St Joan,* 'How can what an Englishman believes be heresy; it is a contradiction in terms,' he was displaying a genetic link with Richard Hooker, who insisted that an Englishman and a Christian were the same animal viewed from different perspectives. Patriotism could assume a spiritual intensity of its own. Cecil Spring-Rice, author of 'I vow to thee, my country,' explained, 'The Cross is the banner under which we fight – the Cross of St George, the Cross of St Andrew, the Cross of St Patrick.'

On the other hand, it is precisely because evangelicalism is so un-compromising in the demands it makes of potential converts and believers that it has become the Church's watchdog. At times it has slumbered, to awaken in noisy and energetic bouts of revival which have issued, not only in the froth and bubble of mass ecstasy, but also in transforming social and political activity. It is of the nature of revival to be sporadic. Solomon Stoddart, minister at Northampton, Massachusetts, witnessed no less than five revivals during his sixty years of service but at the time of his death in 1729 it was noted that, 'the greater part seemed to be at that time very insensible to the things of religion, and engaged in other cares and pursuits.' The pattern continued under the regime of Stoddart's grandson and successor, Jonathan Edwards. He concentrated his evangelistic activities on the 'roistering' and 'licentious' youth of the town. The results in 1733–34 were spectacular and 'soon made a glorious alteration in the town, so that in the spring and summer following . . . the town seemed to be full of the presence of God. . . .' The transformation was short lived. The young bloods of Massachusetts found it no easier to live under a puritanical regime than had the sophisticates of Florence at the time of Savonarola or Cromwell's Englishmen. By 1737 the Northampton revival was 'very much at a stop'. Though the Great Awakening was about to burst upon New England, several ecclesiastical fences had to be rebuilt before Edwards' church was able to participate in it fully.

George Whitefield was the first international Protestant evangelist; a man who saw his calling solely in terms of preaching conversion and who was not involved in founding churches or in pastoral care. Successful revival depends heavily upon novelties. If men and women are to be jolted from the complaisant rut of religious or irreligious conformity something must first

7.2 Jonathan Edwards (1703-58), chronicler of, and participant in, the Great Awakening: 'Whatever imprudences there may have been, and whatever sinful irregularities; whatever vehemence of the passions, and heats of the imagination, transports and ecstasies; whatever error in judgement, and indiscrete zeal; and whatever outcries, faintings, and agitations of body; yet, it is manifest and notorious, that there has been of late a very uncommon influence upon the minds of a very great part of the inhabitants of New England, attended with the best effects.' (*Thoughts Concerning the Present Revival*, 1724).

make them 'sit up and take notice'. It may be the personality of a charismatic preacher, the evidence of signs and wonders, clever publicity or the testimony of those prepared to suffer or die for their faith. Whitefield was a preacher who spoke with eloquence and fervour yet always in a homely idiom. Between 1740 and his death in 1758 he was almost constantly on the move. He travelled all over Britain and over large areas of the American colonies. After his early successes, his fame always went before him. Here was something out of the ordinary; something destined to have a greater impact than the Sunday-by-Sunday sermons of a Stoddart or an Edwards. The knowledge that Whitefield was coming stirred up a sense of expectancy, ensuring the evangelist, not only large audiences, but also audiences psychologically and emotionally geared to respond. When he addressed rallies of up to 15,000 people he made Boston, Massachusetts, seem 'no other than a Bethel and the gate of heaven. Many wept exceedingly and cried out under the Word, like persons that were hungering and thirsting after righteousness. The Spirit of the Lord was upon them all.'

Two factors beyond others made the American revival last. Whitefield inspired and, in some places, instructed the local clergy to continue the work of renewing the churches. At the same time he aroused the hostility of the Anglican establishment by denouncing 'spiritually dead' pastors. Whitefield is 'the most virulent, flaming, foul-mouthed persecutor of the Church of God that ever appeared in any age or country', one senior ecclesiastic fulminated. Such opposition only drove independent-minded colonists into the Nonconformist camp and tended to unite Lutherans, Presbyterians and Baptists in the evangelical cause.

The combination of pulpit oratory and the use of the latest communication techniques remained features of the revival business: the 'colloquial slang and commercial expressions' which Mr Punch attributed to Moody and Sankey, who

> State Scriptural facts in American phrases
> And interpolate jokes 'twixt their prayers and their praises.

Charles Grandison Finney, and Dwight L. Moody in the nineteenth century; Charles E. Fuller, Billy Graham and Robert Schuller in our own provide sufficient evidence of the skilful exploitation of charismatic personality combined with up-to-the-minute technology in the service of the Gospel. In this they were the heirs, not only of the Protestant preachers and pamphleteers of the sixteenth century, but also of the indulgence hawkers, the friars, and the ragged independent itinerants of the Middle Ages. The modern evangelical preacher is probably the last exponent of public oratory. Even American congressional candidates and Glaswegian trade union leaders (an endangered species) do not regularly draw the crowds of ten thousand plus which gather to hear John Wimber, Reinhardt Bonnke or

Morris Cerullo on their national and international tours. Politicians have exchanged the hustings for the TV interviewee's chair while evangelists have actually succeeded in using television to carry their Bible-thumping oratory into millions of homes.

Evangelization of neglected levels of society sounded, in some ears, like drumbeats of class war:

> I thank Your Ladyship for the information concerning the Methodist preachers; their doctrines are most repulsive and strongly tinctured with impertinence and disrespect towards their Superiors, in perpetually endeavouring to level all ranks and to do away with all distinctions. It is monstrous to be told you have a heart as sinful as the common wretches that crawl on the earth.

When one of the aristocratic friends of Selina, Countess of Huntingdon, wrote those splendidly self-condemnatory words she was expressing the fear that religious dissent had provoked ever since Innocent III launched his crusade against the Cathars – the fear of social disruption. Evangelicals addressed several of the same anxieties and aspirations as radical politicians. In Britain the hundred years which began with the Peterloo massacre and ended with the granting of limited female suffrage was the century of political emancipation. It was also, as D.W. Bebbington suggests, 'the Evangelical century'. The years during and after the Napoleonic Wars were the heyday of itinerant Methodist preachers and also of cult founders, such as the 'prophetess' Joanna Southcott, a latterday Maid of Kent, who foretold the overthrow of the nation's political leaders and the triumph of Christ's poor. Opponents of enthusiasm were alarmed at the success of these populists and, like their counterparts in all ages, tended to lump them all together. 'Their heavenly gifts, their calls, their inspirations, their feelings of grace at work within them, and the rest of their canting gibberish are . . . a great scandal to the country,' Cobbett complained. 'It is in vain that we boast of our *enlightened state,* while a sect like this is increasing daily.'

Free Church congregations sponsored lay evangelists and missioners, like Richard Weaver, the 'converted collier', and Philip Phillips, the 'singing pilgrim', who came from humble origins. The Brethren assemblies had no ordained and trained ministers. Leadership and outreach were in the hands of elders. The closing decades of the century saw the establishment of the Salvation Army. Anglicans were not slow to emulate this initiative and set up their own band of full-time evangelists – the Church Army. It was of the essence of evangelicalism that the converted man or woman should discover and apply God-given gifts in the service of the Church. Lay people were employed in house-to-house visitations and the Church of England created the office of reader to provide busy clergy with assistants who could preach and assist in divine worship. All this may have been an aspect of changing social patterns but it was also something of which Hans Sachs would heartily have approved.

THE LAY FRONTIER

Glory be to Jesus
Who in bitter pains
Poured for me the life-blood
From his sacred veins.

Grace and life eternal
In that Blood I find;
Blest be his compassion
Infinitely kind . . .

Oft as it is sprinkled
On our guilty hearts
Satan in confusion
Terror-struck departs.

The words were written, not by a close follower and emulator of Charles Wesley but by a contemporary Italian member of the Passionist Order (Translation by the Tractarian, Edward Caswall). Catholic evangelicalism had much the same message to proclaim as Protestant evangelicalism. It called men and women to intense, inward, personal faith. And it battled against the same enemies – materialism, rationalism, apathy and formalized religion. It shared the fervour, programme and methods of Protestant evangelicals, without, at first, exciting the same threat. The reformist orders had their places within the Catholic authority structure. When they were caught up in political wrangling and rivalry, they tended to submit or retreat. Alfonso Maria de'Liguori founded the Redemptorist order in 1732 for the specific purpose of organizing preaching missions, orginally in the towns and cities of South Italy.

His labours in the port of Leghorn were likened by one enthusiast to the preaching of Jonah in Nineveh and inevitably aroused the hostility and jealousy of others. When Alfonso organized prayer meetings among the Neapolitan beggars, the police raided them, convinced that they were seditious assemblies, and Alfonso was eventually removed from the leadership. Not for him the painful withdrawal from the parent Church which Wesley and his supporters had found necessary, or the bitter self-exile of the *fraticelli*.

This dichotomy is well illustrated by the career of Luther's older contemporary, Giampietro Carafa, the zealous, reformist ecclesiastic who gave up his lucrative and prestigious appointments to form, with Gaetano da Theine, the Theatine order of clerics regular. The brotherhood, which Macaulay likened to the Oxford Holy Club, aimed to continue and extend the charitable work of the Oratory of Divine Love, of which Gaetano was a member, and to couple it with evangelism. For several years Carafa devoted himself to sick visiting and open-air preaching. By calling people to personal piety expressed through the conventional channels, the Theatines hoped, as well as deepening the spiritual life of the laity, to protect them from the blandishments of the heretics. Like every effective evangelist Carafa delivered his orations brass-bound with certainty. He was as fervent in his denunciations of Protestants as he was about championing the affective religion which they also proposed. After the collapse of Cardinal Contarini's attempt to find common ground with the Lutherans at the Colloquy of Regensburg in 1541, Carafa committed himself increasingly to the extirpation of heresy. He was the prime mover in the establishment of the Roman inquisition and went on record as saying that if his own father were found guilty of unorthodox doctrine, he would personally pile the faggots around him. While Gaetano went on to turn his church of St Paul Major at Naples into a centre of Catholic renewal and reform, his erstwhile colleague, increasingly dogmatic and short-tempered as age and rheumatism took their toll, became the intensely reactionary Pope Paul IV, one of the most hated occupants of St Peter's chair.

Catholic evangelicals had one advantage over the proclaimers of Protestant revivalism: they channelled the devotion of penitents and converts into practices rich in personal or corporate drama and did not demand of them literary skills or evangelistic initiatives. As well as the traditional aids of mass, colourful festivals, confession, devotion to saints and telling the rosary, they devised other stereotypes to keep the central facts of redemption before the people's eyes. It was, for example, in the mid-eighteenth century that St Leonard of Port-Maurice gave final form to the medieval Easter ritual of the stations of the Cross and established it as a regular feature of Church life. In these eighteenth-century theatres of devotion, where pity and fear were purged, the congregations had parts.

They were not stimulated to religious initiatives of their own. In their dependence on the parish priest they were expected to be like Hilaire Belloc's 'Jim' and 'never leave a hold of nurse for fear of finding something worse'. The situation had not changed since before the Reformation. The route to a more 'Christian' life still led in the direction of holy orders or an approved lay community. From the Catholic point of view, letting lay spirituality off the leash had, from the sixteenth century onwards, permitted it to foul the footpaths of Christendom with the most obnoxious heterodoxies. Restraining lay activism avoided obvious short-term dangers. But it also deprived the Church of much potential energy and stored up long-term frustration. An inactive laity became the last mission frontier of Catholic evangelicals at home.

The democratization of Church life which, throughout most of the

Protestant world, had come to be recognized as a vital ingredient of renewal was largely resisted in the Roman communion until Vatican II breached the dam. *Lumen Gentium (The Light of the Nations)* advocated that parish priests should

> promote the dignity as well as the responsibility of the layman in the church. Let them prudently make use of his advice: let them confidently assign duties to him in the service of the church, allowing him freedom and room for action. Further, let them encourage the layman so that he may undertake tasks on his own initiative; attentively in Christ, let them consider with fatherly love the projects, suggestions and desires proposed by the laity.

This signalled a squaring-up to previously suppressed truths about the Church. An English Jesuit describes the altered perceptions thus:

> The three major characteristics of the church are sharing in the priesthood of Christ, the kingship of Christ and the prophetship of Christ. And that thinking goes back at least to Calvin. The Second Vatican Council, by rediscovering that the whole church was *priestly* set up a tension between the priesthood of the whole church and that of the ordained ministry. The *kingship* of Christ affects the whole question of decision making and the jurisdiction of bishops, and particularly of the pope. If the whole church is discovered to share in the *prophetship* of Christ, this asks searching questions about the prophetic function of the bishop and notably the pope. Questions of papal infallibility begin to be redefined in terms of the theology of prophecy and are seen to be a particular function of the prophetic activity of the *whole* church . . .

What is emerging as probably the most significant theme in the second half of the twentieth century is the respectability of lay theology – not an emasculated theology, not a second best to academic or clerical theology, but something born out of the experience of living the faith in the world. It goes beyond the admission of unordained men and women to the decision-making bodies. It has a great deal to do with the priesthood of all believers which Luther championed, then shied away from; which Hans Sachs argued for; which John of Leyden exercised so disastrously.

Lay activists have shown growing impatience – with hierarchies, with nice points of doctrine, with clerical rivalries. Lay action and lay theology are dangerous. They have produced and will continue to throw up religious aberrations. But the continual reformation without which the Church will die is now increasingly in the hands of the unordained majority.

THE EVANGELICALS ABROAD

Protestantism began as part of the great evangelizing movement in the late medieval and early modern Church in Europe. But Protestant missions had at first only a small part to play in its transmission overseas. Pietism invigorated Protestant churches and impelled them towards a gradual and eventually momentous missionary expansion during the eighteenth and nineteenth centuries. Pioneers from Halle responded to the call from King Frederick IV for evangelists for the Danish colony at Tranquebar, in 1705. From the missionary college in Copenhagen men were subsequently also despatched to Greenland and the West Indies. When public pressure forced the British East India Co. to relax opposition to Christian work, members of the Danish-Halle Mission were the first to go to the British settlements and garrisons in India. By their willingness to use Anglican rites and formularies they demonstrated that indifference to denominational barriers which marked out many Pietists.

This work in India was backed by the Society for Promoting Christian Knowledge (SPCK). The narrative of the founding of that organization indicates just how hard it was for missionary enthusiasts to build up a head of evangelistic steam. Thomas Bray was an Anglican minister of modest talents but immense tenacity. In 1695 he was appointed as commissary to the Bishop of London, charged with overseeing and staffing the parishes of Maryland. When he set about recruitment he was appalled to discover the poor quality of the clergy presenting themselves for service in the colonies. To help raise the standard he devised a scheme to provide theological libraries in England and America. From this initiative the SPCK emerged. Slowly. Most of the influential people Bray approached thought that his ideas were excellent – as long as they did not have to help fund them. He appealed in vain to the archbishops, to parliament and to the king. There was no official support for the exporting of England's Christian culture. Having virtually impoverished himself in the cause of overseas mission, Bray at last managed to interest a small group of wealthy patrons and it was as a private voluntary organization that the SPCK came into being in 1699. Two years later Bray hived off the specifically missionary activities from the SPCK's literary concerns. The Society for the Propagation of the Gospel in Foreign Parts (SPG) provided hundreds of ordained men to minister to the needs of settlers, slaves and natives in the colonies during the eighteenth century.

Zinzendorf's ecumenism – or, more accurately, pan-Protestantism – was an idea ahead of its time but one which was to influence international evangelism increasingly over succeeding generations. Since the early sixteenth century, attempts to glue back together the fragments of fractured Protestantism had relied on the weak adhesive of doctrinal accord. Zinzendorf and the Moravians proposed a different ecumenical vision – unity

for mission. They urged, what mystics, heretics and other spiritually motivated non-conformists had always urged, that personal salvation and the
propagation of an interiorized religion were more important than dogmas
and ecclesiastical establishments. In eighteenth-century Europe and, to a
lesser extent, America, dogmas and establishments were still too powerful
to permit that dismantling of denominational barriers that Zinzendorf looked
for. Many missionaries bound for foreign parts still packed prejudice and
suspicion with their Bibles. Yet alongside this there also went an inex-
tinguishable desire on the part of others to put Reformation divisions behind
them and make common cause in the Gospel. On the far side of the Atlantic
the cultural fusion of the colonies aided this process. Men and women from
different traditions married and founded 'ecumenical' families. Different
congregations saw the economic sense of sharing their buildings. In this
atmosphere Moravians preached from whatever pulpit was offered to them
and worked alongside their separated brethren in the mission field beyond
the frontier. In addition to this diaspora evangelism, the Moravians also influenced generations of young Americans through their schools and colleges,
a strategy already proven by such bodies as the Brethren of the Common
Life and the Jesuits.

There was in all this that element of lay impatience which, before and
since, has marked periods of Church renewal. Evangelical Christians with a
'passion for souls' (to use a term long current in such circles) united round
a small corpus of core doctrines, pushed to one side what they regarded as
clerical ideologies (which could include even such basic points of difference
as infant baptism) and got on with the job. The job might involve founding
and sustaining such interdenominational bodies as the YMCA, Bible
societies, student Christian unions, temperance organizations, school boards
or societies for home or overseas missions.

The cultures that were exported during the great age of missionary
expansion conveyed to other lands the different attitudes towards revelation.
In Peter Schaffer's *Royal Hunt of the Sun* Atahualpa sniffs and tastes a big
Bible, which a missionary hands him unopened, before flinging it to the
ground in disgust at the unsavoury uselessness of the thing. The Bible did
not quite remain a closed book for Catholic missionaries in the new worlds,
but it is fair to say that it was opened selectively, in line with the restrictive
reverence enjoined by the church in the old. The gospels and epistles were
among the first works to be translated into indigenous tongues in almost
every mission – frequently in lectionary-form, so that readings at mass could
be understood by the congregation; but the dangerously over-stimulating
Apocalypse was often left in the decent obscurity of a learned language, as
usually was most of the Old Testament, apart from Proverbs and the Psalms,
until the late nineteenth century. The Bible was disclosed in the vernacular
– in other words – rather to enrich converts' experience of the liturgy than
to provide texts for private study. Picture stories based on the Bible might

be used instead: a notorious priest in late nineteenth-century Actopan would allow no other catechetical aids in his parish – but Don Francisco Pérez was motivated less by suspicion of Scripture than by dissatisfaction with the translations. His work typified, in an extreme form, one of the best traditions of Catholic missions: an uncompromising belief in the universality of Christianity and an uncompromising desire to make it intelligible to the Indians within the framework of their own traditional culture: he used to box the ears of any Indian he heard talking Spanish.

Sacred dramas in the vernacular also helped to bring the immediacy of Bible stories into the missionaries' message. Some of the earliest survive from early sixteenth-century Mexico or are alluded to in other sources: the Annunciation, presented in dialogue form; complete Nativity cycles, of course; the Temptation and Passion of Christ and works designed to embody untranslated parts of the Bible; a *Last Judgement* with eight hundred parts based on the Book of Revelation, a work on the Fall of Man and an Isaac cycle. To some extent, mission life was immune from the backlash against play-acting which was part of the Church's assault on popular culture in the sixteenth and seventeenth centuries (see below, p. 110ff); and the tradition only withered when Catholic attitudes to the Bible generally became less squeamish and more confiding in the late nineteenth and twentieth centuries.

By this time Protestant colporteurs had made such inroads with vernacular Scriptures, the dissemination of which was so closely tied up with education and 'advancement', that Catholic missions had little option but to adopt similar tactics. That professional iconoclast, Thomas Carlyle, described a Bible society as 'a machine for converting the heathen'. Through almost two centuries there has been about such organizations a whirring relentlessness comparable at some times to the almost imperceptible ticking of a Swiss watch and at others to the onslaught of a jungle-crushing bulldozer. The British and Foreign Bible Society (now the Bible Society) was assembled, at the height of the Industrial Revolution, in 1804. The collaborating engineers were interdenominational evangelicalism, an invincible belief in human progress and colonial expansion. The manufacturers' specification described the device as an organization whose purpose was 'to encourage the wider circulation of the Holy Scriptures, without note or comment'. So effective was the machine and so well-attuned to the needs of the time that within a few years dozens of imitations had been built in countries as far apart as Ireland and New Zealand, Australia and Norway, Philadelphia and Russia, Poland and Canada.

The ambitious commitment to put a copy of the vernacular Scriptures into the hands of every literate human being widened stupendously the vision sustained over the centuries by Jerome, Wycliffe, Erasmus, Tyndale, Jansen and countless others who had laboured or suffered for an open Bible. The translation of Scripture, in whole or part, into more than 1,500 languages in the century and a half after 1804 put a powerful tool into the hands of missionaries and evangelists. It conveyed the Christian message to lands closed to religious propagandists. Its impact has been incalculable. Luther once observed, 'I have done nothing: the Word has done and accomplished everything'. In the nineteenth and twentieth centuries that became true in a way he could never have envisaged.

THE CALL OF THE WILD

The most enduring of early modern European empires was founded by Russians in Siberia. Imperialism has receded from almost all the other European conquests outside Europe but Siberia remains, a vast swathe of Asia immutably Russified. For the makers of this empire its creation was a crusade and its pride was an expanded Christendom. Russians depicted their armies of conquest as protected by visions and the axes of communication between the towns they built as beams from the eye of Christ, cast through the darkness of unevangelized wastes. 'Christian' Siberia was a Siberia of settlers, who rapidly came to outnumber the indigenous people in most parts. The evangelization of the rest was accomplished in the nineteenth century when the orthodox world caught a new, virulent form of the missionary virus which was spreading from the West. In view of the techniques adopted it is not surprising that Christianity acquired, according to the criticisms of the monk Spiridon, a reputation as 'a religion of horse-thieves', evasively adopted by rogues with an interest in the favour of the state, or as a superficial smattering of baptismal waters by missionaries more concerned with quantity than quality. But not all evangelistic endeavour was tainted with secular politics and the sheer energy of the Orthodox mission is impressive. In the early nineteenth century Christianity was planted and nursed on a small scale but carefully by Makary in the Altai mountains. The Siberian-born patriarch Veniaminov carried it, before his translation to the see of Moscow in 1867, among the Aleuts, Koiaks, Tchukches and Manchus – peoples of the fringes of the empire. His vision included the spread of the Orthodox mission beyond the reach of Russian secular power; indeed, he founded a modestly successful mission in Japan. On the whole, however, the history of the spread of Orthodoxy illustrates the advantages and limitations that attended the spread of Christianity in the age of European imperialism. Its successes often depended on the backing of political clout; its configurations were shaped by the movements of settlers or the march of conquistadores.

Some Spanish missionaries in the New World tried to dissociate themselves from imperialism – to spread the faith without the sword; to convert indigenous societies without subjecting them by force or adulterating them with colonists. It worked, if at all, only in small patches and for short periods. When the great advocate of the approach, Bartolomé de Las Casas, retired as bishop in 1552, the Dominicans of the experimental mission of La Vera Paz in Guatemala gave up the effort and called in Spanish troops to help them. The Jesuit reductions in South America became a sort of mini-empire, violently defended against slaver-invaders in battles in which 'St Francis Xavier guided the bullets': in any case they were at best paternalist republics, unequivocally under white men's control. Though the early modern spread of Christianity was to prove the strength of Christian evangelism, its successes were largely owed to colonialism. Conversions were often procured by conquests and the frontiers of the faith, where permanently extended, were usually stretched by settlement from Europe.

Colonial societies could be as much of a challenge to missionaries as the unlighted wilderness. It was Afrikaaner settlers who, in 1852, burned down David Livingstone's post at Kolobeng, not the pagan inhabitants of the land. It is often assumed that the United States, for instance, was founded by religious impulses, created by the consciences of religious refugees. Pilgrim Massachusetts, Quaker Pennsylvania, Catholic Maryland and Mormon Utah are vivid proofs. Yet the usual effect of frontier experience was to dilute Christianity or, at least, to separate the frontiersmen from the discipline of parent-Churches. The Christianization of America was in one sense a work of reclamation, building penfolds for westward-straying sheep. Only 6.9 per cent of US citizens were registered as belonging to churches in 1800. The numbers rose to 15.5 per cent in 1850 and 43.5 per cent in 1910 and only exceeded 50 per cent in 1942.

Faith followed the flag but lingered after it. If the spread of Christianity depended on colonialism, its endurance was of another kind, capable of outlasting its early conditions of growth. No part of the world demonstrates this more than sub-Saharan Africa. To historians in a remote future, perhaps, Christianity will seem as essentially a Black African religion, despite most of the region's late start, just as industrialization, with the same qualification, will seem a characteristically East Asian phenomenon. Outside the antiquity of the Nubian and Ethiopian Churches, Black Christianity in Africa had to wait for white imperialists. Except in coastal toeholds and temperate climes, it had to wait also for the nineteenth century.

The delay was not due solely to the hesitations of imperialism. Protestant Churches' missionary vocations took a long time to mature; those of Roman Catholicism were checked in the late eighteenth century by the disbanding of the Jesuits and the disasters of the French Revolution. Like less benign invaders, missionaries in Black Africa could make little headway without industrial technology and modern medicines: in the first twenty years of its attempted mission in West Africa from 1804, the Church Missionary Society lost fifty men and women to disease. Yet the missionary wave on which the conversion of Africa was launched in the nineteenth century was part of an era of renewed European expansion generally, which covered most of what, in his earlier aggressions, the white man had left unconquered.

This is not to say that missionaries shared all the priorities of imperialism, or that they were not ahead of its forces in many – perhaps most – of the areas where they worked. David Livingstone was motivated by prejudices about 'civilization' and by confidence in commerce as well as by scientific curiosity and by a crusade against slavery which was as much a secular policy as a sacred task. Yet no reader of his journals can doubt the primacy of the missionary vocation among the inner forces which impelled him to make his extraordinary journeys. He behaved consistently with his vow to

> place no value on anything except in relation to the kingdom of Christ. If anything will advance the kingdom, it shall be given away or kept, only as by giving or keeping it I shall most promote the glory of Him to Whom I owe all my hope in time and eternity.

Missionaries were often hostile to lay White power or disposed to serve indigenous state-building as 'Protestant popes in the bush' or servants, even 'slaves', of Black rulers. The White Fathers – still Africa's most successful Catholic missionary society – became almost as unpopular with the secular governments of some imperialist powers as the Jesuits before them. Long before liberation theology was formulated, Catholic mission schools were training a future post-imperial élite to take power back from White rulers. John Colenso, Anglican Bishop of Natal for thirty years from 1853, a man of compassion and integrity who was known to the Zulus as *Sobantu*, 'father of the people', was denounced by his superiors and disowned by the SPG and the SPCK. His 'heresies' were twofold. He was indulgent of such local customs as polygamy because he knew the social evils that would follow their abolition. Enforced divorce, for example, would result in thousands of unwanted women and children. What was more revolutionary was the re-appraisal of orthodox biblical interpretation to which Colenso was forced by answering as honestly as he could the searching questions of African converts. Colenso was solemnly excommunicated by the Archbishop of Cape Town and, for some time, the inhabitants of Durban were treated to the Barchesteresque spectacle of two rival bishops prowling the cathedral precincts.

The Colenso affair, followed a few years later by the humiliation of Isandhlwana and the death of the Prince Imperial drew from Disraeli the celebrated, wry comment, 'A remarkable people, the Zulu; they defeat our armies, they convert our bishops and they have written "finis" to a great European dynasty.' It was precisely this fear of theological contamination that lay behind the official policy of imposing a complete cultural package on 'inferior' races, a policy many missionaries found to be at variance with the love of Christ which they claimed to represent.

Missionary tides ebbed and flowed with local political forces which the preachers only dimly understood. The emissaries of a white god might be welcomed to enhance the prestige of a ruler or to provide magical support in the power struggle between neighbouring tribes. In the sixteenth century, Obas of Benin announced their conversion as often as Portuguese sponsors would send them shipments of arms. Missionaries from Britain were welcomed to the Madagascar of King Radoma I in the 1820s for the same reason; but when Queen Ranavalona was installed by a rival clan, the foreigners were expelled, Christian noblemen were burned alive and a soothsayer who told the queen that all God's children were equal in his eyes was immersed in a pit of boiling rice. In the weak realm of Lewanyika of the Lozi in Nyasaland at the end of the century, British missions were exploited to procure imperial protection against covetous Germans and Portuguese. In the same period, the Kabakas of Buganda played Catholic and Protestant missions off against each other to extract the utmost in gifts.

Despite the entanglement of Christianity and imperialism, Africa's willingness to become Christian was matched by Christianity's ability to become African. African Churches have been created in three ways: by schism, by adaptation and by what might be called spontaneous combustion. The locus classicus of the last type of case is that of William Wade Harris, the Liberian 'prophet' who conducted a singlehanded mission in the Ivory Coast in 1913–15. Robed and stoled, bearing cross and Bible, refusing gifts except for relief of the poor, he founded a shadowy kind of Christianity, with thousands of adherents who sang garbled hymns and venerated a book they could not read. A typical case of schism might be illustrated by two Churches of the 1930s in Makoni in what is now Zimbabwe: the Church of St Francis and the African Catholic Church, both secessions from Anglicanism which rehabilitated the veneration of ancestor-spirits as a form of devotion to be practised by Christians.

Churches like these, sprung of African initiatives, are making an important contribution to the spread of Christianity today. Yet in a way more remarkable still are the African churches born of adaptation: Catholic and Protestant Africa, where the churches have outgrown their need for White personnel, developed distinctive timbres for worship and mounted missions of their own. Missionaries from Africa – the joke is now so often made that it has acquired the force of prophecy – will come to re-evangelize the lapsed-Christian White West. Even the Anglican communion – stagnant or declining in its heartlands – has grown at a rate of 5 per cent a year in its Black African provinces during the 1990s.

Chapter Eight

A SENSE OF BELONGING:
How People Choose their Church

THE SOCIETY OF CHURCH

They were willing to die for Calvinism but they did not know what it was. In the 1560s, leading Netherlandish Protestants, including Jan Denys, who had led rioters in image-breaking in West Flanders and commanded an army of Calvinist rebels, revealed under interrogation that their grasp of the doctrines they professed was negligible. Their confessions summarized long-standing humanist criticisms of clerical privilege, bombast, indolence and expense but omitted any specifically Protestant heresies. If there were leaders so ignorant of the new faith, sharper awareness can hardly have been characteristic of the rank and file. And if faith imperfectly understood could inspire such fatal self-dedication, there must have been something else about it – something felt, not thought – which made up for the lack of rational commitment.

While doctrinal differences mean little or nothing to most people, a kind of change which can immediately be sensed by defectors from one Church to another is the difference in the experience of worship. In some ways, it can be an aesthetic difference, represented, at its extremes, by the appeal to 'high church atheists' of the balletics of a deliciously old-fashioned liturgy, or by the struggles between admirers of the beauty of holiness, who like their churches to look unworldly, and worshippers of the cult of youth who are happier in spaces cluttered with rock amplifiers, big screens and roving microphones. When Chateaubriand wrote the *Génie du christianisme* his defence of Christianity was based on its superior 'beauties' rather than its supposed monopoly of truth or goodness. For the spiritually sensitive, the critical difference between one church and another can be a difference in the quality of the impact on the spirit: the reassurance or consolation, the uplift or ecstasy. In Britain, a popular Sunday newspaper rates rival places of worship according to their 'spiritual high'. Bigger than the gulf between Catholics and Protestants in Britain today is the distaste which separates traditional Protestants, for whom solemnity and decorum are vital for an act of worship, from experimental charismatics who go to church for a regular experiential 'fix'. While practitioners of the 'Toronto Blessing' collapse in giggles, pillars of the Kirk turn in revulsion to their black books of metrical psalms.

In every setting – and, therefore, probably, for most people – the change from one Christian tradition to another is felt as a difference in the *social* experience of worship: in the worshipper's relations with his fellow-worshippers; in the sense of place and of belonging conferred by membership of a congregation; in the affirmation or realignment of worldly rankings that comes with the apportionment of church offices or with the distributions of the pews. Rather than by what you believe, the kind of Christian you are – the tradition, that is, to which you belong – is defined by what you do in church and, for the particular purposes of this chapter, whom you do it with.

In the world of Jan Denys the novelty of the Calvinist experience could be felt with peculiar acuity. Early Netherlandish Calvinism was the religion of a defiantly different community – a summer religion of worshippers under an open sky: Calvinist missions usually started in good weather, with open-air meetings, and seized and 'purified' Catholic Churches only when a congregation had been formed, at the onset of winter. In most places, early Protestants were savourers of danger or, at least, of the disapproval of the socially conventional; the town chronicler of Antwerp in the summer of 1566 reported the citizens' fears of Calvinist meetings, thousands strong, attracting armed worshippers. The excited crowds who thronged to their gatherings must have got an extra injection of adrenalin from the point of every weapon flourished.

The uniqueness of the experience offered by these meetings was enhanced by the attitude of the Catholic authorities: usually, they tolerated the meetings for worship, but would not allow the ministers to celebrate the sacraments; in consequence, there were few echoes of familiar ritual at the open-air services, which generated community atmosphere by uniting the audience in the lusty singing of psalms in French – the language of the only cheap vernacular editions initially available – or urging it to huddle together under the blast of comfortable horrors from hell-fire preaching. The attraction of the experience had something of the same magnetism, for the same kind of people – the independent-minded, the happily marginalized, the sensation-seeking, the susceptible to trends – who frequent political demonstrations or outdoor rallies or 'raves' or open-air 'festivals' today: the thrill of defying familiar conventions is complemented by the solace of immersing oneself in new ones. It satisfied those who love loud scandal: Thomas More prayed for heretics who would be 'reasonable' and 'still' but found that 'in railing standeth all their revel'. Early Protestantism was a 'counter-culture' in its day – even, perhaps, as early Christianity was in an earlier period.

Especially among the young, the pleasure of freakish and outrageous behaviour, sanctioned by the safety of numbers or the protection of powerful patrons, is almost universally attractive. 'Reformation' and 'counter-Reformation' movements in sixteenth-century Europe both mobilized squads of young fanatics to jerk complacent majorities out of orthodoxy or indifference. The Red Guards of reform included the gangs of iconoclasts, sometimes only a handful strong, who vandalized churches for journeymen's pay, subscribed by Calvinist congregations in the Netherlands during the 'fury' of 1566. Their Catholic counterparts were exemplified by the pupils of the Jesuit College of Verdun – spiritual terrorists who conducted their own mission through the town in celebration of the Assumption in 1571, separating brawlers, braving taverns, deflecting priests from brothel doors, exhorting the streets to penance and promising to deliver 3,000 penitents to their teachers' thresholds.

Protestantism and Catholicism appealed to the same constituencies and particular individuals could be equally zealous for each in turn. The most conspicuous example is that of the charismatic maverick and turbulent priest, Stanislav Orzechowski. Born poor but noble in 1513, he had an engaging love of his *patria chica* in the Ruthenian borderlands and a marketable talent for invective. As a student at Wittenberg, he was converted, according to his subsequent confession, by a convincing mixture of youthful restlessness and ambition. 'I became enamoured of innovation; I considered that it would be very honourable to me if, by introducing some German doctrines, I should be distinguished from my equals in age, as for instance: such principles as, to disobey the Pope; to have no respect for laws; to revel always and never to fast; to seize church property; to know nothing about God; to exterminate the monks. After three years of study I arrived at that truth, that all that is old, that is paternal, is not just.'

The Polish Reformation thus began as a religion of *enfants terribles*. But youthful rebels grow into mature opportunists and Orzechowski slid back into Catholicism – and out again and back again – without altering many convictions. In his Protestant youth he won preferment by intimidating patrons; in his Catholic maturity by fawning on them. What he got from Wittenberg was more a matter of style than content – bludgeoning rhetoric rather than radical theology. His spirituality – such as it was – was closest to the Orthodox tradition which was strong in his homeland; the specific issue on which he broke with the Catholic hierarchy and incurred excommunication in 1550 was the marriage of priests, a practice permitted in Orthodox as well as Protestant circles. He could be as condemnatory of 'Lutheran perversion' as of 'Roman corruption' and when he called on Poland to withdraw allegiance from the pope, he advocated adhering instead to the Greek church. Even as a Catholic apologist, he could never stomach monks, from whom he shared an Erasmian aversion: 'numerous and barbarous' they were like 'well fed swine, fattening themselves for the pastures of hell'. On almost all other matters which divided Catholics and Protestants, Orzechowski expressed, at different times of his life, opinions so violent in their mutual contradictions that it is hard to associate him with any consistent beliefs. There were, however, consistencies of theme which disclose what for him were the important issues.

Doctrine did not interest him much. With indiscriminate flair, he could deploy the conventional arguments for and against transubstantiation and consubstantiation, predestination and free will, priesthood and presbytery, mediation and revelation. On the forms of worship he had little to say, beyond a preference, which shows through even his Catholic polemics, for the liturgy in the vernacular. What did concern him were questions of authority and power. In his Protestant phase, 'Consider, O Julius,' he adjured the pope, 'with what a man you will have to deal – not with an Italian, indeed, but with a Ruthene; not with one of your mean popish subjects, but with the citizen of a kingdom, where the monarch himself is obliged to obey the law.' He advocated the exclusion of the clergy from the Diet and from office. 'If, however, they wish to retain the senatorial dignity, let them renounce the allegiance of Rome. Is the Polish church not enough for them? But otherwise, they must not be considered as citizens of the country, because no one can conscientiously serve two masters.' As a Protestant, he was a pre-incarnate Whig; as a Catholic, an unregenerate ultramontane. The publicist who had once advocated the exclusion of the pope on the grounds that royal power was 'independent and derived from God' reverted to the view that 'the king is established only that he should serve the clergy. The supreme pontiff alone establishes kings and as he establishes them, he has authority over them . . . The priest serves the altar, but the king serves the priest, and is only his armed minister.' This had been the refrain of popes' pensioners for centuries.

Poland, despite its reputation as a victorious battlefield of the Counter-Reformation, was really a sheepfold of mild coexistence between rival communions. The clash of reformers, Catholic and Protestant, produced the 'Concors Discordia' – the agreement to differ, a 'beautiful harmony', as a Benedictine called it in 1639, 'born of contrary things'. With only rare lapses, Poles maintained for nearly two centuries the resolve that 'we who differ in religion will keep peace among ourselves.' Lutherans, concentrated in northern cities, were guaranteed freedom of worship by charters and treaties, a basis of civil peace which no regime would risk. In 1645 the civilized if inconclusive 'Colloquium of Love' demonstrated the willingness of Catholic and Protestant divines to strive for mutual understanding. If there was a battle for souls, its weapons were, on the whole, genuinely spiritual. In 1613, the beautiful shrine of Kalwariya Zebrzdowska was laid in the Carpathian foothills to demonstrate the superior beauty rather than the superior might of the Catholic faith; the friars cultivated mystical and ascetic practices as an alternative to violence in their contest of holiness with Protestant pastors; the Jesuits' main instrument was their schools. In 1674 a visiting Spanish diplomat was impressed at the 'free exercise of two religions. . . . All live in great harmony with each other and without disputes or arguments on questions of belief – which is the best way to preserve peace.' Ironically, just as toleration became a fashion in the rest of Europe it broke down in Poland in 1724 when a Jesuit procession bearing an image of the Virgin was attacked and a college burned. Occasional provocations of a similar sort had always been absorbed before; but this time an army was mobilized to quell what was perceived as a sectarian rebellion and Protestant liberties revoked.

In the course of the Reformation, in most of the rest of Europe, the choice of people's religion came to be made for them by the state: *cuius regio, eius religio* became the norm and remained so, with a few exceptions and some gradual modifications, at least until the French Revolution and, in most places, into the nineteenth century. Even today it is possible, with some confidence, to say of Swedes or Danes that they are overwhelmingly likely to be Lutheran, if anything, or that a Spaniard or Austrian will be a Catholic. In the limited times and places in which individuals were genuinely, entirely free to make a choice between Protestantism and Catholicism, the choice was less between systems of belief than between types of fellowship and ranges of fellow-worshippers. When reform movements were launched, under the threat of persecution, in atmospheres of danger and defiance, Protestants were necessarily recruited from among people who relished minority status – its leaven of peril, its luxury of self-esteem. The elect could form, in their own regard, an élite unrepressed by lack of breeding, learning or wealth. Indeed, although Protestant state churches came to enfold entire populations, there is room to doubt whether Protestant self-consciousness has ever been successfully adapted to a majority. The actively committed may always have been outnumbered by the passively conformist, the invincibly indifferent, the quietly secular or the secretly dissident. Even where Protestantism became a part of national identity, as in eighteenth-century England, it relied on nourishment from an heroic self-perception as the religion of a beleaguered band, outnumbered on a global scale, with a mission to resist and survive. In the Netherlands, Calvinism came to shape national culture to an almost monopolistic extent; yet this was already beginning to be the case when Calvinists numbered no more than 10 per cent of the population; and even if nominal conformists are counted, Calvinism never commanded the allegiance of a majority of the population.

Where Catholicism became the minority communion or the object of persecution by the State, it could achieve the same kind of magnetism and attract the same kind of converts – in terms of psychological types – as early Protestantism: English recusants, prepared to pay fines for the privilege of holding themselves aloof from the conventional crowd; keepers of priest's holes, relishing the risk; denizens of English colleges abroad, who got some kind of inverted pleasure from the taste of exiles' bread. Alternatively, where Protestantism took over the establishment, self-separators had the option of withdrawing into more radical forms of dissent and getting their sense of *apartheid* from membership of a sect. An anthropologist from outer space would be more likely to classify Christian traditions into 'minoritarian' and 'non-minoritarian' than into 'Catholic' and 'Protestant'.

CONGREGATIONS IN PROFILE

Seven other kinds of social profile provide examples of how the differences between churches can be appreciated across the conventional boundaries. The Catholic, Protestant and Orthodox communions are made up of congregations, movements and orders of a number of these types; none of the types is necessarily peculiar to any of the three great traditions. The categories are not meant to form a comprehensive typology, only a scheme of convenience; and they have to be understood flexibly, sliding and overlapping like Venn diagrams drawn in quicksilver. For the sake of convenience, before we look at each in turn, they can be labelled: subverted hierarchies; globular communities; cross-class congregations; ersatz families; exclusive brethren; class covens, and gangplank Bethels.

By 'subverted hierarchies' we mean churches which create within themselves patterns of rank or of the absence of rank at variance with those prevailing in society at large. In extreme cases, these are vividly exemplified by egalitarian sects which ape the community of goods attributed to the early Church by the text of Acts: 'And all who shared the faith owned everything in common; they sold their goods and possessions and distributed the proceeds among themselves according to what each needed.' This was the inspiration behind the communism of the Anabaptists; it was practised with remarkable success by the Shakers, eighteenth-century idealists who hailed their foundress as a reincarnation of Christ and nicely combined a Puritanical moral code with rites of collective ecstasy. A similarly pure form of Christian communism impressed Madame de Staël when she saw a community of Moravian brethren near Erfurt: though she thought Protestantism too libertarian for its adherents' good, she found that Moravians inhabited 'the monasteries of Protestantism'. Summoned by a wind band to a church decked with roses, they dressed in identical clothes and were buried under identical tombstones. The Moravian tradition represents Christian communism at its best, but is a kind of piety easily exploited by charismatic conmen: Ananias and Sapphira are always lurking in the vicinity of the account books. It is still found, in a state of surprising purity, among Hutterite communities today. But in variants milder than communism, the subversion of hierarchy has played a big part in the appeal of many forms of Christianity.

It was part of the original appeal of Christianity itself: an edifice of social outcasts – of despised provincials, publicans and sinners, slaves and women, whose Messiah was a carpenter and whose 'foundation stone' a fisherman. Christ promised a heaven in which distinctions of class and of other sources of rank would be obliterated. Few among St Paul's correspondents in Corinth, he admitted, were powerful or highly born. Even in the middle Ages, when the Church had accumulated a crushing weight of respectability, it kept some of the characteristics of an alternative society: defying worldly powers, subordinating lay lords, whenever it could, to prelates of inferior birth, and functioning as a *carrière ouverte aux talents* by which low-born boys could, with suitable gifts and suitable patronage, rise to positions of power and influence. Bishop Peter of Tarentaise, one of the early Cistercians who became a saint, was the son of poor peasants from Dauphiné; his contemporary, Bishop Vicelin of Oldenburg, who made the same transition to sainthood, was 'from parents distinguished rather by goodness than rank'. Saints were 'socially amphibious' characters who, though usually well born, demonstrated their humility by performing menial tasks, usually in monastic kitchens. Though high birth was generally assumed to be a condition of high office, particular orders – Cluniacs, Hirsauers, Cistercians and mendicants – showed a bias in favour of the exaltation of the humble, at least for the first two or three generations of their existence. The vocation of St Francis, who renounced wealth for a beggar's dependence on God, was an aggressive *bouleversement* of the way of the world; a sacralization of the ritual revels at Christmas or Corpus Christi, when masters and servants swapped places; a projection on a massive scale of the Maundy rite when the priest washes the feet of laymen or acolytes. Abelard was suspicious of noble prioresses; the Emperor Henry IV, who knelt in the snow in penance before a pope, liked his bishops to be raised 'from the dust'.

Though ossified ranks could be challenged effectively from within the Catholic church, Catholicism was itself identifiable with a rigid social distinction of enormous power: that between priests and laymen. By deposing the priest from his uniquely numinous role – or, at least, by admitting lay people to a share in his ministry – Protestant reformers were able to offer their converts a subverted hierarchy of enormous appeal. In practice, Protestant churches developed rigid authority structures of their own. Some continued the old hierarchy, from bishops down, almost unmodified. Most acquired pastorates of 'priests writ large'. (see above, p. 155) Some constructed inquisitorial superstructures as forbidding as anything in Catholic tradition: the Board of Directors of Christian Science, for instance, has power to remove all the 'practitioners' and 'readers' of that church without notice or explanation. Sects which have eluded altogether the temptation to erect quasi-priesthoods are relatively rare. Quaker elders, it is true, are generally reluctant to intervene to cut short bogus utterances of the indwelling spirit – but they have the power and, sometimes, the compulsion to do so. Outside Quaker meetings, you have to go to New Orleans to find lay people encouraged in equality of utterance with their ministers: there the People of the Living God, a sect founded in 1932, have open pulpits to check ministerial pride with lay criticism.

Still, even in Protestant churches with powerful pastorates who have a monopoly over the ministry of the sacraments, lay power can be daunting. From the early days of the Reformation Presbyterian Churches had their Kirk-Session or *Kerkegerad* and individual congregations their bodies of elders; lay ordinaries commonly appoint to livings in Protestant State Churches and the Church of England, which has always had a lay 'Supreme Governor', has, for the last twenty-five years, been regulated by a 'general synod' in which representatives of the laity form one of three houses. Membership of the regulatory institutions of a Protestant church not only gives laymen the satisfaction of lording it over the ordained; it can also, where elders form the hierarchy, give fellow worshippers power over people who, outside church, would be considered their social superiors. In Scotland, in recent years, shopkeepers have had the pleasure of sitting in judgement over the Lord Chancellor of England and expelling him from their kirk: as neat a case of the World turned Upside Down as any radical of the Reformation era, or any medieval lord of misrule, could have devised.

Christian movements are both true to the Church's origin and powerful in their appeal when they discard worldly hierarchies and substitute others of their own. Like the elevation of the humble, deference to women is a kind of social subversion which has scriptural roots and enormous power to mobilize devotion. Even St Paul, who thought women should be kept in their place, was alert to the tremendous influence of the sex in spreading the gospel and serving the Church: a third of the fellow-workers to whom he sent greetings by name at the end of the epistle to the Romans were women. Female visionaries could deflect Christians into heresy, like the prophetesses of Montanism who deluded Tertullian, but they were more usually the nursemaids of Christianity, throughout the patristic era, creating Christian households, fostering Christian communities and bringing up future saints of both sexes. Exclusion from the priesthood limited their role to four fields; matronly influence; saintly heroism which gave some of them power over powerful men; mobilization of other women in religious orders; and writing, which underprivileged access to education made rare: the work of St Catherine of Siena, who became a Doctor of the Church, had to be dictated to an amanuensis because she could not write for herself. In these connections – as in the generation of heresy – women's special genius for visionary and mystical experiences played a prominent part.

The associations of the early Protestant reformers are all with stern-faced patriarchy: with Luther's insistence on Paul's strict rules of female conduct in church; with Knox's trumpet-blast against the 'monstrous' deformation that gave women power over men. The Catholic Church was more inventive in exploiting female genius – reforming religious orders, starting schools, harnessing mystical piety in the service of orthodox doctrine. Women became 'the Church's teachers, nurses and social workers and the parish clergy's strong right arm'. The community of English lady missionaries established by Mary Ward at St Omer caused a scandal by eschewing the cloister, dressing like Jesuits and, apparently, usurping the apostolate of men.

Founder-prophetesses and messianic females, however, were sources of energy that could only develop outside the discipline of the Catholic Church and usually beyond the fringe of Protestantism. The Shakers were a relatively small phenomenon compared with some of the huge and outwardly impressive movements inspired by women, as time went on, from inside the Protestant tradition: Adventism is effectively the child of Ellen Gould White, whose revelations superseded those of earlier Adventist prophets; Christian Science was so completely identified with Mary Baker Eddy that she was depicted hand-in-hand with Christ in the movement's early iconography, while preaching at Christian Science services was forbidden lest her doctrines be diluted. Most of the schisms within Christian Science have been led by women.

It may sound odd to maintain, on the one hand, that subverted hierarchies were a recurring characteristic of medieval Christianity and yet, on the other, to ascribe some of the popularity of Protestantism to their appeal. Yet one constant message of this book is that the Reformation was a movement, or a number of movements, entirely typical of the Christian tradition; it should not be surprising to find precedents in medieval Catholicism for everything associated with it. Every form of hierarchical subversion has essentially the same kind of appeal, whether it exalts the poor over the rich, the common over the noble, the lay over the priest, women over men or even children above adults – as in the Catholic movement of dubious orthodoxy galvanized in the Basque country in pursuit of apparitions of the Virgin in 1933. In the cult of the Virgin of Ezquioga, children played the same role, as mediators of sub- or supra-rational perceptions, often assigned to women: their visions, sometimes made with rolling eyes in convulsive fits, were authenticated by innocence and backed by the scriptural evidence of Christ's licence to childish approaches.

One of the most surprising features of hierarchical subversion is its appeal to the subverted: the rich and powerful can find it therapeutic or politically convenient to be humbled within the safe confines of holy precincts. It must be admitted, however, that in general the socially privileged prefer churches which mirror society more faithfully and ensure them a place in the front pew and a squire's monopoly of the right to read the lesson. The period of the Reformation in Europe coincided roughly with a vast, slow social change, which extended over the whole early modern period and in which society was 'de-communalized'. The 'vertical' structures characteristic of medieval society, in which people at all levels of wealth or education could be united in a sense of allegiance to a particular affinity or province or parish or other embracing identity, were replaced by 'horizontal' structures in which people identified rather with their economic or intellectual peers: this was the beginning of the making of the mankind of the Marxist sociologist and the market researcher, resolved into social 'classes'. Nuclear families asserted their prominence over extended lineages; noble houses acquired small dining rooms in place of vast halls for communal eating; Charles I of England and Philip IV of Spain were painted as preincarnations of a Victorian paterfamilias. Socially inclusive arenas, like the fair and the market, were supplemented and driven down the social scale by the assembly room and, ultimately, the club.

Some Protestant congregations worshipped in environments which aped this riven society, enclosing families in church in high-backed pews, where the experience – demeaning or adulterating – of a shared act of worship could be mitigated by the seclusion of privacy; and though social values in the developed world have changed again since then, encouraging congregation members in increasingly expansive exchanges of fellow-feeling, from the kiss of peace to the congregational coffee-party, there are still communities whom this globular structure suits. The Catholic church, with its strong adhesion to the sanctity of the family as the foundation of a moral society, encourages worshippers to attend and sit *en famille;* parish registration cards are divided into sections for 'Father's Name', 'Mother's Name' and 'Children's Names', as if no-one except the clergy were expected to be unmarried and childless; and in churches of all denominations where families sit together, even where high pews have been swept away, one can notice a tendency for family groups to huddle together and leave a space on either side.

Similar to these 'globular communities', composed of discrete globules which generally consist of nuclear families, are the 'class covens' in which worshippers seek the fellowship of their class kindred – people with whom they can identify in terms of wealth, taste, education and outer garb. To some extent, modern cities everywhere produce congregations with this sort of elective social uniformity, wherever churches are numerous, people mobile and neighbourhoods socially homogeneous. Churches with this character are particularly numerous, however, in Britain and the United States, where the proliferation of churches and sects has been so profuse as to provide every set of the like-minded, every social sectile and every ethnic minority with a place and style of worship of its own. In rich and well-provided economies, if no suitable church is to hand, the worshipper can easily find or afford transport to another, more congenial, some way off. Catholic congregations in non-Catholic countries are famously immune to homogenization by snobbery. Aristocrats and Irish navvies, 'county' Catholics and poor immigrants, are accustomed, in the English Catholic tradition, to sitting together in church; yet a kind of differentiation tends to assert itself wherever churches are thick enough on the ground to allow it: in Oxford, where Catholic places of worship are more numerous per capita than anywhere else in Britain, the University Chaplaincy can accommodate a congregation of a thousand on Sundays but only a few people of the town venture across its threshold: it is built like a concrete shed, but keeps the character of an ivory tower. The chapels of the Catholic Halls of the University are favoured by relatively small numbers of an intellectual and economic élite, refugees from the vulgarities of Catholic parish life; only one of the Halls maintains a parish church with a traditional social mix – a 'cross-class congregation'.

While some churches are designed for family worship and emphasize the division of the congregation into family units, others aspire to be the 'Christian family': to take on collectively the characteristics of a close-knit household and even to replace the domestic family life of their members or to operate an ersatz-family in parallel with their members' home lives. This kind of set-up also has a long and honourable Christian tradition behind it, though it has become tainted by association with some of the 'family-breaking' organizations of modern times, like the Unification Church (see below p. 271) and the Catholic lay order Opus Dei, both of which are often accused of alienating children from their parents. Yet the command to leave father and mother is a well-attested saying of Christ's; defiance of parental authority was one path towards sainthood in the early Church; religious orders in the Catholic tradition – though rarely insisting on the severance of family ties, have always tended to attenuate them, substituting a 'name in religion' for the professant's baptismal name, giving him or her a new 'father' or 'mother' and brethren in the community. But the most vivid examples of parallel family life are to be found in the Protestant tradition. Sandemanians in the eighteenth and nineteenth centuries, for instance, spent so long together on Sundays, what with prayers, exhortations, common meal and Lord's Supper, that the day of the week normally reserved for family activities was almost monopolized by the Church. As if to emphasize the pre-eminence of the Church family over the nuclear family, since only adults were admitted to full communion, children were left to eat sandwiches in the pews while the fully-fledged members of the community withdrew for their love-feast. If as Carlyle mused, 'the soul is a kind of stomach', eating together is a means of spiritual union, and the nature of the congregation as a parallel family was shaped and stated in the habit, widely diffused in the

Protestant tradition in the eighteenth century, of substituting or supplementing holy communion with a real common meal, in imitation of what was believed to be the rite of the early Church.

The tendency of particular churches and congregations to attract the like-minded and the similarly inclined has great practical advantages: in a house of many mansions, it provides a conducive environment for Christians of divers preferences; it enriches the life of the whole Church, as many faces add to the lustre of a cut gem. The Church cannot become universal by insisting on uniformity and it was a delusion of the inquisitors and persecutors ever to suppose that it might. A more alarming source of paradox is that Christendom, which aspires to be universal, enfolds groups who are militantly exclusive, and who brandish their exclusivity almost as a weapon against outsiders. The attraction of joining a band of 'exclusive brethren' is obvious – if they will have you. Sects of this type appeal to the clubbability of Groucho Marx. The desire to belong to an esoteric Church, to board a small, trim vessel of salvation with a picked crew always turns out to be an unworthy temptation to join a ship of fools; but yearning for exclusivity is an understandable vice, to which almost all Christians are susceptible. Both writers of this book must confess to wishing at times that their Churches would be deserted by those awkward brethren whose tepidity, perversity or eccentricity, whose ignorance or critical spirit, whose lust for change or whose irrational hostility to it, try our patience and postpone our hopes. The smaller the pilgrim band, the faster it travels; the more united the purpose, the lustier the prayer. The desire for a leaner, fitter Christianity is itself unchristian – a revival for our times of the heresy of the early Christians who reproved Peter and Paul for baptizing Gentiles. Within the Catholic Church, this temptation has been disciplined and even turned to good by equipping religious and lay orders with qualifications for membership, rites of initiation, distinctive liturgies, special habits and oaths: all the apparatus, in short, of the private club and the secret society, while also insisting that members practise demanding exercises in humility which are intended to help keep pride in one's order within proper limits. When the exclusive mentality characterizes a sect, the incitement to spiritual pride can be damning. It is a danger inherent in the doctrine of predestination, which incites those convinced of their own superior worth to set up as the elect.

Congregations in the last class of our types of social appeal often have something of the character of exclusive brethren. We call them 'gangplank Bethels' because, rather than raising a ladder to heaven as in Jacob's dream, they project a gangplank into the unknown, appealing to those with a taste for spiritual adventure to walk the plank together. Opus Dei, for instance, recruits thousands of members to Monsignor Balaguer's 'way' without revealing the destination: the uncertainty is part of the intrigue. Congregations which practise mystical techniques together – like the Catholic Quietists of the seventeenth century, or those voluptuously

8.1 Richard Mather (1596-1669) one of the founders of New England Congregationalism. He was described as possessing 'an awful and very taking majesty' but he was tolerant of immigrants who could not fully accept congregationalist polity.

visionary ex-Calvinists of the same era, the followers of Jean de Labadie – join hands to penetrate a cloud of unknowing with only a nebulous conviction that God will be found within or beyond the cloud. Bus operators fill charabancs for mystery tours, which, however disappointing the destinations, create a sense of camaraderie among the participants. Treading the gangplank on your way to the plunge is an extremely intense way of cultivating a sense of community with fellow worshippers.

SQUARE PEGS

I shall not go to Church again,
They gave the peace you see.
My neighbour put his hands on mine
And spoke to me.
I do not care for that.

Many years have passed
Since I was touched, save by the priest's hand.
Dismissing me.
I do not care for it. I do not care for it.
I have always kept myself to myself . . .

The Peace, the priest said;
Is this, then, peace?
This broken shattered self that cries within?
I have had to touch my neighbour
And he touched me,
I shall not go again . . .

For most of the Christian world at the end of the Church's second millennium the Sunday congregation has ceased to be an accurate expression of the local community. People vote with their feet, choosing not to go to church at all or to travel to a building some distance away where the worship 'suits' them. The quest for individual meaning not infrequently takes seekers across denominational borders. With many religious stores open for business the shopper can seek out the one with the best selection of goods, the most attractive display or the most helpful staff.

The metaphor is neither far-fetched nor disparaging. The Church has always had to attract sinners. That is a large part of its job. Potential converts have always had other preoccupations from which they must be enticed by promises of heaven and threats of hell. In the affluent Western world of today those preoccupations are greater in number and more clamorous. Churches, therefore, have to be more enthusiastic about the advertising and packaging of their wares. Like retail outlets, they approach the problem in different ways. Some high-street shops cling tenaciously to the principle of offering a traditional, personal service to a specialized clientele. Some seek by garishly advertised special offers to attract new custom. But the most successful are, undoubtedly, the supermarkets whose shelves are stocked with a variety of goods to suit all tastes. Churches have had to come to terms with the cult of the individual and the best attended tend to be those offering varied styles of Sunday worship – from a tranquil early-morning communion to a late-night teenage 'rave' – plus a selection of weeknight activities. The Church, which laments the collapse of communities and the decline of family values, yet has to work within the prevailing social parameters and that often means splitting up families for worship and establishing a number of only loosely connected mini-communities.

The Reformation did not create individualism but Protestant reformers were seen as splintering the Church. To traditionalists this breaking of community was unforgivable and any measures were justified in restoring it. In August 1571, Peter Canisius, Jesuit provincial of Upper Germany, preached before Archduke Ferdinand of the Tyrol. His indignation was typical of that which would mark Rome's official attitude for over three centuries.

> The enemies of Christ and the Church should not be borne with and tolerated to the common detriment of the Christian people . . . the untrue and anti-Christian faith . . . is the root from which spring division, disorder, rebellion, insolence and all kinds of excesses . . . what punishment, therefore, is severe enough for those who scorn, deny and reject the sacrament of the altar, and who resist God in his bride, the Church, in his holy general Councils, in his rule laid down by the Church?

Protestant leaders were equally dismayed by those who broke the fellowship of their congregations. Calvin's treatment of Servetus is often quoted as proof that the new churches were just as ardent persecutors of dissent as their Catholic enemies. In the early years of the Reformation the secular arm was often called in to stop extremists further fragmenting the community of the elect. The gradual realization that material and physical restraints were inappropriate means of spiritual discipline left the burden squarely on the shoulders of the pastor. Richard Baxter, in the mid-seventeenth century, tried, in vain, to bring home to an erring member of his Kidderminster flock the seriousness of defection:

> . . . because you have disclaimed your membership in the Church, and denied to express repentance of it, even in private (which you should have done in public) I shall this day acquaint the Church of your Sin and separation (in which you have broken your covenant to God and us), and that you are no more a member of this Church or of my pastoral charge. I shall do no more but leave the rest to God, who will do more.

Only I shall desire the Church to pray for your repentance and forgiveness . . . except you openly lament your sin, you shall be troubled with
my admonitions no more. From this time forward I have done with you;
till either God convert you, or I and my warnings and labours be brought
in as a witness against you to your confusion.

Your compassionate friend
Richard Baxter

What was a sadness for the local congregation was a potential disaster
at the national level. When the Christendom train broke down and its passengers transferred to other transport they wanted to secure their vehicles
against hijackings and on-board disturbances for the bumpy journey ahead.
The most obvious means of securing passenger-solidarity was creating a real
sense of national religion. At the court of Elizabeth I the Earl of Leicester
managed a myth manufactory employing Sir Philip Sidney, Dr John Dee,
Edmund Spenser, Richard Grafton, John Stow and other talented propagandists to create a semi-mystical nation concept. The sovereign was Astraea,
imperatrix and priestess, reformer of the Church, warrior-queen divinely
destined to bear the standard of Protestant truth against the hordes of the
Roman Antichrist. As well as direct political action, the framers of policy and
public opinion employed chronicles, religious pamphlets, sermons and
xenophobic diatribes to arouse and sustain nationalistic and religious
fervour. The romantic idyll of Gloriana was brilliant enough to leave a long
afterglow. It formed part of that self-image of insular superiority Englishmen
assumed when confronting Catholic 'frogs' and 'dagos' over the water. And
even in relationships with those closer to home. As late as 1790 an English
preacher despatched to the Scottish Highlands could describe his mission as

The rescuing of the remoter parts of the Kingdom and its adjacent islands
from barbarism, disaffection and Popery, by infusing into the minds of
the inhabitants . . . the excellence of our civil constitution and the principles of our Protestant Reformed religion, that in process of time, Britons
from North and South may speak the same language, live united and
loyal under the same sovereign, and worship, agreeably to Scripture and
conscience, the same God.

In Geneva the groundwork laid by Calvin and his colleagues similarly
coloured the development of every aspect of life in the city state. Preaching,
the execution of the laws, the proscription of plays and entertainments,
public charity, the extolling of honest toil – all combined to create a unique
ethos. Because commerce was a serious affair, undertaken for the glory of
God and the well-being of his people, Geneva, like Zürich, became a major
banking centre. Because the activities of skilled jewellers and goldsmiths

were no longer directed towards vain personal adornment and because the right use of time was a solemn responsibility Geneva became famous for its clocks and watches.

Stefan Zweig, writing of a visit to Berlin around 1900, contrasted the characteristics of his landlady in that city with the one he had left behind in Vienna:

> The Viennese was a cheerful, chatty woman who did not keep things too clean, and easily forgot this or that, but was enthusiastically eager to be of service. The one in Berlin was correct and kept everything in perfect order; but in my first monthly account I found every service that she had given me down in neat, vertical writing: three pfennigs for sewing a trouser button, twenty for removing an inkspot from the tabletop, until at the end, under a broad stroke of the pen, all of her troubles amounted to the neat little sum of 67 pfennigs. At first I laughed at this; but it was characteristic that after a very few days I too succumbed to this Prussian sense of orderliness and for the first, and last, time in my life I kept an accurate account of my expenses.

Caricature relies for its point on a central core of truth, in this case, the prominence of seriousness, unimaginativeness and efficiency among Prussian values. These can be traced back to the years 1713–40 when Frederick William I deliberately harnessed the Pietism of Francke and Spener to the state. As well as placing Pietists in influential ecclesiastical and academic posts, the king instituted hundreds of preacherships in the army, established compulsory education in schools based on the Halle model and ensured that Pietist principles of honesty and conscientiousness became key virtues throughout the new, centralized civil service. The object of this quite deliberate royal policy was, according to one commentator, 'to draw every last subject not only into the state but also into the Christian community'.

Such examples are not evidence of an underwritten permanence about the religious character of post-Reformation nations. They simply indicate that, given certain political, economic and social conditions, Church and State identities can be fused and help most citizens to achieve a sense of identity. In the 1930s the very church which had played so vital a part in the creation of the Prussian State had to disentangle itself from the Nazi regime and redefine its identity in Reformation terms as 'the visibly and temporally structured reality of the community that has been called, gathered, sustained, comforted and governed by the Lord himself through the ministry of proclamation.' To be a good Lutheran no longer meant to be a good German or vice versa.

Cultural heritage can be a major ingredient of a Church's identity and it can also be divisive. Early in the nineteenth century the autonomous regional assemblies of the North American Lutheran Church achieved a measure of

cohesion. In 1821 a general synod was established which represented virtually all Lutherans in the republic. They were united as much by cultural
ties – a common language (English) and loyalty to the new nation – as confessional identity. Over the ensuing decades the church established its own
seminary as well as missionary and charitable bodies. Yet fragmentation set
in almost immediately. This was not initially because of disagreements
among existing Lutherans. The main cause was the arrival of new settlers.
Between 1830 and the end of the century, approximately six million
Lutherans arrived from Germany, Austria-Hungary, Scandinavia, Finland and
Iceland. Bringing their own languages and customs and predominantly
conservative religious emphasis, the newcomers tended to set up their own
churches rather than support existing ones. In time these assemblies
combined to form unions of their own, such as the German Evangelical
Lutheran Synod of Missouri, Ohio, and Other States, convened in 1847. The
Civil War drove a wedge into the general synod; five southern synods
seceded and never rejoined. Cultural factionalism made it easier for doctrinal
and ecclesiological issues to divide the church further. The admission to the
general synod in 1864 of a group of assemblies which had not sworn
allegiance to the Augsburg Confession led to a series of rifts which resulted
in the establishment of a rival organization, the general council, to which
only eleven members of the general synod adhered.

A much more dramatic contemporary movement was taking place in the
southern states. Negro churches in the North looked with longing eyes on
the huge slave population. Yankee missionaries were as anxious to deliver
the plantation workers from a paternalistic brand of Christianity designed to
keep them in their place as they were to free them from physical bondage.
Literally following the victorious Unionist armies, the African Methodist
Episcopal Church enjoyed immediate, spectacular success. By 1865, AMEC
claimed a membership of 50,000 in Georgia and the Carolinas and was
sending missionaries from this base into Florida, Alabama, Louisiana,
Mississippi, Texas and Arkansas. The African Methodist Episcopal Zion
Church was not far behind. From its command HQ in North Carolina it, too,
had founded hundreds of outposts by 1869.

White Protestants were ambivalent in their attitude towards the establishment of Negro Churches. On the one hand, they regarded the teachings of
northern missionaries as pernicious. On the other, the desire of their ex-
slaves to worship in their own way and in different buildings delivered them
from the painful necessity of treating their Black brothers and sisters as
equals in the sight of God. It was the latter sentiment which prevailed as the
erstwhile masters rebuilt their society on the old foundations of racial
supremacy and intolerance. In the event it was White attitudes which
provided the strongest motive for the creation of a plethora of Black
Churches.

When Negro Baptists withdrew in their thousands to form their own assemblies and associations White preachers welcomed the move. Intermingling for worship could only, in the words of a religious journalist, tend to 'degrade our noble saxon race . . . to a race of degenerate mongrels'. Baptist conventions in all the states passed ordinances legitimizing the separation of congregations. They were forbidden by federal law from expelling their coloured brethren, but they could and did make it as difficult as possible for them to share pews with their betters. The South Carolina convention, for example, stated that Negros were only suffered to stay in White congregations 'provided they studiously avoid occasions of irritation and offence' – a fine catch-all qualification.

A century after the explosion of Black consciousness the unresolved segregationist issue blazed up again in the civil rights movement of the 1960s. Once more, political, social and cultural issues divided Christian from Christian in the South. By no means all Black Non-conformists followed the lead of the Baptist preacher, Martin Luther King. White congregations took up clear reactionary or liberal viewpoints. Whole families transferred their allegiance from one church to another on the basis of their attitude towards mixed schools and shared public facilities. The angry tirade of a Catholic chaplain indicates to what extent the contemporary issue could come to dominate theological thinking:

> When a new Roman Catholic catechism praises Dr Martin Luther King, 'faithful' Roman Catholics object, labelling it 'socialist' and 'leftist', and they object because King is not a 'Catholic' . . . . We try to end denominationalism, when those denominations had little to do with the struggle of good against evil in the first place.
>
> Our concept of ecumenism must go far beyond the borders of the already existing, sterile sanctuaries of segregation and obsoletism. It might be scandalizing for a churchman to realize that a person who publicly denounces the Christian faith might have more in common with Jesus Christ than the most faithful churchgoing, tithing hypocrite that dons the cloak of piety, while he readily hates 'niggers' and the Vietcong.

The Gospel will always be foolishness to the Greeks but it must always be presented in the language and thought-forms of Greeks – and Romans and Jews, Franks and Stalinist Russians and Black Americans and streetwise European junkies. The faith–culture dialogue has been in process ever since the apostles agonized over the terms for Gentile admission to the Church. Hierarchies who drop out of the dialogue end up with schisms on their hands. Churches survive by responding to cultural change. At the end of the eighteenth century, for example, Catholic priests in rural France had to come to terms with new revolutionary saints. In March 1796 Perrine Dugué, an eighteen-year-old girl from Thorigné, near Mayenne, was murdered by royalists. Within weeks local legend told of her ascending to heaven on tricouleur wings. Miracles were recorded at her tomb and a chapel was erected over her remains. Marie Martin of Tresboeuf was another republican martyr whose cult could not be dislodged after the restoration. Until well into the present century devotees still made pilgrimages to the tomb of 'St Pataude' and mothers took their children there if they were slow in learning to walk.

That highlights the Church's perennial problem of how to maintain close contact with the prevailing culture without being contaminated by it – what Jesus called being in the world but not of it. Church members – and the multitudes who have given up on the Church – look for a community that speaks their language, that is relevant to the world in which they live, but which, at the same time transcends it and so can lift them to a higher plane of significance. It is part of the world since of the Reformation that modern seekers have a variety of churches to choose from. It is also a part of that world that they have scores of other movements and philosophies to sample in their quest for meaning and belonging. Many who, in the sixteenth century might have followed Luther, Calvin or Zwingli today find themselves in the ranks of protestantism with a small 'p'. Demonstrating against aspects of the contemporary culture that Christians either do not challenge or only challenge ineffectively can give campaigners a pseudo-religious buzz. Robin Morgan found in feminism fellowship and wholeness – and those are qualities of which Christian denominations of all types have believed themselves to hold the monopoly. She wrote, in what reads remarkably like an evangelical testimony,

> The ensuing years can seem to me a blur of joy, misery, and daily surprise: my first consciousness-raising group and the subsequent groups I was in; the guerilla theater, the marches, meetings, demonstrations, picketings, sit-ins, conferences, workshops, plenaries; the newspaper projects, the child-care collectives, the first anti-rape squads . . . . And all the while the profound 'interior' changes: the transformation of my work . . . . the tears and shouts and laughter and despair and growth wrought in the struggle with my husband . . . . the detailed examinations of life experience, of power, honesty commitments, bravely explored through so many vulnerable hours with other women – the discovery of a shared suffering and of a shared determination to become whole.

In today's voluntarist society of which the Reformation was one (but only one) ancestor, Christian churches of all types try to provide the holes into which oddly shaped individuals can slot comfortably. Ironically, in seeking this particular identity they have wandered far from that concept of 'Church' which the reformers were seeking. Leslie Newbigin, one of the wise men of our times, explained it thus:

. . . . neither a denomination separately nor all the denominations linked together in some kind of federal unity or 'reconciled diversity' can be the agents of a missionary confrontation with our culture, for the simple reason that they are themselves the outward and visible signs of an inward and spiritual surrender to the ideology of our culture. They cannot confront our culture with the witness of the truth since even for themselves they do not claim to be more than associations of individuals who share the same private opinions. A genuinely ecumenical movement, that is to say, a movement seeking to witness to the lordship of Christ over the whole inhabited *oikoumene* cannot take the form of a federation of denominations. It must patiently seek again what the Reformers sought – 'to restore the face of the Catholic Church.'

In the maelstrom of late twentieth-century Christianity it is difficult to identify trends. Just as individuals seek their particular spiritual havens, so whole congregations and even denominations are caught up in the quest for meaning and belonging. For every new church or sect that appears there are two or three which come together in some sort of covenant relationship. The charismatic movement, in the Seventies and early Eighties, enticed many members from older churches. Latterly the flow has been reversed as traditional congregations have shown themselves more receptive to the divine anarchy of the Spirit. A dramatic example is the Church of the King in Valdosta, Georgia. Until 1988 its pastor, Stan White, and the core of its congregations were members of the Evangel, Assemblies of God, Church. This was a flourishing Pentecostal fellowship with a 1,500-seat auditorium, a regular television mission and 3 million dollars' worth of assets. Services had all the conventional Pentecostal characteristics – spontaneity, lively singing accompanied by arm-waving, applause and dancing, public healings and dramatic displays of charismatic gifts. But White sensed a serious gap in the life of the Church. He began studying the Fathers and concluded that what was missing was the richness of sacramental and liturgical experience which the Catholic end of the Christian spectrum had retained. Under his guidance the pattern of worship at Evangel changed until the point was reached at which White was excommunicated by his Assemblies of God superiors. Encouraged by many of his congregation, White started a new church in a nearby warehouse building. Hundreds joined him, excited to 'discover' the use of vestments and the *Book of Common Prayer* in a church that White called 'fully charismatic, fully evangelical, but also fully liturgical and sacramental'. The next logical step – though none the less dramatic for that – came on Good Friday 1990 when the entire congregation of the Church of the King was confirmed by a bishop of the Episcopal church and received into communion.

The story is unusual but the elements comprising it are far from rare. The bogeymen who, for generations, patrolled denominational frontiers scaring off would-be explorers have been exposed as frauds. People are less frightened of experimentation, less locked into convention, more open to new experiences. There is, in some areas of church life, a sense of excitement similar to that which must have existed in parts of Reformation Europe as unfamiliar vistas of spirituality were opened up. Doubtless much of this new fluidity is about insecurity, the quest for novelty, rampant individualism with a religious gloss. But the same was true of the turbulence of the early sixteenth century.

Chapter Nine

BRETHREN AT THE GATE:
From Intolerance to Exclusivism

THE EXCLUDING EMBRACE

A nineteenth-century Baptist minister's wife was explaining to her Bible class the errors of the universalists. 'They believe everyone will get to heaven,' she told her students, 'but we look for something better.' We may smile at such blatant exclusivism until we recollect that her attitude has been officially sanctioned by most of the Christian Church for most of the time. It has been common form for preachers and missionaries to undertake, on God's behalf, the separation of sheep and goats. Indeed, it is difficult to see how any evangelistic religion can operate and succeed without claiming to point men to the only or, at least, the best path to salvation, here and hereafter. If all roads lead to God or if divine love must inevitably embrace all humankind what point is there in preaching, let alone suffering or dying in the pursuit of converts?

The introduction of Jesus to recorded history in the opening verses of Mark's gospel presents him as a herald proclaiming the imminence or immanence (probably both) of the Kingdom of God and calling upon men to submit to divine sovereignty by a process of metanoia (reorientation of the personality) and pistis (steadfast adherence) to the good news, the message he had come to reveal. Immediately, after the declaration of his manifesto,

Jesus is portrayed as recruiting the first Christian evangelists, Simon and Andrew, who are summoned from their nets so that they can give priority to 'catching men'. The apostles and the millions of Christian propagandists who have followed them have never deviated from demanding repentance and faith from would-be converts. The indiscriminate use of baptism, particularly the mass baptisms by which zealous missionaries thought to bring whole tribes into the Christian fold, may have clouded the original intention of the sacrament, but the powerful symbolism of dying to the old life and rising again to the new was always present in the rite.

This implies exclusivity. The salvation, the redemption, the eternal life, offered in the Gospel are only available to those who have turned away from what Paul calls 'fleshly' life to life in the Spirit. The wording in Peter's first sermon was different but the punch line was the same. First-century Christians were denounced as atheists because they rejected the demand (eminently reasonable to the Roman authorities) that they accord other deities equal status with their own.

Yet even within the pages of the New Testament there is already evidence of another attitude which, if not contrary to the unique claims made for Christ, at least sought to avoid confrontation by suffusing Christian witness with a soft layer of pragmatism and sympathy towards those of other cultures. The Petrine epistles urge believers to live at peace with all men and only speak up for their faith when challenged. In the opening chapters of Romans Paul holds out the possibility of salvation to Jews and Gentiles who, though not having heard the Gospel, yet follow their higher impulses. It cannot, however, be said that such an idea sits easily with the dominant message of the New Testament writers that apart from Christ there is no salvation.

A lively apocalyptic and a genuine desire to pluck brands from the burning consistently inspired Christian evangelism. In its march through the world it took on, with equal determination, mystery cults, animism, sophisticated older religions and blatant non-belief. The precise enemy was of little consequence, since all field commanders were serving one and the same generalissimo – Satan, the great deceiver. This conviction was one of the few shared by wild millenarians, cool academics and elegant preachers. 'The devil's most cunning deceit was to extinguish belief in himself.' John Donne accosted the atheist in uncompromising, vivid rhetoric:

> Be as confident as thou canst, in company; for company is the atheists sanctuary; I respite thee not till the day of judgement, when I may see thee upon thy knees, upon thy face, begging of the hills, that they would fall down and cover thee from the fierce wrath of God, to ask thee then, 'Is there a God now?' I respite thee not till the day of thine own death, when thou shalt have evidence enough, that there is a God, though no

other evidence, but to find a devil, and evidence enough, that there is a heaven, though no other evidence, but to feel hell; To ask thee then, 'Is there a God now?' I respite thee but a few hours, but six hours, but till midnight. Wake then; and then dark, and alone, Hear God ask thee then, remember that I asked thee now, 'Is there a God?' and if thou darest, say 'No.'

The history of Christian missions is, if we wish to view it through the spectacles of today's political correctness, also the history of cultural rape. In the years before and after the Second World War, Paul Freyburg was a Lutheran missionary in a remote part of New Guinea. Part of his technique centred on 'renunciation festivals'. He and his native evangelists would preach from a pulpit in front of which a wide pit had been dug. They urged tribal leaders and magic men to renounce the things of Satan. One by one the local people came forward bearing magic totems, charms, herbal remedies and other symbols of age-old beliefs. They denounced these 'things of the devil' in words taught them by the missionaries, cast them into the open grave and spat on them for good measure, before watching them buried. The psychology behind such dramatic demonstrations was the same as that which prompted Savonarola's bonfires of the vanities, and the burning down of sacred groves in Dark Age Europe. It symbolized metanoia and pistis, the determination to turn away from past sin and error and submit to the Christian God. In mission field after mission field convert peoples radically changed their way of life, abandoning cannibalism, polygamy, ritual sacrifice and other evils condemned by the missionaries. In some cases they even gave up nomadism in order to remain close to the mission stations. For two thousand years Christianity has been a major force for cultural change on all the world's continents and most of its islands.

If heralds of the Kingdom were prepared to boldly go where no Christians had gone before, equipped with theological and moral certainty, prepared to face hardship, discouragement, persecution and even death, it is not difficult to understand that they would bring the same conviction, determination and dogmatism to bear on the eradication of error *within* the Church. In *Van Loon's Lives,* a delightful fantasy in which Desiderius Erasmus obligingly summons the shades of great historical personalities, in interesting couplings, to dine with the author, the one evening that was *not* an occasion of reasoned and enlightening debate was that to which two prelates involved in the fourth-century Arian controversy were invited.

. . . . he of Cyrenaica greatly resented some words his colleague from Bithynia had just spoken. The next moment he had grabbed a bottle of French wine, which stood in front of Erasmus, and had hurled it at the head of his enemy . . . . he of Bithynia had reciprocated by picking up Frits' carving-knife and throwing it at the bearded man . . . . and that had been the beginning of one of the finest pitched battles I ever witnessed. Here is the blow-by-blow account.

Bithynia got both his hands into Cyrenaica's whiskers, and Cyrenaica tried to strangle Bithynia. In doing so, they upset the table. The candles fell on the floor and went out, but by the light of the open fire we could observe the two holy men rolling all over the floor. They would undoubtedly have murdered each other if the tablecloth, acting as a sort of swaddling cloth, had not decided to take part in the fun and had so cleverly draped itself around the two struggling figures that neither of them was able to use his arms.

This was only a slight travesty of real life. To their critics in the fourth century Arians were 'a gang to fight Christ', recruited from those the devil had made mad and immoral women had corrupted. In practice, however, below the learned level at which theologians waged their wars, Arians and Catholics could live together without mutual scandal. From the Ravenna of Theodoric, in the late fifth and early sixth centuries, the baptisteries of the two traditions survive, indistinguishable in splendour and almost identical in imagery. Most of the texts about the odium of these communions in the West date from the late sixth century, when two kinds of political dissidence – among Arians in Gaul and Catholics in Spain – got mixed up with religious differences. Even then, the attitude of the chronicler of Arian misdeeds, Gregory of Tours, was uncompromising but forgiving. The Arians were converted by the superior thaumaturgy of Catholic saints and relics. None had to be burned.

Before orthodox belief was defined (see above, pp. 4–7), early Christianity was one of those 'dappled things' in which God glories. Though professions of faith – to judge from the number which survive – were important as badges of identity, the earliest were abundant in slogans, vague on doctrine. The authority of teachers and prelates depended rather on their apostolic credentials and their holiness of life. Neither of these was a guarantee of conformity with what came to be regarded as orthodox belief. Gnostic teachers published pedigrees which traced their learning back to named disciples of Peter and Paul. Ascetics exhibited the 'kingly power' denounced as inappropriate by pagan critics, but welcomed by ordinary people during the decline of the Roman empire as a useful substitute for absent or unsatisfactory civil authority. A Church in which doctrine was diverse and authority atomized had Christ's backing. When John told him the disciples had tried to stop 'someone who is not one of us driving out devils in your name,' Christ reproved him on the grounds that 'no one who works a miracle in my name could soon afterwards speak evil of me.'

On the other hand, John's impulse to exclude people proved hard to control. Nothing – it has been said – so divides Christians as their lust for unity. The best way to achieve unity is to tolerate diversity; but it has usually proved easier to pare the Church down and to limit it to a community of the like-minded. St Paul struggled to find a formula of toleration but ended up admitting that recalcitrant Christians would have to be driven out of the Church. One of his models was the exclusion of moral pollutants. He ordered the Corinthian who was living in sin with his stepmother to be 'turned out of the Church' and the Thessalonians 'to keep away from any brother who leads an undisciplined life'. When he wrote to the Galatians, he was so exercised about the need to exclude heretics that he coined one of his most forceful paradoxes: 'Even if we ourselves or an angel from heaven preaches to you a gospel other than the one we preached to you, let him be anathema' – the same term he used in another context to signify the curse of excision from the body of Christ. In the letters of Titus and John, the same prescription is recommended: to Titus Paul actually uses the word 'heretic' and advises his reader, 'Have no more to do with him: you will know that anyone of that sort is warped and is self-condemned as a sinner.' According to John, 'If anyone comes to you bringing a different doctrine, you must not receive him into your house or even give him a greeting'. Excommunication, indeed, was a sanction older than the Church. It was part of rabbinical tradition and Christ implicitly built it into the community of the apostles by giving Peter power to 'bind' and 'loose': the terms he used were those applied by the Jews to exclusion from and readmission to the synagogue as well as to the authorization and condemnation of opinions. St Benedict's image of the bad monk expelled from the monastery by the 'cutting iron', the surgical knife, proved an irresistibly useful discipline in Church life generally. At one level, it was a practical necessity, at another a ritual obsession – the act arising from a purity taboo.

The knife is followed by the cauterizing brand and the curse of exclusion by 'the curse of destruction'. In the eleventh century the practice of burning heretics was revived in the Western Church after a lapse of more than six centuries. It is hard to resist the impression that the reappearance of this extreme measure was caused not by any new severity of discipline or any new threat to traditional doctrine but rather by the anxiety of the élite at the descent of heresy into a new social milieu. The first recorded peasant-heresiarch was Leutard, in a village of the diocese of Chalons, in about 1000. In a vision, bees – popularly supposed to reproduce sexlessly – swarmed into his body through his penis and obliged him to adjure his wife, smash the images in his local church, and preach a gospel of renunciation of the flesh. It is probably fair to say that medieval heresy persecutions were used at least as much in defence of the balance of wealth and power in civil society as in defence of individual souls or the integrity of the Church.

THE PIT AND THE PENDULUM

The loosing out of Satan . . . . was about the thousandth year after the nativity of Christ . . . .[Then] followed the time of Antichrist . . . . or desolation of the church, whose full swings containeth the space of four hundred years. In which time both doctrine and sincerity of life were utterly, almost extinguished . . . . through the means of the Roman bishops, especially counting from Gregory VII called Hildebrand, Innocent III, and the friars which with him crept in, till the time of John Wickliff and John Huss.

John Foxe's historical drama – an action-packed tragedy in which the spiritual conflict between Jehovah and Satan is fought out on a terrestrial stage – makes no mention of the setting up of the papal Inquisition. The author was primarily concerned with events in England, where the machinery established by Rome for the detection and punishment of heretics was never set up, and he lacked, as he explained, trustworthy documentary evidence for

9.1 The Inquisition. Seventeenth-century engraving by Theodor Goetz. No myth has become more exaggerated or more indelible than that of the atrocities of the Holy Office. The undoubted bestialities perpetrated at some time and in some places in the name of the Catholic discipline gave rise to a lurid and continuing outpouring of anti-Catholic propaganda.

the persecution of Cathars, Waldensians, Bogomils and the confusion of proliferating, late-medieval sects. The martyrologist knew however, that Satan recommenced his vicious attack on the saints in the mid-thirteenth century and that the friars, the principal operators of the Inquisition, were his disciples. Among Protestants, especially in the nineteenth century, the activities of the papal Inquisition and its bastard Spanish offspring provided the ultimate proof that the Roman hierarchy was the devil's spawn.

For secular and ecclesiastical authorities the suppression of heresy was a law-and-order issue. Nor was it just religious dissidents who threatened peace and stability. Orthodox citizens, incensed by the activities of their pious or fanatical neighbours, were just as likely to take matters into their own hands and form lynch mobs. The Inquisition was an attempt to find a unitary solution to this problem. Its introduction was neither a panic measure nor a calculated attempt to increase centralized papal control, though elements of both certainly played their part in the formulation of policy. When Gregory IX, in 1231, authorized a body of agents, answerable only to Rome, to 'enquire into' heretical teaching, he concluded a process of mounting activity which had begun at the third Lateran council, fifty-two years earlier. Gregory was a man of ardent spirituality with a granite will and a keen sense of political realities who did not shrink from excommunicating the formidable Emperor Frederick II – twice. If anyone had ever told him that he had created a monster, Gregory would not have believed him.

The evidence was available soon enough. Within three years some of his inquisitors had created more havoc than the dissidents they were sent to counteract. The first official appointed in the Rhineland was Conrad of Marburg, an ascetic of decidedly sado-masochistic tendencies, already famous as a preacher of the Third Crusade and confessor to the devout young Elizabeth of Hungary, upon whom he enjoined fearsome mortifications. Conrad's tenure of office was bloody and brief. Having condemned scores of humble men and women, he denounced Count Henry of Sayn. Local Church and State leaders were horrified: inquisitors were supposed to underpin the social order not undermine it. An assembly at Mainz reversed Conrad's decision but he insisted that it had no power to do so. His enemies wasted no more time on argument. Conrad and his party were attacked and murdered as they left the city. After this, the Inquisition was never accepted throughout most of Germany.

The first inquisitor in northern France was the fanatical ex-Cathar, Robert Le Bougre. He survived an assassination attempt after securing the incineration of 180 supposed heretics at Mont-Aimé. So great was the outcry that Gregory was obliged to suspend him temporarily. The warning had no effect. In 1239 Robert was dismissed and imprisoned. Thereafter he disappears from the historical record.

Such creatures doubtless stand out from the record because the evidence is sparse and because they were atypically awful. The Dominicans and, to a lesser extent, the Franciscans, to whom extirpation of heresy was largely entrusted, had a mission to preach orthodoxy and to reclaim the misled as well as to hand over the obdurate to the secular arm. The vast majority of sentences imposed fell far short of imprisonment or death; they mostly involved humiliating public penance. Even the mandatory punishment of death by burning for convicted heretics was established by the emperor, not the pope – though Frederick was, very likely, impelled by the political necessity of pleasing Gregory IX.

Inquisitions were meant to be inclusive – not in the sense of extending the sheepfold, but of keeping the sheep penned inside it. In practice, they created large subclasses of probationary, tainted and suspect Christians and, in the hands of fanatics or at times of phrenesis, would heap unreconciled victims on the pyres. At its best the Inquisition was a form of justice which was cheap, popular and conciliatory: the method of proceeding by investigation rather than adversarial trial had a common-sense justification and was gaining ground in the secular administration of justice at about the time it became common in the Church. It was, however, easily warped by abuse. It set aside the checks and balances built into both Roman and canon law, which allowed the defendant at least a semblance of a fair trial. In Inquisition tribunals the investigator was prosecutor, judge and jury. The accused was not allowed to call witnesses in his own defence, to know the specific charges against him or to know the names of his accusers. In 1252 Innocent IV sanctioned the use of torture and thereby put in place the final block in an edifice comparable to those erected in twentieth-century police states, with all their paraphernalia of forced confessions, false accusations, secrecy, paid informers and the deliberate cultivation of fear.

The Spanish Inquisition, a permanent network of tribunals under royal patronage, established on the Roman model in the late fifteenth century, represented the inquisitorial tradition at its best and its worst. It acted as a social safety-valve for the complaints of the poor and unsophisticated, who could never indict their neighbours or challenge their social superiors in ordinary courts. Though it encouraged vexatious and spurious accusations of heresy, it at least protected the old and outcast from the witchcraft persecutions which mopped up so many of them in early modern Europe. It ought to have been socially 'functional'. In practice, however, it had a divisive and depressant effect, spreading insecurity with its vast web of informers, setting neighbours at loggerheads and inducing an atmosphere of fear.

Ultimately repression failed in its objective and rebounded upon its perpetrators. Although several pockets of heresy – most notably the Cathars – were wiped out, other groups of dissidents went underground. In some countries inquisitors were never appointed; in others, their behaviour resulted in the rejection of the institution. Where it did become a permanent feature of the ecclesiastical landscape it often provoked the hostility of local temporal and spiritual rulers towards the claims of Rome. Between 1335 and 1355 Havel of Jindřichův Hradec examined over 4,400 suspects throughout Bohemia and sent about 220 of them to the stake. This vigour did not extirpate heresy and it did nothing to allay those national resentments which surfaced half a century later in Hussitism. Had eradication of dissidents gone hand-in-hand with reform, as wiser administrators intended that it should, some resentment would have been assuaged. But it was easier to use the Inquisition to silence criticism. Even that proved, in the long term, to be a monumental failure. The Inquisition became a black legend.

The two worst aspects of the tragedy of this institution were that it stifled creative dialogue between orthodoxy and dissent and that it committed the central organs of the Church to the belief that heresy could be eradicated. The democratization of mystical spirituality through vernacular treatises, increased literacy, beguinages and other lay communities both evidenced and increased the demand for fresh ways of intensifying religious experience. Many parish clergy and confessors encouraged and channelled such holy desires. But those who persisted in regarding these aspirations as corrosives, eating into the unity of the Church and the authority of the hierarchy, now had ready at hand the techniques of enforcement. Catholic preachers and artists depicted heretics as devil-inspired and destined to occupy the innermost regions of hell. Thomas More exulted in their eternal discomfiture: 'the clergy doth denounce them. And as they be well worthy, the temporality doth burn them. And after the fire of Smithfield, hell doth receive them where the wretches burn forever.' For their part, obdurate heretics could scarcely fail to identify those who persecuted them for upholding 'truth' as the agents of Antichrist. And if the papacy was justifying the use of violence against Christ's poor, in a world of changed political realities, what was to deter the oppressed from retaliating in kind?

THE FIRE OF HUSSITISM

Such a situation emerged in Bohemia in the second and third decades of the fifteenth century. A century before the Lutheran challenge, the appearance of Hussitism and the failure of spiritual and temporal leaders to deal with it wisely and effectively produced a movement bearing most of the hallmarks of sixteenth-century national Protestantism: passion for reform of abuses, anti-clericalism, assertion of regional identity over centralized control, spread of vernacular Scripture, challenge to the Church's temporal power, tendency to fragmentation, emphasis on internal lay spirituality, rejection of the traditional penitential system, outbursts of iconoclasm and mass rallies. The Bohemian revolt was a 'revolution against the established order in the name of religion'. It led to war. Yet, interspersed with the bloodshed and the defiant chanting of party slogans there were several attempts by men of goodwill

9.2 A contemporary woodcut of the burning of Jan Hus.

on both sides to reach negotiated settlements. This, too, prefigured the greater conflict of the sixteenth century.

The congregations which listened to Jan Hus's reformist sermons may rarely have allowed their thoughts to wander but when they did the walls around them provided ample material for meditation. Prague's Bethlehem Chapel had been built by the disciples of Jan Milic, a wealthy churchman who had forsaken luxury and prestige to become a poor preacher of repentance and 'the father of Czech reform'. It was a simple preaching church, decorated, not with spectacular representations of saintly miracles, but with pictures contrasting the power and riches of the contemporary Church with the simplicity and humility of Christ.

Hus living emerges from the fragmentary and biassed records as a sincere enthusiast with no personal ambition and no political programme. Hus dead became a hero of Czech nationalism who inspired twenty years of bloody conflict and, even after the reclaiming of Bohemia for Catholicism, lived on as a legendary standard bearer against tyranny. He is still commemorated in an annual public holiday in the Czech Republic and a Hussite Church was revived in 1920. Long before Hus's sermons and university lectures drew attention to him the Church leadership had become well accustomed to dealing with Czech radicals. Milic and others had been hauled before councils and papal tribunals to be examined and, in some cases forced to recant. Hus, too, might have been summarily dealt with at an early stage had it not been for the political situation. Like Luther, the Czech reformer enjoyed the support of his prince. When the Archbishop of Prague excommunicated Hus, the king ignored the ban. When the university council condemned him, the king sacked them, drew up a new constitution and made Hus the rector. Eventually, however, Hus squandered royal favour over an issue of principle. When the antipope John XXIII issued an indulgence to finance his campaign against Gregory XII, Hus denounced it. This did not please King Wenceslas, who received a commission on all indulgences sold in his territory. The reformer was ordered out of the capital and spent the next couple of years in southern Bohemia preaching, winning support from the local nobility and further defining his views. Ensuing events provide yet another parallel with Luther. Hus's departure left an ideological vacuum in Prague which more extreme campaigners hastened to fill. Preaching and street demonstrations denounced Rome and all her works. Banners depicted Antichrist surrounded by whores and crowned with the papal tiara. Acts of vandalism and violence towards priests became frequent. This was the background to Hus's summons to face his accusers at Constance in 1415.

The Council of Constance did one wise thing and one foolish thing – both in the name of unity. It removed from office, by various means, the three competing popes, thus enabling the cardinals to elect Martin V and end the thirty-nine-year schism. And it burned Jan Hus. It might be truer to say that the Emperor Sigismund (He was actually crowned in November 1414, while the council was in session), half-brother and rival of Wenceslas IV, was responsible for these events. Although Constance was a glittering ecclesiastical gathering attracting to the lakeside city, during its forty-one months, 29 cardinals, 33 archbishops, 150 bishops, 100 abbots and over 300 leading academics, it would have achieved little without the determination, constant prompting and political activism of Sigismund. The new emperor was a soldier-statesman with a passion for administrative tidiness. For him the messy state of the Church was not only a public scandal; it was a personal affront. More importantly it was undermining European morale at a time of relentless Turkish pressure. Sigismund was determined to unite Christendom around the core of a reformed and invigorated Church.

Sorting out the issue of heresy was a necessary part of the process. He provided a safe conduct for Hus and subsequently reneged on it. The reformer believed that he was going to Constance to debate his views openly with orthodox theologians. His opponents were determined to assert the ecclesiastical authority which Hus and his colleagues had flouted. They wanted, and expected to obtain, a recantation. Wycliffe's works had already been condemned and the judges only had to demonstrate that Hus shared the Englishman's errors. Sigismund, if he gave any thought at all to the theological issues, probably accepted that someone needed to be made an example of in the interests of conformity. Evidently his political antennae were not sufficiently well tuned to the Bohemian situation, for he failed to grasp the significance of representations from leading nobles urging him to prevent the 'dishonouring of our nationality' by the ill-handling of Hus. The emperor permitted the accused to be imprisoned and subjected to a farcical public examination in which he could not make his opinions heard above the interruptions and jeers of his accusers.

Not all Hus's interlocutors were intellectual bullies. As far as we know, none of them were trained inquisitors. But the spirit of the Inquisition prevailed over political prudence. Recantation and discrediting of the Bohemian reform were the objectives of the trial. In the end, the Council had to settle for a mere show of strength. By condemning Hus, virtually unheard, for heretical opinions, some of which he certainly did not hold, they made it difficult for him to make a clear abjuration. By underestimating his courage they manoeuvred themselves into creating a martyr.

Back in Bohemia, reformist nobles cried 'treachery'. Nationalism and heresy combined to create a force which successfully resisted pope and emperor for twenty years. Sigismund paid a heavy price for his perfidy. Instead of quietly receiving the Bohemian crown on the death of Wenceslas in 1419, he faced a rebellion which denied him the authority – and the revenues – he desperately needed. Martin V launched no less than five crusades, and approved several smaller expeditions, against the recalcitrant Hussites. Not until after the pope's death did the Hussite wars come to an end in a series of negotiated agreements which granted the Bohemians most of their demands.

When we come to consider what, in terms of Christian belief and practice, the violence and bloodshed were all about we discover very little that was original in the Hussite doctrines. As with other movements it represented a range of reactions to perceived inadequacies of Church teaching and practice and displayed the inevitable tendency to fragment. The symbol of the movement that *was* distinctive and was emblazoned on the banners under which its champions marched to battle, was the chalice. Hussitism was a movement of lay spirituality which placed great emphasis on communion. It claimed for ordinary believers the right to frequent reception *in both kinds*. From this desire for lay involvement sprang the replacement of Latin with Czech in the liturgy and the production of vernacular scriptures and devotional books. Along with this laicization went the usual catalogue of complaints about ecclesiastical wealth, corruption and indolence, ills that could be put to rights by giving lay lords control of all temporalities. The moderate core of Hussites regarded themselves not as separatists, but reformers, recalling the Church to its New Testament purity. Hus, himself, came to regard the papacy as an aberration and, therefore, as an institution which could and should be dispensed with. He did not identify it with

Antichrist. In his lifetime the pretensions of rival 'popes' seemed, in any case, to be collapsing under their own absurdity.

It was the growing conflict, culminating in Hus's death that provided extremists with a platform. Rebel priests rejected all 'defiled' ecclesiastical authority, devised their own vernacular liturgies, administered utraquist communion to their gathered congregations and preached inflammatory sermons in private houses, in barns and in the open air. They attacked traditional central doctrines and spurred their hearers on to acts of iconoclasm.

The vigour and triumphalism of the Catholic reaction handed leadership of the movement to these extremists. In 1417 they held a remarkable series of mass rallies in southern Bohemia. Peasants, apprentices, merchants and nobles left their homes to congregate on hilltop sites which were given biblical names such as Tabor, Olivet and Horeb. There they enjoyed the emotion-charged fellowship of shared worship, shared meals and even shared possessions. These 'Taborite' assemblies were gatherings of the elect, separating themselves from a wicked world and a wicked Church. Some buttressed their high resolve with chiliastic convictions – they were being called out by Christ to prepare for the rule of the saints and the last days. Prophecies of the end of the world increased when the Taborites' enemies marshalled against them the arguments of artillery and sharpened steel.

The crusades brought together in a militant union those holding all shades of Hussite opinion. Moderates joined Taborites in a series of armed conflicts to defend their homeland and their reformed religion. Victory resulted in both compromise and the separation of the Czech movement into its component parts. It was political realities and not any concession to unorthodox beliefs which obliged the Hussites' enemies to do what they had vehemently refused to do since Constance – negotiate. For Sigismund it was the only way to have his rule acknowledged in Bohemia. Ecclesiastical agreement to a settlement was given by the Council of Basel and though the new pope, Eugenius IV, rejected their decision, he had no alternative but to accept the *fait accompli*. By the terms of the *Compactata* utraquism was permitted in those parishes which wanted it and Church lands were placed under secular control. The Bohemian Church became a reformed or heretical (depending on your point of view) enclave.

Whatever else the settlement was it was not a victory for toleration. Two irreconcilable principles had come into conflict. Czech tribalism had asserted that, within broad doctrinal limits, national Churches should be free to order their own affairs. The position taken in Rome was that, without the unity and uniformity emanating from Christ's vicar, there was no Church. The Bohemian leaders regarded the *Compactata* as a peace treaty, guaranteeing perpetual privileges. To the Vatican it was no more than a truce to be repudiated as and when opportunity served.

From Massacre to Pragmatism

In the late summer of 1572 a bitter ballad, *The Second Jezebel,* was being hawked on the streets of Paris. 'The first one ruined Israel; the other has ruined France,' it proclaimed, 'By one the prophets consecrated to God were massacred; by the other a hundred thousand followers of the Gospel were done to death.' The subject of this indignant lament was Catherine de Medici, the queen mother, who was widely believed to have planned and instigated the recent St Bartholomew's Day massacre. In the small hours of 24 August, a directed but eventually uncontrollable, blood-crazed mob careered through the quarter where Protestant supporters of Admiral Gaspard de Coligny were lodged and indulged in an orgy of murder and looting that left narrow streets clogged with stripped corpses, pitiable family groups clinging together in huddled death. The final solution was applied with similar ferocity throughout much of France in the ensuing days. A contemporary, non-partisan guesstimate put the final death toll at around

9.3 The St Bartholomew's Day Massacre, 1572, shocked much of Europe, Catholic and Protestant, but the pope and Philip II applauded the Guise plot to break the Protestant factions in Paris. In this contemporary engraving Huguenots are cut down in the streets while Admiral Coligny is murdered in his bed.

30,000. The Massacre of St Bartholomew ranks in the annals of licensed bestiality with Kristallnacht and the slaughter of the Mamelukes.

Immediate reactions were varied. The news soured diplomatic relations with Protestant countries and alarmed several Catholic commentators. But there were quarters in which it was received with immense satisfaction. Pope Gregory XIII, proclaimed it 'a hundred times more pleasing than fifty victories like Lepanto.' Philip II considered the hostile reaction provoked in London as a bonus for his policy of Catholic *realpolitik*. 'Yes, stir up the English against the French. Very Good. I approve of this,' he scribbled in the margin of a report dealing with the aftermath of the massacre. In France there was no let-up in the campaign led by the Guise faction against the Huguenots. Throughout the country they attempted to consolidate the gains made on St Bartholomew's Day.

Yet the massacre was not the kind of turning point the Catholic party hoped for. It temporarily deprived the Protestants of their aristocratic leadership. Coligny and his suite were butchered. The princes of Condé and Navarre were forced to convert. The revulsion the massacre inspired helped to contribute to an attitude of inner detachment from the warring confessions: the tendency of the 'Family of Love', whose members – princes, aristocrats, rich men and scholars – might conform outwardly to Protestantism or Catholicism indifferently while cultivating an internalized religion of direct approach to God. The 'Valois Tapestries' show the French royal family and its friends united, regardless of religion, in a series of magnificent chivalric festivities. On the other hand, the removal of leaders committed to Protestantism gave greater prominence to the movement's idealists, theologians, propagandists and middle-class activists who, not being politicians, saw the issues in clear black and white. The great families of France were in the business of power and influence. They, therefore, spoke the language of compromise and toleration. Not so the pamphleteers, who now loosed a snowstorm of paper. Huguenot writers, who had previously, for the most part, paraded their loyalty to the Crown, now called for the deposition or assassination of a godless king who had either authorized or permitted the slaughter of the saints. Catholic controversialists countered by urging the government to continue fearlessly its divine mission to root out every last heretic.

All religious activists agreed that religion was the mortar of the state and that it was the sovereign's task to uphold truth and eradicate error. There could be no unity or lasting peace in a state where 'orthodoxy' and 'heresy' flourished side by side. 'Jesus Christ will conquer! Jesus Christ will reign! Jesus Christ will be King of France! He will install his viceroy to administer his very Christian laws.' That rallying cry of a Catholic pamphleteer could just as easily have been written by his Huguenot opposite number. Such were the slogans of conviction politics in the era of Trent and second-generation Calvinism. It was an age for defining truth and re-establishing consistency of religious belief after tumultuous decades of ideological conflict. That hobgoblin of consistency, 'adored by little statesmen and philosophers and divines', frightened into silence many common-sense Frenchmen. Over the next couple of centuries its grotesque grimace was to be sporadically seen in the land, encouraging religious men in cruelties which drove thousands of Huguenots from their homeland and contributed to the enforced secularism of 1789.

If its triumphs were sometimes reversed or modified it was because not everyone who wore the label 'Catholic' or 'Protestant' accepted the logic of the extremists. The rulers of France certainly could not afford to do so. In 1561 the eleven-year-old Charles IX perched nervously upon an impressive chair of state in the Benedictine abbey at Poissy and addressed a solemn assembly of Catholic and Protestant clergy. His mother, Catherine de Medici, had drilled him well in his prepared speech and he tried hard to impress his authority on his venerable audience: 'The reason I have decided to bring you here, is that you should reach some conclusion, so that my subjects can live in peace and union with each other.' Catherine had convened the meeting in defiance of the pope, the theologians of the Sorbonne and Philip II, who had all insisted that it was heresy even to talk to heretics. Her primary concern was the survival of the dynasty and the last thirty years of her life would be spent in a losing battle against death, which claimed each of her childless sons before they reached the age of forty. That meant balancing the power of the Catholic Guises and the houses of Bourbon and Châtillon which were drawing increasing strength from the growing body of Huguenots. A measure of theological agreement at Poissy would eat into the ideological granaries from which both factions were fed. It was a forlorn hope. 'Compromise' was a word which did not figure prominently in the vocabulary of theologians. 'Idiot' and 'blasphemer' were more typical of the profundities exchanged in the debate, which ended on a completely negative note. Catherine fell back on toleration. Determined that political expediency should triumph over religious malice, Catherine issued an edict granting limited rights of assembly and worship to adherents of the *religion prétendue réformée*.

Toleration was recommended by its advocates not as a religious principle but a tool of practical statecraft. Montaigne, who experienced at first hand the horrors of the conflict, urged liberty of conscience as a means of starving the fires of fanaticism and balking those 'whom passion thrusts out of the bounds of reason, and often forceth them to take and follow unjust, violent and rash counsels'. Freedom of conscience was also urged by some of the main combatants. François d'Andelot, younger brother of Coligny, once demanded of Henry II, 'I pray you, Sire, leave my soul alone and make any use you wish of my body and my earthly goods, which are entirely yours.'

One problem with toleration as *a tool of practical statecraft* is that it can be laid back in the box whenever changed situations suggest that other tools might be more effective. In the broad alliances that made up the 'Huguenot' and 'Catholic' parties, activists were constantly changing not only their tactics but even their religious and political convictions. For example, the Catholic nobility ardently supported the principle of hereditary monarchy and divine right against Huguenot theories of the sovereignty of the people – until Henry of Navarre, a Protestant, became heir to the throne, at which time both sides suddenly saw the flaws in the political principles they had previously espoused. Both sides protested their loyalty to the Crown. Yet both sides were prepared to arrange foreign alliances and bring mercenary troops onto the soil of France. So it was with toleration. Always an attractive option to the Protestant minority, it figured less in their propaganda when the war was going well for them. Always anathema to Catholics, they yet advocated it when an interlude of peace suited their book.

Only when, after a quarter of a century, neither side had been able to batter the other into total submission did toleration make some sense simultaneously to both – for a time. The Valois dynasty having perished in an orgy of murder, treachery, lust and disease reminiscent of the contemporaneous *Titus Andronicus,* Henry of Navarre, the Huguenot leader became heir to the throne of France. His horrified opponents managed to secure a papal excommunication but, like a Judas pistol, this exploded in the face of the one who aimed it. The pope's 'interference' in national affairs was bitterly resented and brought several waverers to Henry's side. But not enough to ensure his peaceful accession. The French would not accept a non-Catholic king. So Henry converted. He may or may not have said that Paris was worth a mass but he certainly held the sentiment the words expressed.

The pragmatism and ambition of the new king found support in the war-weariness of the combatants. The extremists on both sides were becoming increasingly marginalized. The Sorbonne theologians exposed the hollowness of Henry's conversion and insisted that they would not accept it even if the pope did so. Philip II urged his co-religionists not to waver. Henry IV had to fight four-and-a-half years for recognition. But religious alliances fell to pieces under the pressure of the desire for peace. When papal absolution was granted in 1595 the king was able to direct the nation's military energies against Spain and initiate talks with Huguenot leaders which resulted in the Edict of Nantes.

It was only a truce. Sporadic resort to arms continued until 1629, by which time the Huguenots had ceased to be a significant military force. Now there was no *raison d'état* for continued toleration. Determined reactionaries were able to whittle away the Huguenots' hard-won gains. A campaign of harassment and forced conversion culminated in the revocation of the Edict of Nantes in 1685. Louis XIV's triumphant advisers told him that he had achieved the miracle of reclaiming all his people for the true faith. The king was stupid enough to believe them. The reality was the mass exodus (variously assessed at between 200,000 and 400,000) of Huguenots, with continued resistance of embittered Protestant groups in remoter areas and further sporadic outbreaks of persecution. The tragedy for France was that dissent now had nowhere to go. It could not find expression in regular non-conformist worship. It could not be channelled through the life of minority communities enjoying at least some civil liberties. It could not be softened by peaceful enjoyment of the fellowship of like-minded neighbours. It became part of the growing resentment felt by many towards the *ancien régime*.

Catholic protagonists who rejected freedom of conscience for those in error believed they were defending the integrity of Christendom. Alexandre Correrius, writing in 1599, could assert that the pope was equivalent to God on earth and that kings were merely his valets. The unity of the Christian world, defined by a body of doctrine and ruled from Rome, was an idea that had great staying power and still has its defenders. The Christendom myth was not given the lie by the Protestant nations which seceded from Roman allegiance. The religious monopoly of Catholic Europe was broken by Catholic monarchs striking their own bargains with the manufacturers of religious dissent and the Catholic rank and file who, when forced to choose between loyalty to pope or king, opted for the latter. What happened in France happened in all Western European nations, Catholic and Protestant. Because religious toleration is the only political solution possible for states which want to preserve internal harmony, all the fragments of Western Christendom found their own paths towards it. Established Churches were obliged to make room for denominations they had once outlawed as seditious and demonic.

Toleration for reasons of state was a staging post to secularism. It encouraged people to confuse political secularism, which asserts that all religious convictions are, under the law, of equal value, with philosophical secularism, which suggests that they are all equally worthless – or, at least, equally questionable. For the Christian this halfway house of pragmatic toleration is an unsatisfactory habitation. It takes a high degree of sainthood to live cheek-by-jowl with someone fundamentally *wrong* on the most important issues of faith without slipping into contempt and suspicion, if not open hostility. Only some understanding of toleration *as a Christian virtue* provides a starting point for reversing the errors of the past. The churches bear a large share of responsibility for the despiritualization of Western society because too many of them for too long concentrated on their differences and, by so doing, magnified them.

Not that differences could, or should, be ignored. For the Church to make a reasonable fist of fulfilling its mission its various parts have to reach a basic understanding of their common message. That means finding a new perspective from which to view those beliefs on which they are at variance.

VOICES OF PEACE

Several of the sixteenth-century reformers were fully aware of this. Men of eirenic disposition and passionate concern for the spread of the Gospel strove to hold in common harness the horses of Rome, Wittenberg, Zürich, Geneva and London and prevent them skittering off in different directions. The Confession of Augsburg of 1530 was a heroic attempt to express the essence and insights of Lutheranism without saying anything objectionable from a Catholic point of view. It was largely the work of Philip Melancthon, who had arrived in Wittenberg as a young professor of Greek and Hebrew and who immediately identified Luther as a Catholic teacher with a message truly based on Scripture. 'In doctrine', he acknowledged, 'we agree with the true Catholic Church. The false teachers' – by which he meant Anabaptists and heretics who denied the Trinity and the divinity of Christ – we ourselves have fought. We are ready to obey the Roman Church as long as we are permitted to abolish all abuses in practice.' He used his personal influence with Luther to try to restrain him from the showdowns to which the older man's temperament was inclined. He spent the night before the public reading of the Confession of Augsburg weeping at the divisions of the Church. He uttered the language of compromise without weasel words and obscured differences without obscuring truth: 'We become righteous through grace and faith' was the Confession's statement on justification. The use of the chalice at mass and the rights of married clergy – two concessions the Catholic church had already made in certain provinces – were the only specific reforms he demanded to which Rome was unwilling to agree. The Confession of Augsburg became the foundation document of many Protestant communities later tolerated in Catholic states. Even after the Council of Trent had drawn up battle lines which were extremely hard to cross, the eirenic Catholic theologian Georg Witzel continued to recommend it as a statement of common faith.

The young Calvin – even without the emotional investment in the past which Melancthon made – might almost have been a peacemaker. His exchange of letters with Cardinal Sadoleto in 1539 reads like a bridge-building exercise. Though both correspondents scored cunning points, their rhetoric was mild by the standards of the day and their rancour, though visible, restrained. Calvin was genuinely indignant at Sadoleto's claim that 'authors of dissension' were motivated in part by anger at their own unmerited exclusion from office and honours. On the contrary, Calvin presents a credible picture of the sacrifice of tranquillity and comfort demanded by a stand like his own. This misunderstanding, however, did not colour the correspondents' courtesy or poison their arguments. The effort to express dogma in common language was striking on both sides. 'We obtain salvation by faith alone,' agreed Sadoleto, adding that, 'when we say that . . . . we hold that in that very faith love is comprehended.' 'We deny that good works have any share in justification,' replied Calvin, 'but we claim full authority for them in the lives of the righteous,' where 'faith and works are inseparable.' On the eucharist, Sadoleto deplored materialism and profane logic as unhelpful and Calvin agreed: 'We loudly proclaim,' he wrote,

> the communion of flesh and blood which is exhibited to believers in the Supper; and we distinctly show that that flesh is truly meat and that blood truly drink – that the soul, not content with an imaginary conception, enjoys them in very truth. The presence of Christ, by which we are ingrafted in Him, we by no means exclude from the Supper nor shroud in darkness.

On confession and the invocation of the saints, Calvin conceded Sadoleto's points in principle, explaining only why Geneva excluded them in practice.

Calvin limited his justification of Geneva's secession almost entirely to a list of abuses which Catholics could also acknowledge as such. The correspondence exposed only two differences of principle: first on the doctrine of purgatory, which Calvin merely dismissed as 'unproved' rather than false, suggesting that prayers for the dead in the early Church were signs only of 'passing affection'. More seriously, he objected that 'in the room of the sacred Supper has been substituted a sacrifice by which the death of Christ is emptied of its virtues.' On that point, he could perhaps only have been reconciled with Sadoleto by an agreement to differ. The most encouraging feature of all was the remarkable overlap in the two writers' conception of the Church. They both rightly identified this as the critical issue. For Sadoleto, 'the point in dispute' was whether tradition or 'innovation' represented a model 'more expedient for salvation'. Though Calvin replied with a challenging definition of the Church as 'the society of all the saints', he fairly repudiated the charge of innovation on the grounds that 'all we have attempted has been to renew the ancient form of the Church . . . . We deny not that those over which you preside,' he conceded, 'are Churches of Christ,' and promised to obey the pope 'so long as he maintains fidelity to Christ and the gospel.'

The friendliness of the exchange was affected by temporary conditions: both men were anxious about the proliferation of 'sects' whose Christianity neither recognized: Anabaptists and antinomians, deniers of the Trinity, the sacraments and the divinity of Christ. Calvin's letter includes a strong hint of a rapprochement with Rome in the interests of common defence against these heretics. Yet the prospect of toleration between Catholics and Protestants was genuine: grounded in their common background, common faith and common prospects. Documents like the Confession of Augsburg and the correspondence of Calvin with Sadoleto showed that such tolerance could be allowed without compromising the unity of the Church. Despite the conflictive conditions of the rest of the sixteenth century and most of the seventeenth, the voices of tolerance were never silent. Perspectives were gradually devised from which even the 'sects' denounced by Calvin could be comprehended in the ecumenism of the future. The Erasmian tradition – the tradition of Melanchthon and Sadoleto, which put a higher value on human dignity and Christian charity than on the detection of heresy, remained at work even when dogmatists on both extremes were trying to suppress it.

In 1555, however, it became apparent that, at least in the lands of the German empire – where the mixture of confessions was greatest and the practical case for tolerance therefore strongest – that eirenic future would be postponed. The Peace of Augsburg guaranteed freedom of worship to princes and condemned their subjects to conform. This was an anticipation of the principle Hegel uttered with respect to his king: 'in Prussia, only one man is free.' The peace assumed that religious uniformity was politically desirable and encouraged the persecution of minorities for reasons of state. The principle that 'the prince will decide the religion' reversed the priorities of the traditional formula, 'Une foi, un roi' and empowered rulers to cloak policy with piety. There were many princes who could see the practical advantages of toleration. Philip II of Spain was able to scorn the chance to be 'a king of heretics' because, until late in his reign, he had relatively few heretical subjects. Elizabeth I of England, on the other hand, whose people were a confessional mixture of increasing complexity, could see the wisdom of refusing 'to open windows into men's souls'. Maximilian II of Austria, similarly, thought 'there is no tyranny more intolerable than to want to dominate over people's consciences' and departed from the principle of the Peace of Augsburg by granting selective toleration to Lutherans. Every realm, however, had an entrenched élite that benefited from the exclusion of heretics: in seventeenth-century England, every ruler except Charles I wanted to relax the disabilities of religious minorities; none of them succeeded in implementing the policy as widely as they would have liked or for as long.

Meanwhile, the dogmatic work of the Council of Trent had made toleration harder by accentuating differences of doctrine and strengthening the terms in which heretics were anathemized. On the other hand, the case for tolerance was made out with increasing urgency and inventiveness by those who suffered from persecution or witnessed the wickedness of religious wars. In 1561, that great deflector of conflicts, Peter Gienger, advised the Emperor Ferdinand I that 'goodwill is always more effective than severity, exhortation more than threats, charity more than power.' In 1562, recoiling from the outbreak of religious violence, Sebastián Castrillo addressed his *Conseil à la France désolée* with a gloss on the proverb from Tobit, 'Do not unto another what thou wouldst not have done unto thee.' Shortly afterwards Bodin began to work out his theory of an entirely secular state, withdrawn from the religious arena. In 1566, Anabaptists petitioned William of Orange for toleration on the grounds that Christ had foretold a divided household and Calvinists made the same appeal to Philip II on the grounds that Jews were tolerated in the Papal States. By 1578, the example of France convinced William's advisers that 'rivers of blood flow until freedom is granted, which always brings peace in its train.' In 1598, Cornelis Peterszoon Hooft, burgomaster of Amsterdam, expressed the commitment to toleration which tended to thrive in self-governing cities, where strife inhibited trade and where neighbours of differing views were crammed in mutual dependence: God forbade David to build the Temple because he had shed much blood. After that, 'could we be so presumptuous as to build living temples with violence?' In 1619 the commune of Leyden attributed the growth in wealth and number of its inhabitants to 'freedom of conscience or the toleration of different Christian sects.' By then, toleration was beginning to appeal even in Lutheran circles, where it had formerly seemed to pose a threat. 'It is better,' suggested the 'arch-theologian' of Lutheranism, Johann Gerhard of Jena, in 1614, 'to offer protection and security to subjects who are loyal to the true religion, even if they mix with members of other denominations, like lilies among thorns, than to wreck the ship of state by violence.'

THE NARROW GATE

> When Lady Powerscourt told Mr Daly that she had determined on joining the Plymouth Church . . . . he said to her: 'You expect to meet with perfection, and you will be disappointed; it is not to be met with among any body of Christians in this sinful world. After a little time you will separate yourself from some whom you will find not to be as perfect as you thought them to be . . . . at last you will be left alone; and when you look into yourself, you will not find perfection there.

Such conversations have happened countless times when members of moribund congregations have felt the allure of some exciting new Christian movement.

The Philippian jailer demanded of Paul and Silas, 'Sirs, what must I do to be saved?' He received the answer that faith in Christ was the only requirement, but, clearly, there was more to it. Before that dramatic night was out, the official and 'all that were his' received baptism, and that sacrament implied membership of the little, potentially persecuted, Christian community in the city.

Assurance of salvation has always had its individual and corporate aspects. Augustine's assertion that there is no salvation outside the Church in no way excused the believer from personal commitment and a life producing the fruits of the Spirit. Earnest souls over the centuries – not the

Korea is the scene of the most dramatic Christian expansion at the end of the twentieth century. Here 1.1 million people gather in Seoul for an evangelical convention, addressed by Dr Billy Graham. *(Crusade Information Services (photo by Russ Busby))*

Both a cause and an effect of the Reformation was Christocentric preaching. Here Jakob Seisenegger, the court painter, depicts the papal nuncio preaching before Emperor Ferdinand I, c.1560. *(Graf Harrach'sche Familiensammlung (photo Meyer Vienna))*

William Carey (1761–1834), regarded as the father of British missions, spent forty years in India and had much success with evangelism and Bible translation despite the 'cool attitude' of the East India Company and the colonial administration. In this portrait he is depicted with a convert from Buddhism. *(Mansell Collection)*

Death of five missionaries on 'Palm Beach'. In the second half of the twentieth century some Christians still work in traditional ways based on traditional assumptions and face traditional hazards. *(Orange County Register)*

The frontispiece of Daniello Bartoli's *History of the Jesuits* (1650) shows the light of pure Catholic doctrine irradiating the world and its four known continents thanks to the endeavours of Ignatius Loyola and his colleagues. *(Biblioteca Nazionale Braidense, Milan)*

William Booth – and, later, his son Bramwell headed the Salvation Army which, in the late nineteeth century, was simply the latest manifestation of an ancient phenomenon – earnest Christians determined to grapple with the problems of a society largely ignored by the established churches. *(Hulton Getty)*

Salvation Army lasses like these officer-cadets at Tring (1889/90) were the object of much coarse humour, but were at the same time widely respected in the depressed areas where they worked. *(The Salvation Army)*

Men said that there was no pope in Philip II's Spain. Within his dominions the king exercised greater control of church affairs than that claimed by some Protestant rulers. From his palace/monastery/bureaucratic centre at the Escorial (here shown a-building in a contemporary drawing) he attended minutely to administrative detail in religious and secular affairs. He commissioned *The Adoration of the Name of Jesus* (c.1577) from El Greco which depicted himself and the pope united in adoration. In reality the two men were often at loggerheads. *(National Gallery, London)*

Philip Melanchthon (painted by Lucas Cranach the Elder) and Desiderius Erasmus (depicted in a woodcut dictating to his secretary, Gilbert Cousin, c.1530) were both humanist scholars passionately committed to religious truth and church reform. Both were also dismayed at the schismatic effects the new insights were having. *(Staatliche Kunstsammlungen, Dresden; Universitats-Bibliothek, Basel)*

COGNATVS

ERASMVS.

Pedro Berruguete (fl. 1483-1503) was the official court painter of Spain but his portrayal of the callousness of heresy trials strikes an independent line and may reflect criticism of the Inquisition in some official circles. *(Museo del Prado, Madrid)*

Followers of the authoritarian and conservative Monsignor Josemaria Escriva de Balaguer, the founder of Opus Dei, pressed for his canonization. Within months of his death in 1975 reports were current of miracles wrought as a result of his heavenly intercession. *(Opus Dei)*

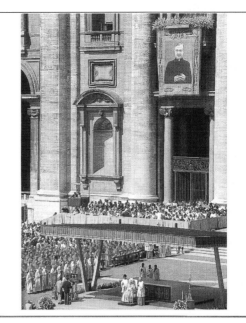

Blessed
JOSEMARÍA ESCRIVÁ
Founder of Opus Dei

NEWSLETTER No. 14

The rebel French Roman Catholic Archbishop Marcel Lefebvre walking in procession at an open-air service in Switzerland in 1977. In spite of a ban on all priestly duties placed on him by the pope, the archbishop carried out ordinations, confirmations and masses. *(Hulton Getty)*

Catholic propaganda. In this 1612 engraving heretics and their books are consigned to the innermost ring of hell. *(Instituto Nazionale per la Grafica, Rome)*

Eugenio Lucas (1824–70), *The Dungeons of the Spanish Inquistion.* As late as the mid-nineteenth century this follower of Goya was still perpetuating earlier Protestant ideas about Catholic persecution. *(Musées Royaux d'Art et d'Histoire, Brussels)*

In his last years Dürer found in
Luther's writings a system of belief
which provided new channels for his
passionate intensity. His portrait of
Nürnberg councillor Hieronymus
Holzschuher (1526) reveals what
Otto Benesch called 'the look of the
men who made the Reformation'.
*(Staatliche Museen Preussischer
Kulturbesitz, Berlin)*

Robert Schuller epitomizes the age-
old determination of missionaries to
use the spectacular and employ
whatever communication techniques
are available. Having built his Crystal
Cathedral in California and become
known nationwide through books
and radio programmes, he later took
his triumphant evangelism worldwide
via satellite television. *(Crystal
Cathedral Ministries)*

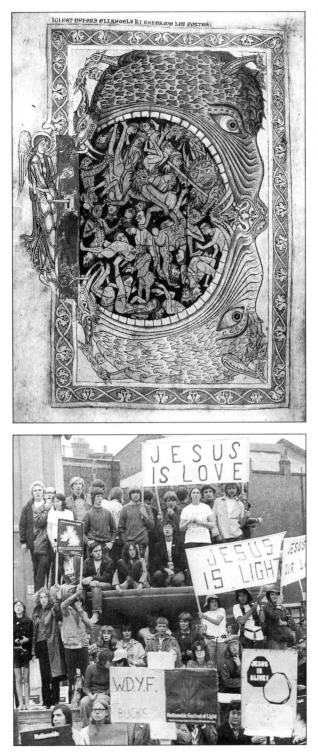

The picture of the damned being locked into hell is twelfth-century but the message has been repeated over and again by religious leaders – mainstream and sectarian – wishing to drum up support. *(British Library)*

The Festival of Light was a Christian moral backlash in Britain of the 1960s and 70s. Its supporters were protesting at declining standards and particularly at the pollution of public morals by inadequately controlled media. *(Hulton Getty)*

Vatican II. This council in 1963 replicated the conflict of some medieval councils between the Curia and the wider Catholic church. It produced sweeping changes within the church and made considerable ecumenical advance, but the papacy found some of its statements difficult to live with. *(Hulton Getty)*

The tragic end to the siege of the Branch Davidian's compound near Waco, Texas in April 1993 was the latest in a very long line of sanguinary consummations experienced by millenarian movements for centuries. *(Hulton Getty)*

Issues such as the campaign against legal abortion unites many Catholics, Protestants and Jews in the United States. *(Hulton Getty)*

A nineteenth-century cartoon portraying Uncle Sam as a latter-day Moses scarcely exaggerated the biblical terms in which the founders of the republic understood their mission. In fact the ideals of liberal toleration were far removed from the Christian concept of toleration. *(American Jewish Archives, Cincinatti)*

Robert Fleury *Galileo Before the Inquisition*. By the mid-nineteenth century the conviction had become firmly established that Galileo's trial was the classic confrontation of pure scientific enquiry and religious bigotry. *(Mansell Collection)*

Rembrandt van Rijn, *Faust in his Study*, c.1651. The Christian cabalist receives a flash of divine illumination. By the seventeenth century two schools of thought had emerged concerning independent scholarship which rejected the confines of ancient dogma: some saw it as the Faustian pathway to diabolical error; others regarded it as the highest and best road the human spirit could follow. *(Trustees of the British Museum)*

Dr Martin Luther King – one of the outstanding twentieth-century examples of a Christian leader impelled into political action by his beliefs. *(Popperfoto)*

The Catholic Charismatic Conference is an annual event in Italy which attracts tens of thousands of ardent supporters who, like their Protestant counterparts, express their faith through ecstatic worship, preaching, healing services and evangelism. The theme of the 1994 conference at Rimini was the Holy Family, reflecting the emphasis many Christians regard as vital in an age when marriage and family life are under intense pressure. *(Father Michael Harper)*

least among whom was Martin Luther – painfully aware that outward conformity was not enough, pledged themselves to more intense devotion, usually in the company of others equally eager to acquit themselves well in this proving ground for eternity. Thus, all the fraternities, communities, sects and heretical groups to which we have frequently referred. Belonging to such fellowships provided part of the answer to the anxious individual's cry 'What must I do to be saved?' It was immensely reassuring to know that one was a part of a holy (in the original sense of the word) people whose beliefs and practices marked them out as particularly (in some cases, exclusively) deserving of divine favour.

For most pre-Reformation people eternal bliss could not be guaranteed even by belonging to the Catholic church, believing as it taught and observing its prescribed patterns of devotion. 'In the visible church the bad be ever mingled with the good.' No Catholic teacher would have disagreed with Anglicanism's Thirty-Nine Articles on that point. This was why charismatic preachers, hawkers of heretical tracts and gospellers reciting from the open Bible made such an impact. There were always those in any town or village who wanted to be sure; to find out something more that they could do to be saved. It was in these lakes of uncertainty that Protestant pioneers netted many of their converts.

The elements of sixteenth-century dissent which could not be retained within the radical Catholic reform movement had to find new ways of reassuring those who had left the Church, as traditionally defined, that only they were the faithful remnant saved from the ranks of false faith. Where did that leave the orthodox majority? If the pope was Antichrist, were all who followed him doomed to hell? Sectarian leaders and crude rabble-rousers did not hesitate to say 'yes'. Thomas Müntzer, determined to hasten the sanguinary Day of the Lord, preached before Duke John of Saxony:

> . . . . a godless man has no right to live if he hinders the godly . . . The sword is necessary to exterminate them. And so that it shall be done honestly and properly, our dear fathers the princes must do it, who confess Christ with us. But if they don't do it, the sword shall be taken from them . . . If they resist, let them be slaughtered without mercy . . . . At the harvest-time one must pluck the weeds out of God's vineyard . . . . the ungodly have no right to live, save what the Elect choose to allow them.

Müntzer did not hesitate to use against Rome the methods and the language that the papacy employed against its opponents. The commonplaces of Catholic propaganda included the contention that obdurate heretics must not be suffered to live and that it was the duty of princes to destroy them.

For more responsible Protestant thinkers the implications of withdrawal from the visible church needed to be thought out rather more carefully. For

9.4 In *The Four Horsemen of the Apocalypse* (1498) Albrecht Dürer (1471-1528) captured all that was most terrifying in the late medieval vision of heaven, earth and hell.

Luther the members of the true Church were obvious to a seven-year-old; they were the lambs who heard the Shepherd's voice. That was typical of the throwaway line that Luther loved but it fronted a mystery which he was equally happy to acknowledge: 'Oh, it is a high, deep, hidden thing is the Church, which nobody may perceive or see, but can only grasp by faith in Baptism, Word and Sacrament.' Calvin, like Luther, was not prepared to consign to perdition all who were not of his party:

> To judge whether others be of the Church, or no, and to distinguish the
> elect from the reprobate, is not for us. This is God's prerogative alone.
> The eyes of God alone see who are to endure to the end.

Calvin's progressive treatment of the related themes of election and predestination in succeeding editions of the *Institutio* has been frequently examined.

In this assertion that salvation lay in the sovereign will of a loving God and was appropriated by faith Calvin was saying nothing new. But, in itself, it could not satisfy every anxiety, every quest. The reformers' contemporaries wanted assurance just as much as those of earlier generations who had followed mystical paths to the presence of God. Indeed, Protestant teaching made the high-wire act of faith even more dangerous by removing the safety net of purgatory, requiem masses and the invocation of the saints. If the individual's eternal wellbeing depended entirely on decisions made in response to the divine call and could not be affected by the mediation of priests or the prayers of the faithful, then the cry 'What must I do to be saved' took on an even more terrifying urgency.

Membership of a Church, separated alike from unbelievers and misbelievers was one strong guarantee. For Catholics it was self-evident that this was the visible, historic Church with Christ's vicar at its head. For Protestants it was just as obvious that the vehicle of salvation was the gathered *ecclesia* where, as Calvin insisted, 'the Word of God is sincerely preached and heard, and where the Sacraments are administered according to the institution of Christ'. Calvin did not intend that definition to be exclusive but it was rapidly interpreted as such. Calvin also meant all decisions about proper preaching and administration to be decided by ministers but these judgements very easily came to be made by unauthorized laymen, visionaries, self-important fuglemen and leaders of personality cults. Just as medieval religious orders had tended to subdivide as members sought out ever more rugged, ascetic pathways, so post-Reformation Protestantism fragmented because believers wished to be identified as adherents of stricter individual doctrines or more faithful followers of the Gospel.

Some separatists have been genuinely unaware that they were causing fresh schisms. The Brethren (or Plymouth Brethren) movement was avowedly quite the opposite in its origins.

You say I quitted *your* communion; if you mean by that, that I do not now break bread with the Church of England, this is not true; but if you mean that I do not *exclusively* join you, it is quite true, feeling this spirit of exclusiveness to be of the very essence of schism, which the apostle so strongly reproves in the Corinthians. I therefore know no distinction, but am ready to break the bread and drink the cup of holy joy with all who love the Lord and will not lightly speak evil of his name. I feel every saint to be a holy person, because Christ dwells in him, and manifests Himself where he worships; and though his faults be as many as the hairs of his head, my duty still is, with my Lord, to join him as a member of the mystical body, and to hold communion and fellowship with him in any work of the Lord in which he may be engaged.

Anthony Norris Groves, who wrote thus to a friend in 1828, was an earnest Bible student, determined to live as closely as possible by the plain word of Scripture. He was a successful Plymouth dentist with a wife and family who turned his back on wealth and position, laboured among the poor, gave almost all his income away and eventually felt the call to overseas mission work. It was while studying in Dublin that he found his spiritual roots being shaken loose from their Anglican soil. Doubts about the Christian duty to bear arms and, more importantly, about infant baptism obliged him to forsake his commitments to ordination and to the Church Missionary Society. Henceforth, he would belong to no party but would embrace in Christian fellowship 'all who love the Lord'. In practice that meant Anglicans and Non-conformists of an evangelical persuasion. He subsequently went as an independent missionary to the Middle East and India.

First in Dublin, then in Plymouth, Groves was joined by others from a wide spectrum of Catholic and Protestant congregations who were dissatisfied with their own Churches and came together for fellowship, study and breaking of bread. It was in 1831 that the inevitable happened. A group of Christian Brethren took over a Plymouth chapel. At first, it was just for weeknight preachings but before long it had become a centre of regular worship. The early days of the movement coincided with a period of disarray in British Churches. The problems of the established Church provoked the emergence of Tractarianism and some spectacular defections to Rome. Emancipated non-conformist and Catholic congregations were tending to become 'respectable'. The simplicity and vigour of the Brethren attracted many disillusioned Christians from the historic Churches and the number of assemblies multiplied rapidly. And not only in Britain. Missionaries, supported by the prayers and sacrificial giving of their home assemblies, were despatched, not only to all the traditional 'heathen lands afar', but also to the continent to convert 'papists'.

The moving spirit behind the expansion into Europe, and the most dynamic figure in the movement was John Darby, a strong-minded and argumentative ex-Church of Ireland minister. Inspired by his own reading of Scripture, the troubled state of many Churches and his own success in attracting members from other denominations, Darby developed principles that would permanently split the Brethren. A letter written by Groves during one of his visits to England describes the change that Darby had brought about in his assemblies.

> I ever understood our principle of union to be the possession of the common life or common blood of the family of God; these were our early thoughts, and are my most matured ones.. . . . then, all our thoughts were conversant about how we might *ourselves* most effectually mani-fest forth that life we had received by Jesus, and where we might find that life in others; and when we were persuaded we had found it, bidding them, on the Divine claim of this common life, to come and share with us, in the fellowship of the common Spirit . . . . The moment the witnessing for the common life as our *bond* gives place to a witnessing *against* errors by separation of persons and preaching, every individual or society of individuals, first comes before the mind as those who might need witnessing against, and all their conduct and principles have first to be examined and approved before they can be received; and the position which this occupying the seat of judgement will place you in will be this: the most narrow-minded and bigoted will rule, because his conscience cannot and will not give way.

Darby's magnetism and his powerful apocalyptic preaching attracted thousands. He welded them into a network of assemblies, much more organ-ized and tightly controlled than the earlier worshipping communities. What he offered his followers was the ultimate assurance of complete exclusivity. The soul that would be saved must abjure the company of worldly people and misguided Christians (i.e. all those not of Darby's sect):

> The path of the saints is most simple; their portion is heavenly; to be not of the world, as Christ is not of the world . . . . [the saint's] path is very clear, to wit the spirit of separation from the world, through the knowl-edge of death, and power, and glory, and coming of the Lord Jesus Christ . . . . and hence growing *positive separation from them all.*

Groves' prophecy lost little time in the fulfilment. Darby had an extremely bitter altercation with other leaders in Plymouth and the tremors from this epicentre vibrated throughout the movement. Thus did the Exclusive Brethren and the Open Brethren part company. Darby's rigidity and his making a positive virtue of the closed mind ensured that his feder-ation would further fragment. It has continued to do so to the present day and periodic media exposés tell sad tales of families divided and minds controlled by 'sinister brain-washers'. Open Brethren, by contrast, have, for the most part, remained true to the original vision of collaboration with other Protestant evangelicals. They have been and are prominent in philanthropy and mission.

THE MAN WHO IS SUFFERING

There is a kind of exclusivist logic imbedded in Protestantism. The self-conscious elect are likely to be impatient of the rest. The appeal of an apostolic model of Church life is inseparable from an historical context in which Christians were a small minority, a pilgrim band journeying through a hostile environment. On the face of it, Catholicism ought to be less prone to this vice: the aspiration to universality, the willingness to defer enumeration of the invisible Church – these unfastidious traditions suggest a relatively open community with undemanding conditions of membership. In practice, however, for most of the time since the Reformation, the Catholic Church has been as tough on non-members as the fussiest of small sects and was the last of the major churches to extend fraternal sympathy to other communions. Only in the 1960s was triumphalism – the aspiration to unity by 'converting' and absorbing followers of other traditions – replaced by ecumenism – a policy of enfolding other Christians by extending the church's embrace.

At the Second Vatican Council, one of the delegates who voted in favour of this revised posture was Archbishop Marcel Lefebvre. Yet he went on to lead traditionalists opposed to ecumenism in a movement of secession which has come very close to schism. He was raised in a brood of seven siblings which produced two priests and three nuns: all his early experience showed him that traditional piety worked. In the era of the rise and crimes of fascism he was working in the mission field in Africa. He never saw the horrible unravelling of the right-wing politics in which he was brought up, never discarded his old colonialist's view of the nature of 'Christian civilization', never escaped the lingering influence of the rhetoric of Action Française. Communism, liberalism and freemasonry remained allied bogeys in his mind. He was a spokesman of fossilized prejudices but also of a noble and typical kind of Catholic spirituality: devotion to the changelessness of God, un-compromising rejection of the mutability of the world. Even if they did not share his views or approve his defiance, other Catholics could sympathize with him, because they all had to endure the trauma as well as the joy of the Second Vatican Council. Lefebvre spoke for the millions who felt alarmed or abandoned at being deprived of the lovely liturgy of their childhoods, or challenged in their adherence to verities they thought were unassailable. Miraculously – it almost seemed – nearly all Catholics accepted these trials as a test of faith and offered up the sacrifices the Church demanded from them. Lefebvre became the leader of those who could not or would not do so.

To begin with, he welcomed the council; but he wanted it to be a council of spiritual energy, enforcing standards of discipline among the clergy, and a council of dogmatic entrenchment, denouncing modern heresies – like communism and materialism and, perhaps ecumenism and liberalism – just as Trent had denounced the heresies of Protestants. He was in favour of Pope John XXIII's policy of bringing the church 'up to date'; but by that, Lefebvre understood turning the church against up-to-date enemies, not making compromises with modern fashion or what he called 'today's tastes'. He voted for the decree *'Lumen Gentium'*, which admitted that the Church included Christians of 'holiness and truth' outside the ranks of professed Catholics, because, strictly speaking, that had always been Catholic teaching; but he did not support the spirit in which it was formulated or concede to other denominations the liberty and courtesy implied.

Because he was moved, in part at least, by a revulsion of spirit and taste rather than by strictly rational arguments, it is hard to identify Lefebvre's specific objections to the council's work. Understandably, given the long span of his defiance and the changes going on in the background, his own pronouncements on the subject were not entirely consistent. It seems fair, however, to highlight three critical points of controversy. First, Lefebvre believed that the council had subverted the structure of authority in the church, transferring the power of the pope to the bishops collectively. In reality, the pope's authority depends not on the institutional framework but on the responses of Catholics to the initiatives he takes. To judge from the evidence of the pontificate of John Paul II, a pope can still guide the church according to his own vision and inspiration, against political, social and economic trends of apparently irresistible power. Councils of war aboard the flagship always, of their nature, galvanize the solidarity of the subordinate commanders; in the long run, the effect boosts the authority of the admiral who stays on the bridge when the officers have retired to quarters. Though it is impossible to test, this proposition is persuasive: the post-conciliar papacy is stronger than it would have been without the council. In any case, even if Lefebvre's judgement on this point was correct, it led him into a logical absurdity: defending the pope's authority by defying it, adhering to it in principle while disobeying in practice.

His second sticking-point was religious liberty. Lefebvre could not admit that Catholics, who ought to be convinced of the unique truth of their faith, should be willing for 'other cults' to share an equal measure of liberty. On this matter, the arguments on both sides were bad. Lefebvre accused the council of excesses it never uttered: the church would not and could not say that religious choices could be free because they did not matter, or because they were all equally good or because people have no obligations to God. On the contrary, freedom is a condition of Catholic evangelization because it is a sacred principle of canon law that coercion cannot induce conversion and that the choice to be a Catholic is meaningless unless it is made freely. The early seventeenth-century Jesuit theologian Martin Becanus helped to convince Catholics that religious liberty is not just a 'lesser evil' for Catholics' own protection where they are in a minority but also a 'greater good' which makes it possible to convert others by peaceful means. Catholic tradition did temper the commitment to liberty with a serious qualification: it was not to be extended to blasphemers or apostates. 'You are free to accept Christianity,' said Thomas Aquinas 'but obliged to keep it.' This is reminiscent of Brezhnev's dictum, 'Communism is a choice for life' and of the logic that prompted Ayatollah Khomeini's fatwahs of death. But even if one were willing to admit it in principle, it would not seem that toleration could properly be withheld from Protestant churches, once they were established. Enthusiasm for religious liberty naturally accompanies confidence in one's own faith, just as the makers of the best products are keenest on free markets.

Finally, Lefebvre rejected the new liturgy promulgated by Pope Paul VI, the Missa Nunctiva. In practice, this proved to be the most serious conflict. Adherence to the old liturgy gave Lefebvre's cause a rallying-call and rite with which people could identify and brought him followers in numbers otherwise inconceivable. The Catholic church has never achieved liturgical uniformity and there is no good reason why it should. If both liturgies, old and new, had been available in parallel, to be chosen according to the preference of particular congregations, provinces or dioceses as they wished, the trauma of Vatican II would have been much easier to cope with. In England and Wales, where bishops were allowed to authorize the old liturgy, and in the Uniate and Maronite communities, which continued to have their own liturgies, Lefebvre got little or no support. Pope Paul VI and his advisers, however, seemed to think that the new liturgy would not get a fair chance to be widely adopted unless the use of the old one was suspended. Ironically, Lefebvre's obstinacy postponed the effect he desired and the old liturgy, despite the present pope's obvious wish, has not yet been restored to equality with the new.

Lefebvre detected doctrinal subversion and, specifically, 'Protestant influence' in the text the pope promulgated. 'The new rite,' he said, 'expresses a new faith, a faith which is not ours.' This seems unfair. As has been argued throughout this book, the theme of reformation is one the Protestant and Catholic traditions have shared since the sixteenth century. Even when Protestants and Catholics were keenest on mutual self-differentiation, they were accessible to mutual influence. Pius IV granted the use of the lay chalice to the provinces of the Holy Roman Empire in 1564, though the practice was gradually discontinued. By the time of Paul VI's reforms, especially in provinces where both communions were well represented and worshipped side-by-side, the modification of Catholic behaviour in church and the borrowing of Protestant hymns and music had a history of generations and, in some places, of centuries behind it. To pretend that Protestants had no share in Catholic tradition, no insight into Christian truth and no good lessons to teach other Christians would not only be crassly at variance with the evidence but also contrary to Catholic teaching, which has always allowed that partial revelations, gifts of the Spirit and words and works of Christian witness can be communicated by God to people outside the church.

Even if Lefebvre's analysis of the text had been right, the new liturgy would not necessarily have been a bad thing. Yet other careful scrutineers could detect no dilution of Catholic orthodoxy in it. The Missa Nunctiva is firm on all the essential doctrines: the mass as sacrifice, the uniqueness of the priesthood, prayers for the dead, the place of the sacraments, the saints and the Mother of God. Those who dislike it usually do so for aesthetic reasons: the undistinguished quality of most of the translations into the vernacular grates on their ears; or reasons of snobbery: they are uneasy about exchanging a kiss of peace with a neighbour to whom they have not been introduced; or simply because they balk at the unfamiliar.

Lefebvre, however, had a further and, in some eyes, a sinister agenda. He resented the style of the new mass as 'democratic'. In some respects, the new style and some of the new words were indeed less hieratic than the old. The altar was shifted away from the east wall. The priest faced the congregation. The worshipper made his confession to 'brothers and sisters' as well as to the priest; the kiss of peace emphasized the status of the community. The priest invited the congregation to pray for the acceptance of 'this sacrifice, mine and yours'. To call this 'democracy' would, however, be to appropriate secular language in an attempt to describe the sacred – the very kind of profanation Lefebvre himself would most claim to abhor. Lefebvre's distaste for democracy was grounds for his quarrel with secular trends, not with the Church; ironically, this was a quarrel in which few of his followers were on his side. Traditionalists in the Church could be, and by the 1960s usually were, democrats in politics.

Lefebvre struggled to find a form of words with which to acknowledge the authority of the council, but his heart was not in it. He let slip his real feelings when he denounced the council as 'neither inspired nor led by the Holy Spirit'. Similarly, he made many conventional submissions to the pope, but implicitly admitted his reservations about the status of Paul VI when he said he could not 'accept a pope who appoints bishops who practise Marxism'. He trapped himself in the paradox of heretics and schismatics throughout the ages when he declared, 'We are not in schism; we are the continuators of the Catholic Church.' In what was effectively his declaration of independence on 21 November 1974, he made an alarmingly subjective distinction:

> We adhere with all our heart and soul to Catholic Rome, guardian of
> Catholic faith and traditions. . . . . Eternal Rome, mistress of wisdom and
> truth. We refuse, however, and have always refused to follow the Rome
> of neo-modernist and neo-Protestant tendencies.

In some ways, like all rebels, Lefebvre did the church good. By causing a
conservative scare, he exercised a restraining influence. It may be in part
thanks to his rebellion that the church has not made the worldly compromises he feared. The pontificate of John Paul II has taken the edge off the
appeal of conservative secession: the pope seems always to have had in
mind Christ's warning to St Peter, 'Get thee behind me, Satan, for your
thoughts are the thoughts of men and not the thoughts of God.' He has been
inflexible in defence of traditional teaching on faith and morals against
adulteration by expediency or surrender to secular clamour. During his
pontificate the spirit of Vatican II has continued to shape reform: lay
participation has gone on increasing, ecumenism has opened a widening
embrace. But the pope himself has been the living proof that these trends
are unsubversive. Most of the priests Lefebvre ordained are finding or will
find their fears dissolved and their vocations fulfilled.

Of Lefebvre himself, John Paul said, 'There is a man who is suffering.'
He tried hard to reconcile the archbishop. It was a genuinely hopeless task.
Lefebvre – at some uncertain point – ceased to want to be reconciled. When
he thought he was succeeding, his demands became more strident, his
language more shrill. As early as 1974, when commissioners appointed by
Paul VI came to investigate his seminary, they were impressed by the
sincerity and austerity of Lefebvre's students but alarmed by the whiff of
exclusivist fanaticism. The school at Écône nourished an atmosphere of
sauve qui peut – a sense of being a beleaguered refuge of orthodoxy, from
which the saints in security could behold others' self-destruction. The
mark of the beast of exclusivism is just that superior conviction: the self-
seclusion of the self-identified elect.

Chapter Ten

ALL CHANGE:
Ecumenism and its Limits

THE RELIGION OF THE AMOEBA

In a forgotten story by John Betjeman, the narrator is a member of a society
of Oxford dons, dedicated to the charitable work of giving an occasional
square meal to impecunious scions of the Anglo-Irish aristocracy. Of the
many indigent peers in that category, the only one they have never been
able to track down is Lord Mount Prospect, who never answers letters. The
sole clue to his whereabouts is the line about his religious affiliation in *Who's
Who*, where he declares himself to be an 'Ember Day Bryanite.'

After looking the sect up in the telephone directory, the narrator sets off
in search of the only congregation of Ember Day Bryanites listed as extant,
beneath 'Other Denominations', below the Particular Baptists and the
Peculiar People, below the Sandemanians and Independent Calvinistics. He
tracks them down to a grimy green in a working-class area of north London,
where non-conformist chapels line the square in various shades of inappropriate grandeur. The most austerely classical of them all is that of the
Ember Day Bryanites, black and pedimented, 'more like a warehouse than
anything else'. The gates are secured by a padlock choked with rust but in
the gathering twilight the narrator gets in by scaling the pitted railings. As
he crosses an unkempt courtyard towards a vast, windy, gloomy colonnade
he is gripped by misgivings: 'the chapel loomed so large and high that it was

almost as if it had moved forward to interrupt me'. Only one faded, curling notice crackles in the portico. But on a wooden board, the remains of painted lettering can be read by matchlight; 'Those Who Are Chosen for His Courts Above Will Meet Here (God Willing) on The Lord's Day at 11 a.m. and at 6.30. Holy Supper by Arrangement.' Resignedly, the narrator admits to himself that the Lord has summoned the last of His Ember Day Bryanites to Him.

Betjeman's imaginary green, its worn grass 'bright with the rays of gas-light from the places of worship' was a brilliant device for conjuring up the fragmented condition of English Protestantism, the sectarian spectrum into which the light of the gospel was refracted by the long and undisciplined history of the Reformation in England. 'From all over Hungerford Green came the whooping of hymns loud enough to stream through ventilating spaces in the pointed windows of Baptist and Wesleyan chapel . . . . I scanned the names on black and gilded noticeboards. "Congregational", "Primitive Methodist", "United Methodist", "New Jerusalem", "Presbyterian Church of England".' Even all these, and the "Other Denominations" of the telephone book, were only a few sherds of the shattered vessel of English Church Unity.

Schism in the Church is like a shivered mirror. The breaks multiply along the lines of the cracks. The images reflected back get smaller as they multiply. Within schismatic communities, schism becomes a habit. The world of fragments Betjeman observed had spread slowly from some sixteenth-century cracks. Schisms were started by reformers impatient for a 'reformation without tarrying'; others by purists, drunk on the doctrine of predestination, who craved apartheid from the reprobate. In 1579 Robert Browne repudiated episcopal authority and founded congregations outside official parishes, where 'the worthiest of the Kingdom of God' could 'covenant to walk together', before exile to Holland and the dissolution of his sect by the momentum of schism. Sir Andrew Aguecheek would 'as lief be a Brownist as a politician', but the reforming mentality, with its emphasis on the primacy of conscience, bred revulsion from authority and stimulated what came to be known as separatism. Within or alongside the nominally uniform reformed Church of England, as life-blood seeped from the Church through wounds opened by the Reformation, 'privy churches' or fellowships of reformers clotted around particular preachers. Many of them evolved into separate churches or independent gatherings. 'Pause awhile with me,' Bishop Pilkington of Durham wrote to a friend in 1573,

> and mourn over this our church at this time so miserably divided, not to say, wholly rent in pieces. Commend her to the Lord your God, and entreat him that, having compassion upon us, he may very soon provide some godly remedy for the healing of her wounds, that she may not be utterly destroyed.

This friable texture, this tendency to fragment, was already typical of Protestantism. Every effort of continental reformers to draw up a common confession had foundered; every diplomatic initiative to ally in the Protestant cause had struck limits. The Huguenot Church, founded by eighty-eight missionaries from Geneva, threatened to dissolve after Calvin's death in 1564, as Béza struggled to hold the line of Presbyterian organization against secessions by individual congregations encouraged by Villiers. In the next century, however, independentism, 'the sink of all heresies and schisms', came to seem a characteristically English disease, especially after the Civil War of 1632–53 was won by manpower recruited from independent congregations. The rule of Oliver Cromwell, who made toleration for Protestant radicals the defining policy of his government, dappled English religion, once uniform, with unchangeable spots. For a moment, a new concept of the Church seemed possible, in which diversity could be encompassed in a wide-embracing kind of unity: toleration, fairly considered, could be a uniting arch, rather than a separating structure. But in 1662 reimposed uniformity of the liturgy effectively expelled independent-minded radicals from the Church of England. The freedom of the preceding years was too precious to give up. Some honest oxen felt the sting of the pricks more than the weight of the yoke. Joseph Caryl spoke for them when he resigned his living in August, 1662: experience of Christ 'hath left such a relish upon their souls that they would not lose it for all the dainty morsels of this world; they had rather indeed walk with Christ in white than walk with the world in scarlet'.

In the late 1680s, James II, a Catholic who saw radical Protestants as his allies in an attempt to revive toleration on an even wider basis than Cromwell's, could not refrain from gloating at the reformed Churches' inability to enforce a discipline of their own. In his view, the Church of England was being repaid in kind for her own offences against the unity of the universal Church. 'You cut the banks of infallibility,' he told fellow-Englishmen, 'and let in the waters which must drown you.' The Protestant habit of mutual exclusion seemed for a long time to justify this sort of taunt. The Independents were exiled or self-exiled from the Church of England. Baptists of different degrees of strictness excluded each other. Methodists, once they had repudiated the disciplines of the established church, could not keep their own churches in one fold. The 'connection' founded by the Countess of Huntingdon, at enormous personal expense, precisely with the aim of transcending differences between Protestants, dissolved with its own dissensions in the 1770s. The Church of Scotland struck secessionist sparks and 'wee frees'. One of its splinter-sects, the Glasites, generated a splinter-group of its own when its followers in Edinburgh unilaterally abjured other congregations' understanding of the Lord's Supper as excessively cultic: the discords of the Reformation indeed seemed, like Aristotle's apple, infinitely divisible. As if in parallel mirrors, the sects proliferated and dwindled, and dwindled as they proliferated, to the numbers of legion and the dimensions of specks.

Yet diversity is not necessarily self-destructive and the traditions which genuinely arose from the Reformation never quite lost touch with the ideal of Christian unity. Paradoxically, it was excessive reverence for scriptural exhortations to unity that provoked some schisms among fundamentalists who demanded unrealistic standards of unanimity from fellow-worshippers. 'Brothers, I urge you, in the name of our Lord Jesus Christ,' wrote Paul to the Corinthians, 'not to have factions among yourselves but all to be in agreement in what you profess; so that you are perfectly united in your beliefs and judgements.' Taken literally, in one sense, this text left the freedom of conscience stranded in never-land and authorized the sanctions of spiritual outlawry in any case of disagreement. The ultimate logic of this interpretation would lead to the unity of the dot that thinks itself the universe. In Chile in 1910 the Iglesia Metodista Nacional split from a Methodist parent-church dominated by Yankee missionaries. In 1932 the Iglesia Metodista Pentecostal seceded from the Iglesia Metodista Nacional. By 1962 fifteen more Churches had been founded by dissenters from the Iglesia Metodista Pentecostal, each generating more schisms of its own.

Paul was writing about the unity of a local ecclesia. The greater unity of the Catholic Church had scarcely yet arisen, though it is clear that, even in its embryonic stage, it was marked by differences of emphasis between the converts of various evangelists. All the New Testament letter writers juggled with the individual and corporate elements of the faith. Yet for all of them the drive towards *personal* commitment and holiness was paramount. For example, I John exhorted his fractious flock, 'Love one another'. But that *philadelphia* was dependent upon *agape*. Existence of the former was evidence of the pre-existence of the latter: 'We know that we have passed from death to life because we love the brotherhood.'

EXPERIMENTS WITH ADHESIVES

The Protestant tradition has always included a tendency to try and break the schismatic habit in two ways: by recementing splits and by redefining church unity. The independent congregations of England set up common institutions for their own collective guidance. At the height of his fame as a scientist, Michael Faraday shuttled between London, Edinburgh and Dundee to heal the schism among the Glasites. In 1817 the Reformed Church in Prussia formally united with the Orthodox Lutherans, albeit under orders from the government. In 1947 the Church of South India succeeded in enfolding Presbyterians, Congregationalists and Anglicans and inspired a series of attempts to build 'united' or 'uniting' churches in Canada, Australia, Britain and the United States.

Luther and Calvin were probably not secessionists, by temperament, but evangelists; they wanted not to split the Church but to convert the whole of it to their own way of thinking. The letters Sadoleto exchanged with Calvin were based on the assumption that schism was bridgeable and that the wounds inflicted by the sharp words and burning brands of the Reformation conflict could be healed (See above, p. 241–2). The seventeenth-century exchanges between Archbishops of Canterbury and Patriarchs of Constantinople were not only a ganging-up of self-consciously apostolic Churches against Roman claims but also part of a genuinely ecumenical movement, which, as Archbishop Laud hoped, would erase the scandal of a disunited Christendom. In the late seventeenth century, parallel spiritual movements within the Protestant and Catholic traditions – rather like the spanning effect of the charismatic movement today – stirred hopes that confessional divisions would be transcended by a larger unity. In 1699, Johannes Kelpius, who had sought freedom among the Quakers of Pennsylvania, saw, in 'ecstasies, revelations, apparitions, changings of minds, transfigurations, translations' and 'paradisical representations by voices, melodies and sensations', a 'revolution in Europe . . . . which in the Roman Church goes under the name of Quietism' and, among Protestants, under those of 'pietism, chiliasm and philadelphianism'. The Philadelphians were not a sect but, by self-definition, a society 'preparatory' to the cosmic Church predicted in the third chapter of Revelation. Leibniz was born during the Thirty Years' War – reputedly the most destructive conflict of religions in European history; yet much of his maturity was spent negotiating for collaboration between Protestants and Catholics to counter what was perceived as a Muslim threat from the Ottoman Empire.

In the mid-eighteenth century, Frederick the Great proclaimed himself 'neutral between Rome and Geneva. I try to unite them by showing them they are fellow-citizens.' At about the same time, a German Catholic who longed to bring Lutherans back into the fold urged the pope to return to the early Church concept of his primacy as first among equals. The author was committed and persuasive. He was also nobody's fool: he published his book pseudonymously (under the name Justinus Febronius Jurisconsultus) and with a false printer's mark.

A writer of the preceding generation, who regarded himself as a pure academic rather than a controversialist, took no such precautions. Lodovico Muratori spent most of his working life as librarian to the Duke of Modena. His prodigious output of works covering history, politics and economics and his publishing of ancient texts won him a deserved place in the annals of European scholarship. But the lessons he calmly drew from history and contemporary affairs gave great encouragement to radical reformers and Jansenists. Muratori criticized superstitious saint-worship and insisted that adoration of Christ should be paramount and in no way shared with his mother. In his tract *On the Moderation of Minds in Matters of Religion* he attacked the so-called 'blood vow', an oath demanded of entrants to some university courses committing them to support the dogma of the immaculate conception.

Muratori's book, *On a Well-ordered Devotion* linked him directly with the Erasmian humanists of two centuries earlier. The writer had gone through a conversion experience in his middle years and the whole thrust of his work thereafter was towards the encouragement of life-transforming personal piety. He argued for vernacular translations of the mass, Bible-based preaching and devotional books for lay people which did not rely on absurd legends and outrageous miracles. *On a Well-ordered Devotion* narrowly escaped being banned by the Inquisition but this did not stop Muratori and his works being attacked by reactionaries.

One result of the Reformation divide was that Catholic radicals and even champions of intelligent moderation (as Muratori certainly considered himself to be) were inevitably branded as covert Protestants. The mud thrown by generations of polemicists has built up and hardened into a solid wall. Until the twentieth century practical measures of ecumenism hardly ever crossed the Protestant–Catholic divide. The late seventeenth and early eighteenth centuries are often characterized as the period of the 'rise of toleration'; but the conflicts of the Reformation continued almost unabated. In 1685, Louis XIV expelled Protestants from France. In 1715 his successor celebrated the supposed extermination of those who remained and in 1724 renewed the decree against them. In the same year a government-sponsored campaign to eliminate Protestantism from Poland began. In 1725 Catholic and Protestant alliances were formed by European powers, each expressly for the defence of its religion against the other. In the 1730s the exile of Protestants from Lorraine and Salzburg inspired a vivid literature of exodus. The eschatological dreams of exiled Huguenots helped to excite the 'enthusiasm' which eighteenth-century churchmen suspected as inherently excessive.

Early in the second half of the century, Protestants in many parts of Europe experienced a great fear of an imminent war of annihilation to be unleashed on them by Catholics. The American War of Independence was, at least in part, a 'war of religion' and as late as the 1840s religion was the main issue in the Swiss Civil War. The Christian genius seemed at least as well adapted to trench-digging as to bridge-building. When open warfare subsided, rancour remained – the habits of exclusion, perpetuated in hurtful, hateful practices that divided families, as they divided the Christian family. On the Friday of Samuel Wilberforce's funeral in 1873, his Catholic relations held aloof from the Protestant prayers, while his Protestant relations had cutlets served for lunch.

Throughout the period 1600–1900, moves towards union or closer co-operation were usually little more than tactical manoeuvrings on the ideological battlefield. Perhaps they should not be graced with the title 'ecumenical' at all. Some early experiments in Protestant states were undisguised anti-

Catholic gestures, such as the moves patronized by Prussian secularists in the 1870s to strengthen the hand of the Reich against the pope by encouraging a movement of reunification between Protestants and disaffected Catholics. Trapped in the long legacy of intolerance, the Roman communion reacted with hostility which lasted until the second half of the twentieth century.

Political realities were a positive discouragement to theological and ecclesiological rethinking. Rulers in the Age of Enlightenment drew the line at burning people for their faith but they were prepared to employ the forces of law and order against religious dissidents. As long as Habsburgs and Bourbons were ready to turn their state machines against Protestants and coerce them into reconversion, drive them into foreign havens or force them into transatlantic obscurity, there was little reason for church leaders to question Catholicism's serene exclusivity. During the troubled decades when the Western nations struggled to discard the concept of rule by divine sanction and assume the principle of government by common consent, the papacy naturally found its allies in the representatives of autocracy. Radicals, liberals and republicans, with their insistence on the separation of Church and State and the toleration of religious minorities, were seen as the enemies of the Christendom myth to which many Catholic thinkers still clung.

Pius IX, who certainly did not begin his pontificate as a reactionary, was forced by the logic of the official Vatican line, the turbulence of the times and his own temporary exile from Rome during the 1848 revolution to dig his papal slippers in very firmly. His *Syllabus of Errors* of 1864 consigned to a common gaol the host of ethical and philosophical criminals Pius considered responsible for terrorizing and seducing the faithful. Into the catalogue of eighty 'errors of our times' went freedom of worship and belief, renunciation of the use of force by the Church, the suggestion that the papacy should carry its share of blame for schism, the abandonment of temporal power and the separation of Church and State. As the *Church Times* observed, the implied all-embracing condemnations of other churches and most European governments failed to square with the pope's claim to be the focus of Christian unity. In terms of relations with other churches Pius IX set the pattern followed by Rome for almost another century. It was Leo XIII, a pope personally inclined to diplomacy and dialogue, who had the effrontery to pronounce Anglican orders invalid in 1896. It was Pius XI whose encyclical *Mortalium Animos,* of 1927, observed on the subject of ecumenical gatherings, 'The Apostolic See can by no means take part in these assemblies, nor is it in any way lawful for Catholics to give to such enterprises their encouragement or support.'

The situation was different in North America. Social fluidity and the absence of many of the establishment shibboleths which marked out old world religious communities allowed room for experimentation. Communities were increasingly distinguished by language and social customs – German, English, Dutch – rather than by allegiance to particular churches. Lutheran, Reformed and Anglican families readily intermarried. Some Lutheran ministers received Anglican orders so that they could find paid employment with English congregations. By 1776 45 per cent of church buildings used by Reformed and Lutheran worshippers in Pennsylvania were shared. 'The sense of denominational exclusiveness rapidly collapsed, showing incidentally how far the orthodox platforms of Europe were simply clerical ideologies.' Yet such pragmatic experiments in survival cannot be regarded as attempts to address the 'scandal of disunity'.

The impetus towards an ecumenism that, although sporadic, went deeper than convenience came from Protestant evangelicals. It was from the beginning mission-oriented: Christians from different traditions coming together in order to fulfil more effectively what they conceived to be the Church's primary function. (see above, p. 194f) Of all approaches to ecumenism that has always been the simplest and most effective. The Moravians paid little attention to denominational barriers in pursuing their brand of evangelistic pietism. Methodists and evangelical Anglicans made common cause in the late eighteenth-century revivals despite John Wesley's earlier experiences of rejection by evangelical clergy which led him to describe them as 'a rope of sand'. A tradition of fluidity developed in many Church of England parishes. Thus, if a gospel-centred incumbent was succeeded by an ineffective preacher or an active opponent of 'enthusiasm' several members of the congregation might decamp to a dissenting chapel. A constituency built up which identified itself by adherence to basic Reformation theological principles rather than by loyalty to any particular religious establishment.

In the nineteenth century evangelicals came together with increasing readiness in interdenominational bodies such as the YMCA, temperance organizations, university Christian unions, Crusaders Bible classes, school boards, and societies for home and overseas mission, where Anglicans, Baptists, Methodists, Presbyterians. Congregationalists and independent Church members pursued specific objectives. They were only open to 'Bible-based' Christians subscribing to conservative evangelical tenets. Yet they were genuinely ecumenical because, as well as drawing membership from a wide denominational constituency, they embraced people with basic doctrinal differences. There were Calvinists and Arminians, devotees of varied apocalyptic interpretations, upholders of believers' baptism and those who practised the 'sprinkling' of infants. Evangelicals frequently showed themselves ready to set aside the issues of sacramental theology and doctrine that had divided their sixteenth-century forbears in order to get on with the task in hand.

In 1846 a large conference in Liverpool gathered together representatives from all British Churches which considered themselves to be evangelical. Its convenors were concerned about the drift away from biblical

Christianity, Romanizing tendencies in the Church of England and the denominational divisions which prevented like-minded believers making a united stand for the Gospel. The outcome of the conference was the founding of the Evangelical Alliance which was pledged:

> . . . . to aid in manifesting as far as is practicable the unity which exists among true disciples of Christ; to promote their union by fraternal and devotional intercourse, to discourage all envyings, strife and division.

The EA was one of many organizations aimed at healing the breach between church and chapel, achieving communal evangelistic activity and co-ordinating opposition to the political, social and moral evils of the day.

It was from this ethos, this evangelical sense of priorities, that the event sprang which is usually taken as marking the beginning of the ecumenical movement proper. The leaders of several missionary societies were concerned that rivalry in the field was hampering both their existing work and any evangelistic thrust into new areas. So a World Missionary Conference was summoned to meet in Edinburgh in 1910. It was remarkable as being the first large gathering of Western non-Roman Catholics of all shades of churchmanship. It had authority, stature and influence but its vision was contained within well-defined limits. It was another example of unity for mission. It made no attempt to tackle issues of faith and order and it was content to live with doctrinal differences among its members. There was, for example, no service of Holy Communion because Baptists and Anglo-Catholics would have been unable to gather round the same table.

The impetus given by the Edinburgh conference was deep and long lasting. An International Missionary Council emerged to continue the work of co-ordination via journals, occasional papers and conferences. But the wider impact was a greater openness between Churches and a desire to explore together their theological differences. Some leaders began to talk about the 'sin of division'. J. H. Shakespeare, Secretary of the Baptist Union after the First World War, called for the unification of all the Free Churches. The idea disturbed many of his followers, though not as much as the fact that he was prepared to accept episcopacy in order to bring the Anglican communion into his reordered church.

Ecumenism was still a minority taste but it was favoured by the mood of the times. It was argued that if politicians could form the League of Nations in order to safeguard world peace, then the Christian community should point the way to harmony and reconciliation. It was still only Protestants who were ready to take up the challenge. The Orthodox churches sent observers to conferences in the interwar years and were generally encouraging of the movement. But the Vatican remained inflexible.

On the eve of the Second World War the enthusiasms and heartsearchings of three decades focused in the formation of the World Council of

Churches. Its formal inauguration was prevented by the outbreak of hostilities but a secretariat was established in neutral Geneva. This was sufficient to keep up the momentum. While Europe crumbled into bloody chaos the embryo WCC was, in its small way, helping to draw up the blueprint of a more hopeful future. The institution came into being formally in 1948.

It was a long, purposeful and optimistic stride but the direction it was taking was far from clear. The WCC developed a very different attitude to reunion from anything that had been tried before. Sixteenth-century attempts to create cohesion had concentrated on satisfactorily defining certain core doctrines. Joint action by certain Protestant bodies was based on a commitment to mission but had an agreed Bible-based agenda. Eighteenth- and nineteenth-century Catholicism was, similarly, an alliance of churches loyal to certain centrally promulgated dogmas. The WCC by contrast, in its desire to embrace all, had at its centre a theological vacuum. It is significant that the Roman Catholic church was not alone in holding aloof from it; the Evangelical Alliance would not touch it either.

Observers at either end of the spectrum were concerned about the WCC's drift towards liberalism and social radicalism. Theology, like nature, abhors a vacuum. The central councils of this inter-church body came to be dominated by men and women, unkindly dubbed 'ecumaniacs' by the doubters, who sought to impose policies with which Christians of various traditions felt uncomfortable. The WCC favoured radical belligerents in Third World conflicts. It adopted many of the tenets of liberation theology and committed funds to causes hateful to the people in the pews. In the seventies it channelled money directly to the ANC to finance the armed struggle in South Africa.

The World Council of Churches both responded to and helped to create a radically changed climate of opinion. It was one which no Christian body could afford to ignore. The official Catholic reaction was set in train by John XXIII. When Angelo Roncalli was elected pope he was one month short of his seventy-seventh birthday and an extremely unlikely agent of revolution. Nor had this gentle, wisecracking, down-to-earth priest of Lombard peasant stock any intention of turning his church upside-down. When he summoned the Second Vatican Council he had in mind an opportunity for cardinals, bishops and theologians to take stock of a changing world and to consider how the Roman Catholic church might best serve that world. Doctrinal revision and relaxing of discipline were not on the agenda. The Council responded to changed Protestant perceptions by treating Protestants in a spirit of collegiality rather than with magisterial assumptions of superiority. The respectability of diversity within a generously defined concept of the Church was made apparent when mass was celebrated every day according to a different traditional rite: all of these were formally Catholic and canonical; some at times had been revised or even abolished; but the richness of gifts they disclosed strongly implied that only the accidents of history had separated some traditions and relegated them to a Protestant néant. With so much diversity within the church, a bit of redefinition could embrace the diversity that happened to have fetched up outside it.

Once, the Reformation had been seen as a kind of cancer from which the Catholic church had been saved by the *ferrum abscissionis* – the surgical knife. Now it was seen as a limb of which that church had been deprived. The Catholic church signified its absorption of the Reformation's most important lesson in the Declaration on Religious Freedom, promulgated in 1965, which enshrined primacy of conscience as a Catholic doctrine: repudiators of Protestant influence could prove that this had always been what Catholics thought; hostility to Protestantism, however, had previously inhibited them from saying so. The proclamation of conscience as supreme was, in practice, as much a part of what Protestants had taught the Catholic church as the singing of hymns, the desirability of personal Bible study, the use of vernacular liturgies and making children sit quietly in church. The fact that Catholics could feel free to do the things Protestants did, without feeling threatened or corrupted, was a sign that in one sense the Reformation had ceased to be feared as a source of division and had come to be accepted as the common property of Christians.

It would be agreeable to believe that the religious landmasses forced apart by the intense seismic shocks of the Reformation were being pulled back together solely by the magnetism of Christian charity. The truth is that other forces were at work. The political changes of the first half of the century profoundly affected Rome's attitude towards its world mission. When hereditary monarchs were forced into political oblivion or brutally hustled across the great divide, they carried with them the tattered, trailing banner of *cuius regio eius religio*. No longer could the Vatican rely on friendly autocrats to continue ancient Catholic privileges; to give flesh to the spiritual exclusivity claimed by Rome. After the crumbling of thrones the Vatican struck deals with the new breed of tyrants – Mussolini, Hitler, Franco – and learned from its mistakes. In the new world Christian leaders had to reckon with secular, democratic states, banded together in pacts and alliances – NATO, Common Market, EFTA, SEATO – on the free side of the iron curtain. Postwar governments were not interested in concordats. Churches might try to exercise influence by infiltrating political parties, as the Catholics did in Italy and the evangelicals did in America, but for the most part they had to rely on moral suasion. That meant that most Christian bodies were in the same boat battling with the winds of materialism and trying to avoid the sandbanks of communism. Pulling together now seemed to make very good sense.

In some areas unity was the sickly offspring sired by survival out of insolvency. Throughout the Western world every major denomination, with the exception of the Baptists and the new charismatic Churches, has been in decline for much of the last three decades. This situation has called forth mergers and deals which are little concerned with theology and only tangentially connected with mission. It is no coincidence that 'ecumenism' was the great buzz word in Christian assemblies throughout most of this period. A great deal was heard of 'covenants', 'local ecumenical projects' and proposals for organic union between major bodies. In 1972 the majority of English Presbyterians and Congregationalists came together as the United Reformed Church. A few years later enthusiastic attempts at rapprochement between Methodists and Anglicans were staved off by the Church of England's Anglo-Catholic diehards. At the local level, where crisis situations were more pressing and theological niceties seemed irrelevant church people were less inhibited. By 1990 over five hundred experiments had been set up involving various degrees of sharing of buildings, ministry, worship and mission. These involved members of Methodist, Roman Catholic, Anglican, URC and Baptist congregations.

These arrangements, no less than those in seventeenth-century Pennsylvania, combined pragmatism and an impatience with theological issues which had seemed important at the Reformation and still obsessed the professionals. But that is not to deny their significance. The most heavily publicized example of collaboration, inaugurated in Liverpool by the Roman Catholic archbishop and the Anglican bishop, was seen as a major event and not only for the north-west of England. The covenant ceremony which also involved Baptist, Methodist, URC and Salvation Army leaders made a great psychological and emotional impact:

> There was a huge congregation for the opening of the service in the Metropolitan Cathedral . . . . Then we moved in procession to the Anglican Cathedral, gathering still greater numbers on the way. When we reached the end of Hope Street we looked back to see the whole route filled with a joyful surge of people, from all parts of Merseyside and of all ages. Afterwards we were told, 'If at that moment the Church leaders had wanted to turn back, they couldn't have. The crowd would have carried them forward.' In the Anglican Cathedral we solemnly signed the Covenant. Towards the end of the service, we all sang 'Bind us together, Lord' and the Church leaders spontaneously joined hands. Immediately an old lady reached out and moved across the nave aisle – a distance of some twenty feet – towards the person on the other side. Within half a minute the whole aisle down the length of the cathedral had disappeared as the entire congregation joined hands and the great divide closed.

Clifford Longley, religious affairs correspondent of *The Times* and editor of *The Tablet,* was not far wide of the mark when he described 'ecumenism' as 'yesterday's word'. The truth of that remark lies not in the sense of the unity debate being *passé.* What has happened is that ecumenism, like the charismatic movement which was contemporary with it, has entered the system and begun to attack its debilitating prejudices and emotional viruses. It is now commonplace for theologians from different communions to meet together in mutual quest for face-saving theological formulae; for Church leaders to meet fraternally; for Christians of different traditions to pray, study, worship and mission together. 'Ecumenism', once a battle cry for some and a term of ribald graffiti for others, has now become a word with various grades of meaning. Most believers can identify with it at some point.

Petty forms of spiritual apartheid do persist in places, even among some otherwise respectable Christians. In 1991 the British Lord Chancellor was expelled from the wee-free Church in which he was an elder for attending the requiem mass of a colleague. For many Protestants, however, the whore of Babylon seems to have matured miraculously into a respected maiden aunt. In 1982 the pope worshipped in an Anglican cathedral. In 1994 the Catholic and Southern Baptist Churches in the United States pooled resources for a pro-life campaign. These are the twin aspects of modern ecumenism: reconciliation in approaching God; fusion of resources in confronting the world.

From Sects to Cults

Sects have not lost their fissiparous properties. They are still breeding like amoebas. But Betjeman's abandoned chapels are signs of their fragility, their tendency to disappear or to be reabsorbed in older traditions. Indeed, if a measure of the vitality of the Protestant tradition is its ability to generate sects, it could be that the Reformation is now over. The current mode of sect-formation seems to belong to a different pattern from that of the Reformation centuries – developing not so much from the schismatic properties inherent in Protestantism as from one of two wholly different sources: first, the re-emergence of wildly radical, millenarian and irrational mass delusions of a kind just as prevalent before the Reformation as after it; secondly, the creation of syncretic religions, which may not, to a Christian, be recognizably Christian, but incorporate some ill-digested matter in regurgitated form.

The locus classicus of the first type – the model by which such movements can be identified – is the millennial kingdom of Münster of 1525–26: a messianic theocracy, formed in the shadow of the Reformation and under cover of the Peasants' War, which Protestant preaching had helped to incite, but without reference to the teachings of Luther. Münster's chiliastic agony was the result of a political experiment by Anabaptists, whose heresy preceded the Reformation – perhaps by centuries – and who regarded Protestants and Catholics as equally damned: their distinctive doctrine was that no baptism was valid but their own. Their self-elected

IOHAN·VĀ·LEIDEN·EY·KONINCK·DER·WEDERDOPER·
THO·MONSTER·WA   ERHAFTICH·CŌTER·

HÆC·FACIES·HIC·CVLTVS·ERAT·CV·SEPTRA·TENE^{RE}
REX·αναβαῶJισῶψ·SED·BREVE·TĒPVS·EGO·
HENRICVS·ALDEGREVER·SVSATIĒ·FACIEBAT·
·ANNO·M·D·—·XXXVI·
GOTTES·MACHT·IST·MYN·CRACHT·

10.1 Preachers of apocalyptic delusion.
Jan Bockelson (ob.1536), a tailor, made himself 'King' of Münster.
Thomas Müntzer (c.1490-1525) proclaimed a new age of the Church to be inaugurated by bloodshed. He was executed after the slaughter of his rebel host at Frankenhausen.
Hans Beheim (ob.1476), the Drummer of Niklashausen, was the puppet of a renegade Dominican, here seen whispering the message proclaimed by the orator to an impressed congregation. Beheim was revered long after his execution.

king in Münster was Jan Bockelson of Leyden, an illegitimate bankrupt who had failed in business as a tailor but whose charismatic gifts, overlooked in times of peace and prosperity, became conspicuous in a community gripped by strife.

He seized power with the aid of a gang of armed Anabaptist immigrants in the town. Money had been abolished, property communalized, and marriage was relaxed into virtual free love. Bockelson renamed the days of the week, chose all children's names himself, appropriated all the prettiest women for his harem and dispensed bloody and arbitrary justice in the market square from a towering throne draped in cloth of gold. His policies were legitimized by the exhortations of pet prophets and enforced by daily public executions.

These are familiar features from the horrific histories of some modern cults: messianic ravings turned into cohesive politics by violence, psychological intimidation and selective licence. Jim Jones led his gun-toting followers to mass suicide in a Guyanese swamp in a fever of millenarian expectation in 1980. Under the spell of a sexually predatory messiah who called himself David Koresh, hundreds of people were immolated in a fire during a siege of their armed compound in Texas in 1993. From one perspective, these looked like splinter-groups in the Protestant tradition, having started among Pentecostalists and Seventh-Day Adventists respectively. But in both cases, the 'parent'-Churches were only surrogates for the monstrous offspring of an alien tradition that had more in common with Jan Van Leyden than with Ellen Gould White or the nineteenth-century practitioners of 'Holiness'. Mrs White represented the respectable face of millenarianism: she would never have recognized the sort of Messiah a lady could not ask to tea. The poor Black 'speakers in tongues' who were the first Pentecostalists were recovering buried gifts of Christian spontaneity, not deliberately providing the raw material of false prophecy.

In the penumbra of Christendom, the shade favours the growth of syncretic shrubs. East Asia, where European evangelization was patchy and European imperialism weak, has produced some startling examples in the last century and this. In mid nineteenth-century China, for instance, the Taiping movement resembled the rebellions of peasant visionaries which have been common in Chinese history, but was inspired by a garbled version of Christianity. The uncertain word was transmitted by missionary tracts and selective Bible readings to Hung Hsiu-ch'üan, a peasant-born schoolteacher embittered by rejection from the imperial civil service. During a 'long march' from its heartlands in Kwangsi to the capture of Nanking the movement acquired 2,000,000 converts, disciplined by visionary utterances from a handful of charismatic leaders. The Taipings had almost conquered the Chinese empire by the time their prospects were wrecked in bloody squabbles among leaders each of whom proclaimed himself spokesman or incarnation of one of the Persons of the Trinity. Later syncretic movements in East Asia have been almost as powerful and almost as bizarre. In Caodai, a religion born in Vietnam in the 1920s, the raft of salvation was piloted jointly by Christ, Buddha and Taoist sages through messages received by ouija-board. Starting in Korea in the 1950s the 'Unification Church' has attracted members in every continent. To an impartial eye, it has little overlap with traditional Christianity, but its founder and pontiff, Sun Myung Moon, is said to believe himself to be a reincarnation of Christ.

Colonial and post-colonial worlds have also been fertile ground for syncretic cults. Voodoo, Umbwanda, 'Afro-Catholic' spiritualist sects and their cognates, often regarded as blends of pagan and Christian traditions, probably have too little genuinely Christian input to be considered properly syncretic but the Christian content of other movements, equally rich in mixture and menace, has been more prominent. In the Cruzob movement – a millenarian renaissance of Maya nationalism which emerged from the caste war of the 1840s in Yucatán – authority was mediated through a miraculously 'Speaking Cross'; the fervour of its devotees survived the exposure of the device as a sham and the movement was finally suppressed by armed conquest in 1905. In the 1930s in Peru Victor Raúl Haya de la Torre frankly presented his campaign for personal political power as a new religion. Some of its ingredients were borrowed from political creeds – Bolshevism and anarcho-syndicalism; some came from ancient orphic and hermetic traditions; some from modern gropings towards a non-Christian understanding of transcendence, such as Freemasonry and spiritualism. The whole caboodle was presented in language which mixed social-gospel Protestantism with the imagery of Inca paganism and the book of Revelation; it came dressed up with mysterious talk – supposedly based on the science of Einstein – of raising consciousness to the fourth dimension. None of it made sense but Haya was one of nature's cult-figures who almost mustered enough votes to make him president.

The line between syncretic cults and Christian Churches is always hard to draw and nowhere more so than in Africa, where, long and honourably, missionary tradition has adapted indigenous concepts and images as means of Christian expression. When Colenso in southern Africa revived principles which had animated Matteo Ricci's mission among Confucians and that of Robert de'Nobili among the Brahmins, he preached Christianity on the basis of respect for native traditions, tolerating polygamy and using a Zulu name for God. (see above, p. 199) More than a hundred years later, Emmanuel Milingo, a Roman Catholic archbishop of Lusaka, was deprived for heresy after accusations that he had encouraged pagan survivals in a pastorate increasingly preoccupied with his personal healing ministry. In the extensive twilight zone between evangelical light and pagan 'darkness', one of the most successful movements, with hundreds of thousands of adherents, is the Aladura Church of West Africa, founded in 1929 by Joshua Oshitelu, an Anglican seminarian called in visions to a life of prophecy:

10.2 The Church of Jesus Christ of Later-day Saints (Mormons) showed the classic signs of cult development and aroused the hostility which led to the assassination of its founder. (Opposite) Mormons rejected society and headed for the wilderness in search of their own promised land.

though the rituals, vestments and much of the language and spirit of the 'church' are Christian, with a heavy debt to the sumptuous garb and liturgy of the High Anglican tradition, this was a cult of a messianic healer with its vital roots in the sort of peasant millenarianism found in almost every culture. Its rituals include precautions against witchcraft by ministrations of holy water and by prayers recited in the nude. The Nazareth Movement in South Africa is, by its members' profession, Christian, but it deifies its own founder, Isaiah Shembe, who died in 1960, as a miraculously born 'spirit'.

There is perhaps another kind of syncretism, which is more at home in Europe and North America, the long-Christian 'West', as well as in the more prosperous, economically developed parts of the rest of the world. Superficially, this claim may seem paradoxical, since syncretic religion is commonly identified with 'primitive' cultures, recently emerged from paganism or retarded by impoverished education systems. Yet it is the rich man who has to struggle into heaven like a camel through the needle's eye

and economic sophistication is no proof against an imperfect grasp of Christianity. Rich men's heresies and sophisticates' sins are responsible for some of the fastest-growing, newest-looking departures today from the Christian tradition as it has developed since the Reformation. The syncretic pollutants which attenuate their Christianity come from the secular value-scales of consumerism, materialism and hedonism. Some of these movements preach a gospel of worldly success, others of bodily health, others of sexual antinomianism. Preachers of the 'gospel of prosperity' are particularly common in the United States. In Orange County, California, which became a byword for the free-enterprise magic of instant riches in the 1980s, the Reverend Robert Schuller has built a 'crystal cathedral' of glass and chrome, capable of housing thousands of worshippers who regard business success as a mark of divine election. There are tele-evangelists who carry the prosperity-gospel to unscrupulous lengths, hosting phone-ins from grateful adherents whose public confessions are of confidence in the divine origin of their business windfalls. Commonly, such profits are represented as returns on the value of donations made to prosperity-cults. Despite the Christian rhetoric, this sort of religion seems more readily classifiable as a form of commodity-fetishism, analogous to the cargo-cults of the South Pacific. It has its folk-religion equivalent in the 'banknote baptisms' practised by Blacks in the southern Cauca valley in Colombia: by palming a banknote during the baptism ceremony, godparents divert the sacrament from the child to the bill, which is then expected continually to return from circulation to its owner, bringing interest with it.

The notion that temporal pains and penalties are divinely inflicted as punishment for sin has a respectable pedigree in ancient Judaism and in simplistic forms of Christianity. Concern for worldly rewards and physical well-being parts company from Christian tradition when it becomes the worshipper's first or sole objective – when the comfort of the body displaces the health of the soul to a remote plane of interest. The Full Gospel Central Church of Dr Yonggi Cho in South Korea combines the prosperity-gospel with a healing cult in which bodily health seems to be pursued for its own sake. The healing ministry of Morris Cerrulo has something of the flavour of a part of a private health-care sector. Emmanuel Milingo's ministry was curbed in the Catholic church partly because it seemed to be acquiring the character of an extra-Christian cult.

If the denunciations of strait-laced orthodoxy can be believed, erotic excess also has a long history of abuse among heretical Christian sects, usually incited by a promiscuous paraclete. Two kinds of error inspire sexual licence. The doctrine of predestination can leave the believer with the impression that he might as well do his damnedest. A mystical conviction of divine union can seem to sanctify all one's inclinations, however base. The accusation, however, that heretics habitually have orgies has to be treated with care. Sometimes it reflects the fears of orthodox onlookers rather than the practices of the heretics; sometimes it is a propaganda device. There is no conclusive evidence that the Free Spirit heresy of the fourteenth century, to which inquisitors ascribed athletic feats of sexual indulgence, ever existed at all. Seventeenth-century stories of Quaker orgies are prima facie unconvincing, like the absurd and tragic allegations of satanic rituals of child-abuse made against Quaker families in the Orkneys in 1992.

The cases of Quakers are cautionary: they are communities of unimpeachable moral traditions who nevertheless attract the prurience of outsiders by their quiet common life and their sense of housing the 'indwelling spirit' of God. Sexual antinomianism, however, can happen in a supposedly Christian context. The best-attested case is still going on. In the 1960s, when sexual permissiveness came to acquire widespread assent as a good in the social value-scale of the Western world, it was likely that it would seep through and stain some part of Christian tradition. The cult founded by 'Moses David' – whose choice of name suggests messianic delusions – may have been harshly judged; the spokesmen of the 'Children of God' claim to belong to a fundamentalist Christian Church in the Protestant tradition. But their media-soubriquet as 'hookers for Jesus' seems justified by an avowed policy of using sex-appeal to entice potential converts; and Moses David seems to have borrowed from psychology and perhaps pornography the message that sexual pleasure should be unrepressed. When professedly religious movements proclaim as their goals material enrichment, bodily well-being and physical gratification, some kind of profanation – a syncresis with secular trends – has surely taken place. Get-rich, feel-good, come-often 'gospels' owe nothing to the honourable Reformation tradition. Rather, they are signs that the first Reformation is over and that we need another.

Chapter Eleven

KINGDOMS OF THIS WORLD:
Reformation and Secular Society

THE FRUIT OF ACORNS

Importance is unfashionable. Historians shy from the cosmic events that filled the textbooks of earlier generations and reach for comfortingly low-key, human-scale events, specific to particular localities. Like community architects, fashion designers and regionalist politicians, they are in thrall to the aesthetics of beautiful smallness. In the breakers' yard of history, the Reformation has got pounded into fragments, reduced from a cosmic event to a series of local or individual experiences. What formerly seemed a world-shattering revolution has been reclassified as a 'transition' in devotional style or taste. Yet the importance of episodes in the past still tends to be judged according to popular perceptions of its consequences; and the reputation of the Reformation continues to trail clouds of ascribed effects.

In long-range perspective or critical spirit, the Reformation looks less potent for change than it seemed to Christians caught up in it or to historians contemplating it from inside the confessional arena. As the changes wrought by the movement subside in significance, the wider effects commonly ascribed to its influence on the secular or non-Christian worlds therefore begin to look curious or at least unexpected. It is a common fallacy to suppose that great effects must always have great causes. History is like the weather – a chaotic system in which a cyclone can arise from the flap of a butterfly's wings. Yet, while events happen at random or issue from causes so remote, obscure and tiny that they are effectively undetectable, the assumption that the Reformation had great secular consequences begins to look less secure as its religious consequences are demoted. Once it has been reclassified as a transition rather than a revolution, the revolutionary changes commonly said to have flowed from it – deism, secularism and atheism; individualism and rationalism; the rise of capitalism and the decline of magic; the scientific revolution and the American dream; the origins of civil liberties and shifts in the global balance of power – all appear less convincing as time goes on. One by one, in recent years, the links by which these chains of consequence are bound have been loosened or cut by revisionist thinking and critical scholarship.

Protestantism and capitalism, for instance, have become unthinkingly connected by the kind of incantatory repetition that associates sugar with spice or time with tide or officers with gentlemen. While people still think of them as a pair, the logic and history connecting them have been prised apart. Outside a Marxist scheme of history, the very concept of 'the rise of capitalism' is useless: if capitalism is seen as Marx saw it – an inevitable phase of universal historical development – it becomes a quarry to be tracked through time; its origins and spread signposted by revolutions. If on the other hand it is a habit or a scale of values or an economic relationship not necessarily specific to any particular type of society, then it might be found anywhere at any time in varying degrees. The decline of Marxism has made the rise of capitalism a less attractive quarry than it once appeared to historians of the early modern era, when they were convinced that it was an event traceable to their own period, to be linked with the other revolutionary convulsions they thought they could detect.

In 1904, when Max Weber formulated the link between Protestantism and capitalism, the Reformation looked like just such a revolution: sudden, sweeping, transforming. It seemed to come at the right time, ahead of the vast expansion of credit in sixteenth- and seventeenth-century Europe, before the intense and ever longer-range commercial activity of the period, the rapid urban development and the entrepreneurial culture which followed. Weber thought he could see further grounds for pressing an investigation: in the seventeenth century, Protestant peoples – or peoples among whom Protestants were copiously represented – had fared better in commercial empire-building than their Catholic competitors. The Dutch empire expanded at Portuguese expense. The new commercial and imperial powers of the period included England and Sweden; old ones supposedly in decline included Venice, Poland and Spain. Protestant Christendom seemed to boom while the Catholic world stagnated.

The correspondences were not quite exact. Muscovy 'rose' without the benefit of Protestantism; Turkey 'declined' without the curse of Catholicism; France was a successful power, by Weber's standards, where Protestantism was first checked, then excluded. Nevertheless, the match between Protestantism on the one hand and successful commercial empire-building on the other was good enough to be suggestive. Weber believed, moreover, that he had found the key to the door which opened from Protestantism into capitalism. He felt that the 'genius', the *Geist*, of capitalism was essentially religious and that it dwelt in communities which practised a devotion of contempt for ostentatious luxury, conserving funds for saving and investment. This 'inner-worldly asceticism', as he called it, was characteristic of Jews – which accounted, he believed, for Jews' early discovery of capitalism and long expertise in its practice. It was also proper to Protestants, whose religion elevated simplicity of life into a sign of divine election, and, by denying the efficacy of individual works of mercy, spared money for self-help.

These were not very accurate characterizations of either of the religions they covered. If Jews have tended to eschew ostentation, it is more likely to have been a camouflage against the envy of potential persecutors than because of anything inherent in their religion; if they have shown, in some cases and places, a capitalist genius, it may have something to do with the old-testament tradition of wealth as a mark of divine favour, or with their exclusion, in hostile societies, from the professional careers at which they have so often been extraordinarily adept when given the chance. In any case, rich Protestants are as likely to be big spenders as big savers. In the Europe of the early modern period, no country's culture was as deeply informed by self-consciously Protestant values as that of the northern Netherlands; yet Amsterdam, which was the capital of a commercial empire and a symbol of the commercial success of a Calvinist élite, was a sumptuous city of conspicuous consumption.

To be sent to the Hague was exile for an Amsterdam patrician who needed to be near the Bourse and the harbour, but at least a third of the city's office-holders in the late seventeenth century had pleasure-houses along the Amstel; by the late eighteenth century owners of country houses comprised more than 80 per cent of the patriciate and the town council rarely met in July and August. Taste is the best clue to values and in all Europe, according to one of the most perceptive economic theorists of the late seventeenth century, 'you will find no private buildings so sumptuously magnificent as a great many of the merchants' and other gentlemen's houses are in Amsterdam.' The burghers managed to retain an image of parsimony because a great deal of the display was withheld inside their dwellings. Planning regulations kept façades narrow, though determinedly ostentatious householders could create double-width garden fronts or double their frontage by collaboration with neighbours. Exteriors could be enlivened by armorial gables, richly moulded entablatures or decorative urns and busts, of the sort favoured by the early seventeenth-century arbiter of elegance, Hendrick de Keyser. There are examples still standing today on the Keizersgracht and the Herengracht. The baroque taste of Andries de Graeff rivalled Venetian palaces of the period. The simplicity and austerity commonly associated with Dutch art patrons of the early modern period have been largely in the eyes of the beholders.

In one of the most devastating of the many critiques of Weber's thesis, Hugh Trevor-Roper showed in 1961 that many leading capitalists of early modern Europe were neither particularly Protestant nor particularly ascetic. At first sight, the hold of Calvinist financiers on the international banking system of mid seventeenth-century Europe looks impressive. Nominally Calvinist bankers kept the armies of the Thirty Years' War in the field – on the Catholic as well as the Protestant side. But they were, in most cases, shaky in their Calvinism or gaudy in their way of life. Hans de Witte, whose financial wizardry kept Habsburg armies supplied, had his son baptized a Catholic. François Grenus committed no comparable defection but he supplied loans to such Catholic champions as the King of Spain and the Duke of Savoy. Louis de Geer, the King of Sweden's paymaster, bought estates 'surpassing in extent the dominions of many small German princes' and affected an aristocratic title and demeanour typical of his fellow-financiers. Barthélemy d'Herwarth, Mazarin's fixer, demolished a duke's palace to rebuild it for himself on a more lavish scale. In Amsterdam, the grave of Isaac Le Maire proudly records the wounds of entrepreneurship – the loss of one-and-a-half million guilders. This capitalism was ancient rather than 'modern' – capitalism to the taste and, perhaps, in the tradition of Trimalchio.

If Protestantism at its most lucrative was not particularly austere, Protestantism at its most radical was actually anti-capitalist. The Fifth Monarchy Men and Levellers, the Moravian Brethren and Shakers hardly advertised the capitalist ethic in their emphasis on equality and common goods. 'Buying and selling', declared the Leveller Gerrard Winstanley, 'is an art whereby people endeavour to cheat one another of the land.' The Fifth Monarchists scandalized Oliver Cromwell by 'telling us that liberty and property are not the badges of the Kingdom of Christ'. Protestantism, in its more radical forms, was as likely to develop towards socialism as to justify capitalism. The early socialist communities, strenuously formed by nine-teenth-century idealists, slotted into a long history of backwoods utopias constructed by religious fanatics. Remnants of one of them can be seen, for example, at Ephrata, Pennsylvania, where despite the founders, exhortations to celibacy, an austere Eden lasted from 1728 until 1904; wooden buildings survive in the style of the prayer hall, built to the plan of Solomon's Temple, so that 'neither hammer nor axe nor any tool of iron was heard in the house while it was building.' Socialism followed with secular utopias, which, in the opinion of one of their great projectors, Étienne Cabet, would breed true Christianity. In Christian tradition, the truth is that neither capitalism nor socialism is original to Protestantism. Both touch different Christian nerve-centres: faith in the love of a personal God breeds a conviction of individual worth which is at the heart of the inspiration of a successful entrepreneur. The apostolic example of a shared life is a model for socialists.

Marxist rhetoric has given capitalism the connotations of an opprobrious term. But even by Marx's standards it had the advantage over preceding systems of bringing the proletarian revolution a stage nearer. For those who accepted Marx's scheme of historical development while rejecting his value-judgements, capitalism was unqualified progress. It was modern. It was dynamic. It was forward-looking. By accumulating wealth and stimulating industry it could support growing populations and buy the raw materials of power. By the presumed connection with capitalism, Protestantism could improve the lot of man and enhance the power of states. And by the test of military effectiveness, the demonstrability of Protestant superiority seemed to get more pronounced as time went on.

The ascent of the United States to the rank of a world power looked like a triumph of the Protestant ethic in a period when America was still over-whelmingly a Protestant country and the Protestant input into its 'national' culture was universally regarded as essential. The nineteenth-century record of victory and defeat in war – which includes English success in imperial competition with France, US victories over Mexico and Spain, and Prussian victories over Austria and France – was sometimes used to justify theories of 'Nordic' or 'Anglo-Saxon' racial superiority; but it was also convenient for upholders of the doctrine that Protestantism was progressive. Anti-Catholic crusades, like the Know-nothing movement in America or the German *Kulturkampf,* were, in part, efforts to preserve national purity from the supposedly debilitating effects of Catholicism. 'Can one throw mud into pure water and not disturb its cleanliness?' asked Samuel Morse, arguing that America was the intended victim of a Jesuit plot.

Against this background, over the period when our historical traditions about the Reformation were formed, it is hard to resist the impression that a prejudice in favour of Protestantism has influenced the way some far-reaching effects have been ascribed to it. Individualism, the rise of civil liberties, the cult of reason, the spread of a scientific outlook and culture are generally presumed to have been benign changes for mankind and there-fore – by those it suits to think so – indebted to a Protestant heritage. In all these cases, the presumed connection with Protestantism is traced through the same line of descent. The Reformation is held to have been a liberating force: liberating conscience from obedience to authority; liberating reason from clerical repression; liberating research from inquisitorial surveillance; liberating critical opinion from immersion in the vast solvent of Christian unity, liberating self-awareness from the smother-love of the Church.

Yet reason, individualism and the worship of conscience all have long histories, which were gathering pace before the Reformation started. Their place in the penumbra of Protestantism is likely to have been a part of an old process, rather than the start of something new. Indeed, like so many aspects of the 'modern' world, they were all prominent features of the twelfth-century renaissance – the movement which produced the letters of Heloise, with their conviction of the sanctity of carnal love, the lectures of Abelard, with their pride in the reach of reason, and the ladder of perfection of St Bernard, with self-love as its first rung.

Nor was Protestantism as firm a step forward in respect of these traditions as has often been supposed. Except by radical thinkers who were as unwelcome in reformed as in Catholic communities, the authority of the Church was attenuated, perhaps, but not abolished by the Reformation: it was diffused among the authority of churches. The elevation of the Bible, represented as the sufficient disclosure of divine revelation and as a source of authority higher than tradition, actually demoted a source of guidance in which human reason had always had a big part. Biblical fundamentalism is not a necessary part of Protestantism but it is a danger inherent within it: no Catholic discipline could ever be as hostile to the exercise of reason as the tyranny of an unquestionable text. It was the self-styled Protestant prophet, Thomas Muggleton, who identified Reason as the beast in the book of Revelation. Nor was the throne room of conscience an exclusively Protestant sanctum. Conscience can play as big a part in a Catholic's decision to submit to the authority of Rome as in a Protestant's to reject it.

In the aftermath of the Reformation, intellectual innovation and invention in science, religion and the arts were at least as lively in the Catholic as the Protestant world. The monetary theory of value, the concept of international law, the heliocentric theory of the universe, the study of comparative ethnology, the notion of sovereignty as absolute legislative authority – all were new departures in intellectual history formulated in Catholic milieus in the sixteenth century. Investigation of an inquisitorial kind did not inhibit St Teresa of Avila, for instance, from attaining new heights of mystical expression, or Fallopio from discoveries in anatomy or Galileo from revolutionary contributions to astronomy or Cervantes from new explorations in creative writing or Caravaggio from bold initiatives in painting. The only university in Europe where the theories of Copernicus reached the syllabus in the sixteenth century was Salamanca. In the seventeenth century papal Bologna was pre-eminent in anatomy and distinguished in cosmography. The astronomers who took over the imperial observatory of Peking were Jesuits. The data bank for the delineation and measurement of the earth was in the Paris of that scourge of Protestants, Louis XIV. Much of the literature of the Enlightenment was published, it is true, in Protestant countries; but at least as much of it was the work of Catholic as of Protestant writers.

Galileo's recantation has given early modern Catholicism a bad press as an incubator of scientific achievement. But in the Catholic world science could and did move. The presumption that the Reformation was a necessary

The Tragicall Histoy of the Life and Death

of Doctor Fauſtus.

With new Additions.

Written by *Ch. Mar.*

LONDON,
Printed for *Iohn Wright*, and are to be ſold at his ſhop without
Newgate, at the ſigne of the Bible. 1620.

11.1 Dr Faustus conjuring a devil from the title page of Christopher Marlowe's play, 1620 edition. Lutheran preachers were largely responsible for creating the Faust legend but Catholics and Protestants were equally interested in limiting the scope of intellectual enquiry. Magic and science have never been as far apart.

precondition of the scientific revolution is now as battle-weary as the idea that Protestantism led to capitalism. 'Scientific revolution' is an awkward term, resistant to definition and inappropriate in a context where knowledge accumulates slowly and mind-sets tend to lag behind; but it is a traditional name for the rise of empiricism and for the triumph of sensed experience over received wisdom. The connection with the Reformation is specious. The Reformation – the argument goes – freed religious thinkers to innovate in defiance of authority; the scientific revolution freed scientific thinkers from the same kind of inhibition. Therefore they are likely to have been connected.

Yet Protestant thought is not peculiarly empirical: obedience to the Bible is a form of deference to the authority of a text more compelling than any of those on which medieval science relied; the empirical habit of mind was much older than the Reformation. It had a continuous history in Europe at least from the time of those resolute thirteenth-century experimenters, Robert Grosseteste and Frederick II; if it grew in popularity as a scientific method in the sixteenth and seventeenth centuries, two developments unconnected with the Reformation were probably responsible. First, the cumulative effect of the authority of Aristotle had a paradoxical effect: because his own authority as 'the philosopher' par excellence was un-challengeable, his recommendation of the empirical method gave it an authority-dispelling prestige. Secondly, the experimental approach grew out of the Hermetic tradition: chemistry out of alchemy, astronomy out of astrology, physics out of Faustian magic.

Instances of specifically Protestant influences on scientific thinking are hard to come by. It is tempting to suppose that unorthodoxy in one respect will accompany originality in another. Newton's secret lucubrations, for instance, included alchemy and recalculations of sacred chronology; but, of his religious beliefs, his entirely orthodox confidence in the divine origin of the architecture of the universe most obviously underpinned his investi-gations of the mathematical principles of nature. If religious proclivities and scientific method are connected it can only be in a very general way, through the respect for truth which is common to the values of religion and science. Benjamin Franklin's Quakerism contributed nothing in particular to his science, but did dispose him to confront nature with uncompromising honesty. It is often regarded as surprising that a scientist as rigorous as Michael Faraday should have belonged, in his own words, 'to an obscure sect' of Protestant fundamentalists, albeit an exceptionally tolerant one, prepared to acknowledge evidence of God's grace in others; but Sandemanianism was entirely compatible with a scientist's vocation for integrity.

The indebtedness to Protestantism of a scientific outlook has also been discerned in the 'decline of magic' – one of the great, pervasive changes in outlook to have overtaken Western European culture in the early modern

11.2 Hans Baldung, called Grien, *A Witches' Sabbath*, 1514. One conviction shared by many Protestant and Catholic authorities was a belief in and abhorrence of witchcraft. No European state was free from the existence of harsh laws against the practitioners of *maleficium*.

period. Disbelief in magic can be a symptom or consequence of the scientific point of view. At the margins, however, magic and science are not easily distinguishable and the Renaissance magi were struggling to control nature by means they considered entirely rational. For Tomasso Campannella, the search for a means of measuring longitude and the quest for the philosopher's stone were part of the same enterprise; for Thomas Harrington, a perpetual-motion machine and a system for telling the future were both legitimate objectives of an ingenious mind.

Nevertheless, at relatively high levels of intellect and education, the distinction gradually imposed itself and a 'scientific outlook' became consciously exclusive of 'magical' effects – unverifiable connections of cause and effect, that is, attributed to otherwise unrelated phenomena. Two kinds of magic, in particular, became objects of scientific contempt: the first ascribed power to symbolic objects, the second attributed force to rituals. In the first, for instance, a hare's foot might make a wish come true; in the second, say, a pentangle drawn with suitable accompanying incantations might make or break an enchantment. The Catholic tradition, in which saints' relics mediate healing strength, and in which the ritual of the Mass attains its climax when bread and wine are miraculously altered, is vulnerable to condemnation as magical by a sceptical mind. This raises the presumption that the Reformation favoured the spread of science at least in a negative sense, by discouraging belief in magic. The most exhaustive trawl of the evidence for this presumption in England was made by Keith Thomas in one of the great history books of recent times, *Religion and the Decline of Magic*. Thomas finished the book with the conviction that there must be some connection between the Reformation and the attrition of folk magic, though he remained unable to specify it. There surely is a connection but it is not peculiar to the Protestant strain in early modern Christianity. Non-Christian rituals, as we have seen, were outlawed as much in Catholic as in Protestant Europe. Folk magic was one of the victims of the great campaign of evangelization of which the Protestant movements were only one aspect.

THE STABLE OF LIBERTY

One of the most widely appealing recommendations of the Reformation is the claim that it promoted political freedoms. The logic underlying the claim is simple: despotism and popery are natural allies; political servitude is the consequence of enslaved faith. The struggle for liberty of worship fed demand for other freedoms and inspired the development of a doctrine of civil liberties. It is not easy, however, to match this reasoning to the facts. The virtue of abnegation of the will is beautifully expressed by St Benedict: 'renouncing your own will, ready to fight for Christ, the true king, take up the famous and formidable weapons of obedience.' It is an obligation of

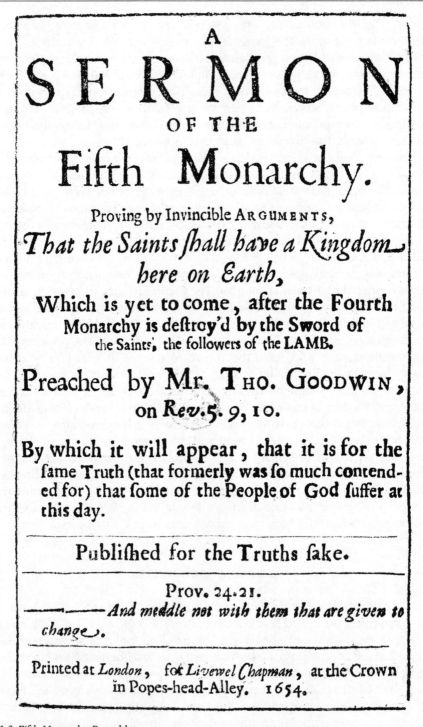

A

SERMON

OF THE

Fifth Monarchy.

Proving by Invincible ARGUMENTS,

That the Saints shall have a Kingdom here on Earth,

Which is yet to come, after the Fourth Monarchy is destroy'd by the Sword of the Saints, the followers of the LAMB.

Preached by Mr. THO. GOODWIN, on *Rev.* 5. 9, 10.

By which it will appear, that it is for the same Truth (that formerly was so much contended for) that some of the People of God suffer at this day.

Published for the Truths sake.

Prov. 24. 21.
———— *And meddle not with them that are given to change.*

Printed at *London*, for *Livewel Chapman*, at the Crown in Popes-head-Alley. 1654.

11.3 Fifth Monarchy Pamphlet.

followers of religious rules, who swear obedience to their abbots or the heads of their orders; but this is a discipline reserved for relatively few dedicated souls and the notion of the Catholic church as a tight-linked chain of command, like a Christian Tong or a fascist party, is laughably silly.

So is the image of much of the Catholic world in the early modern period cowering under the shadow of censorship and inquisition, cringing from the swing of the pendulum in the pit. In practice, though inquisitions were usually repressive, they spent more time, where extant and active, on the enforcement of social norms than on policing thoughts or exacting political obedience. They were cheap tribunals, useful for defusing irrational neighbourly rancour. Sometimes, as in the commission of the inquisitor Salazar among the alleged witches of the Basque country in the early seventeenth century, they freed innocent victims of lay resentment. They were prone to abuse because of their secretive procedures, their networks of informers, their unlimited jurisdiction and their financial methods, which gave them an incentive to prolong cases and impose fines and sequestrations for the profit of their coffers. Overwhelmingly, however, the penances they imposed were mild. Their tally of torture and bloodshed has had a vivid press but religious repression, although it took different forms, was no less prominent in the Protestant world, especially if witchcraft persecutions are included.

Most scrutineers will be fair enough to judge the record of the Catholic church in promoting and defending liberty not by the tabloid history of cloister and hearth or pit and pendulum but by genuine intellectual pedigree of liberal political theory. Two intellectual challenges often flung against the state on subjects' behalf in the era of the Reformation were the theories of tyrannicide and of the right of resistance. For obvious reasons, they were particularly attractive to persecuted religious communities. In practice they were as widely canvassed among Catholic minorities or subject-populations as in Protestant circles.

The right of resistance to a tyrannical ruler was, indeed, a long part of Christian tradition, enshrined by Thomas Aquinas. Luther himself initially subscribed to the doctrine in unmodified Thomist terms, sharing the definition of a tyrant as a ruler who served his own interests against those of the people. He was wary, however, of jeopardizing his relationships with princely patrons by appearing to condone rebellion. After the alarming bloodshed of the Peasants' War of 1524–25, his emphasis on the subjects' duty of obedience to the powers that be, as ordained by God, became extreme. Calvin, for most of his life, was unwilling to justify rebellion even in the face of persecution for the sake of the faith. He regarded Christ's command to turn the other cheek as unnegotiable. Protestant political vision was trapped behind a near horizon: the assumption that men are placed by God in subjection as a remedy for their sins. The right of resistance developed not as an extension of Protestant premises but as a response to the need to justify defiance of confessionally alienated rulers in an age of religious warfare; and as a reaction against the sufferings of beleaguered communities in an age of persecution.

Thus in the 1530s, when Protestant princes were in revolt against the emperor in Germany, Lutheran theologians developed a theory of the right of resistance by 'inferior magistrates' to 'the lusts of a godless tyrant'. In the second half of the century, in the context of the revolt of the Netherlands and the French wars of religion, the extension of the same right directly to the people was canvassed by Calvinist writers. But their opponents were quite capable of marshalling the same arguments when the political tide turned. Tyrannicide, a doctrine associated with Calvinists under Henry III, became associated with Jesuits under Henry IV. If resistance-theory had been a Protestant prerogative we should expect the political revolutions of the period to be exclusively Protestant work. Yet Catholics justified the subversion of dynasties, the assassination of monarchs and even, in one case, the proclamation of a republic in England, France, Portugal, Catalonia and Naples in the late sixteenth and seventeenth centuries.

If Catholic thought could be revolutionary, that of some Protestants was extremely hostile to political freedom. The power of the Church in the Middle Ages had been a check on the potential absolutism of the State. By denying the Church a role in the regulating of lay society and by subordinating spiritual authority to that of the prince, Luther created a potential bond between Protestantism and absolutism. Though in practice secular rulers achieved almost as much sway over Catholic as over Protestant ecclesiastical establishments in the early modern period, the formal reach of civil authority was always greater by rights as Protestants judged them: the elimination of papal jurisdiction concentrated power in the ruler's hands; secularization of Church property – which happened in the period in Catholic countries too, but on a smaller scale – enriched the state; the loss of the pope's powers as universal ordinary, however residual, added to the State's stock of patronage. Bossuet, writing the greatest Catholic apologia for absolutism of the seventeenth century, based his arguments on texts selected from the Bible by Luther.

The origins of modern absolutism are too diffuse and complex to be blamed on any one Christian tradition; but Protestantism was at least as servile as Catholicism in the face of the state's pretensions, and advocacy of untrammelled state power was a Protestant initiative. To adapt a famous phrase, without Luther, perhaps, Louis XIV would have been unthinkable. Yet individualism and civil rights were in the DNA of Protestantism, in which redemption depends on personal response to the mighty acts of God in Christ, sanctification on the personal development of the inner life and knowledge on personal meditation on the word of God read or preached. The implications for communal life in this world exercised Protestant Reformers. The ideal commonwealth beloved of sixteenth-century theorists was a willing combination of individuals, bound together by love, in which each fulfilled responsibilities and enjoyed rights. This applied just as much to the sovereign as to the lowliest peasant: 'Though no manner of person be unsubject to the king's power, yet so is the power of the king over all and in all limited, that unto all his proceedings the law itself is a rule.' Like Hooker, Calvin absorbed from a long tradition the principle that the State existed to make people virtuous. From these convictions sprang such diverse doctrines as republicanism, laissez-faire capitalism, socialism and totalitarianism, all of which were championed by evangelical Protestants. The contradictions of political theory for Protestants and Catholics alike sprang from the desire to achieve an end common to both sides: the maintenance of a truly Christian state. Whether the arguments were couched in terms of the 'two swords' or the 'godly commonwealth', propagandists shared the vision of a state where the proclamation of faith received government support and where public and private morality were enforced in accordance with divine law.

In the long run, the liberty of the subject was not guaranteed by the doctrine of resistance and the threat of revolution, but by types of political solution broadly to be characterized as constitutionalism: throughout Western Europe, gradually or fitfully, over a long period extending from the seventeenth century to the nineteenth, sovereignty was to be shared between a variety of institutions, and the freedom of rulers curbed in favour of the subject by respect for the rule of law or by written constitutions. The model of a 'mixed polity', in which power was shared among the various communities of which the state was composed, was a medieval ideal; a justification of it – almost universally accepted in late medieval Christendom – was adapted from Aristotle by Thomas Aquinas in the thirteenth century. The saint promoted the mixed polity from the modest place assigned to it in the rankings of the philosopher to be 'the best type of constitution'. The notion of the rule of law – the regulation of rulers by a traditional body of wisdom which could be modified only by consensus – was mediated through Aristotle and was not discovered or even rediscovered by Protestantism. On the contrary, in the late Middle Ages it was in a Catholic context that constitutionalism can be seen to have developed and grown. Its great incubator was the conciliar movement, which called for the reform of Church government by diffusing responsibility ever more widely beyond the Roman curia. Conciliarist theory overspilled into thinking about the secular commonwealth. Jean Gerson, who believed that general councils should be the highest governing authority of the Church, believed that the symmetry of the divine mind demanded also that the state should be governed by a representative assembly; personal power – whether of prince or pope – should be bound by the law. Constitutional experiments in the State, based on Thomism, conciliarism or pragmatic adjustments to the effect of unreflective power-struggles, predated the Reformation in the dominions of the medieval Crown of Aragon, where royal power was limited by the presumption that aristocrats held their estates directly of God; in late-medieval England, where parliaments made sporadic attempts to bind kings to their or their predecessors' promises; in Hussite Bohemia; and in the Holy Roman Empire in the late fifteenth century, where Berthold, Archbishop of Mainz, tried to resolve the stagnating conflicts of rival sources of authority by reforms aped from conciliarist models.

THE FOUNT OF ILLS

Just as Protestants credit the Reformation with all sorts of improving consequences for the world, so, from a Catholic point of view, great effects of a less welcome character have been ascribed to it. It is a common failing of Catholics to suppose that sheep change colour when they stray from the fold of the Church. When Ronald Knox was planning his great work on eighteenth-century illuminism be expected to give it a cautionary moral. 'Here, I would say, is what happens inevitably, if once the principle of Catholic unity is lost! All this confusion, this priggishness, this pedantry, this eccentricity and worse, follows directly from the rash step that takes you outside the fold of St Peter!' In practice, he managed to remain objective, but he was resisting an almost universal Catholic temptation. Those characteristic vices of the modern world – secularism, deism and atheism – have been blamed on the Reformation on the grounds that once authority is repudiated, error is unrestrained. In recent years non-partisan historians and sociologists have taken up the same thesis, though arguing it on slightly different grounds. Voluntarism, which in Protestant understanding characterizes the believer's compact with God, ultimately robs society, they suggest, of all the agreed religious, moral and cultural components which give it meaning. Thus the secularism which churches deplore springs, it is said, from the fragmentation of Protestantism and the tolerance accorded in Protestant countries to a variety of practices and doctrines.

In the case of secularism, the charge might, at first sight, appear to stick. From the earliest days of the Reformation reformers and rulers needed each other and Protestant theologians, in the larger interests of religion, were willing to flatter the vanity and vindicate the ambitions of princes of this world. The early Protestants could not afford to be choosy about the provenance of their support: they had the fate of too many burned heresiarchs and crushed secessions from the Church before their memories. Luther's patron, Frederick of Saxony, seemed by inclination a Christian of conservative devotional tastes, whose collection of relics was the largest in the world: 17,443 items, including angels' feathers, hair from Christ's beard and 204 assorted bones of massacred innocents; yet he soon established a community of interest with the Protestants. Of all the rulers who defected from the allegiance of Rome in the early years of the Reformation, Henry

VIII of England was by far the most important – ruling the biggest realm, commanding the greatest resources: he, too, was conservatively inclined – a 'Defender of the Faith' who had received a papal accolade for his refutation of Lutheran heresies - yet he was quick to exploit reformist doctrines which could be made to favour his own vast pretensions to power. Protestant theology bought princely protection by placing the jurisdiction, resources and patronage of the Church at secular rulers' disposal and cutting the popes out of their traditional share in revenues, appointments and appeals. Examined under the glare of Catholic prejudice, it looked as if the Protestants had set a corrosive example to lay people: not just setting profane rulers above the Church but also putting worldly anxieties above spiritual priorities.

In the absence of biblical precedents, Protestant satisfaction with secular control of the Church was pragmatic. Protestant thought was not inherently, necessarily or essentially secularizing. Like the good consequences misascribed to the Reformation, the bad ones had earlier pedigrees or had been seen before in the course of Christianity's long compromise with the kingdoms of this world. The prototype of 'cesaropapism' belonged to the reign of the emperor Constantine in the early fourth century – in that patristic phase of early Church history which Protestants generally accused the Roman Church of respecting too highly in spite of biblical evidence. Constantine was barely literate and seemed, in some ways, a shakily converted Christian, who appeared on his coins in the sun-god's garb; yet he dictated theology to the fathers assembled at the Council of Nicaea and was honoured with the title 'like an apostle'; the Christians of his day were beholden to him in the same way as the sixteenth-century reformers would be to their lay patrons. They gave him deference, first in payment for being protected from persecution, then in gratitude for being preferred above the pagan establishment. In the Middle Ages, the game of politics was played between churchmen and rulers with results that changed with the state of the pitch and the prowess of the players. David submits to Nathan on the doors of the abbey of Ripoll, but Ottonian kings tower above their supporting bishops in the illuminations of gospel-books of the same period. Henry IV knelt in the snow at Canossa in 1054; Boniface VIII battered his head on the door in frustration at Agnani in 1308. The Reformation may have contributed marginally to the subjection of Church to State by weakening the former and fawning on the latter; but the adjustments which followed were part of the revolutions of a long-spinning wheel of fortune.

When Charles I of England declared war on his parliament, he unfurled a banner emblazoned with a bloody hand reaching to sieze the crown over the motto 'Give Caesar his due'. This was a hopeless gesture and an offputting programme – like political parties today fighting an election campaign on a pledge to increase taxes. We recall a sermon, once heard at the Dominican priory at Oxford, on the same text: the preacher suggested that Christ's injunction to render unto Caesar the things which are Caesar's should be understood ironically, and that Jesus really was the political revolutionary Iscariot took him for. Irony is the hardest kind of nuance to detect in the literature of another age and it may be that this was one of our Lord's jokes, too obvious to deceive an audience of Jewish patriots. But he spoke with a voice more easily recognized by most of his followers ever since when he proclaimed a kingdom not of this world, which it was the Christian's first duty to seek. Disciples who urged him to lead a revolution were rebuffed. The kingdom of heaven could be realized on earth, but not by political action. When Jesus thought his followers wanted to crown him, he fled back to the hills alone. There is no such thing as an essentially Christian political ideology and therefore, *a fortiori,* none is essentially Catholic or essentially Protestant. Neither tradition deserves the credit or blame for the politics foisted on it.

The charge that Protestant divisions and Christian toleration feature prominently on the genealogical tree of today's secularist and pluralist societies rests on a misunderstanding of Christian theology. In an early chapter we made the distinction between toleration as an aspect of pragmatic politics and toleration as a Christian virtue. They are very different. One seeks to unite citizens on the basis of shared uncertainty. The other tries to hold Christians together despite their clashing convictions. Secularism has everything to do with non-Christian philosophy and politics and little to do with Christian divisions and toleration.

It has been observed that the telescope was one of the most revolutionizing inventions in human history because it shattered our illusions about the universe, the world and our place in the scheme of things. Every discovery that widens the bounds of knowledge, by the same token, widens the bounds of ignorance: we know that there is even more that we do not know. Seventeenth-century philosophers faced with this awe-inspiring realization were obliged to question, not only what can be comprehended, but also the mechanics of comprehension. Descartes resolved to begin his quest for meaning with an empty book; 'reason already convinces me that I must withhold assent no less carefully from what is not plainly certain and indubitable than from what is obviously false', a line of reasoning that led him to the conclusion, 'What then is true? Perhaps only this one thing, that nothing is certain.' Thinkers of the Age of Reason and the Enlightenment used empirical and deductive method to conclude that the Christian God did or did not exist, that the doctrines evinced by the Church to explain his dealings with men were or were not acceptable, that spiritual criteria were or were not relevant in matters of law, morality and state policy. It was the permeation of the educated and ruling classes by rationalism that led to increasing toleration. Human affairs were to be guided by reason and in those things which are beyond reason citizens should be allowed the maximum latitude consonant with public order. When religious dogma ceased to be the source of objective truth it also ceased to be the accepted basis for government policy. It is not just a century that separates Louis XIV's revocation of the Edict of Nantes from Joseph II's edict of toleration. So far from supporting such developments, Protestant and Catholic leaders, where their churches enjoyed majority status, tended to oppose them. In Britain every extension of civil rights to 'dissenters' and 'papists' was hotly contested. When the issue of admitting Jews to parliament emerged in the 1840s, the Bishop of London prophesied apocalyptic doom: 'If you destroy the groundwork of Christianity upon which the legislature is based, in order to gratify for a time a handful of ambitious men, you will destroy Christian England.'

In a sense the bishop was right. If 'Christian England' means a nation-church as defined by Hooker, then certainly it lies in ruins. The point was succinctly made by the heir to the throne in a 1994 television interview when he said that, as king, he would want to be known as 'Defender of Faith' rather than 'Defender of The Faith'. Admitting to full citizenship men and women of all beliefs and none has played a major part in the demolition process.

Secular toleration abandons objective truth and espouses relativism; denies moral absolutism and affirms freedom of choice; dethrones God in order to crown the individual. It is a flabby, unrestrictive, all-embracing corset which lacks the whalebones of discipline and compassion and can never adequately contain the bulging flesh of an over-indulged society. The most ardent peace-maker of the Reformation era would not have contemplated assuming such a feeble philosophy. Protestants and Catholics took their stand on revealed truth. Each party believed the other to be wrong on issues that mattered – and mattered profoundly. Therefore when negotiators came together to seek a *modus vivendi* they were motivated by a granite charity. They identified and set aside *adiaphora*. They re-examined their theological presuppositions in order to find maximum agreement. Where stubborn differences remained they advocated to their respective hierarchies the hard task of pilgrimaging together in love. For most Christians most of the time this proved too difficult.

If few contenders for Christian truth have had the courage to appeal their disputes to the high court of love it is because in that tribunal every cause, every prosecutor and every defendant is subjected to the most relentless scrutiny. Judgement is there given against persecution-mania, bigotry and self-righteousness. Those who have genuinely encountered the Cross know that striving for the well-being of the wilfully ignorant is more important than demonstrating their errors or silencing their propaganda. John Foxe might be supposed, from a reading of *Acts and Monuments,* to have been a Protestant 'hard case', ready to take revenge on those who shed the blood of Christ's saints. Yet this was the man who, without abandoning any of his Calvinist convictions, interceded for the Jesuit, Edmund Campion, and entreated Elizabeth's Council to spare the lives of five condemned Dutch

Anabaptists. Foxe was a man who hated violence. He confessed that he could not ever pass a slaughterhouse without feeling squeamish. Yet it was not a weak stomach that motivated his pleas for clemency. As long as men lived there was time for them to repent and to be persuaded of the truth. Once dead, there remained only judgement. Even when he composed his mournful catalogue of martyrs, indicting Rome for the spilling of holy blood, he did so, or so he claimed, to bring his Catholic enemies to repentance. Toleration was but a staging post on the road to repentance and forgiveness, a hard road of love. Politicians, sociologists and pedlars of cheap grace, who regard it as the destination, indulge themselves in an emasculated concept of love – a concept the reformers would not have recognized.

CHRISTUS CONTRA MUNDUM

When Jesus promised the gift of the Holy Spirit to his disciples it was so that a highly dangerous message might be proclaimed: 'He will prove to the people of the world that they are wrong about sin, righteousness and divine judgement.' From its inception the Church was committed to confrontation with, not only the flesh and the devil but also the world.

In the spring and summer of 1994, Italy was frequently the focus of international media attention. The people were electing their thirty-third postwar government and looking to a new electoral system and the campaign of a non-political media tycoon (who went on to win) to deliver their nation from decades of corruption and collaboration between ministers and leaders of syndicated crime. Characteristically, few reporters and programme editors paid any attention to the 90,000 Catholic charismatics who assembled enthusiastically in April at Rimini and outnumbered many times over any crowd that any of the political aspirants could attract. The representatives from hundreds of charismatic prayer groups all over the country had assembled to hear uplifting addresses, sing uproarious praises, witness miracles of healing, recommit themselves through confession and eucharist to the work of evangelism – and to make a socio-political statement. The theme for the 1994 annual conference was *Famiglia – Icona della Trinità*. Like the pope and like most Protestant charismatics, the delegates at Rimini were asserting their belief in the family unit and their opposition to everything that wages war against it. The central image on the wall behind the conference platform was one which is becoming popular among Christians of all denominations worldwide – the holy family.

Spiritual renewal always issues in social comment and not infrequently in political action. That was certainly true of the Reformation. Hugh Latimer castigated Edward VI's courtiers over enclosures and price inflation. Luther pressed the German nobility to be ruthless in suppressing civil unrest. Philip II's confessor warned him against tyrannous taxation of the poor. António

11.4 Preaching against 'the vanities' was part of the friars' stock in trade long before Savonarola. John Capistrano (1386-1456) was a Franciscan who enjoyed considerable success in turning his hearers away from wordly snares and wickedness.

Vieira denounced slavery in the seventeenth-century Portuguese empire. In 1610 the inquisitor Sálazar exposed witchcraft-accusations in the Basque country as delusive.

Irrespective of whether they stand in the Protestant or Catholic tradition, churches have been fairly robust springboards for political action in recent times, even after nearly half a millennium of triumphant secular values and Christian subjection in ever-more powerful states. Confrontation with anti-religious ruling ideologies at the high tide of fascism and communism turned Christianity into an opposition creed in much of twentieth-century Europe. In more recent times, Protestant pastors were among the revolutionaries who unseated communism in Hungary and East

Germany; Catholic bishops helped to perform the same role in Poland, Hungary and Czechoslovakia: the endurance of Orthodoxy under communism played a less active but perhaps no less vital part in other east European countries. The Catholic church was the most left-wing political organization tolerated in the Philippines under Ferdinand Marcos and, for a while after the Second Vatican Council, in Franco's Spain. The Church was a fundamental ally of the Sandinistas in promoting the Nicaraguan revolution; and, after it, instrumental in criticizing the revolutionary regime and promoting democracy. The largely Protestant 'moral majority' movement in America has been highly influential in moulding government policy and swinging election results. In Latin America, 'liberation theology' – the doctrine that sin was not just a personal problem and that society had to be reformed to eliminate 'structural' guilt – looked more potent as a revolutionary force than decrepit Marxism. In parts of Mexico and Guatemala, competition for souls between Catholic and Protestant missionaries took on the tints of a conflict of left against right.

In our own time the focus is on the battle with secularism. In its all-embracing modern sense 'secularism' became a sociological buzz word in the late 1960s but T.S. Eliot had enumerated the main symptoms of what he identified as a spiritual malaise thirty years earlier. A society will have ceased to be Christian, he asserted

> when . . . . prosperity in this world for the individual or the group has become the sole conscious aim . . . .
>
> The realisation of a Christian society must lead us inevitably to face such problems as the hypertrophy of the motive of Profit into a social ideal, the distinction between the use of natural resources and their exploitation, the use of labour and its exploitation, the advantages unfairly accruing to the trader in contrast to the primary producer, the misdirection of the financial machine, the iniquity of usury, and other features of a commercialised society which must be scrutinised on Christian principles . . . . A great deal of the machinery of modern life is merely a sanction for un-Christian aims.

The Church has always had its own word for the phenomenon – 'worldliness' – and has opposed it ever since Jesus told his disciples to live by the rules of the Kingdom of God in the kingdoms of men; ever since Paul urged Christians in the imperial capital, 'Do not conform yourselves to the standards of this world, but let God transform you inwardly by a complete change of your mind'. Preachers before, during and since the Reformation lamented the godlessness and moral decadence of their own times. Historians, reading the evidence and trying to answer the question, 'How did the devil come – when first attack?' have produced a bewildering array of answers.

'Many medieval clergy and laity had been beset by overwhelming temptations to blasphemy and atheism,' Keith Thomas tells us, 'and a wide range of popular scepticism was uncovered by the fifteenth-century church courts.' Laurence Stone reached the conclusion that the reign of the first Elizabeth was 'the age of greatest religious indifference before the twentieth century.' Yet the myth persists of a high flood mark of religious intensity from which the waters rapidly receded. Most people who think about it still assume that it was really the pincer movement of Enlightenment and industrialization that devastated native Christianity and that materialism and consumerism have cleared away its remains. In 1862 a religious journalist could assert, 'the beginning of the end is indeed approaching.'

> . . . . there are large classes not ostensibly connected with any denomi-
> nation, and to whom religion has long since become an unreality . . . .
> In the upper ten thousand, when there is no church or chapel atten-
> dance, there is still generally a piety of feeling, and a vague artistic sort
> of faith . . . . But among the working classes indifferentism and utter
> unbelief extensively prevail . . . .

And a recent analysis assures us, 'it is clear that both institutional religion and popular religiosity, of whatever hue and texture, has [sic] declined significantly in the twentieth century.' This is the history of *1066 and All That:* an 'Age of Faith' followed by an 'Age of Reason'.

When we look at the real history of Western countries we do not observe peoples who were once spiritual and became secular; quite the reverse. It is secularism that is the bedrock and spirituality which, generation by generation, beats upon it like a restless ocean – sometimes crashing with a reshaping force; at others retreating to the distant sandbanks. We have argued that the Reformation was part of a long, vast evangelizing effort (see above, pp. 165–200) but even by the beginning of the seventeenth century attendance at church was no guarantee of spiritual understanding or motivation. A Yorkshire boy quizzed by a minister could not say 'how many gods there be, nor persons in the god-head, nor who made the world nor anything about Jesus Christ, nor heaven or hell, or eternity after this life, nor for what end he came into the world, nor what condition he was born in.' A Lancashire woman, asked who the Jesus Christ mentioned in the Creed was, said 'she could not tell, but by our dear Lady it is sure some good thing, or it should never have been put in the Creed.' A Kent rector reckoned that less than 10 per cent of his congregation had any understanding of Christ, sin, death and the afterlife. In the closing decades of the century, the dissenters, for whom religious commitment was a costly business, made up only about 6 per cent of the population of England and it is unlikely that a higher percentage of Anglicans were equally devout. After two hundred years of intense, if sporadic, religious activity Britons fiercely identified themselves as a Protestant people but what that actually meant in terms of changed faith and spirituality is problematic.

So are the implications for the relationship of religion to public mores. Recent analyses of sexual behaviour in England suggest a long-term reform of attitudes extending from the fifteenth to the seventeenth centuries and influenced as much by economic changes as Christian indoctrination. France, by contract, seems to have experienced a more dramatic regularizing of sexual relationships in the period after 1600. For five or six generations – most notably during the periods of Puritan ascendancy – strenuous efforts were made by preachers, politicians and justices to ensure that England was a Christian country in more than name. Gospel values and beliefs permeated society but imperfectly, which is why varied impressions are gleaned from contemporary accounts and historical analyses. Whatever successes were achieved were the results of constant vigilance on the part of those who took seriously their call to be 'salt' and 'light', and who were prepared to be laughed at and condemned as busybodies, killjoys, hypocrites, humbugs and interferers with other men's liberties.

Members of the religious establishment are often in the front row of the jeering crowd. Whether the campaigner is Teresa of Avila or Mary Whitehouse, William Wilberforce or Girolamo Savonarola, the condemnation is raucous from their enemies and from some who should be their friends. As in the Reformation, individuals tend to make the running, usually with little or no support from religious establishments. Billy Graham, Mother Teresa, C.S. Lewis, Malcolm Muggeridge – these are the sort of people who, in their own day, are recognized as those who can challenge prevailing cultural norms. More rarely – except where Church and State are in conflict – are such charismatic figures to be found within the official hierarchies. William Temple, Donald Soper, John Paul II are among the few obvious examples that come to mind.

In the 1980s in England the Christian voice was raised to a shout in the political arena, discomfited the wielders of power and made an impact on policy. What church leaders objected to with increasing fervour was Thatcherite canonization of individualism and the free market. Early causes of disquiet were the government's willingness to pay the price of lengthening dole queues for a falling inflation rate, the growth of inner-city tension, the need to restrain public expenditure and the Falklands War. The Archbishop of Canterbury declined to play the role of triumphalist cheer leader at Britain's 'spectacular' defeat of a tenth-rate military power but Church and State were still pledged to working together. For example, after the 1981 Toxteth riots the Church leaders of Liverpool personally conducted the prime minister and the home secretary around the deprived areas and introduced them to community spokesmen.

It was the plight of these 'urban priority areas' (UPAs) as they came to be called that really focused the incompatibility of right-wing politicians and the majority of church people. If they did not win the arguments Christian critics of the British government gradually influenced the rhetoric. By the autumn of 1988, the prime minister's speech writers were instructed to lay more emphasis on social responsibility. Attention should be turned away from individual freedom and wealth creation to individual responsibility. One of the Church's main complaints had been the corrosive effects of her policies on community life. Now Mrs Thatcher became the apostle of social cohesion. It was no accident that a major element in the new programme was more aid for the inner cities: the Church of England had already very successfully launched its Church Urban Fund, pledged to raising £18 million in two years.

The Schoolroom of History

In Flora Thompson's village,

> The Catholic minority at the inn was treated with respect, for a landlord could do no wrong, especially the landlord of a free house where such excellent beer was on tap. On Catholicism at large, the Lark Rise people looked with contemptuous intolerance, for they regarded it as a kind of heathenism, and what excuse could there be for that in a Christian country? When, early in life, the end house children asked what Roman Catholics were, they were told they were 'folks as prays to images', and further inquiries elicited the information that they also worshipped the Pope, a bad old man, some said in league with the Devil. Their genu-flexions in church and their 'playin' wi' beads' were described as 'monkey tricks'. People who openly said they had no use for religion themselves became quite heated when the Catholics were mentioned . . . .
>
> The Methodists were a class apart. Provided they did not attempt to convert others, religion in them was tolerated. Every Sunday evening they held a service in one of their cottages, and, whenever she could obtain permission at home, it was Laura's delight to attend . . . .
>
> Permission was hard to get, for her father did not approve of 'the ranters'; nor did he like Laura to be out after dark. But one time out of four or five when she asked, he would grunt and nod, and she would dash off before her mother could raise any objection.

A hundred years later Lark Rise would have had little time for or interest in denominational divisions. In the global community of the late twentieth century local church rivalries are hugely irrelevant. The world is smaller. The vision of the Church is wider. There are still ghetto-minded sects. There are still people who need or think they need the kind of spiritual insurance which only comes from taking out heavenly policies through exclusivist religious brokers. But two radical changes have come over the Church scene since the 1960s. The first is the charismatic movement. Pentecostalists communicated it to the American Episcopal church. It spread rapidly to Roman Catholic congregations and subsequently appeared in all mainline Churches in every corner of the world. Nothing has done more to change attitudes, particularly among evangelicals. If the Holy Spirit manifests himself in similar ways in both orthodox and heretical assemblies those labels begin to look very suspect. The charismatic subculture has spread freely over confessional boundaries. Its members speak the same language, acknowledge the same priorities (praise, prayer, evangelism and healing), and share in the work of mission. It has found its way through the nooks and crannies of many congregations which by no stretch of the imagination could be called 'charismaniac', invigorating worship, creating tension, arousing a deeper commitment to mission.

The other change is that which has taken place in Roman Catholic attitudes, largely as a result of Vatican II. The mainline Protestant leaders of the sixteenth century were agreed that the institution of the papacy was the abode of Antichrist but they studiously avoided denouncing all 'papists' as heretics. The inheritors of the Kingdom were known to God alone. Catholic protagonists insisted that Protestants had deserted the ship wherein alone salvation was to be found and were floundering in the waves of damnable error. It was the official Catholic line until the 1960s that there could be no ecumenical dialogue with heretics. When this intransigence evaporated in the warmer climate of the postwar world all manner of new initiatives became possible. Not least among them was an edging towards mutual repentance and forgiveness.

One reason why for four hundred years the Catholic world saw no reason to embrace the deceived and deceiving assemblies of Protestantism was their habit of continual bifurcation. The regular appearance of new, warring sects seemed so obvious a denial of divine order that no other proof of their demonic masterminding was necessary. Rome's new openness to the Protestant world, its acceptance of many of the insights enjoyed by the spiritual heirs of Luther, Calvin and Zwingli, is an acknowledgement – implicit, at least – of a truth we referred to in the opening pages of this book. The Church is, and always has been, an agglomeration of parts. Most exist within the frameworks of Western Catholicism and Eastern Orthodoxy. Some rattle around within the smaller communions stemming from Wittenberg, Geneva and Canterbury. Others are independent or linked in tiny confederations. The 'scandal of disunity' is a mantra often recited with little understanding. The only basis mere humans are given upon which to make judgements has nothing to do with doctrines, traditions or forms of worship. Jesus said 'You will recognize them by their fruits.'

NOTES

1. SPLINTERS OF THE CROSS

PLUS ÇA CHANGE
'. . . Snakes Won't Bite': Tom Sharpe, *The Great Pursuit* (1979), p. 219.
'. . . peace and virtue': *D. Martin Luthers Werke. Kritische Gesamtausgabe* (1883 – in progress), xxvi, 530–3 [Preface to S. Klingebeil, Von Priester Ehe (1528)].
'. . . Council of Christendom': R.W. Chambers, *Thomas More* (1938), p. 341.
'. . . poor of Christ': W.L. Wakefield and A.P. Evans, eds, *Heresies of the High Middle Ages* (1969), p. 129.

Protestant princes: F. Fernández-Armesto, 'Cardinal Cisneros as a Patron of Printing' in D.W. Lomax and D. MacKenzie, eds, *God and Man in Medieval Spain: Essays in honour of J.R.L. Highfield* (1989), pp. 149–68.
'. . . in the Lord': A Grion, *La dottrina di Santa Caterina da Siena* (1962), pp. 87–108.
'. . . law of Moses': Acts 15:5.
'. . . in the wrong': Galatians 1:7, 2:11.
'. . . gust of teaching': Ephesians 4:14.
'. . . wrong doctrines': Titus 3:10.
'. . . could be identified: I Corinthians 11:19.

THE COLOURS OF THE CANVAS
'. . . they were ignorant': Bede, *A History of the English Church and People*, tr L. Sherlley-Price (1968), p. 68.
'. . . church of Gaul': ibid., p. 73.
'. . . good things': ibid., p. 73.
'. . . colonizing them with relics: ibid., p. 87.
'. . . immaculate conception: E.A. Johnson, 'Marian Devotion in the Western Church' in J. Raitt, ed., *Christian Spirituality: High Middle Ages and Reformation* (1988), p. 411.
'. . . *be despoiled*': R. Bainton, *Here I Stand: Martin Luther* (1983), p. 80

SACRED TOPOGRAPHY
'. . . household gods': M. Duran i Bas, *Discursos en el Senado y en el Congreso* (1883).

'. . . say regular masses: E. Duffy, *The Stripping of the Altars: Traditional Religion in England, c. 1450–1580* (1992).
'. . . bowel complaints: ibid., pp. 166 ff.

THE GRAIL QUEST

'. . . taste of it also': J.C. Olin, *The Catholic Reformation: Savonarola to Ignatius Loyola: Reform in the Church 1495–1540* (1971), p. 36.
'. . . future remedy': ibid., p. 55.
'. . . *beast you'd be!*': Robert Browning, *Bishop Blougram's Apology*.
'. . . fifteenth-century church courts': K. Thomas, *Religion and the Decline of Magic* (1971), p. 199.
'. . . about the English Reformation': Duffy, op. cit., p. 6.
'. . . come forth': A.G. Dickens, *Lollards and Protestants in the Diocese of York* (1959), p. 40.
'. . . directly and without mediation': S. Ozment, *Age of Reformation* (1980), p. 129.

2. STAYING FOR AN ANSWER

THE ECCLESIASTICAL MONOPOLY
'. . . sole rulers': F.M. Dostoevsky, *The Brothers Karamazov*, tr. S.S. Kosteliansky (1930), pp. 11–12.

TRUTH AS A GIVEN
'. . . human nature': F. Bacon, *Essays on Counsell, Civill and Morall*, ed. M. Kiernan (1985), p. 8.
'. . . such things': L. Febvre, *The Problem of Unbelief in the Sixteenth Century* (1982), p. 404.
'. . . profane into chaos': Erasmus, *Opus Epistolarum*, ed. P.S. Allen, 12 vols (1992), vi, 306.
'. . . Esau or Jacob': G. Rupp, *The Righteousness of God* (1953), p. 342.
'. . . word shall fell him': *Werke*, ed. cit., xxxv, 455-7.

THE WORD
'. . . knowledge and inquiries': E.F. Sutcliffe, 'Jerome' in G.W.H. Lampe, ed., *Cambridge History of the Bible*, ii (1969), 101.
'. . . toads and frogs': W.A. Pantin, *The English Church in the Fourteenth Century* (1962), pp. 132-3.
'. . . of the original': G. Shepherd, 'English Versions of the Scriptures before Wycliffe' in G.W.H. Lampe, ed., op. cit., p. 363.
'. . . St Paul in English': *The Acts and Monuments of John Foxe*, ed. S.R. Catley, 8 vols (1837–41), iv, 218.
. . . most convenient: E. Cameron, *The European Reformation* (1982), p. 120.
'. . . all truth': John 16:13.

STRICTLY BY THE BOOK
'. . . belongs to nobody': Rousseau, *Discours sur l'origine et les fondements de l'inégalité parmi les hommes,* ed. J. Starabinski (1985), p. 94.
'. . . apostles and the martyrs': M. Lambert, *Medieval Heresy* (1992), p. 56.
'. . . mother tongue': Archbishop Arundel to 'John XXIII' quoted by H. Hargreaves, 'The Wycliffite Versions' in Lampe, ed., op. cit., ii, 388.
'. . . in their wills: K.B. McFarlane, *Lancastrian Kings and Lollard Knights* (1972), pp. 207-20.
'. . . literacy was incipient: Lambert, op. cit., p. 271.
'. . . meaning thereof: H. Walter, ed., *Doctrinal Treatises and Introductions to Different Portions of the Holy Scriptures by William Tyndale, Martyr,* 1536 (1848), p. 394.

SCRIPTURE IN TRADITION
'. . . invites him': J. Calvin, *The Institutes of the Christian Religion,* tr. H. Beveridge, 2 vols (1962), i, 22.
'. . . *for the individual'*: 2 Peter 1:20.
'. . . *sermon on the mount:* O. Chadwick, *From Bossuet to Newman* (1957), pp. 127–8.
'. . . attached to them: V. Krasinski, *History of the Reformation in Poland,* 3 vols (1836–9), i, 329–30.
'. . . human commandments': Matthew 15: 1–9
". . .editorial hands: John 21:24.
'. . . we have taught you': 2 Thessalonians 2:15.

3. ACCESS TO GOD

EXPERIENTIALISM
'. . . pious deeds': R.L. De Molen, 'The Interior Erasmus' in *Leaders of the Reformation* (1984), p. 24.

MYSTICS
'. . . some experience': *The Complete Works of St Teresa of Jesus,* ed. E. Allison Peers, 3 vols (1946), i, 192–3.
'. . . no suitable ones': [Castillo Interior, VIII, 2].
'. . . *Chief of Sinners*: C. Hill, *A Turbulent, Seditious and Fractious People* (1988), pp. 75–6.
'. . . tossings to and fro': C. Hill, ibid., p. 199.

COMMUNITIES OF EXPERIENCE
'. . . spirit with us': W. R. Ward, *The Protestant Evangelical Awakening* (1992), p. 117.
'. . . on any altar: *Fire from a Flint,* ed. R. Llewellyn and E. Moss (1986), pp. 93, 127.

'. . . is to become': I. Kant, *Religion within the Limits of the Reason Alone*, ed. T. M. Green and H.H. Hudson (1960), p. 40.

'. . . remarkable organizer: Ward, op. cit., p. 61.

'. . . not by the reason': B. Pascal, *Pensées*, tr. A.T. Krailsheimer (1960), p. 154.

THE COMMON PURSUIT

'. . . your captain': J.C. Wengler, ed., *The Complete Writings of Menno Simons* (1956), p. 621.

'. . . growth in church': A. Walker, *Restoring the Kingdom* (1985), p. 187.

'. . . something better': J.W. Allen, *A History of Political Thought in the Sixteenth Century* (1960), p. 40.

'. . . right meaning': R.M. Jones, *Spiritual Reformers in the Sixteenth and Seventeenth Centuries* (1914), p. 50.

4. HERESY: SO WHAT?

DOCTRINE IN ITS PLACE

'. . . prospect of death: J. Brown, *Images and Ideas in Seventeenth-century Spanish Painting* (1978), pp. 129–46.

'. . . Bedforshire in 1636: K. Sharpe, *The Personal Rule of Charles I* (1992), p. 335.

'. . . heretic at all: O. Pesch, *Die Theologie der Rechtfertigung bei Martin Luther und Thomas von Aquin* (1967).

'. . . in the streets: A. Lynn Martin, *The Jesuit Mind: the Mentality of an Elite in Early Modern France* (1988), p. 9.

THE ONE BREAD

'. . . blood of the Lord': I Corinthians 11:27.

'. . . memorial of me': I Corinthians 11:23–25.

'. . . reign of Antichrist': M. Chemnitz, *Examination of the Council of Trent*, 2 vols (1971–8), i, 441.

'. . . was designed': L. Hernández, 'El culto divino en El Escorial' in *Iglesia y monarquia: la liturgia* (1986), p. 44.

MEANS OF GRACE

'. . . increase sins': Luther, *Werke*, ed. cit., xxix, 37, 45.

'. . . disinherited by God': S. Ozment, *The Reformation in the Cities* (1975), p. 81.

'. . . gracious God': Chemnitz, op. cit., i, 271.

'. . . tells him to do': Romans 3:27–28.

'. . . our saviour Jesus': *Le Sommaire de Guillaume Farel*, ed. J.G. Baum (1867), p. 22.

'. . . debate in Rome: D. Fenlon, *Heresy and Obedience in Tridentine Italy* (1972), pp. 6–23.

'. . . begun in us': Chemnitz, op. cit., ii, 467–8.

'. . . seventeenth century: K. Thomas, *Religion and the Decline of Magic* (1971).
'. . . find it simple: A. McGrath, *Justification by Faith* (1991).

THE PREDESTINED SOUL
'. . . which Luther hatched': Allen, ed., op. cit., v, 609.
'. . . Change your minds!': Matthew 3:2.
'. . . in gold pots'. *Luther's Works,* ed. H.T. Lehmann et al., 55 vols (1958–86), xxxiii, 16, 29.
'. . . through Jesus Christ': J. Calvin, *The Institutes of the Christian Religion,* tr. H. Beveridge, 2 vols (1962), ii, 213–14.
'. . . clothed in him': ibid., ii, 169.

BACK TO THE FUTURE
'. . . tolerated Luther': Allen, ed., op. cit., viii, 434.
'. . . Vatican itself: J. Toynbee and J. Ward Perkins, *The Shrine of St Peter and the Vatican Excavations* (1956), p. 117.
'. . . an earlier grave: M. Guarducci, 'L'eroica impresa di Pio XII: gli scavi sotto la basilica vaticana' in *Pius XII: in memoriam* (1962), pp. 277–307; Toynbee and Ward Perkins, op. cit., pp. 127–67.

ATTITUDES IN PRACTICE
'. . . impressive surplus': *The House of Mirth* (1989), p. 27.

5. A GIFT WRAPPED

SERMONS IN STONE
'. . . plaything of the celebrants': A. Kavanagh, 'The Conciliar Documents: Liturgy (Sacrosanctum Concilium)' in A. Hastings, ed., *Modern Catholicism: Vatican II and After* (1991), pp. 72–3.
'. . . for its worship': *A New Catechism* (1969), p. 229.
'. . . thirsty auditory': P. Collinson, *Godly People: Essays on English Protestantism and Puritanism* (1983), p. 493.

REFORM BY THE AXE
'. . . what else to do': C.M.N. Eire, *War against the Images: the Reformation of Worship from Erasmus to Calvin* (1986), p. 146.
'. . . which are similar': *Registres du Conseil Générale de Genève,* ed. E. Rivoire et al., 13 vols (1900–40), xiii, 576.

THE SINS OF THE IMAGES
'. . . on divine things': J.H. Schrieder, ed., *Canons and Decrees of the Council of Trent* (1960), p. 147.

'. . . benefites unto us': *The First and Second Prayer Books of Edward VI* (1957), p. 235.

'. . . hunger and thirst': Eire, op. cit., pp. 28, 44.

'. . . lowest classes?': Olin, op. cit., p. 52.

THROUGH A GLASS DARKLY

'. . . clothed as a beggar': P. Villari, *Life and Times of Girolamo Savonarola,* tr. L. Villari (1888), p. 499.

INTO THE PIT

'. . . properties, too: K. Ware, *From Byzantium to El Greco* (1987), p. 39.

'. . . an horse indeed': T. More, *Complete Works* (1963 – in progress) vi, 156, 231.

'. . . the Holy Spirit: Romans 8.

'. . . Michael Hug: P.A. Russell, *Lay Theology in the Reformation* (1986), p. 143.

'. . . devil's tomfoolery: Eire, op. cit., p. 95.

'. . . their miseries: G.E. Corrie, ed., *Sermons by Hugh Latimer* (1844), pp. 36–7.

'. . . power of the image': F. Braudel, *The Mediterranean and the Mediterranean World in the Age of Philip II,* tr. S. Reynolds, 2 vols (1982), ii, 832.

'. . . special faith': C. A. Bolton, *Church Reform in Eighteenth-century Italy* (1969), p. 104.

ALTAR AND TABLE

'. . . our intermediaries': J. Campbell with B. Mayers, *The Power of Myth* (1989), p. 63.

'. . . and its sacraments': F. Vandenbroucke, 'Lay Spirituality: Fourteenth to Sixteenth Century' in J. Leclerq, F. Vandenbroucke and L. Bouyer, *A History of Christian Spirituality,* 3 vols (1968), ii, 498.

'. . . profit them both': *The First and Second Prayer Books of Edward VI* (1957), p. 324.

'. . . communion of a church': Calvin, op. cit., [IV,i,12].

'. . . errour or Supersticion': *First and Second Prayer Books,* p. 326.

EVERYBODY SING

'. . . human heart': R. Bainton, *Here I Stand: Martin Luther* (1978), p. 341.

'. . . slip in a missal': M. Hebblethwaite, 'Aspects of Church Life since the Council: Devotion' in Hastings, op. cit., 241.

'. . . diversity in unity': G. Hughes, *In Search of a Way* (1981), p. 88.

6. Servants and Sacrificers

THE REVENGE OF THE PHARISEES
'. . . not willing': Matthew 23:37.
'. . . your God': Joel 2:12–13.

THE AUTHORITY TEST
'. . . one who serves': Luke 22:25-6.
'. . . permitted in heaven': Matthew 16: 17–19.
'. . . not forgiven': John 20: 22–3.
'. . . an 'abnormal birth': I Corinthians 15:8.
'. . . critics in Corinth: II Corinthians 11-12.
'. . . heard me say': II Corinthians 12:6.
'. . . in the face': II Corinthians 11:20.
'. . . in the Spirit: Jude 19.
'. . . the Christian community': W.H.C. Frend, *The Rise of Christianity* (1984), p. 143.
'. . . everyone by himself': J. Stevenson, ed., *A New Eusebius: Documents Illustrative of the History of the Church to AD 37* (1968), p. 165.
'. . . rule of truth': ibid., p. 378.

THE CRITIQUE OF PRIESTHOOD
'. . . took their origin': C. Morris, *The Papal Monarchy: The Western Church from 1050 to 1250* (1989), p. 30.
'. . . a member of Antichrist': C.N.L. Brooke, 'Priest, Deacon and Layman, from St Peter Damian to St Francis' in W.J. Sheils and D. Wood, eds, *Studies in Church History*, xxvi (1989), 67.
'. . . to this office': K. Holl, *Gesammelte Aufsätze zur Kirchengeschichte*, 3 vols (1948), i, 326.
'. . . face of the Church': J.K.S. Reid, ed., *Calvin's Theological Treatises* (1954), p. 231.
'. . . form of rule': ibid., p. 58.
'. . . necessary to the Church': H. Höpfl, *The Christian Polity of John Calvin* (1982), p. 60.

RIVAL KINGDOMS
'. . . gobbling up cabbages': G. Vendotis quoted in T. Ware, *Eustratios Argenti* (1964), p. 5.
'. . . of the World': P. Rycaut, *The Present State of the Greek and Armenian Churches* (1969), pp. 11–12, 107; quoted Ware, op. cit., pp. 3–5.

DRIVER AND PASSENGERS
'. . . of the people': G. Rupp, *The Righteousness of God: Luther Studies* (1953), p. 316.

'. . . into something else': C.A. Pater, 'Lay Religion in the Program of Andreas Rudolff-Bodenstein von Karlstadt' in R.L. De Molen, ed., *Leaders of the Reformation* (1984), p. 117.

'. . . and his neighbour': G. Rupp, *Patterns of Reformation* (1963), p. 123.

'. . . acceptable to God': W.R. Ward, 'Pastoral Office and the General Priesthood in the Great Awakening' in Sheils and Wood, op. cit., p. 304.

WRIT LARGE?

'. . . sacrifices of old': J. Keble, *On Eucharistic Adoration* (1857), p. 70.

'. . . draws strength': J.B. Lightfoot, *St Paul's Epistle to the Philippians* (1869), p. 179.

'. . . they have imagined': Jeremiah 14:14.

'. . . take away sins': Hebrews 10:4.

'. . . for generations: Acts 6.

'. . . order of Melchizadek': Hebrews 7; Genesis 14:17–20.

'. . . fixed on Jesus: Hebrews 12:1–2.

'. . . to the world: I Peter 2.

'. . . pleasing to Yahweh': Leviticus, 3:55.

'. . . share the altar?': I Corinthians 10:18.

'. . . offered the gifts': Stevenson, op. cit., p. 14.

'. . . prophets and teachers': ibid., p. 14.

'. . . duly ask it': J.E. Cox, ed., *The Works of Thomas Cranmer*, 3 vols (1844–6), i, 88.

'. . . Son once offered': J. and C. Wesley, *Hymns on the Lord's Supper* (1745), preface. See J. S. Simon, *John Wesley and the Methodist Societies* (1923), pp. 303–10.

'. . . interpret them?': I Corinthians 12: 29–30.

THE CLERICALIST TRAP

'. . . may not meddle': R. Hooker, *The Law of Ecclesiastical Polity*, 2 vols (1907), ii, 417–18 (V, lxxvii).

'. . . body of Christ': H.E. Manning, *The Eternal Priesthood* (1883), pp. 12f.

'. . . execrable thing': P. Collinson, *Godly People* (1983), p. 448.

'. . . Catholic priest': J. Mirbt, *Quellen zur Geschichte des Papistums* (1905), p. 499.

'. . . Scandalous Lives': R. Baxter, *A Third Defence of the Cause of Peace* (1681), pp. 17–18.

'. . . take a good nap': B. Reay, *Popular Culture in Seventeenth-century England* (1985), p. 98.

7. The Evangelical Impulse

The Penumbra of Christendom

'. . . very hard': Public Record Office, London, S.P. 94/5, fos 54–5 (524).

'. . . fifteenth and sixteenth centuries: A. Reid, *South-east Asia in the Age of Commerce*, 2 vols (1989–93), ii, 135.

'. . . with dog-dung': W. Heissig, *The Religions of Mongolia* (1980), pp. 24–38.

'. . . of this world: F. Fernández-Armesto, *Millennium* (1995), pp. 271–96.

'. . . a foul race': *A Chronicle of the Carmelites in Persia*, 2 vols (1939), i, 157, 236–9.

'. . . to work on: E. Maclagan, *The Jesuits and the Great Mughal* (1936), p. 284.

'. . . manner of the English': N. Salisbury, 'Red Puritans: the "praying Indians" of Massachusetts Bay and John Eliot', *William and Mary Quarterly*, 3rd s., xxxi (1974), 27–54.

'. . . particular gods': R. Ricard, *The Spritual Conquest of Mexico* (1966), p. 269.

'. . . on their bodies': I. Clendinnen, *Ambivalent Conquests* (1987), pp. 74–6.

'. . . of the eye': T. Gage, *A New Survey of the West Indies* (1655), pp. 148, 151.

'. . . pagan gods: K.R. Mills, 'The Religious Encounter in Mid-colonial Peru', D. Phil, thesis, Oxford University (1991), pp. 290–94.

'. . . pagan deity, Tonantizín: M. Gamió, *La población del valle de Teotihuacán*, 2 vols (1922), i, paer II, 479–81.

'. . . worship in practice: A Métraux, 'Croyances des Indiens uro-Cipaya', *Religion et magie indiennes* (1957), p. 253; *Black Peasants and their Religion* (1960), pp. 60–1, 92–4.

'. . . partiality to this Virgin: F. Fernández-Armesto, *The Canary Islands after the Conquest* (1982), pp. 188–91.

The Indies Within

'. . . believe in God': H. Kamen, *The Phoenix and the Flame* (1993), pp. 82–4, 378.

'. . . among the Indian': P. Burke, *Popular Culture in Early Modern Europe* (1979), p. 208.

'. . . word of faith': A. Lynn Martin, *The Jesuit Mind: the Mentality of an Elite in Early Modern France* (1988), p. 68.

'. . . understand at all': L. Abelly, *La vie de Saint Vincent de Paul*, 3 vols (1891), i, 55.

'. . . entirely absent: C. Ginzburg, *The Cheese and the Worms: the Cosmos of a Sixteenth-century Miller* (1992).

'. . . innocent of Christianity: F. Delicado, *Retrato de la lozana andaluza*, ed. J. del Val (1980), pp. 70ff.

. . . among the rich: J. Delumeau, *Vie économique et sociale de Rome dans la seconde moitié du XVIe siècle,* i (1957), 14.

'. . . of the catechism: G. Strauss, *Luther's House of Learning* (1978), pp. 160–75.

'. . . in circulation: S. Ozment, *The Reformation in the Cities* (1980), pp. 152–64; Strauss, op. cit., pp. 161, 164.

'. . . worshippers from church: Ozment, op. cit., pp. 27–8.

'. . . in licence': Burke, op. cit., p. 209.

'. . . spattered anathema: ibid., pp. 207–43.

'. . . clerical bans: M. Ingram, *Church Courts, Sex and Marriage in England, 1570–1640* (1987).

'. . . to the 1590s: B. Benassar, *L'Inquisition–espagnole: XVe–XIXe siècles* (1979).

'. . . to their perdition': A. Marín Ocete, *El arzobispo Don Pedro Guerrero,* 2 vols (1970), i, 182.

''. . . festivities and drunkenness': J. Alberigo et al., eds, *Conciliorum Oecumenicorum Decreta* (1973), pp. 775–6; J. Waterworth, ed., *The Councils and Decrees of the Sacred and Oecumenical Council of Trent* (1888), pp. 263–6.

'. . . kinds of sausage': Kamen, op. cit., p. 146.

'. . . wants to know?': W.A. Christian, *Local Religion in Sixteenth-century Spain* (1981), pp. 187, 208.

'. . . *memoriae gratia*': R.W. Scribner, *Popular Culture and Popular Movements in Reformation Germany* (1987), p. 339.

'. . . making sacrifices': H. Heppe, *Geschichte der evangelischen Kirche von Cleve-Mark und der Provinz Westphalen* (1867), p. 188n.; quoted with differences of translation in W.R. Ward, *The Protestant Evangelical Awakening* (1992), p. 37.

'. . . had been washed: Scribner, op. cit., p. 259.

'. . . rather than the church': Kamen, op. cit., p. 436.

'. . . aftermath of Trent: W.A. Christian, *Person and God in a Spanish Valley* (1972).

THE OUTSIDERS AT HOME

'. . . converted to Protestantism: E. Cameron, *The Reformation of the Heretics* (1984).

THE ARENAS OF THE GLADIATORS

'. . . of the nation': V. Krasinski, *A History of the Reformation in Poland,* 3 vols (1836–9), i, 3–9.

'. . . with Holy Scripture': J.M. Neale, *A History of the Holy Eastern Church,* 3 vols (1847), ii, 398–9.

. . . in the seventeenth: N. Davies, *God's Playground,* 2 vols (1981), i, 173.

EVANGELIZATION BY EVANGELICALS

'. . . praise for evermore': T. George, 'The Spirituality of the Radical Reformation' in J. Raitt, ed., *Christian Spirituality: High Middle Ages and Reformation* (1989), p. 338.

'. . . greeted like angels': Roelke, op. cit., p. 262.

'. . . her religious beliefs: D. Wilson, *A Tudor Tapestry: Men, Women and Society in Reformation England* (1972).

'. . . been with Jesus: P.A. Russell, op. cit., pp. 165ff.

'. . . cares and pursuits': S.F. Dwight and E. Hickman, eds, *Works of Jonathan Edwards,* i (1834), 364.

'. . . presence of God': ibid., i, 347–8.

'. . . upon them all': W. Wale, ed., *Whitefield's Journals* (1905), vii, p. 28.

'. . . ecclesiastic fulminated: Ward, op. cit., p. 289n.

'. . . crawl on the earth': J.H. Whiteley, *Wesley's England* (1938), p. 328.

'. . . Evangelical century': Bebbington, op. cit., p. 149.

'. . . increasing daily': W. Cobbett, *Political Register,* 12 June 1813.

THE LAY FRONTIER

'. . . by the laity': *Lumen Gentium* (1965), pp. 4, 37.

'. . . the whole church': Professor J. Mahoney in conversation with Derek Wilson.

THE EVANGELICALS ABROAD

'. . . beyond the frontier: Ward, op. cit., pp. 249–51.

'. . . talking Spanish: R. Ricard, *La conquista espiritual de México* (1947), p. 140.

THE CALL OF THE WILD

'. . . quantity than quality: S. Neill, *Christian Missions* (1964), pp. 448–9.

'. . . guided the bullets': J. Hemming, *Red Gold* (1978), pp. 266–71.

'. . . in 1942: K. Latourette, *History of the Spread of Christianity,* iv, 385; vii, 124.

'. . . women to disease: Neill, op. cit., p. 306.

'. . . of Black rulers: ibid., pp. 380–2.

'. . . practised by Christians: T.O. Ranger, 'Medical Science and Pentecost: the Dilemma of Anglicanism in Africa,' *Studies in Church History,* xixi (1982), 333–65.

8. A SENSE OF BELONGING

THE SOCIETY OF CHURCH

'. . . Protestant heresies: G. Parker, *The Dutch Revolt* (1977), p. 59.

'. . . their revel': Chambers, p. 265.

'. . . teachers' thresholds: Martin, op. cit., pp. 64–6.

'. . . is not just': Krasinski, op. cit., i, 179–80.

'. . . liberties revoked: Davies, op. cit., 160, 167, 179.

'. . . resist and survive: L. Colley, *Britons: Forging the Nation, 1707–1837* (1994).

'. . . of the population: S. Schama, *The Embarrassment of Riches: An Interpretation of Dutch Culture in the Golden Age* (1988).

CONGREGATIONS IN PROFILE

'. . . identical tombstones: Mme de Staël, *De l'Allemagne,* 2 vols (1932), ii, 215–17.

'. . . 'from the dust': A. Murray, *Reason and Society in the Middle Ages* (1978), pp. 317–415.

'. . . apostolate of men: E. Rapley, *The Dévotes: Women and Church in Seventeenth-century France* (1988), pp. 8, 30.

SQUARE PEGS

'. . . I shall not go again': J. Brockelsby, *Step into Joy,* quoted J. Bax, *The Good Wine* (1986), pp. 170–1.

'. . . by the Church?': J. Lecler, *Toleration and the Reformation,* 2 vols (1960), i, 280.

'. . . Richard Baxter': R. Baxter, *Gildas Salvianus: the Reformed Pastor,* ed. J.T. Wilkinson (1950), p. 191.

'. . . religious fervour: D. Wilson, *Sweet Robin: A Biography of Robert Dudley, Earl of Leicester, 1533–88* (1981), pp. 151ff.

'. . . the same God': J. MacInnes, *The Evangelical Movement in the Highlands of Scotland, 1688–1800* (1951), p. 98.

'. . . my expenses': S. Zweig, *The World of Yesterday* (1943), p. 113.

'. . . Christian community': M. Fulbrook, *Piety and Politics: Religion and the Rise of Absolutism in England, Würtemberg and Prussia* (1983), p. 169.

'. . . ministry of proclamation': J. Pelikan, *The Christian Tradition: a History of the Development of Christian Doctrine,* v (1989), 291.

'. . . synod adhered: W.K. Gilbert, *Commitment to Unity* (1988), pp. 9ff.

'. . . catch-all qualification: H. Shelton Smith, *In His Image, But . . . : Racism in Southern Religion, 1780–1910* (1972), pp. 223ff.

'. . . and the Vietcong': J.E.P. Woodruff, 'Black Power vis-à-vis the Kingdom of God' in M. Boyd, ed., *The Underground Church* (1969), pp. 97–8.

'. . . to become whole': J. Alexander, *American Personal Religious Accounts, 1600–1980* (1983), pp. 403–4.

'. . . face of the Catholic Church': L. Newbigin, *Foolishness to the Greeks: the Gospel and Western Culture* (1986), pp. 145–6.

'. . . into communion: R. Balmer, *Mine Eyes Have Seen the Glory: a Journey into Evangelical Subculture in America* (1993), pp. 109ff.

9. BRETHREN AT THE GATE

THE EXCLUDING EMBRACE

'. . . 'catching men': Mark 1: 14–18.

'. . . in the Spirit: Romans 8: 1–13.

'. . . first sermon: Acts 2: 14–36.

'. . . no salvation: Acts 4: 10–12.

'. . . say, 'No.': L. Pearsall Smith, ed., *Donne's Sermons* (1920), p. 156.

'. . . 'use his arms': H.W. van Loon, *Van Loon's Lives* (1943), pp. 182–3.

'. . . 'kingly power': Eunapius, *Vitae Sophistarum,* ed. J. Giangrande (1956), p. 39 (VI, 11).

'. . . evil of me': Mark 9:38.

'. . . .out of the Church': I Corinthians 5:2.

'. . . an undisciplined life': II Thessalonians 3:6.

'. . . be anathema': Galatians 1:8.

'. . . body of Christ: Romans 9:3.
'. . . him a greeting': Titus 3:10; II John 10

THE PIT AND THE PENDULUM
'. . . and John Huss': J. Foxe, op. cit., i, 4–5.
'. . . burn forever': R. Marius, *Thomas More* (1993), p. 406.

THE FIRE OF HUSITISM
'. . . name of religion': M. Lambert, *Medieval Heresy* (1992), p. 326.

FROM MASSACRE TO PRAGMATISM
'. . . done to death': C. Haton, *Mémoires* (ed. F. Bourquelot) (1857), i, p. 1110.
'. . . chilvalric festivities: F.A. Yates, *The Valois Tapestries* (1975), esp. 102–6.
'. . . very Christian laws': Allen, op. cit., p. 347.
'. . . with each other': T.E. D'Aubigné, *Histoire universelle,* ed. A. de Ruble, (1886–1909), i, 314.
'. . . rash counsels': *Montaigne's Essays,* ed. J. Florio (1965), i, 395.
'. . . entirely yours': N.L. Roelker, 'The Châtillon Brothers in the French Reformation' in De Molen, ed., op. cit., p. 262.

VOICES OF PEACE
'. . . abuses in practice': R. Stupperich, *Melanchthon* (1966), p. 87.
'. . . bridge-building exercise': J. Calvin, *Tracts and Treatises,* 3 vols (1844), i, 1–68.
'. . . *une roi*': J. Lecler, *Toleration and the Reformation,* 2 vols (1960), i, 260.
'. . . more than power': ibid., p. 262.
'. . . peace in its train': ibid., p. 211.
'. . . temples with violence?': ibid., p. 295.

THE NARROW GATE
'. . . perfection there': F.R. Coad, *A History of the Brethren Movement* (1968), p. 207.
'. . . allow them': N. Cohn, *The Pursuit of the Millennium* (1957), p. 239.
'. . . Word and Sacrament': G. Rupp, op. cit., pp. 317–18.
'. . . frequently examined: F. Wendel, *Calvin: the Origins and Development of his Religious Thought,* tr. P. Mairet (1963), pp. 263 ff.
'. . . may be engaged': Coad, op. cit., p. 23.
'. . . not give way': ibid., p. 288.
'. . . *from them all*': ibid., p. 116.

THE MAN WHO IS SUFFERING
'. . . to keep it': *Thomas Aquinas: Summa Theologia,* II.ii. Q.10, art. 8; ed. T. Gilby et al., 61 vols (1963-80), xxii, 63.
'. . . neo-Protestant tendencies: A. de Penanster, *Un papiste contre les papes* (1988), pp. 85, 108, 113, 145.

10. ALL CHANGE

THE RELIGION OF THE AMOEBA

'. . . momentum of schism: R. Tudor Jones, *Congregationalism in England* (1962), pp. 16–17.

'. . . utterly detroyed': to Rodolph Gaulter, 20 July 1573. *The Zürich Letters,* ed. H. Robinson, i (1842), p. 287.

'. . . world in scarlet': Jones, op. cit., p. 60.

'. . . must drown you': G. Davies, ed., *Papers of Devotion of James II* (1925), pp. 23–6.

'. . . beliefs and judgements': I Corinthians 1:10.

'. . . of its own: E. Willems, *Followers of the New Faith: Culture Change and the Rise of Protestantism in Brazil and Chile* (1967), pp. 110–13.

'. . . love the brotherhood': I John 3:14.

EXPERIMENTS WITH ADHESIVES

'. . . chiliasm and philadelphianism': W.R. Ward, *The Protestant Evangelical Awakening* (1992), p. 51.

'. . . they are fellow-citizens': ibid., p. 53.

'. . . served for lunch: D. Newsom, *The Parting of Friends: a study of the Wilberforces and Henry Manning* (1966), p. 412; cf. P. Johnson, *A History of Christianity* (1976), p. 384n.

'. . . encouragement or support': G.K.A. Bell, ed., *Documents on Christian Unity* (1930), p. 620.

'. . . clerical ideologies': Ward, op. cit., p. 250.

'. . . great divide closed': D. Warlock and D. Sheppard, *Better Together: Christian Partnership in a Hurt City* (1988), p. 96

FROM SECTS TO CULTS

'. . . public executions: N. Cohn, *The Pursuit of the Millennium* (1957), pp. 281–306.

'. . . properly syncretic: see A. Métraux, *Black Peasants and their Religion* (1960).

'. . . the fourth dimension: *Oxford Illustrated History of Christianity,* ed. J. McManners (1990), p. 440; J.L. Klaiber, *Religion and Revolution in Peru* (1977).

'. . . interest with it: M. Taussig, *The Devil and Commodity Fetishism in South America* (1980), p. 46.

11. KINGDOMS OF THIS WORLD

THE FRUIT OF ACORNS

'. . . in Amsterdam': B. de Mandeville, *The Fable of the Bees,* ed. D. Garman (1934), p. 144; quoted S. Schama, *The Embarrassment of Riches: an Interpretation of Dutch Culture in the Golden Age* (1987), p. 297.

'. . . eyes of the beholders': ibid., pp. 311–14.

'. . . more lavish scale: H.R. Trevor-Roper, *Religion, the Reformation and Social Change* (1967), pp. 12–15.

'. . . another of the land': G. Winstanley, *Works,* ed. G.H. Sabine (1941), p. 373.

'. . . Kingdom of Christ': *Cromwell's Letters and Speeches,* ed. T. Carlyle, iv (1948), 35.

'. . . it was building': W.A. Hinds, *American Communities and Co-operative Colonies* (1908), pp. 16–24; C. Wittke, *We Who Built America* (1946), pp. 339–61.

'. . . a Jesuit plot: S.B. Morse, *Imminent Dangers to the Free Insitutions of the United States through Foreign Immigration* (1835).

THE STABLE OF LIBERTY

'. . . weapons of obedience': *The Rule of St Benedict,* ed. J. McCann (1952), p. 6.

'. . . a godless tyrant': Q. Skinner, *The Foundations of Modern Political Thought,* 2 vols (1978), ii, 206.

'. . . Bible by Luther: ibid., ii, 114.

'. . . is a rule': R. Hooker, *Works,* ed. J. Keble et al., 3 vols (1888), iii, 353 *(Ecclesiastical Polity,* VIII.2.13).

'. . . type of constitution': *Summa,* ed. cit., xxxix, 266-73. See P.E. Sigmund, 'Law and Politics' in N. Kretzmann and E. Stump, eds, *The Cambridge Companion to Aquinas* (1993), pp. 219–22.

'. . . representative assembly: Skinner, op. cit., p. 116.

THE FOUNT OF ILLS

'. . . fold of St Peter!': R. Knox, *Enthusiasm* (1950), p.v.

'. . . were rebuffed: Acts 1:6.

'. . . hills alone: John 6:15.

'. . . nothing is certain': E. Anscombe and P.T. Geach, *Descartes' Philosophical Writings* (1970), pp. 61, 66.

'. . . destroy Christian England': A. Gillan, *The Emancipation of the Jews in England, 1830–60* (1982), p. 100.

'. . . enemies to repentance: Townsend, ed., op. cit., i, 512.

CHRISTUS CONTRA MUNDUM

'. . . divine judgement': John 16:8.

'. . . un-Christian aims': T.S. Eliot, *The Idea of a Christian Society* (1939), p. 12.

'. . . change of your mind': Romans 12:2.

'. . . fifteenth-century church courts': Thomas, op. cit, p. 199.

'. . . before the twentieth century': L. Stone, review of W.K. Jordan, *The Charities of London,* in *English Historical Review,* lxxvii (1962), p. 328.

'. . . rapidly recede: B. Coward, *Social Change and Continuity in Early Modern England, 1550–1750* (1988), p. 96.

'. . . extensively prevail;': W. Binns, 'The Religious Heresies of the Working Classes' in J.R. Moore, ed., *Religion in Victorian Britain* (1988), iii, 371.

'. . . in the twentieth century': D. Hempton, 'Popular Religion, *1800-1986*' in T. Thomas, ed., *The British, their Religious Beliefs and Practices, 1800–1986* (1988), p. 200.

'. . . death and the afterlife: B. Reay, 'Popular Religion' in Reay, ed., op.cit., pp. 94–5.

'. . . after 1600: M. Ingram, 'The Reform of Popular Culture: Sex and Marriage in Early Modern England' in Reay, op. cit., pp. 129ff.

THE SCHOOLROOM OF HISTORY

'. . . any objection': F. Thompson, *Lark Rise to Candleford* (1973), pp. 213f.

'. . . by their fruits': Matthew 7:16.

INDEX

TEXT PICTURE ACKNOWLEDGEMENTS

Bodleian Library, Oxford 1.1, 2.6; Trustees of the British Museum 2.1, 4.3 top left and bottom, 6.1, 6.5 top, 9.4, 10.1 left, 11.2; A C Cooper 4.3 top right; Germanisches Nationalmuseum, Nuremberg 5.2; Hulton Getty 3.1, 7.2, 8.1; Kupferstichkabinett Staatliche Museen zu Berlin-Preussischer Kulturbesitz (Photo by Jorg P Anders) 4.1; Mansell Collection 6.3, 10.2 left and right; Metropolitan Museum of Art, New York 2.5; Universitatsbibliothek, Tubingen 3.2 p. 62 top and bottom.